STUDIES IN
HEBREW
AND
ARAMAIC
ORTHOGRAPHY

BIBLICAL AND JUDAIC STUDIES FROM THE UNIVERSITY OF CALIFORNIA, SAN DIEGO

Volume 2

edited by
William Henry Propp

STUDIES IN HEBREW AND ARAMAIC ORTHOGRAPHY

by
David Noel Freedman
A. Dean Forbes
Francis I. Andersen

EISENBRAUNS
Winona Lake, Indiana
1992

Published for Biblical and Judaic Studies
The University of California, San Diego

by

Eisenbrauns
Winona Lake, Indiana

Library of Congress Cataloging-in-Publication Data

Freedman, David Noel, 1922–
    Studies in Hebrew and Aramaic orthography / by David Noel Freedman,
A. Dean Forbes, Francis I. Andersen.
        p.   cm. — (Biblical and Judaic studies ; v. 2)
    Includes bibliographical references.
    ISBN 0-931464-63-3
    1. Hebrew language—Orthography and spelling.   2. Aramaic language—
Orthography and spelling.   3. Bible. O.T.—Criticism, Textual.   I. Forbes,
A. Dean.   II. Andersen, Francis I., 1925–.   III. Title.   IV. Series.
PJ4583.F74   1992
    492.4′152—dc20   91-32408

CONTENTS

viii

PREFACE

On April 11–13, 1986, the Judaic Studies Program of the University of California, San Diego, hosted a Conference on the History of Hebrew Spelling. The participants were an assortment of researchers in the fields of biblical studies, Northwest Semitic epigraphy, and linguistics: Francis I. Andersen (University of Queensland), Frank M. Cross (Harvard University), A. Dean Forbes (Hewlett-Packard Laboratories), David Noel Freedman (UCSD, The University of Michigan), Richard E. Friedman (UCSD), W. Randall Garr (University of California, Santa Barbara), Baruch Halpern (York University), William H. Propp (UCSD), Stanislav Segert (UCLA), Ziony Zevit (University of Judaism), and Bruce Zuckerman (University of Southern California); Laurel J. Mannen handled the logistics of the meeting (and subsequently created the illustration on page 27 with her trusty Macintosh). The deliberations were devoted entirely to consideration of the use of *matres lectionis* in Northwest Semitic texts, particularly those in Hebrew, whether biblical or inscriptional.

Among the featured speakers were the authors of this volume; Freedman presented his current understanding of the development of Hebrew spelling based upon epigraphic remains and the MT, and Andersen and Forbes reported on their statistical computer analysis of the Leningrad Codex that had just appeared as **Spelling in the Hebrew Bible**, *Biblica et orientalia 41*; Rome: Biblical Institute Press, 1986. (Henceforth, **SHB**.)

The public and private discussions during that meeting as well as the later reviews of **SHB** indicated that a further volume would be in order. The aims of this collection are to summarize clearly the previous work of Freedman, Forbes, and Andersen, responding to criticisms where appropriate; to introduce refinements; to examine manuscripts and inscriptions besides **L**; and to adumbrate remaining problems for future investigation. Except for four essays which, as indicated below, have recently been published elsewhere, these studies are new, being the latest reports by the authors on the state of their research.

The volume is divided into four parts. Part I introduces the subject and presents, in effect, what we know so far. Freedman (Chapter 1) propounds a general model for the evolution of biblical Hebrew spelling, in particular the expanding use of *matres lectionis* from the archaic to the Hellenistic periods. Forbes and Andersen (Chapters 2–3) recapitulate the method and broad results of **SHB** in "friendly" language that should make sense even to math-phobes. Those unfamiliar with the earlier work will be impressed by its rigorous method and surprising results. Who would have guessed, for example, that while Exodus is the most archaically spelled book of the Bible (but not in all respects), Joshua 1–12 exhibits extremely divergent orthography? Behind the tables and graphs of Andersen and Forbes we dimly perceive the work of number-less and nameless scribes torn between tradition and fashion in their restrained attempts to update the orthography of Scripture, each in his own manner.

In Part II, Andersen and Freedman address various issues raised but not resolved by earlier investigations into the use and non-use of *matres lectionis*, whether in the pronominal suffixes (Chapter 4) or in words containing diphthongs (Chapter 5). In Chapter 6, Andersen faces honestly the problems in assigning absolute dates to the phases of Hebrew orthography, still an unattained goal. Finally (Chapter 7), Andersen and Freedman tackle the controversial status of terminal *aleph* in Old Aramaic and along the way make a bold, new proposal concerning the relation between particles with *aleph* prefixes and affixes.

Part III may be the most difficult for many readers, but despite their daunting appearance these essays are not too hard for the layman to follow. In Chapter 8, Forbes experiments with other statistical methods besides that chosen for **SHB**, and in Chapter 9 he and Andersen explore the variant orthography of duplicate passages within the Bible, an enterprise analogous to the identical twin studies of psychologists and biologists and possessing the same inherent fascination and utility. To conclude, Forbes (Chapter 10) shows the difficulty of arranging texts in chronological sequence on the basis of orthographic profile. Although to common sense this might seem a simple task, the stark mathematical realities are otherwise.

Part IV carries forward the task of obtaining a comprehensive profile of *all* Hebrew and Aramaic orthography, not just the spelling of **L**. Our volume can only make a start in this direction, but Andersen and Freedman have selected several new or neglected documents of particular interest: the lately uncovered Tell Fekherye inscription (Chapter 11), Samaria Papyrus 1 (Chapter 12), and two Qumran scrolls, 4QSam[b] (Chapter 13) and 4QTestim (Chapter 14). Finally, in Chapter 15, Andersen treats the fabulous Karasu-Bazar Codex of Leningrad. This little known tome, briefly described but never before examined in detail, may be the oldest extant biblical codex in Hebrew, although the ostensible date (pre-847) is tainted with a hint of skulduggery.

In short, **Studies in Hebrew and Aramaic Orthography** serves as a bridge from older methods for the study of orthography to newer, from the manual treatment of relatively brief documents to the computerized, statistical analysis of vast tracts of text. By bringing together the results of these two enterprises we can, maintain the authors, at least begin to place chronologically the spelling of early Hebrew and Aramaic texts, not least importantly the Bible. Throughout the sixteen essays that comprise this volume, the authors list, count, calculate, and plot, often employing the computer to perform Herculean labors. The value of such rigorous quantification is manifest: we can obtain exact answers, and, even when a matter is fuzzy, we can precisely define its fuzziness, not allowing anomalies to obscure an overall pattern. Obviously the micro-chip is no panacea; the maxim "garbage in, garbage out" will ever apply, and what is made of results always will depend on the insight of the scholar. Nevertheless, one can scarcely imagine what future generations of scholars may discover through "crunching" Scripture, if the present essays are any indication of the method's potential.

Though computer-assisted analysis of the Bible is over a quarter-century old (Hughes 1987: 491–545), the field is in its infancy; most biblical scholars, the editor included, are still bashful illiterates. Our authors are chronologically beyond the computer punk generation, but they share its exuberant spirit. Before many younger scholars had mastered word processing they already had embraced and espoused the new vistas opened by the computer and ever since have been among the pioneers in its use. Freedman, Forbes, and Andersen are thus true heirs of those proto-statisticians, the Masoretes. In fact, readers who have always wondered how the Jewish scribes arrived at their verse, word, and letter counts will be enlightened (and slightly disillusioned) by the appendix "What *Did* the Scribes Count?" in which the authors simultaneously pay homage to their intellectual forebears and dispel much mythology.

Non-students of orthography and non-computer junkies may wonder what motivates Freedman, Forbes, and Andersen to pursue studies both laborious and arcane. Is it a conviction that "God is in the details"? Do they find in quantification a retreat from the harsh uncertainties of traditional biblical exegesis? Have they joyfully succumbed to the allure of new gadgetry? Do they simply love counting and gathering statistics? Whatever their motivation, the happy result is **Studies in Hebrew and Aramaic Orthography**, the production of which is supported by the Jerome and Miriam Katzin Publication Fund of the UCSD Judaic Studies Endowment.

—William H. Propp, Editor

SIGLA

References to ancient sources and modern publications follow
the recommendations of the Society of Biblical Literature.

A	Aleppo Codex
AHS	Archaic Hebrew Spelling
B	British Museum Or 4445
BA	Biblical Aramaic
BH	Biblical Hebrew
BH³	**Biblia Hebraica** (3rd. edition)
BHS	**Biblia Hebraica Stuttgartensia**
C	Cairo Codex
D62	Karasu–Bazar Codex
HHS	Hellenistic Hebrew Spelling
L	Leningrad Codex
L¹⁵	Karasu–Bazar Codex
LHS	Late Hebrew Spelling
MT	Masoretic Text
Mm	Masorah Magna
Mp	Masorah Parva
P	Petrograd Codex
R	Second Rabbinic Bible
S¹	Sasoon MS 1053
SHB	**Spelling in the Hebrew Bible**
SHS	Standard Hebrew Spelling
SP 1	Samaritan Papyrus 1
SQS	Sectarian Qumran Spelling

Part I

Background

Chapter 1

The Evolution of Hebrew Orthography

David Noel Freedman

1.1 Introduction

The basic objective of this chapter is to trace the development of Hebrew spelling from one end to the other, from pure consonantism or no use of vowel letters to the systematic use of both final and medial vowel letters. Phoenician is the best example of pure consonantism, derived from old Canaanite, the original system dating as far back as the fifteenth century BCE (or even earlier). Phoenician carried on this practice down to late times. Using only consonants is a viable form of shorthand, but there are shortcomings.

At the other extreme is Masoretic vocalization in which all vowels are indicated in terms of quality and/or quantity. This approach is already visible in Greek, which from the time of the adoption of the alphabet had a full set of vowel letters. So the options were already available at both extremes almost from the beginning and certainly from about 1000 BCE. The complete evolution covers about 2500 years. We will concentrate attention on a narrower range, namely the West Semitic languages using the Phoenician (= Canaanite) alphabet.

1.2   Phase I: Pure Consonantism

1. *Origins*: The earliest alphabetic usage is found in all Canaanite inscriptions of the archaic period, 17th–11th centuries. There is no evidence of vowel letters.

2. *Proto-Sinaitic*: The spelling is purely consonantal so far as we can tell (Albright 1966).

3. *Ugaritic*: With a few possible exceptions, it also is consonantal (Blau and Loewenstamm 1970).

4. *The famous or infamous Gezer Calendar*:

   (a) The date is 10th century(?).

   (b) The language is Hebrew or Canaanite or Phoenician or what?

   (c) The spelling is purely consonantal, or does it use vowel letters? We cannot make *a priori* assumptions, and we are particularly concerned about final *waw*, which is attached to the noun **yrḥ**, *month*. The word occurs eight times, four times with final *waw* and four times without it. Scholars generally are agreed, but have not proved, that the four with *waw* are dual forms and the four without are singular. The possibilities for final *waw* are as follows:

      i. Consonantal **w**, which includes diphthongal forms.

      ii. Vowel letter. In my opinion the only viable possibility is **û**. Some scholars argue for the equation **w** = **ô**, but I see no unambiguous evidence for this usage at such an early date. Masoretic vocalization, without supporting data, is not sufficient to establish the case.

   (d) It would be very helpful if we could find some inscriptions that were clearly Hebrew or could determine without doubt whether there were any vowel letters. I would say that the Gezer Calendar is not decisive one way or another, although I lean toward Hebrew and pure consonantism.

5. *The Isbet Sarte inscription*: This is not much help. We may question whether there is a coherent text at all and also who wrote it. The date is early, certainly.

1.3   Phase II: Vowel Letters

The introduction of vowel letters is about as old as the adoption of the Phoenician alphabet by other groups, ethnic or linguistic. It seems clear that especially the Aramaeans and Greeks adapted the alphabet for such usage at the same time that they adopted it, or very soon after. In neither instance is there evidence of a transitional usage, i.e., texts in Greek or Aramaic which use no vowel letters whatever, whether from the earliest times, immediately after importing the alphabet from the Phoenician, or as a continuation of this primal usage, even after they had begun to use vowel letters. It is this possibility that makes the Gezer Calendar so tantalizing and our failure to get a handle on it so frustrating. If we knew that the language was Hebrew, and if we could be certain that the final *waw* on **yrḥw** (4 times) was not a vowel letter, then we would have one piece of evidence for such a transitional phase, at least for Hebrew. But it would be the only known case of the use of purely consonantal (Phoenician) spelling for a language other than Phoenician. The similarity (amounting almost to identity) of the earliest attested Hebrew spelling forms to Aramaic suggests either that the system was taken over *in toto* from the Aramaeans, and not directly from the Phoenicians, or, if there was an initial borrowing of both alphabet and system from Phoenician, it was soon replaced by the superior Aramaic system. A more nuanced question is whether Hebrew trailed behind Aramaic in the scale of the use of internal vowel letters. We will speak primarily of Semitic practice, since Greek usage takes us to a different area, namely, the use of letters solely for vowels, whereas from beginning to end in West Semitic inscriptions, certain letters served as both consonants and vowels.

In the light of recent discoveries it seems clear that the whole system of vowel indication was devised at one time. The basic principles and applications were as follows:

1. Final vowels were indicated by appropriate vowel letters *he*, *waw*, and *yod*.

2. There is no clear indication that terminal vowels primally short, such as case endings, were written in the first millennium BCE. Hence we assume that they have been lost. When such a vowel is written, we assume that it has become long, not that a vowel letter could represent a short terminal vowel. That becomes an equation, if not a tautology.

   The distinction between long and short vowels is an obligatory one, since the representation of short vowels by appropriate vowel letters is an extremely rare and late phenomenon in the evolution of alphabetic orthography in Semitic—to this day.

   It can be argued, and it is, that short vowels may have survived in the final position, and scholars often vocalize inscriptions on the basis of Masoretic models, e.g., the pronominal suffixes. These, however, are anomalous in MT, prove nothing, and as I have often observed are not short vowels.

3. The system was briefly as follows:

   (a) *waw* for û.
   (b) *yod* for î.
   (c) *he* for â.

In the final position, ē and ō were also represented by *he*. While the case for these equations is reasonable, it has also been claimed that *waw* is used for ô and *yod* for ê. The argument is based entirely on the contention that the diphthongs *aw* and *ay* had been contracted with the retention of the original consonants as vowel letters, i.e., historical spelling. Ultimately, contraction occurred but at different times in different dialects of NW Semitic and there is no unequivocal evidence for it in the early period, apart from Phoenician.

4. The system of internal vowel letters was more restricted since only *waw* and *yod* were pressed into service for such vowels:

   (a) *waw* represented û.
   (b) *yod* represented î.

Naturally they could also represent consonants and diphthongs: the latter have to be regarded as consonants until and unless contracted, when they become long vowels.

All remaining vowels were not indicated at this stage of development: ā was left unrepresented because it was not considered feasible to use *he* internally, so in effect ā was relegated to the zero-classification like the short vowels. As for ō and ē, their time would come, but so far we have no decisive evidence for their representation in this period. What is needed is the occurrence of non-etymologic vowel letters that were not part of the consonantal structure of the word and whose vocalization is equally certain.

The inscription from Tell Fekherye offers numerous instances of *waw* for û and *yod* for î. Other cases are less certain:

   (a) The *waw* in **šwl** (Akkad. **šāla**) can hardly represent ā, but may reflect –**āw**.

   (b) The *waw* in **gwzn** (Akkad. **guzana**), *Gozan*, may also reflect an earlier –**āw**.

(See Chapter 11, "The Tell Fekherye Bilingual.")

5. *Aleph* was never a true vowel letter until very late in the history of spelling. It occurs as a vowel letter only in words where it originally served as a consonant and quiesced. Then it became a marker for the preceding vowel. (See Chapter 7, "Aleph as a Vowel Letter in Old Aramaic.")

   Much later it was used in a variety of ways to represent the vowel **a**, long or short. The Greeks picked this up from the beginning but for different reasons: they had no clearly distinguishable *aleph* sound and the vowel associated with *aleph* was naturally **a** by the principle of acrophony. So from the beginning the Greeks understood the letter as representing the vowel **a** just as *iota* represented the vowel **i**.

For Hebrew orthography we argue that the official system called for the representation of all final vowels by appropriate vowel letters (**h**, **w**, **y**). All known Hebrew inscriptions from the 9th to 6th centuries follow this pattern and confirm this procedure. I know of no exceptions. The dubious or questionable cases are the result of the misapplication of Masoretic vocalizations to the inscriptional material. Scholars who adopt this practice fail to recognize that such vocalizations have a long and complex history and are the end result of a process of evolution. They therefore incorporate changes and developments that have little if any connection with the older system.

When it comes to internal vowel letters it is clear that they were used, but before the Exile the practice was sporadic at best. Such vowel letters are attested as early as the 8th century and their use may go back further. Unequivocal examples are found in proper nouns and in distinctive verbal (and nominal) forms where the function and probably the purpose are unmistakable. For example:

- ᵓrwr = ᵓarûr, *accursed*, in the Shebna inscription (8th cent.)

- hbqyd = hibqîd, *he appointed*, from Arad (7th–6th cent.)

But systematic use is unattested in any Hebrew inscriptions or those of closely related dialects. Recent discoveries, including Quntillet ᶜAjrud and Deir ᶜAlla as well as the latest unpublished inscription from Transjordan, show a fairly standard pattern.

In Aramaic inscriptions there is a greater tendency than in Hebrew to use medial vowel letters, and the general array of such helps to pronunciation is in place at an early date, as shown by the inscription from Tell Fekherye. But even in Aramaic, that inscription did not become a model for succeeding generations.

Summarizing, all final vowels were indicated by appropriate vowel letters:

- $w = \hat{u}$

- $y = \hat{i}$

- $h = \hat{a} \, (+ \bar{e} + \bar{o})$

Diphthongs were represented by the consonantal elements *waw* for **w** and *yod* for **y**. The only evidence for **w** = ô and **y** = ê is from much later vocalization of the diphthongs (chiefly MT) showing both contraction and historical spelling. Such data cannot be used for the early period, and such argumentation is circular and self-defeating.

1.4 Phase III: Post-exilic Orthography

Three stages can be distinguished:

1. Early (6th–5th centuries): Archaic Hebrew Spelling (AHS), attested by 4QSam[b]. (See Chapter 13, "Another Look at 4QSam[b].")

2. Middle (5th–4th centuries): Standard Hebrew Spelling (SHS), generally attested by MT.

3. Later (3rd century and following): Hellenistic Hebrew Spelling (HHS).

The progression here is from sporadic to more extensive to full use of vowel letters internally. Only *waw* and *yod* are involved, but increasingly long vowels and vowel letters define each other: if there is a vowel letter it is for a long vowel and if there is a long vowel there will be a vowel letter to mark it. The major exception is the ā vowel, which remains unrepresented, except for some rare very late occurrences of *aleph* to mark it.

While the evolution of spelling is a continuous process, there are nevertheless periods of accelerated change and development, usually connected with important changes in other areas; at other times there may be little or no change. The Exile, especially if we associate the production of a number of biblical books in the form we know them with the exilic community, produced some significant changes in the manner of spelling. It seems probable if not inescapable that the expansion in the use of vowel letters had something to do with the change of setting and the gradual decline in the use of Hebrew in daily life. It therefore became incumbent upon if not urgent for those working with the Scriptures to provide a more elaborate system for spelling words than had been used when the language was current among the people. Thus there are significant changes in the system, but generally there is greater use of internal *matres lectionis*. We consider 4QSam^b as the most archaic exemplar of biblical spelling, but its very existence shows, in all likelihood, that the same system was in use for all of the books of the Primary History (Torah and Former Prophets). This spelling is more archaic than MT generally and, just as important, is quite regular, whereas MT is less regular in the matter of certain vowel letters.

1.4.1 Archaic Hebrew Spelling (AHS)

We can summarize the case for internal *matres lectionis*:

1. **w** for **û** and **y** for **î** are now regular. Curiously, MT has archaic stretches in Exodus and Leviticus where the vowel letters do not show up as expected (especially in the m. pl. forms of nouns) pointing to the existence of older perhaps pre-exilic or early-exilic MSS. One striking example is the spelling of the name *David* with three letters in 4QSam^b. MT, in Samuel and Kings, also preserves this archaism. We could expect and do find the four-letter spelling **dwyd** in post-exilic compositions such as Chronicles, Ezra-Nehemiah. It is noteworthy that all other occurrences of the name *David* in Qumran MSS have the four-letter spelling (Freedman 1983a).

2. No **y** for **ē** or **w** for **ō** except when these are or were diphthongs. (See also number 5 below.)

3. Rare use of *waw* for **ō** derived from **ā**.

4. No use of *waw* for **ō** from **u** or of *yod* for **ē** from **i**.

5. The suffix **w** for **ô** after singular nouns in place of pre-exilic *he* is an important switch and not easily explainable. If we knew more about pre-exilic vocalization of Hebrew we might be able to reconstruct the pattern of orthographic change. The survival of *he* attached to various words shows again that some pre-exilic or early-exilic MSS survived as partial models for post-exilic writings.

6. More remarkable is the spelling –**yw** for the 3 m. s. suffix with plural nouns. After long struggle with this one, I conclude that the *yod* is an unvocalized plural marker, the first of its kind so far as I know, and apparently designed to distinguish these forms from singular nouns with the same suffix, a refinement made necessary only with the adoption of *waw* for the 3 m. s. with s. nouns.

When the first change was made, the second one became both an opportunity and a necessity if the two forms were to be kept separate. There are enough cases of *ktyb/qry* confusion in MT, in which K has −**w** and Q reads −**yw**, to illustrate both the problem and the solution. So far as I am aware, we do not have inscriptional evidence for this development outside of the biblical MSS themselves or inscriptions derived from them, so it may be a literary and scriptural affectation.

I associate these developments with the composition and compilation of the text of the Primary History, which I continue to date in the period between 560 and 540 at the latest (Freedman 1983b). The publication of an authoritative text would tend to establish an official spelling, the basic character of which does not change significantly, at least for biblical texts, for a long time. I think this first canonical standard largely survived in (the more archaic parts of) the Pentateuch, and was in place by 515 when there was a good occasion to issue an official text.

1.4.2   Standard Hebrew Spelling (SHS)

There are in fact four parts to this stage: the basic division here is between the Torah on the one hand, and the Prophets and Writings on the other. In the present MT, even in the best manuscripts, there are disconcerting divergences showing that there is a distinct, even unique history for each book of the Bible. This distinction exists because they were not books at all, but scrolls; hence each was partly independent of the others. We know that this is true in textual terms, and it is also true orthographically. Overall, the orthography of the Torah is the most conservative, having fewer vowel letters, while that of the remaining books is richer in vowel letters. Similar distinctions may be observed among the remaining parts: the spelling of the Former Prophets is less full than that of the Latter Prophets, although there are variations between individual books in both groups. The spelling of the Writings is fuller still, with variations among the several books. Generally in this group the poetic books are somewhat more conservative than the prose works (e.g., Ezra-Nehemiah), which reflect the latest and fullest spelling in the Hebrew Bible. This development is also historical, the fuller spelling generally being later than the more defective spelling.

The pattern of MT is basically the same as what we have maintained for early post-exilic spelling. The chief difference is the greater use of *waw* internally for ō, but it is still not widespread. Trying to define a rule is difficult, but essentially this means that using *waw* for ō from ā is now more fully recognized, but not *waw* for ō from u. All this suggests that since the ancient scribes were not scientific linguists or serious (as against popular) etymologists, the reason that the distinction is maintained is that the phonetic shift in the second case had not yet taken place (or that the vowel was not long). There are also numerous qualifying factors that enter into the equation and that undermine consistency, such as the apparent avoidance of duplicating vowel letters in the same words, or of repeating letters when consonantal *waw* or *yod* would be preceded or followed by the corresponding vowel letter. These are exceptional cases, however, and the general rule holds. Since stress and length are somehow associated if not quite interchangeable, accent shift likewise affects spelling, but it remains to determine both the cause and effect in such cases.

The chief difference among the biblical divisions lies in the increased frequency in the use of *waw* internally for ō. The development is significant on a statistical basis, although there is considerable variation from book to book within the larger divisions as well as among the divisions.

My thesis about the consonantal spelling of MT or the Rabbinic Bible, or what I regard as the text already available in the days of Ezra and Nehemiah, is that it conforms to the standard spelling of that period. In other words, I believe that Ezra promulgated the official version of the Torah, which we now have, and that it has not changed appreciably since that date. There are only slight variations in spelling from book to book in the Torah. We may assume that the standard or official spelling of biblical books in Ezra's time is reflected in the orthography of such an old manuscript as 4QSam[b]. The surviving manuscripts of the Hebrew Bible of MT (from the Middle Ages) can be compared in their spelling with 4QSam[b], and the distance from its pattern of spelling can be calibrated. Thus for the Torah there is a preponderant correspondence, with MT varying in certain respects, but in both directions. It contains more archaic features (e.g., the omission of *yod* in m. pl. nouns) showing that earlier versions of the text go back to early-exilic or even pre-exilic times, as well as some later features (i.e., more extensive use of internal vowel letters), reflecting the inevitable accretion of vowel letters in the course of transmission. As we continue through the Prophets (Former and Latter) and Writings, the divergences between their orthography and that of 4QSam[b] become more pronounced, mostly in the direction of fuller and later spelling. The effect of the formal promulgation of the Torah by Ezra was to preserve the text and stabilize the spelling from that point on. The remaining parts of the Bible were more susceptible to the drift or movement towards fuller spelling. What that means is that the Torah, at least in its most conservative parts, reflects the actual text with its spelling as of that date. The differences in orthography of the Former Prophets between 4QSam^b and MT are not great, but we can pinpoint the official spelling of biblical Hebrew in the middle of the 5th century in this fashion. There can be little doubt that the whole of the Primary History was written with the spelling we have found in 4QSam^b, and it stands to reason that Ezra would have used the best of the older texts available to him with their orthography. Nevertheless there is some tendency toward more elaborate use of *waw* for $\bar{o}$ (not associated with diphthongs past or still present in the language) and this expansion may have evolved during the 6th or early 5th century, unless it derives from inadvertent scribal alterations of a later time. Nevertheless, the conservatism of the Torah in contrast with the rest of the Bible shows that special care was taken with it from a very early time.

The latter part of the Hebrew Bible shows more extensive use of *waw* for $\bar{o}$, but otherwise there are no striking changes. We have noted the four-letter spelling of the name *David* which persists in the second half of MT, but this shift was already foreshadowed in the 6th century with the regular use of *yod* for $\hat{\imath}$ in medial positions. It should be noted, however, that nowhere in MT do we find a four-letter spelling of *Moses* (**mšh**, never **mwšh**) although that too would have occurred in time. This shows that the more conservative spelling was frozen probably in the 5th century for the whole Bible, and it was only with a dramatic development in the 4th or more likely the 3rd century that the basic pattern was changed.

The proposal here is that the whole spelling structure of MT can be explained and accommodated by the developments and decisions of the 6th–5th centuries, that with very minor exceptions MT as a whole and in particular 4QSam^b reflect that period—the period during which first the Torah and then the text of the rest of the Hebrew Bible (excluding only Daniel and perhaps one or two other books) reached substantially their present form.

There are all kinds of exceptions and practically any kind of Hebrew spelling can be found, from the most archaic to the most recent (i.e., from purely consonantal to the extended use of vowel letters including *aleph* for long and even short vowels) but statistically these variations are no more than rare aberrations and do not affect the pervasive regularity of the orthography of the surviving text. We may add that the other old MSS (4QEx^f and 4QJer^a), while clearly fuller and later in their spelling than 4QSam^b, nevertheless fall well within the range of SHS.

1.4.3   Hellenistic Hebrew Spelling (HHS)

It is not until we come to the Qumran MSS that we find the really full spelling of the Maccabean Age that inaugurates what we may call

Hellenistic, Qumran, or Maccabean spelling as over against the Persian orthography of the MT.

The spelling of this period is the logical development from the earlier practice and the realization of the potential already present in the earliest spelling with vowel letters, namely to represent all long vowels. While it can be endlessly debated, I think that the occasional representation of short vowels (in MT) by vowel letters is not the result of deliberate choice but accidental in the sense that the scribes who put in the vowel letters thought the vowels were long (and pronounced them that way) while the Masoretes, having a different text or a different spelling, thought the vowels were short. Conflation would produce similar results. But there is no strong evidence for the regular representation of short vowels by vowel letters any more than there is today in modern Hebrew, although there are such examples. Certainly in post-biblical texts and especially in Talmudic or Medieval Hebrew the practice is common, but the evidence from Qumran remains ambiguous. There the effort was to complete the task begun centuries before and that was to represent all long vowels (other than medial ā) by the appropriate vowel letter. Thus the biblical texts were recopied in the new modern spelling, much as the King James version is spelled now according to modern principles and rules of spelling, even if the language remains Jacobite. The objective was fairly simple: to mark all long vowels. Thus *waw* is now used ubiquitously for ō of whatever origin, and former short u is regularly represented by *waw*, showing that the shift u → ō has taken place. There is some evidence for i → ē, but I believe this is less clear, and *yod* is not generally so used, not as widely as *waw* for ō. Perhaps the shift had not yet occurred, or the vowel was still considered to be short. There was also no restraint about duplicating letters or including as many letters as there were long vowels. Scribal niceties (reflected in MT) were not recognized or observed.

At the same time, it is clear that at Qumran they continued to preserve older biblical MSS with their archaic orthography, although when they copied them they probably made little effort to preserve the older spelling. We have said nothing about a widely perceived difference in spelling at Qumran involving among other things the longer forms of pronouns, suffixes, and the like, in which vowel letters were added at the end, producing forms such as **hûʾâ**, **hîʾâ**, **–kâ**, etc. I hesitate to talk about this phenomenon, because there is widespread confusion about the matter, but the main point is that there were in reality different forms in the language: long and short, used perhaps in different ways, and faithfully reflected in the orthography. I do not believe it proper to say that the forms were all the same or that the spelling was optional. The opposite was true. If the final *he* was written the form was long, if not it was short. The Masoretes normalized in both directions, using texts with the short forms written, vocalizing them as though they had the long forms. I think that they felt that the texts with the short forms were better and older, while at the same time they thought that the long forms were more elegant and literary, more like classical Hebrew than the short forms, which they may have regarded as Aramaizing. So they conflated the two forms in such a way as to make it difficult for many to grasp the nature of the anomaly and to understand what has happened.

In recent magisterial articles on the orthography of the texts of Qumran, Emanuel Tov (1986, 1988) points out that there is a Qumran spelling with the peculiarities and idiosyncrasies we have noted—fuller use of vowel letters and the widespread use of longer forms of pronouns, suffixes, and other particles. He lumps everything else into a category that does not follow spelling rules or customs. While for the most part the division is sound and justifiable, the implied rationale is not, namely that Qumran spelling reflects a kind of strange dialect of Hebrew spoken, read, and written at Qumran. In this fashion the orthographic patterns of Qumran are relegated to a cultural as well as geographic backwater and banished from the interplay of currents and crosscurrents in social history.

In my view, Qumran spelling, while idiosyncratic in certain respects, nevertheless with regard to overall features, principally fuller spelling, reflects accurately the general pattern of Hebrew or Aramaic speaking communities all across the Near East. The phenomenon of fuller spelling is not peculiar to or isolated in Qumran but reflects the general development in spelling practices used by the Jewish nation and people. The spelling of the non-Qumran documents fits the framework suggested, but generally these are older documents or copied from earlier examples. These documents are neither heterogeneous nor miscellaneous but reflect the general spelling principles and practices described previously, only they belong to an earlier period of orthographic evolution. Qumran spelling, however, belongs to the post-biblical phase.

1.5   Conclusion

We have traversed half the distance originally set forth, but that is all we intended. We are primarily interested in vowel letters, not vowel sounds, in the preserved biblical text. We have tried to trace the history of Hebrew spelling from the beginning to the point at which the vowel system was fully realized and to place the spelling of MT in that framework.

The conclusion is as follows: the spelling of the Hebrew Bible conforms closely with its literary history. There is no strong evidence for pre-exilic spelling in the Bible, meaning that the literature of the Bible was not fixed until after the Exile. Sporadic survivals of pre-exilic spelling show that the Bible was not created in the 6th century but was built up out of and based upon written sources. What we have, beginning with the Primary History, is a work composed in the exilic or early post-exilic period. MT preserves a type of spelling that was normative in the 5th–4th centuries, which coincided with a great revival of classical Hebrew, clearly post-exilic and just as clearly pre-Qumran or Maccabean. The fuller spelling doubtless reflected the interest and desire on the part of the sponsors to make the language of the Bible accessible to the people as a whole.

When the rabbis fixed the canon and text, they rested their case on the most ancient and best-attested MSS they could locate, avoiding or rejecting MSS of recent date and late spelling. On the whole they managed to recover and retain and preserve for posterity the text that had been chosen and promulgated by their great leader and master scribe, Ezra, in the 5th century.

Chapter 2

A Tutorial on Method: A Guide for the Statistically Perplexed

A. Dean Forbes

> Leaving aside the mathematical material...
> —Barr's review of **SHB** in **JSS**

> ...intimidating...
> —Emerton's review of **SHB** in **S.O.T.S. Booklist**

> The authors, for all their good will, did not succeed in making statistics instantly digestible for this reader.
> —Pardee's review of **SHB** in **CBQ**

2.1   One More Time...

The story of the Hebrew Bible can be traced for the last three thousand years. It took about a thousand years to compose the books. These were handed down by repeated copyings over the next thousand years. For the last thousand years, surviving manuscripts and printed editions show that the text has been pretty well fixed.

Spellings change with time. For example, the name *Moses* (pronounced *mō-šeh* in Hebrew) was originally spelled with only three consonant letters: **mšh**. By the time of the Dead Sea Scrolls, the dominant spelling used four letters **mwšh**, the added **w** indicating the vowel ō. Given the fact of spelling change, one wonders if variant spellings coexist in the received text of the Hebrew Bible or whether spellings have been completely modernized in the process of repeated copying. If variant spellings have survived, their patterns of occurrence can be used to cluster text portions into groups having similar spelling practices.

Spelling differences do not result solely from differing origins in time. Local practice can influence spelling (American "honor" versus British "honour"). Alternate spellings may coexist ("labeling" and "labelling"), leaving the author a choice. Suffixation may (systematically) modify spelling ("try" versus "tried").

These ideas can be illustrated by considering a pair of experiments involving English translations rather than Hebrew texts of the Bible.

2.2   Finding Spelling Patterns

Suppose that some early-seventeenth century compiler put together an English translation of the Hebrew Bible by selecting, for each verse, his preferred translation from either the Great Bible of 1539 or the Geneva Bible of 1560. Suppose further that the first edition of this composite translation fell into our hands. Could we use spelling patterns to disentangle the strands making it up? Probably.

If, by examining many verses, we concluded there were two sources, X and Y, then, upon being presented a new verse, we might well be able to assign it to X or Y. Consider the following trio of verses:

> Why do the Heathen grudge together? and why do the people ymagine a vayne thynge?
>
> —Psalm 2:1, source to be determined.

> And Ioseph sayde vnto hys brethren: come nere to me, and they came nere. And he sayd: I am Ioseph youre brother whom ye solde in to Egypte.
>
> —Genesis 45:4, source X (the Great Bible of 1539)

> The time of our life *is* threscore yeres & ten, and if they be of strength, foure score yeres: yet their strength *is* but labour and sorowe: for it *is* cut of quickely, and we flee away.
>
> —Psalm 90:10, source Y (the Geneva Bible of 1560)

The challenge is to decide whether the first verse (Psalm 2:1) is from source X (the Great Bible) or from source Y (the Geneva Bible). If you saw the spellings with *y* in Psalm 2:1 as paralleling the spelling of *sayde* in Genesis 45:4 and so classified Psalm 2:1 as being from source

X, you would have leapt to a shaky, yet correct, inference. Making any classification with so little information is bound to be impressionistic. To do a proper job, the spelling characteristics of many verses should be catalogued, and rigorous methods of classification based on extensive study should be used.

2.3 Grouping Copies of Copies

The previous experiment was designed to illustrate how spelling behavior might be used to classify portions of text. The English translations of the Hebrew Bible made at two different times were analogs of portions of Hebrew text composed at differing times, each embodying the spelling practice of its era. But the analogy was incomplete: it assumed that we had the first edition to work with. To parallel the situation with the Hebrew Bible, we should have introduced *transmission by copying*. To improve the analogy, suppose that we have not the first edition, but a copy of a copy of...a copy of a copy of the original text. We wish to group verses, as before, but now must base our work on a copy of unknown fidelity to the original. One can envision two extreme theories describing the state of affairs.

At one extreme, if each copyist in the chain of copyists was extremely careful and held it his duty to reproduce *precisely* the copy from which he worked, then our text could be identical with the original. This is the *error-free theory of text transmission*.

At the other extreme, if the copyists were concerned to preserve the meaning of the text but felt free to update its archaic spelling to current usage, then the text could arrive in our hands with completely homogeneous spelling. The spelling practice would reflect the copyists' behavior, not the authors'. It would be theoretically impossible to use spelling to assign verses to sources. We call this the *indifference theory of text transmission*.

By examining texts, it should be possible to determine whether one of the extreme theories or some intermediate *mixed theory of text transmission* holds. All this suggests the following research plan:

1. select a representative manuscript of the Hebrew Bible;

2. identify factors which might have affected its spelling;

3. isolate those items in the text having variable spelling;

4. label these in terms of suspected conditioning factors;

5. use the labeled data to study spelling practice in the text;

6. if nonuniform practice is demonstrated, cluster text portions into groups showing similar spelling practice.

We executed this plan and reported on it in our book **Spelling in the Hebrew Bible** (Andersen and Forbes 1986).

2.4 Hebrew Spelling

The first Hebrew writing was likely purely consonantal; vowels were not indicated. That consonants alone suffice to convey the sense of a sentence is illustrated by producing statements such as:

Mst nglsh spkrs cn ndrstnd ths sntnc.

But there is more to be said. There are many situations where the meaning cannot be determined without vowels. Consider:

Th ct ws n th ht, nd th ht ws n th ct.

Is this "The cat was in the hat, and the hat was on the cot" or "The cot was in the hut, and the hut was in the city" or yet something else? Context might help sort things out in many cases, but other cases would be intrinsically ambiguous without vowels.

Fairly early in its development, the Hebrew consonantal spelling system was expanded to help resolve such ambiguities and to assist proper pronunciation in reading. Based on extra-biblical materials, it is generally held that the Hebrew writing system was purely consonantal until about the tenth century BCE. Some time in the ninth century BCE, the letters transliterated **h,w**, and **y** acquired the secondary function of representing some vowels. These reading aids are called *matres lectionis*, "mothers of reading" or "vowel letters." (It was only in the Middle Ages that the Jewish scholars, the Masoretes, introduced their complete system of dots-and-dashes vowel pointing into manuscripts intended for study.) Thus, *David* (dāwīd) has two ancient spellings: an older one with no *mater lectionis* for ī, **dwd**, and a newer one with a *mater lectionis* **y** for the ī, **dwyd**. When the helping *mater lectionis* is included (as in **dwyd**), the spelling is said to be *plene* ("full"). When no *mater lectionis* is used (as in **dwd**), the spelling is said to be *defective*. Both spellings are "correct." We should not transfer our notions of "correct" spelling onto the writers and transmitters of the Hebrew Bible. As we shall see, there are many cases where instances of a word are spelled differently in close proximity. (We note that the King James Version of 1611 has "The dayes of our **yeres** *are* threescore **yeeres** and ten..." at Psalm 90:10 [our emboldening].)

2.5 Data Preparation

2.5.1 Which Text?

For a complete investigation of the use of *matres lectionis* in the Hebrew Bible, one obviously needs to decide which text of the Hebrew Bible is appropriate. Do we select one complete manuscript or pick and choose parts of this and parts of that manuscript? The *Leningrad Codex* (also known as *Codex B*19[A] or **L**), which dates from 1008 CE, is complete and is generally judged to be of high quality. This manuscript is the basis of the scholarly edition **Biblia Hebraica Stuttgartensia** and is the manuscript we have spent many years preparing for computer analysis. For parts of the Hebrew Bible, there are contending manuscripts: the **Cairo Codex of the Prophets** of 895 CE (**C**), the **Petersburg Codex of the Latter Prophets** of 916 CE (**P**), the **Aleppo Codex** of around 930 CE (**A**), **British Museum Or 4445** (Genesis 39:20– Deuteronomy 1:33) of around 950 CE (**B**), and various texts from Qumran. **A** is an especially strong contender but now lacks most of the Pentateuch and many of the Writings. For the most part the spelling of the Qumran materials is far less conservative than that of the foregoing Medieval manuscripts. That is, Qumran texts tend to use *matres lectionis* profusely. They appear to be in a tradition that did not hesitate to modernize spellings.

Because of its completeness and wide acceptance, we based our work on the *Leningrad Codex*. As a check, we collated other manuscripts with **L** for selected spelling phenomena to judge the extent of the differences in spelling practice. We found quite astonishing unanimity among the manuscripts for the spelling phenomena sampled.

2.5.2 What Might Determine Spelling?

One of the essentials of good statistical practice is that all variables directly affecting the variable(s) under study must either be taken into account in the analysis or be shown not to have a significant influence. Otherwise, quite misleading conclusions may be reached. For example, a proper analysis of automobile fatalities should consider not only speed at impact, but also vehicle weights, passenger restraints in use, *et cetera*.

We found three variables that must be taken into account (type of vowel, stress on vowel, portion of text) and three whose effects are of minimal importance (word aesthetics, the proximity of occurrences of the same word, and *local* word frequency).

Vowel Type

The changes in letters used in writing words occur at varying times. For example, the "u" in "haue" became "v" giving "have" early in the sixteenth century. There has since been no option to write "haue." "Musick" finally lost its "k" and became "music" in the eighteenth century while "honor" may or may not have a "u" to this day. Similar situations occurred in Hebrew. The spelling of various words developed at differing rates. Therefore, we distinguished sixty-five vowel types, defined on the basis of current knowledge of the history of Hebrew spelling. A vowel type may correspond to a vowel in one particular much-used Hebrew function word. (For example, our Type 33 is the ō in the form Hebrew uses to mark a pronoun direct object.) Or it may cover entire classes of dictionary items. (Our Type 46 is the stem ō [first vowel] in nouns.)

Vowel Stress

We distinguish three kinds of stressed vowels: 1) a vowel in a word with an attached stressed suffix and hence itself under low stress; 2) a vowel in a word which is structurally dependent on a following word and hence is under intermediate stress; 3) a vowel in a free, unsuffixed form and hence under high stress. Some vowel types are more likely to be spelled *defective* when they are not stressed than when they are. For example, the ō in the word *fathers* (ʾābōt) is stressed. It is written *plene* (using the *mater lectionis* **w**) seventy-seven times (ʾbwt); it is written *defective* twice (ʾbt). The same ō in the word *his fathers* (ʾăbōtāyw) is unstressed and has a *plene* spelling five times (ʾbwtyw); it is written *defective* seventy-three times (ʾbtyw). (The ending –**yw** signifies *his.*)

Text Portion

The great nineteenth-century Hebraist Wilhelm Gesenius observed that *plene* spelling "is more usual" in the later books of the Hebrew Bible while *defective* spelling "is more usual" in the earlier. To assess the validity of this assertion, we let one of the variables in our analysis be text portion. One should not subdivide the text into too many portions since the smaller a portion, the fewer vowels it contains and the less reliable the statistical results. When we examine our store of vowels, conservative statistical practice dictates that, for overall analyses of the Hebrew Bible, we work with no more than seventy-six portions. These we define by subdividing large books at natural boundaries or by combining similar small books. For example, Genesis 39–50 (most of the Joseph Cycle) is one portion; Amos, Obadiah, and Micah combine to form another portion. When we analyze single vowel types, good statistical practice may require that fewer than seventy-six portions be used. For example, in analyzing our Type 30, which only involves eighty-four vowel-choice opportunities, we are allowed no more than eight portions. In fact, we use only five portions (Pentateuch, Former Prophets, Latter Prophets, Poetry, and Other Writings).

Word Aesthetics

Gesenius made three other assertions about Hebrew spelling that we subsume under the term "word aesthetics": 1) word-terminal vowels are *plene*; 2) in words where *plene* spelling would cause a letter to be immediately repeated, the tendency is to use *defective* spelling; 3) *plene* spelling in successive syllables is avoided. Having the text of the Hebrew Bible in computer-manipulable form allows us to test Gesenius' statements.

Gesenius' first assertion is correct. Aside from word-terminal ־ֶךְ, ־ֶם, and ־ֶן (see §4.1), only six of 55,439 words have a terminal vowel written without a *mater lectionis*. We declare word-terminal vowels to be of fixed spelling and drop them from our analysis as being devoid of discriminating information.

Viewed in terms of gross counts, Gesenius' second assertion is also correct. Of the 523 words whose *plene* spelling would involve **ww**, 413 (79%) are spelled *defective*; of the 18,688 words whose *plene* spelling would involve **yy**, 17,963 (96%) are *defective*. However, only a couple thousand of these words allow a choice of spelling. Of these, sixty percent are spelled *plene*. There thus appears to be no particular avoidance of immediately repeated letters when a genuine spelling option exists.

To avoid repetition, Gesenius' third assertion is taken up in § 3.2.1 below. The upshot of the analysis is that Gesenius' notion of an avoidance of doubly-*plene* words is too simple an explanation of the facts.

Word Proximity

It is natural to inquire how the spellings of a word depend on the spacing between its repetitions. One might expect increasing differences as spacing increases. As the number of intervening *segments* (pieces of words having identifiable functions) varies from none through forty (so the two instances of the repeated word are separated by at most two verses), the percent which are spelled differently, which exhibit *discordant* spelling, increases only slightly, as Figure 2.1 shows. Contrary to intuition, word proximity has very little influence on spelling practice.

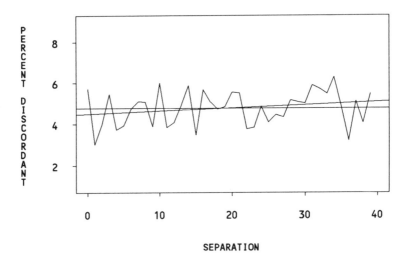

Figure 2.1 Percentage of forms with differing spellings versus separation (in segments). (Jagged line: actual data. Horizontal line: mean of the data. Upsloping line: best approximating straight line.)

Local Frequency

A study of the spelling choices made for items which are of high frequency in given portions (words which make up more than one percent of a portion's word stock) discloses no additional effects not accounted for by the three main controlling variables: type, stress, and portion.

2.5.3   The Mechanics of Data Preparation

Identifying Vowels Having Fixed Spelling

The spelling of some words or types of vowels is fixed throughout our texts and throughout the available extra-biblical materials. For example, final long vowels in almost all words are spelled *plene* (with a *mater lectionis*). When a vowel is known to have allowed no option for spelling choice, it is marked as fixed and dropped from further consideration. There are other vowels in specific words which in theory could have presented a spelling choice but which, in fact, are always spelled one way. For example, the consonantal spelling for *day* could have been **ym** or **ywm**, the former *defective* and the latter *plene*. In fact, *day* is spelled **ywm** in all 1,505 of its occurrences. On such statistical grounds, twenty-six dictionary items accounting for 36,094 text items get marked as having fixed spelling.

Labeling Vowels

All historically- or statistically-fixed vowels are dropped, leaving only vowels for which a scribe could choose between acceptable alternative spellings. Each remaining vowel is labeled as to which vowel type it is, which stress it is under, in which text portion it occurs, and which spelling choice it is. Along the way, many interesting observations regarding spelling choices in terms of type, stress, and portion emerge.

2.6 Methods of Data Analysis

While the methods of data analysis used in our research can be understood by most readers, detailed exposition is beyond the scope of this tutorial. Suffice it here to indicate the basic ideas underlying the techniques used. *Contingency table analysis* examines tables of counts of vowels corresponding to all possible combinations of attributes and determines whether the counts disclose relationships among the attributes. For example, one may determine if choice of spelling is or is not dependent on text portion. *Multidimensional scaling* creates plots in which similar items are near each other. It is then left to the analyst to decide which items form natural clusters. *Hierarchical clustering* uses the "distances" between pairs of objects to establish which objects are most similar, which objects are clustered. For example, clustering text portions reveals which are most similar in terms of their spelling-choice patterns. This technique will be explained in some detail in § 2.8.

2.7 Results

2.7.1 A Helpful Analogy

An analogy is helpful in visualizing how the text of the Hebrew Bible has been transmitted to us. Picture an urban complex consisting of sixty-five tenements, one for each of the vowel types. Each tenement has three stories, one for each level of stress a vowel can experience. Each story has a central corridor running through it. There are seventy-six positions along the corridor, one corresponding to each text portion. Each corridor position is flanked by two cubicles, one for each of the possible spelling choices. To the reception area of the complex of tenements arrives a visitor, Mr. Vowel. He is assigned to the unique cubicle corresponding to his vowel type (tenement), the stress he is under (story), the portion from which he comes (position along corridor), and which spelling choice he represents (cubicle). Every vowel involving a spelling choice is sent to its appropriate cubicle. For example, in the Hebrew

Bible the first spelling choice is the *plene* **y** representing ī in the final
vowel of the first word *In the beginning*, **br²šyt**. This vowel is sent to
tenement 11 (Type 11. Suffix –īt of feminine nouns), to the middle story
(as it is under middle stress), to the first position along the corridor (as it
occurs in the first portion of the Hebrew Bible), and to the *plene* cubicle
(as it is indicated by the *mater lectionis* **y**).

2.7.2   Possible Effects of Transmission

By analyzing the patterns of cubicle occupancy, we can determine
how spelling choice depends on the other variables. There is a further
complication. As Figure 2.2 illustrates, each copying of the text involves
relocating the vowels from one set of tenements (corresponding to the
manuscript being copied) to a new set (corresponding to the resulting
new copy). That a low-stress Type 49 noun suffix –ōn has been correctly
copied is shown by Mr. Solid Vowel taking the solid-line path from the
tenement corresponding to his vowel type in the manuscript being copied
to the identical cubicle in the tenement corresponding to his vowel type
in the new copy. That a high-stress Type 49 noun suffix –ōn has been
incorrectly copied is shown by Mr. Dotted Vowel taking the broken-line
path from a *defective* cubicle in the tenement corresponding to his vowel
type in the manuscript being copied to a *plene* cubicle in the tenement
corresponding to his vowel type in the newly written manuscript.

Error-free Theory

At one extreme, if all copying is *error-free*, the pattern of vowels in
the final complex (our copy) will be unchanged from that corresponding
to the autograph (original). A survey of the major manuscripts (**A**,
B, **C**, **L**, and **P**) discloses variations from manuscript to manuscript
in the spelling of particular words. Thus, the error-free theory of text
transmission is not tenable.

Indifference Theory

At the other extreme, suppose each time the texts are copied, there
is a tendency to introduce *matres lectionis*. Then, over the long run, the
population of the *defective* cubicles will tend to migrate over into the
opposite *plene* cubicles. If the *plene*-izing process continues long enough,
the received spelling will reflect not the spelling practices of the texts'
originators but rather those of the copyists. In such a situation, spelling
practice will be homogeneous across the portions.

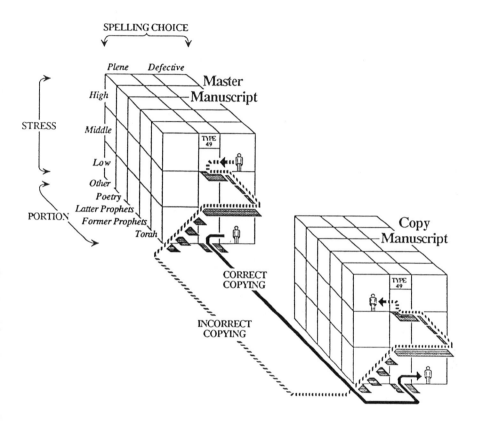

Figure 2.2 Tenement analogy for the copying process

Mixed Theory

Encompassing the *error-free theory* and the *indifference theory* is the *mixed theory* which allows the extent of copyist changes to various text portions to have ranged from very few, through sufficiently few to preserve significant traces of the spelling practices of the originators of the texts, to complete modernization of the spelling.

2.7.3   Examples of Text Portion and Spelling Choice Association

When we analyze the spelling data, we find that a few vowel types show little association between spelling choice and text portion, their spelling being essentially homogeneous across the Hebrew Bible. A few other vowel types show a spuriously strong association between spelling choice and text portion due to very localized, idiosyncratic spelling of a few dictionary items. But the majority of vowel types display a genuine association between spelling choice and text portion.

Since associations between spelling choice and text portion exist, it is meaningful to examine the similarities among text portions regarding spelling practices. To illustrate such examination, we first discuss spelling practices for two particular words and then show the clusters formed by text portions when *overall* spelling practice is assessed.

David

This name is spelled two ways in the Hebrew Bible: **dwd** (*defective*) 789 times and **dwyd** (*plene*) 286 times, about a quarter of the total. Most occurrences are in the parallel histories: Samuel–Kings and Chronicles–Ezra–Nehemiah. Their spelling choices are shown in Table 2.1. The distribution is quite clear-cut and makes historical sense. In Samuel–Kings the MT retains the older spelling almost entirely. In Chronicles–Ezra–Nehemiah the spelling is consistently modern.

Table 2.1 Spelling of 'David' in parallel histories

Portion	*Defective*	*Plene*	Total
Sam–Kings	669	3	672
Chron–Ezra–Neh	0	272	272
Total	669	275	944

The Object Marker

Hebrew has a preposition which marks the object of a verb. When the object is a pronoun, the (pronoun-suffixed) marker (ʾōt–) may be spelled either ᵓt– (*defective*) or ᵓwt– (*plene*). The marker's distribution is uneven, there being 656 (almost half) in the Pentateuch but only 64 in the Writings. Of the 1,387 such markers in the Hebrew Bible, 357 (nearly twenty-six percent) are spelled *plene*.

ᵓōt– occurs only twice in Job, twice in Proverbs. Where a word is this rare, *statistical* study is meaningless. To put in popular language a principle we followed rigorously in our book, the larger the sample, the more confidence we can have in statistics. Here we shall restrict our attention to the ten books in which ᵓōt– occurs at least sixty times.

Table 2.2 shows the percentage of *plene* spellings in these books, ranked from lowest (Exodus, with 4.4%) to highest (Ezekiel, with 62%). The range is wide. The scores are generally low in the Pentateuch and Samuel–Kings. The Latter Prophets and Joshua are high.

Table 2.2 Spelling of ᵓōt– in ten books

Book	Defective	Plene	Total	% Plene
Exodus	130	6	136	4.4
Genesis	156	9	165	5.5
Samuel	81	5	86	5.8
Leviticus	131	9	140	6.4
Kings	101	8	109	7.3
Numbers	116	15	131	11.5
Deuteronomy	69	15	84	17.9
Jeremiah	75	56	131	42.7
Joshua	27	40	67	59.7
Ezekiel	62	102	164	62.2

2.8 Hierarchical Clustering

2.8.1 A Geographical Example

In our book, we systematically studied sixty-five different types of vowels, assessing the statistical significance of the data by means of stringent criteria and controls. Here we provide only the barest summary of our procedures and results.

As was noted earlier, *hierarchical clustering* is a way of charting the similarities among sets of objects described by attributes. Its result is visualized via a diagram called a *tree* or *dendrogram*. An understanding of the analysis process and associated tree can be gained by considering a situation involving a single attribute: geographical separation.

Figure 2.3 Twenty selected continental U.S. cities

Figure 2.3 indicates the locations of twenty U.S. cities. The *tree* in Figure 2.4 shows the hierarchy of clusters formed by the cities when we characterize them solely in terms of their geographical separations. The tree is obtained as follows. First, a distance measure is defined. Even for our simple geographical example this is not a trivial matter as we must define the distance between groups (clusters) of cities. (A single city is a cluster having but one member.) Put concretely, how far apart is the cluster consisting of our four West Coast cities from that consisting of our three Northeastern cities? For the limited purposes of this paper, we may choose our definition of inter-cluster distance as either: 1) the mean of the distances between each of the cities in one cluster and each of the cities in the other cluster; or 2) the distance between the two closest cities, one from each cluster; or 3) the distance between the two furthest cities, one from each cluster. Each of these definitions has its advantages and disadvantages. We choose the third definition (for reasons discussed below in § 8.3). Thus, the distance between our West Coast and Northeastern groups of cities is the distance between Portland (Maine) and San Francisco, around 2,700 miles.

Next, a tree scale is defined by determining which pair of cities is furthest apart. For our twenty cities, San Francisco and Portland (Maine) are the furthest apart. This allows us to begin our tree by drawing the linear scale in Figure 2.4. (In Figure 2.4, a range of 0 to 2,500 miles has been used.)

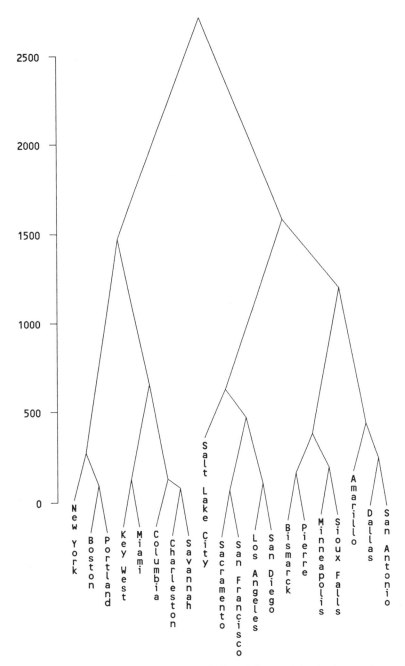

Figure 2.4 Tree diagram describing hierarchical clustering of cities

Next, clustering begins. At each stage of the analysis process, clustering involves merging the two clusters which are closest to each other (most similar). For the first stage, each individual city is a cluster consisting of but one item. (The original objects are often called *leaves* since they appear at the "highest" branches of the trees.) So, to find the two closest clusters, we find the two closest cities. For the great-circle distances used in our example, these are San Francisco and Sacramento. The names of the two cities are positioned adjacent to each other at the zero end of the distance scale, and line segments are drawn from each which join at the level of the distance scale corresponding to the geographical separation (in miles) of the two clusters (cities). The merging of the two cities indicates that they form a cluster. In all subsequent merges this pair of cities is treated as a single entity. As the merging process continues, a stage will finally be reached when only two clusters remain. As the final stage, these are merged into a grand cluster containing all twenty of the cities. This merge occurs at a distance of about 2,700 miles since the distance between the two clusters being combined is defined by the distance between the pair of cities, one from each cluster, most remote from each other (San Francisco and Portland, Maine, as noted above).

Examination of the tree resulting from the clustering reveals the patterns of similarity among the cities. The Northeastern cities merge together early as do the Southeastern cities, the West Coast cities, the Texas cities, the midwestern cities. The Northeastern and Southeastern clusters merge, as do the midwestern and Texas clusters. The Western and Central clusters next merge. Finally, the East Coast and Central/Western clusters merge to form the single continental U.S. cluster. All this makes sense and confirms observations readily made from the map.

Had we suitably combined a set of attributes designed to reflect multiple characteristics of the cities (educational opportunities, crime rates, per capita incomes, and so forth), the resulting tree would have grouped the cities into clusters based on the whole range of attributes.

2.8.2   Text Clustering Based on Spelling Practice

When hierarchical clustering is applied to our data on spelling, the tree in Figure 2.5 results. (This figure is reproduced in § 8.3 of this volume, where a detailed discussion of its characteristics is given.)

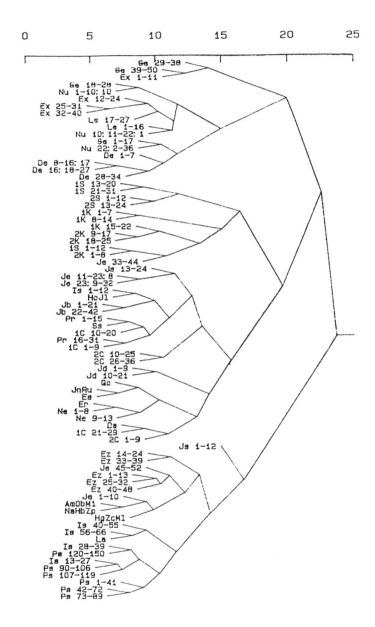

Figure 2.5 Tree of spelling practices for 76 text portions (The most similar portions are Exodus 25–31 and 32–40 as branches joining these are "highest" in the tree. Joshua 1–12 is the most disparate portion as it is last to merge into the tree.)

The tree's leaves are text portions. Its branches link similar text portions or groups of portions. Leaves joined by branches high in the tree (i.e., to the left in Figure 2.5) are very similar. Branches which join low in the tree link relatively dissimilar portions or clusters of portions.

Such a diagram contains details which make immediate sense, as when portions of the same book turn out to be similar. Other joins invite closer scrutiny. For example, the several portions of Isaiah are closer to portions of other books than they are to one another.

The most robust result of our work is the clustering of all portions of the Pentateuch together, away from the rest of the Hebrew Bible. (The uppermost major branch in the tree includes all the portions of the Pentateuch.) This fact can be associated with another feature: The pattern illustrated in Table 2.2 turns up again and again. The Pentateuch prefers old-fashioned spellings in many cases. There could be several explanations for this. Perhaps the manuscripts of the Pentateuch came from a different community, one with different spelling practices, than the source(s) of the rest of the Hebrew Bible. Perhaps the Pentateuch enjoyed greater veneration and so resisted modernization. Perhaps it is older than the rest.

2.9   Where Matters Stand

The spellings of Hebrew words actually used during biblical times are known from ancient inscriptions and manuscripts unearthed by archeologists. For the early period, up to the destruction of Jerusalem by the Babylonians in the sixth century, there is enough evidence from these documents to show that Bible spelling is later; it has been adjusted fairly uniformly to the standards of post-exilic times. For the turn of the era (200 BCE–200 CE), we have the Dead Sea Scrolls and other documents from the period. In them the vowel letters are used more copiously than anywhere in the Bible, although some of the earliest manuscripts found at Qumran show a restraint close to that of the Masoretic Text. The changes in spelling can thus be charted from the earliest rule ("Write consonants only!") to the latest practice ("Write long vowels with the help of consonant letters!"). Can we date biblical spelling more precisely within this range?

Unfortunately there are practically no Hebrew manuscripts or inscriptions from the time when the Hebrew Bible was taking its final shape, that is, from the fifth to third centuries BCE (the Persian Period). Aramaic was then the dominant language. To the extent that Hebrew was influenced by Aramaic, the abundant Aramaic inscriptions of the Persian Period would supply the needed points of reference.

In order to make further progress, it will be necessary to study the history of Aramaic spelling. Our impression is that both languages had similar spelling rules and that these were fairly stable over the crucial period. This suggests that the corpus of the Hebrew Bible was finally closed, and its text—including its spelling—was fixed sometime in the fourth century BCE.

The results obtained so far are a promising beginning. They display the power of the computer in this kind of research, and they uncover all kinds of problems which invite further investigation.

Chapter 3

Review: MT Spelling and Statistics

Francis I. Andersen & A. Dean Forbes

3.1 Survey of Our Previous Work

3.1.1 Background Materials

In **SHB** (Andersen and Forbes 1986), we first introduced some examples of spelling practice, identified some problems, and developed ways of analyzing spelling behavior (Chapter 1). We next reviewed the history of Hebrew spelling (Chapter 2) and expounded the development of the use of *matres lectionis* (Chapter 3). In Chapter 4, we introduced a theory of text transmission and used it to illustrate how repeated copying of the texts could easily have led to the loss of all text-differentiating orthographic information (**SHB** § 4.9). We also illustrated that such randomization need not have occurred (**SHB** § 4.10). We emphasized the importance of taking seriously the cumulative effects of repeated copying. Impressionistic approaches to spelling which rely on isolated examples have their place. But because of the ever-present possibility of copying error, their results have only limited force. The virtue of the statistical approach is that it uses all the evidence, leading to global conclusions which are less sensitive to *random* copying errors.

3.1.2   Preparing the Data for Analysis

The next three chapters of **SHB** explained data preparation tasks. We showed how writers of Hebrew developed options for spelling some vowels. There was virtually no choice for the spelling of short vowels, of diphthongs, and of vowels at the end of words, the last always long (Chapter 5). The Masoretes assumed that there had been a choice in the case of some word-terminal long ā's (**SHB** § 6.5.4). We recognized the spelling of some word-internal long vowels as virtually fixed on historical or statistical grounds (**SHB** § 5.6). On the basis of history, word class, and word shape, we classified the remaining vowels, which presented a writer or scribe with an opportunity to make a spelling choice, into the sixty-five types listed at the end of this chapter in Tables 3.2 and 3.3 (abstracted from **SHB** Chapter 6). We divided the Hebrew text into four nested sets of portions of suitable length (**SHB** Chapter 7). The sets are shown at the end of this chapter in Tables 3.4–3.6 (adapted from **SHB** Tables 7.1a-c and 7.2a-b, used with permission). ("OPPS" is the number of spelling choice opportunities.) Tables of counts were created by classifying the 108,943 opportunities for spelling choice thus identified with respect to four variables: *type* of vowel, *stress* "level," *portion* of Bible, and *choice* of spelling (**SHB** § 1.7).

3.1.3   Analyses of Spelling Practice

In **SHB** Chapter 8, we considered the possible effects on spelling of proximity, local frequency, and stress. We found that nearby repetition of similar forms influences spelling choice only slightly. We also found that stressed vowels are not relatively lengthened; at least there is no strong evidence that this circumstance increases the likelihood of *plene* spelling. Also shown in Chapter 8 (and Chapter 1): construct nouns behave more like absolutes than suffixed forms, contrary to expectation.

In **SHB** Chapter 9, we examined the behavior of each vowel type across the portions previously specified. Statistical models for the data were set up (§ 9.1; see also § 1.8). Each vowel type had its own three-dimensional table of counts (stress, portion, choice); or, if the vowel had only one stress (Types 1, 5, 6, *et cetera*), two-dimensional (portion, choice). If it could be shown for any given type that stress was an unimportant variable, the table was collapsed on stress. (That is, we summed over the stress dimension, yielding a two-dimensional table [portion, choice] of counts. See **SHB** § 9.1.) This often happened when one stress was over-represented, dominating the table (Types 2, 3, *et cetera*). The tables of counts were analyzed to determine which model best accounted for the spelling pattern of each type (§ 9.2). The analysis showed that significant orthographic information persists in the spelling patterns of many of the vowel types (**SHB** Figure 9.1).

We studied types for homogeneity and for model fit, and we detected outlier portions (stretches of spelling which accounted for an undue fraction of the inhomogeneity for a given type of vowel). We were specially interested in those portions of the Hebrew Bible which made a major contribution to the inhomogeneous spelling of any given vowel type. When the outliers were numerous, we reported only the five most conspicuous and listed them in decreasing order of contribution to inhomogeneity. Tables 3.7–3.15 gathered at the end of this chapter result from grouping the outliers of **SHB** Chapter 9 by portion rather than type. For each outlier, we report its "Deviation" in terms of overuse or underuse of *defective* or *plene* spelling. $N(D)$ and $N(P)$ give *defective* and *plene* spelling counts. (For new material on the notion of outlier and on the use of the tables, see below.) An asterisk indicates a type omitted from our analysis in Chapter 10 of **SHB**.

In Chapter 10 we studied the similarities in spelling habits among the text portions. The results were exhibited in the form of cluster diagrams, tree structures showing the affinities among portions. We found that biblical spelling is not haphazard, as hierarchical clustering led to coherent, stable groupings of text portions.

Chapter 11 summarized results and offered conclusions. Finally, the *Epilog* indicated that there is ample scope for debate and abundant room for ongoing work.

3.2 Further Explanation

In spite of our efforts to make the statistical arguments in **SHB** accessible, some reviewers have found them difficult to follow. Here, we offer further explanation on three sticking points: 1) the spelling of vowels in successive syllables, 2) the effects of Markov chains, and 3) the definition of outliers and their detection.

3.2.1 *Plene* Vowels in Successive Syllables

On **SHB** page 112, *apropos* of the Gesenius–Kautzsch–Cowley assertion (§ 8 1 (a)) that "the scriptio plena in two successive syllables was generally avoided," we displayed the double-vowel data for the Hebrew Bible (reproduced as Table 3.1 on the next page). We then observed:

> Overall, 9,874 of the 67,844 paired instances are doubly *plene* (14.6%). Thus, there are about two-thirds the number of *plenes* in successive syllables as we would expect were the

choice of *defective* or *plene* equiprobable. This is hardly evidence that double *plenes* were avoided.

Having made this observation *sans* discussion, we immediately focused on the facts which make any generalization about the spelling of double vowels in the Hebrew Bible, considered as a unit, misleading: the extent to which double-vowel spelling practice differed among the MT sections.

Table 3.1 Double-vowel incidence counts

Section	DD	DP	PD	PP	Total
Torah	8953	5100	2403	1533	17989
Former Prophets	7646	4276	1613	1733	15268
Latter Prophets	5869	4496	2342	2702	15409
Poetry	2633	2976	960	1769	8338
Other Writings	4129	3352	1222	2137	10840
Total	29230	20200	8540	9874	67844

We showed, for example, that the Torah was over-rich with DD-pairs, under-rich with PP-pairs and the Poetry was under-rich with DD-pairs, over-rich with PP-pairs. Lumping these disparate behaviors together as the GKC generalization does (*i.e.*, performing a marginal analysis) loses important facts regarding the differing practices. A reviewer missed this (admittedly insufficiently explicit) logic:

> A nonstatistician might easily have interpreted these figures (9,874 out of 67,844) as mathematical confirmation of GKC's impressionistic and traditional assertion. (Hamilton 1988)

This comment reveals a common confusion: that a phenomenon is rare does not necessarily imply that it was avoided. Temporarily putting aside—for the sake of argument—the central fact that the GKC generalization inappropriately ignores a *crucial* source of spelling variation (section of the Hebrew Bible), further discussion may be helpful. The GKC generalization is twofold: something is generally being *avoided*, and that something is *plene spelling in successive syllables*. Suppose the *plene* or *defective* writing of any vowel is equiprobable. Then we would expect half of the vowels to be written *plene* and half to be written *defective*. In fact, overall for vowel pairs, only thirty-six percent (rather than fifty percent) are *plene*, suggesting that *plene* vowels are—in some circumstance(s)—"avoided." This leaves the question as to what the circumstances of avoidance are. Just because the "PP" sequence is rare (9,874 out of 67,844) does not allow us to infer that *plene-plene* is avoided. The "PD" sequence is even more rare (8,540 out of 67,844). Look at the counts for the second vowel in the pairs. 37,770 are spelled *defective* (56%), and 30,074 are spelled *plene* (44%). As compared with the prediction based on randomness, there is a mild "avoidance" of *plenes* in the second vowel of a pair. Compare the counts for the first vowel in the pairs. 49,430 are spelled *defective* (73%), and 18,414 are spelled *plene* (27%). As compared with the prediction based on randomness, there is a strong "avoidance" of *plenes* in the first vowel of a pair. In light of these facts, did the scribes generally avoid *plene-plene* in successive syllables (as GKC assert) or did they generally avoid a *plene* spelling as the first of a pair of vowels? In fact, the question is ill-posed since the foregoing discussion has—to simplify the exposition—ignored vowel type, stress, and portion.

3.2.2   The Effects of Markov Chains

On **SHB** pages 115–125, we introduced the notion of the copy channel. We set forth an algebraic apparatus for describing it. We used tabular displays to show the effects of repeated copying on the vowel distributions for a quartet of hypothetical portions. When the error rates were high (**SHB** Table 4.6), the four portions emerged from repeated copyings with identical vowel distributions. The error-rich copyings had obliterated all evidence of differences in vowel distributions present initially. When the error rates were low (**SHB** Table 4.7), the portions emerged with statistically detectable differences.

For some reviewers, the basic ideas of the Markov channel and its behavior were obscured—not clarified—by the equations and tables. This is unfortunate, for the basic ideas are very simple. In an effort to set matters right, we shall re-explain the ideas here, using a parlor game analogy whose analysis requires only arithmetic.

Consider a game of gossip with seventeen players. (According to Webster, *gossip* is "a humorous party pastime in which a sentence or anecdote is whispered from one person to the next around the group and the final version compared with the original.") Let the "sentence" consist of a string of randomly intermixed D's and P's (standing, of course, for *defective* and *plene* vowels). For simplicity of analysis, suppose the players are uniform in their tendency to make errors. Namely, suppose each player misrepeats 20% of the D's as P's and 10% of the P's as D's. Now, send three different messages through the group (through the Markov channel). Let the first message consist of 20 D's and 20 P's. Let the second consist of 5 D's and 35 P's. Let the third consist of 35 D's and 5 P's. With how many D's and P's are the messages likely to emerge? The first trio of diagrams (Figure 3.1) shows the likely composition of each message as it leaves each player. (For ease of comprehension, the D's and P's are gathered.) Generation of the diagrams involves simple arithmetic. The first message leaves the first speaker as a 20D/20P message. Twenty percent of the D's (4) are heard as P's, and ten percent of the P's (2) are heard as D's. This means that the second speaker transmits an 18D/22P message, as the diagram shows. And so on. The point of all this is that each of the messages, although of quite different composition initially, emerge from the channel with exactly the same composition: 13D/27P, as Figure 3.1 illustrates. The ratio of D's to P's is completely determined by the error characteristics of the channel. In each case, the final message contains *no* information about the original message!

The second trio of diagrams (Figure 3.2) shows what happens when the error rates are reduced by an order of magnitude, so each player misrepeats 2% of the D's as P's and 1% of the P's as D's. With these lower error rates, seventeen repeatings do not suffice to destroy all information about the original messages, the drift toward equilibrium being much slower.

3.2.3   Outliers and Their Detection

Clarification regarding the *outlier* portions listed in **SHB** § 9.2 (and reorganized and gathered as Tables 3.7–3.15 at the end of this chapter) may prove helpful.

We consider first the notion of *outlier*, in general and as used in our work. A few examples will make the general idea clear: A one-hundred-year-old man is an outlier as regards age. An individual who earns a million dollars a year is an outlier as regards income. These are instances of *univariate outliers*, objects which exhibit atypical behavior when judged in terms of single attributes. A ten-year-old child is not an outlier as regards age. Nor is an individual who earns \$30,000 a year as regards income. But a ten-year-old child who earns \$30,000 a year *is* an outlier as regards age and income considered jointly. This is an instance of a *multivariate outlier*, an object which exhibits atypical behavior when judged in terms of multiple attributes. An object may be quite unremarkable as regards its attributes taken separately but be quite remarkable when the attributes are taken together.

In **SHB** § 9.2, we document the outcome of contingency table analyses for each relevant spelling sub-type. For each sub-type, we report the allowed departure from agreement with the relevant model beyond which we declare portion and spelling associated for the given sub-type; this threshold is $\chi^2_{99\%}$. Immediately to the left of each threshold value, we report the observed departure from the relevant model, G_s^2. If $G_s^2 > \chi^2_{99\%}$, portion and spelling are declared associated. When one or a few portions contribute excessively to the total G_s^2 (*i.e.*, when portions are outliers as regards the spelling of the type under consideration), we list the portions, reporting their contribution to the total discrepancy. Each individual contribution is G_1^2. For example, for Type 25 (stem-terminal $\bar{e}$ in nouns), we report that the model of independence properly fits our data provided G_s^2 does not exceed $\chi^2_{99\%}$, which equals (in this case) 106.4. But $G_s^2 = 356.7$, so portion and spelling are strongly associated for Type 25. However, when we look at the outliers whose particulars are given on **SHB** page 260, we see that one portion (Js 13–24) contributes a $G_1^2 = 290.7$ to the total $G_s^2 = 356.7$. Were the spelling data from this one portion suppressed, the spelling of Type 25 would be homogeneous across the portions, as $G_s^2 - G_1^2 = 356.7 - 290.7 = 66$.

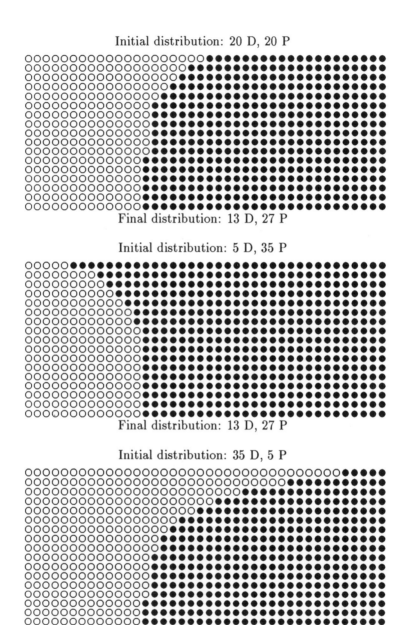

Figure 3.1 Three portions through error-rich channel. Error
rates: 20% D → P, 10% P → D

Initial distribution: 20 D, 20 P

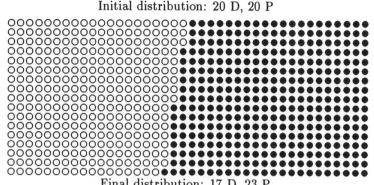

Final distribution: 17 D, 23 P

Initial distribution: 5 D, 35 P

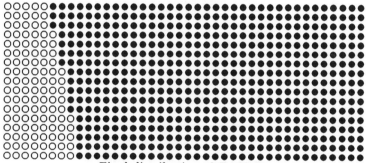

Final distribution: 8 D, 32 P

Initial distribution: 35 D, 5 P

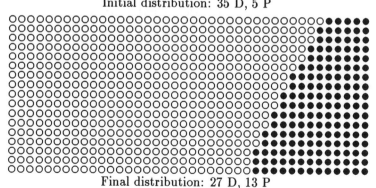

Final distribution: 27 D, 13 P

Figure 3.2 Three portions through error-sparse channel.
Error rates: 2% D → P, 1% P → D

Table 3.2 Vowel types for ī, ē, ἐ, and ā

Type 1.	Suffix ī on finite verbs
Type 2.	Stem ī in *qal* of hollow roots
Type 3.	Stem ī in perfect of ל״ה roots
Type 4.	Stem ī in *hiph⁽ᶜ⁾il* forms
Type 5.	Stem ī in forms from פ״י roots
Type 6.	Suffix –ī(m) of plural nouns
Type 7.	Stem ī (first vowel) in other nouns
Type 8.	Stem ī in nouns with hollow roots
Type 9.	Stem ī (second vowel) in nouns
Type 10.	Stem ī in other proper nouns
Type 11.	Suffix –ī(t) of feminine nouns
Type 12.	Residuum of ī opportunities
Type 13.	Stem-terminal ē in prepositions
Type 14.	Stem-terminal ē in nouns
Type 15.	Stem-initial ē in verbs
Type 16.	Stem ē in verbs from ל״י roots
Type 17.	Stem ē in verbs from other roots
Type 18.	Stem ē in nouns from hollow roots
Type 19.	Stem ē (first vowel) in other nouns
Type 20.	Stem ē (second vowel) in nouns
Type 21.	Stem ē (first vowel) in proper nouns
Type 22.	Stem ē (second vowel) in proper nouns
Type 23.	Stem ē (first vowel) residuum
Type 24.	Stem ē residuum
Type 25.	Stem-terminal ἐ in nouns
Type 26.	Stem ἐ in verbs
Type 27.	Suffix –tā of perfect verbs
Type 28.	Suffix –nā of feminine plural verbs
Type 29.	Suffix ā of intensive imperatives

Table 3.3 Vowel types for ō and ū

Type 30.	The preposition **kāmō**
Type 31.	Words ending in ō (not *his*)
Type 32.	The negative particle *not*
Type 33.	*Nota accusativi* ʾōt-
Type 34.	Stem ō (first vowel) in prepositions and nouns
Type 35.	Stem ō in *hiph^cil* of יʾʾפ roots
Type 36.	Suffix ō in *hiph^cil*s, etc.
Type 37.	Suffix –ō(t) of לʾʾה infinitives
Type 38.	Stem ō in infinitives absolute
Type 39.	Stem ō in *qal* active participles
Type 40.	Stem ō in *qal* imperfect regular verbs
Type 41.	Stem ō in *qal* imperfect פʾʾן roots
Type 42.	Stem ō in *qal* imperfect verbs of hollow roots
Type 43.	Stem ō in regular imperative and infinitive
Type 44.	Stem ō in imperative and infinitive of hollow roots
Type 45.	Stem ō in *pōlēl*
Type 46.	Stem ō (first vowel) in nouns
Type 47.	Plural suffix –ō(t) of nouns of hollow roots
Type 48.	Plural suffix –ō(t) of nouns, regular roots
Type 49.	Suffix –ōn of nouns
Type 50.	Stem ō (second vowel) in nouns
Type 51.	Stem ō in other proper nouns
Type 52.	Stem ō in *niph^cal*s of irregular roots
Type 53.	Stem ō (first vowel) residuum
Type 54.	Stem ō in verbs—residuum
Type 55.	Stem ō residuum
Type 56.	Suffix ū on finite verbs
Type 57.	Suffix –ūn on finite verbs
Type 58.	Stem ū in imperfect verbs
Type 59.	Stem ū in imperative and infinitive
Type 60.	Stem ū in *hoph^cal*s
Type 61.	Stem ū in *qal* passive participles
Type 62.	Stem ū in nouns of hollow roots
Type 63.	Stem ū (first vowel) in other nouns
Type 64.	Stem ū in other nouns
Type 65.	Stem ū residuum

Table 3.4 The seventy-six portions

P#	BOUNDARIES	OPPS	CONTENTS
1	Ge 1-17	1554	Creation → circumcision covenant
2	Ge 18-28	1362	Hebron visit → Jacob at Bethel
3	Ge 29-38	1419	Jacob at Paddan-aram → Tamar
4	Ge 39-50	1928	most of Joseph cycle
5	Ex 1-11	1207	Moses' beginnings → plagues
6	Ex 12-24	1550	Passover → covenant
7	Ex 25-31	1418	P cultic laws
8	Ex 32-40	1489	restoration of covenant → end
9	Le 1-16	1881	worship → rite of atonement
10	Le 17-27	1520	Holiness Code plus appendix
11	Nu 1-10:10	1682	sojourn at Sinai [P]
12	Nu 10:11-22:1	1549	Sinai-Paran → Kadesh-Moab
13	Nu 22:2-36	2144	Balaam story → end
14	De 1-7	1359	God's acts → conquest of Canaan
15	De 8-16:17	1213	past lessons → yearly pilgrimages
16	De 16:18-27	1315	officials' duties → Shechem ceremony
17	De 28-34	1295	blessings and cursings → Moses' death
18	Js 1-12	1818	conquest of western Palestine
19	Js 13-24	1722	division of land → end
20	Jd 1-9	1541	Canaan invasion → story of Abimelech
21	Jd 10-21	1608	tale of Tola → end
22	1S 1-12	1453	Samuel's birth → his farewell
23	1S 13-20	1366	independence war → Jonathan
24	1S 21-31	1427	Saul & David at war → Gilboa battle
25	2S 1-12	1561	David at Hebron → Nathan's rebuke
26	2S 13-24	1938	David's court problems → end
27	1K 1-7	1707	David's last days → building of temple
28	1K 8-14	1386	temple dedication → story of Rehoboam
29	1K 15-22	1221	North-South wars → Jehoshaphat
30	2K 1-8	1062	Elisha narratives
31	2K 9-17	1599	Jehu's revolution → fall of North
32	2K 18-25	1289	Assyrian period → end
33	Is 1-12	1231	superscription → thanksgiving
34	Is 13-27	1379	doom of Babylon → last trumpet
35	Is 28-39	1358	lesson for dissolute → end, 1st Isaiah
36	Is 40-55	1833	Second Isaiah
37	Is 56-66	1150	Third Isaiah

Table 3.5 The seventy-six portions

P#	BOUNDARIES	OPPS	CONTENTS
38	Je 1-10	1533	superscription → prayer
39	Je 11-23:8	1552	Jeremiah's life → Judah's king
40	Je 23:9-32	1611	prophets → purchase of field
41	Je 33-44	1604	restoration → Jeremiah in Egypt
42	Je 45-52	1543	oracles against nations, appendix
43	Ek 1-13	1650	superscription → against prophets
44	Ek 14-24	1900	idolators → Jerusalem's fall
45	Ek 25-32	1242	oracles against foreign nations
46	Ek 33-39	1200	restoration of Israel
47	Ek 40-48	1588	restored community
48	Hs/Jl	1269	Hosea and Joel
49	Am/Ob/Mi	1541	Amos, Obadiah, Micah
50	Na/Hb/Zp	877	Nahum, Habakkuk, Zephaniah
51	Hg/Zc/Ml	1653	Haggai, Zechariah, Malachi
52	Ps 1-41	2169	Book I
53	Ps 42-72	1785	Book II
54	Ps 73-89	1276	Book III
55	Ps 90-106	1042	Book IV
56	Ps 107-119	1119	Book Va
57	Ps 120-150	1172	Book Vb
58	Jb 1-21	1632	prose prolog → 2nd cycle
59	Jb 22-42	1678	3rd cycle → prose epilog
60	Pr 1-15	1460	title → Solomon's wisdom, I
61	Pr 16-31	1489	Solomon's wisdom, II → end
62	Jn/Ru	674	Jonah and Ruth
63	SS	624	Song of Songs
64	Qo	922	Qohelet
65	La	694	Lamentations
66	Es	1014	Esther
67	Da	965	Daniel less 2:4-7:28
68	Er	1065	Ezra less 4:8-6:18; 7:12-26
69	Ne 1-8	1246	Jerusalem → reading of law
70	Ne 9-13	1171	marriage reform → end
71	1C 1-9	1629	genealogies
72	1C 10-20	1453	end of Saul → David's victory
73	1C 21-29	1342	census → David's farewell
74	2C 1-9	1379	reign of Solomon
75	2C 10-25	1853	reign of Rehoboam → Amaziah
76	2C 26-36	1793	Uzziah → last kings of Judah

Table 3.6 Hierarchy of 5/10/30 divisions

5	10	30	BOUNDARIES	OPPS
Torah	A	i	Ge 1-28	2916
		ii	Ge 29-50	3347
		iii	Ex 1-24	2757
		iv	Ex 25-40	2907
	B	v	Le	3301
		vi	Nu	5375
		vii	De 1-16:17	2572
		viii	De 16:18-34	2610
FP	C	ix	Js	3540
		x	Jd	3149
		xi	1S	4246
		xii	2S	3499
	D	xiii	1K	4314
		xiv	2K	3950
LP	E	xv	Is 1-39	3968
		xvi	Is 40-66	2983
		xvii	Je 1-32	4696
		xviii	Je 33-52	3147
	F	xix	Ek 1-24	3550
		xx	Ek 25-48	4030
		xxi	Hs-Mi	2810
		xxii	Na-Ml	2530
Poetry	G	xxiii	Ps 1-72	3954
		xxiv	Ps 73-150	4609
	H	xxv	Jb	3310
		xxvi	Pr	2949
Other	I	xxvii	Jn/Ru-Da	4893
		xxviii	Er-Ne	3482
	J	xxix	1C	4424
		xxx	2C	5025

Table 3.7 Outliers for five portions

Portion (5)	Deviation	N(D)	N(P)	G_1^2	Type	Stress
Torah	+D -P	17	8	12.3	30	H
Is-Je-Ek-MP	+D -P	11	4	8.8	63	M
Ps-Jb-Pr	+D	2	12	6.7	8	M
Ps-Jb-Pr	-D +P	0	12	11.9	63	M

Table 3.8 Outliers for ten portions

Portion (10)	Deviation	N(D)	N(P)	G_1^2	Type	Stress
Ge-Ex	-P	160	0	24.9	22	H
Ge-Ex	+D -P	33	0	28.7	36	LMH
Ge-Ex	-P	19	0	8.2	41	H
Ge-Ex	+D -P	23	1	13.9	44	L
Ge-Ex	+D -P	29	36	20.0	47	M
Ge-Ex	-P	21	0	9.7	54	LMH
Ge-Ex	+D -P	15	6	22.2	63	L
Le-Nu-De	+D -P	8	27	19.8	8	H
Le-Nu-De	+D -P	4	31	8.7	36	LMH
Le-Nu-De	+D -P	30	2	33.3	37	L
Js-2S	-D +P	23	12	39.7	22	H
Js-2S	+D -P	49	0	23.0	41	H
Js-2S	-D +P	14	16	7.8	44	L
Is-Je	+D -P	21	7	41.2	20	M
Is-Je	-D +P	12	10	9.3	41	H
Ek-MP	+D	7	32	11.3	8	L
Ek-MP	-D +P	9	44	9.6	16	LMH
Ek-MP	+D -P	14	1	23.5	20	M
Ek-MP	-D +P	4	25	20.0	37	L
Ek-MP	-D +P	3	38	8.2	47	M
Ek-MP	+D -P	16	13	7.1	52	LMH
Ek-MP	+D -P	11	4	16.2	61	M
Ek-MP	+D -P	8	14	15.0	65	LMH*
Ps	+D -P	4	1	7.2	20	M
Ps	-D +P	1	10	9.2	37	L
Ps	-D +P	0	3	7.0	44	L
Jb-Pr	+D -P	6	4	14.4	23	L*
Jb-Pr	-D +P	14	11	9.8	41	H
Jb-Pr	-D +P	4	31	10.3	52	LMH
Jn/Ru-Ne	+D -P	22	2	41.3	16	LMH
Jn/Ru-Ne	-D +P	0	22	12.1	47	M
Jn/Ru-Ne	-D +P	2	29	10.4	63	L
1-2C	-D +P	4	19	26.3	36	LMH

*—Type omitted from analyses in Chapter 10 of **SHB**.

Table 3.9 Outliers for thirty portions

Portion (30)	Deviation	N(D)	N(P)	G_1^2	Type	Stress
Ge 1-28	+D -P	5	3	11.9	28	L*
Ge 1-28	+D -P	36	2	17.8	55	H*
Ge 29-50	+D -P	8	12	11.1	28	L*
Ex 1-24	+D -P	6	7	9.9	28	L*
Ex 1-24	+D -P	8	0	12.8	44	H
Ex 25-40	+D -P	4	4	10.8	1	H
Ex 25-40	+D -P	4	1	12.1	5	L
Ex 25-40	+D -P	5	0	21.8	28	L*
Ex 25-40	+D -P	16	4	7.4	61	L
Ex 25-40	+D -P	9	6	28.3	62	L
Le	+D -P	13	46	19.3	11	LMH
Nu	+D -P	11	24	23.5	11	LMH
Nu	+D -P	39	18	25.7	50	M
Nu	+D -P	70	32	47.3	61	L
De 1-16:17	-D +P	0	16	10.3	34	M
De 1-16:17	+D -P	6	2	22.6	62	L
De 16:18-34	+D -P	2	0	8.6	28	L*
Js	-D +P	0	9	10.0	38	H
Jd	+D -P	46	15	55.1	10	H
Jd	-D +P	19	12	12.8	39	M
1S	+D -P	6	14	9.8	1	H
1S	+D -P	7	10	20.0	2	LMH
1S	+D -P	8	10	11.9	5	L
1S	+D -P	15	6	7.7	38	H
2S	+D -P	5	13	8.0	9	M
2S	+D -P	4	3	8.3	64	M
1K	+D -P	11	3	6.6	44	H
2K	+D -P	51	12	26.5	21	L
2K	-P	30	0	9.0	39	M

*—Type omitted from analyses in Chapter 10 of **SHB**.

Table 3.10 Outliers for thirty portions

Portion (30)	Deviation	N(D)	N(P)	G_1^2	Type	Stress
Is 1-39	-D +P	0	16	12.3	10	H
Is 40-66	-D +P	0	17	21.3	50	M
Je 1-32	+D -P	10	20	20.8	9	M
Je 33-52	-D +P	2	29	9.0	34	M
Je 33-52	+D -P	15	6	7.7	38	H
Je 33-52	+D -P	12	21	10.9	53	H*
Je 33-52	+D -P	9	20	13.4	59	LMH
Ek 1-24	-D	0	42	6.7	1	H
Ek 1-24	+D -P	13	5	33.2	49	M
Ek 25-48	+D -P	10	12	9.8	34	M
Ek 25-48	-D +P	0	33	10.4	53	H*
Ek 25-48	-D	1	54	8.8	64	M
Na-Ml	+D -P	4	4	7.0	64	M
Ps 1-72	-D	0	29	8.2	5	L
Ps 1-72	-D +P	11	10	19.3	19	L
Ps 1-72	-D +P	11	39	14.0	45	L
Ps 1-72	-D +P	13	46	57.6	55	H*
Ps 73-150	-D +P	8	40	20.6	45	L
Ps 73-150	-D +P	27	31	12.1	55	H*
Ps 73-150	-D +P	1	15	9.2	61	L
Pr	+D -P	10	4	12.2	34	M
Pr	-D +P	4	3	7.2	55	L*
Pr	-D +P	4	10	9.2	55	H*
Pr	+D -P	5	2	20.7	57	H
Er-Ne	-D +P	5	28	12.0	10	H
Er-Ne	+D -P	28	9	9.4	21	L
Er-Ne	+D -P	27	5	21.7	45	L
Er-Ne	+D -P	23	7	20.8	50	M
Er-Ne	+D -P	15	5	39.8	53	H*
Er-Ne	-D +P	2	4	14.4	55	L*
1C	-D +P	16	38	13.2	21	L
1C	-D +P	0	11	10.8	61	L
2C	-D +P	29	17	17.2	39	M
2C	-D +P	3	16	7.9	44	H

*—Type omitted from analyses in Chapter 10 of **SHB**.

Table 3.11 Outliers for seventy-six portions

Portion (76)	Deviation	N(D)	N(P)	G_1^2	Type	Stress
Ge 1-17	+D -P	6	9	29.2	14	L
Ge 1-17	+D -P	44	44	23.9	34	H
Ge 1-17	+D -P	14	4	21.2	48	M
Ge 18-28	+D -P	6	7	11.1	37	H
Ge 29-38	+D -P	44	2	68.0	34	L
Ge 29-38	+D -P	110	3	123.2	51	LMH
Ge 39-50	+D -P	20	18	30.6	13	L
Ge 39-50	+D -P	92	2	114.4	31	H
Ge 39-50	-D +P	4	150	69.2	46	L
Ex 1-11	+D -P	17	11	31.7	13	L
Ex 1-11	+D -P	25	1	39.0	34	L
Ex 1-11	+D -P	6	5	14.1	47	H
Ex 1-11	+D -P	39	11	78.2	50	H
Ex 1-11	+D -P	8	1	10.3	56	H
Ex 12-24	+D -P	12	8	21.7	13	L
Ex 12-24	+D -P	10	4	30.5	37	H
Ex 12-24	+D -P	8	16	10.3	47	H
Ex 12-24	+D -P	21	1	68.6	48	H
Ex 25-31	+D -P	4	5	7.0	37	H
Ex 25-31	+D -P	45	8	123.6	48	H
Ex 25-31	+D -P	52	8	106.2	49	H
Ex 25-31	+D -P	26	13	31.1	64	L
Ex 25-31	+D -P	12	3	25.4	64	H
Ex 32-40	+D -P	5	2	13.3	13	L
Ex 32-40	+D -P	12	11	26.2	37	H
Ex 32-40	+D -P	10	9	22.9	47	H
Ex 32-40	+D -P	23	6	36.8	48	M
Ex 32-40	+D -P	52	6	155.9	48	H
Ex 32-40	+D -P	34	7	63.0	49	H
Ex 32-40	+D -P	23	20	16.6	64	L

Table 3.12 Outliers for seventy-six portions

Portion (76)	Deviation	N(D)	N(P)	G_1^2	Type	Stress
Le 1-16	-D +P	4	92	107.7	31	H
Le 1-16	+D -P	5	5	10.1	37	H
Le 1-16	+D -P	67	89	19.4	46	L
Le 1-16	+D -P	28	6	72.6	48	H
Le 1-16	+D -P	71	7	161.8	49	H
Le 1-16	+D -P	50	34	63.5	50	H
Le 17-27	+D -P	10	6	19.1	13	L
Le 17-27	+D -P	7	0	13.7	56	H
Nu 1-10:10	+D -P	39	1	29.2	47	L
Nu 1-10:10	+D -P	60	1	45.3	48	L
Nu 1-10:10	+D -P	21	2	44.9	48	M
Nu 1-10:10	+D -P	22	5	55.9	48	H
Nu 1-10:10	+D -P	55	25	71.6	49	H
Nu 1-10:10	+D -P	16	13	12.4	64	L
Nu 10:11-22:1	+D -P	59	27	76.8	49	H
Nu 10:11-22:1	+D -P	14	6	18.1	58	LMH
Nu 22:2-36	+D -P	34	232	28.7	6	H
Nu 22:2-36	+D -P	47	3	16.3	39	H
Nu 22:2-36	+D -P	39	0	34.4	48	L
Nu 22:2-36	+D -P	32	7	55.7	48	M
Nu 22:2-36	+D -P	27	27	23.9	50	H
De 1-7	+D -P	11	26	11.7	4	H
De 1-7	+D -P	9	2	32.6	47	H
De 8-16:17	+D -P	7	4	19.4	47	H
De 28-34	-D	0	107	7.0	25	H*
De 28-34	+D -P	13	8	18.0	64	H

*—Type omitted from analyses in Chapter 10 of **SHB**.

Table 3.13 Outliers for seventy-six portions

Portion (76)	Deviation	N(D)	N(P)	G_1^2	Type	Stress
Js 1-12	-D +P	14	23	22.4	33	L
Js 1-12	-D +P	25	141	145.7	50	L
Js 1-12	+D -P	13	4	20.0	58	LMH
Js 1-12	+D -P	130	15	367.9	64	H
Js 13-24	+D -P	49	22	290.7	25	H*
Js 13-24	-D +P	6	20	18.1	47	L
Jd 1-9	-D +P	2	19	40.3	33	L
Jd 10-21	-D +P	2	35	83.2	33	L
1S 1-12	+D -P	13	0	12.9	4	L
1S 13-20	+D -P	15	48	11.3	4	H
1S 13-20	+D -P	24	13	16.8	7	L
1S 13-20	+D -P	122	27	252.3	9	H
1S 21-31	+D -P	14	1	25.3	7	L
1S 21-31	+D -P	174	62	309.5	9	H
1S 21-31	+P	59	9	11.2	32	L
1S 21-31	+D -P	6	16	10.2	61	H
2S 1-12	+D -P	20	40	26.4	4	H
2S 1-12	+D -P	195	54	385.8	9	H
2S 1-12	-D +P	39	8	13.3	32	L
2S 1-12	+D -P	14	13	20.0	35	L
2S 13-24	+D -P	7	11	6.8	9	L
2S 13-24	+D -P	95	73	97.9	9	H
2S 13-24	+D -P	13	14	16.5	35	L
2S 13-24	-D +P	82	16	66.4	51	LMH
1K 1-7	+D -P	11	24	13.2	4	H
1K 1-7	+D -P	95	1	125.9	31	H
1K 1-7	+D -P	83	6	53.0	50	L
1K 8-14	+D -P	164	31	55.3	50	L
1K 15-22	+D -P	12	0	7.8	4	L
1K 15-22	+D -P	34	5	63.3	46	L
2K 1-8	-D +P	42	8	12.4	32	L
2K 9-25	-D +P	1	21	9.1	10	H

*—Type omitted from analyses in Chapter 10 of **SHB**.

Table 3.14 Outliers for seventy-six portions

Portion (76)	Deviation	N(D)	N(P)	G_1^2	Type	Stress
Is 40-55	+D -P	12	3	14.5	7	L
Is 40-55	-D +P	19	7	7.9	40	H
Is 56-66	+D -P	16	101	14.8	6	H
Is 56-66	-D +P	10	5	7.5	40	H
Je 1-10	-D +P	125	21	29.7	32	L
Je 1-10	-D +P	6	11	10.0	42	LMH
Je 1-10	-D +P	1	16	25.9	47	L
Je 11-23:8	+D -P	14	0	6.7	4	L
Je 23:9-32	+D -P	20	15	36.3	9	L
Je 33-44	+D -P	14	0	14.8	4	L
Je 33-44	+D -P	8	0	18.1	7	L
Je 33-44	+D -P	8	8	11.8	9	L
Je 33-44	-D +P	11	5	12.8	17	LMH
Je 45-52	+D -P	17	8	11.6	3	LMH
Je 45-52	+D -P	9	16	7.6	9	L
Je 45-52	+D -P	7	6	10.5	35	L
Ek 1-13	-D +P	3	33	22.3	34	L
Ek 1-13	-D +P	9	24	19.9	48	L
Ek 14-24	-D +P	14	40	57.9	33	L
Ek 14-24	-D +P	2	40	69.2	47	L
Ek 14-24	-D +P	16	38	29.1	48	L
Ek 14-24	+D -P	21	17	22.7	50	H
Ek 25-32	+D -P	9	21	10.1	4	H
Ek 25-32	+D -P	26	146	28.3	6	H
Ek 33-39	+D -P	30	102	53.8	6	H
Ek 33-39	-D +P	0	8	20.4	42	LMH
Ek 40-48	-D +P	2	8	11.7	42	LMH
Hs-Jl	-D +P	12	12	29.1	40	H
Hg-Zc-Ml	+D -P	23	194	13.4	6	H
Hg-Zc-Ml	-D +P	65	10	12.5	32	L
Hg-Zc-Ml	+D -P	12	8	15.7	64	H

Table 3.15 Outliers for seventy-six portions

Portion (76)	Deviation	N(D)	N(P)	G_1^2	Type	Stress
Ps 1-41	-D +P	11	5	8.2	27	LMH*
Ps 1-41	-D +P	0	53	17.9	35	L
Ps 1-41	-D +P	6	26	29.5	48	L
Ps 1-41	-D +P	1	25	16.2	56	H‡
Ps 42-72	-D +P	21	12	12.4	39	L
Ps 42-72	-D +P	0	26	15.4	58	LMH
Ps 73-89	-D +P	12	10	14.6	39	L
Ps 90-106	+D -P	17	12	13.7	34	H
Ps 120-150	-D +P	8	10	12.5	49	L
Ps 120-150	-D +P	2	27	15.4	56	H
Jb 1-21	-D +P	35	20	35.2	40	H
Jb 22-42	+D -P	16	21	17.0	35	L
Jb 22-42	-D +P	4	9	16.3	49	L
Pr 1-15	-D +P	12	12	12.0	49	L
Pr 16-31	-D +P	16	12	16.1	39	L
Pr 16-31	-D +P	4	12	24.7	49	L
Jn/Ru	-D +P	6	5	7.2	39	L
Qo	-D +P	25	29	15.9	39	H
Qo	-D +P	21	27	35.4	43	LMH
La	-D +P	4	15	21.3	39	H
Es	-D +P	2	12	20.6	42	LMH
Es	-D +P	0	65	37.9	64	L
Ne 1-8	-D +P	40	16	10.4	39	L
Ne 1-8	-D +P	1	9	17.2	42	LMH
1C 1-9	-D +P	3	47	21.8	7	L
1C 21-29	+D -P	12	2	22.0	34	H
1C 21-29	+D -P	15	10	14.1	64	L
2C 1-9	-D +P	6	13	13.4	39	H
2C 1-9	-D +P	4	6	8.4	43	LMH
2C 10-25	+D -P	18	9	19.6	34	H
2C 10-25	-D +P	9	10	11.2	43	LMH
2C 10-25	-D +P	1	5	12.6	49	L
2C 10-25	-D +P	31	92	60.8	50	L
2C 10-25	+D -P	29	14	17.7	56	H‡
2C 26-36	+D -P	6	7	7.8	9	L
2C 26-36	+D -P	11	6	11.1	34	H
2C 26-36	-D +P	2	11	18.2	39	H
2C 26-36	-D +P	10	11	12.2	43	LMH
2C 26-36	+D -P	6	3	6.9	58	LMH

*—Type omitted from analyses in Chapter 10 of **SHB**.
‡—Exchange error corrected, Type 56, **SHB**, page 278.

Part II

Extensions

Chapter 4

The Spelling of Suffixes

Francis I. Andersen

4.1 More on Terminal ā

We are dubious about the conventional accounts of the apparently *defective* spelling of terminal ā in some words (**SHB** § 6.5.4). See our misgivings at **SHB** page 180. Why should ā be the only word-terminal long vowel that is not always spelled with a vowel letter? Zevit (1980: 10) asserts:

> The common defective orthography of this suffix [–kā, *thy*] in the biblical text must then be considered a scribal convention which did not, as a rule, append *m.l.* [*mater lectionis*] to the pronominal suffix *kā*.

This begs the question. And why mention only this one morpheme, when there are two or three others: –tā, *thou*, –nā, suffix of feminine plural verbs, and possibly ā, intensive imperative? And why did the Masoretes level the pronunciation of these three or four suffixes but not do it for other pairs which are spelled both with and without –h? The Masoretes apparently believed that it was permissible to write these three or four kinds of ā without –h, but when other words were found with both spellings, that is, pairs differing only in terminal –h, they assumed that the different spellings reflected different pronunciations.

There are some pairs of related spellings which did not come under our study because they do not qualify as *defective*-versus-*plene* variants

in the strict sense. That is, the Masoretes did not recognize them as
alternate spellings of the same word but as variants of the same lexeme
with slightly different pronunciation, reflected in the variant spellings.
They did not recognize cohortatives, locatives, or feminines ending in –ā
unless the word ended in –h (na^cărâ is the one exception, discussed at
SHB, 133).

Pairs such as **hm/hmh** and **hn/hnh** were not pointed as if the
first were *defective* spelling of the second; two distinct pronunciations
were accepted. Likewise **ᵓyk/ᵓykh**. Both the suffixed and unsuffixed
forms of these pairs of words are met in all sections of the Hebrew Bible,
as shown in Tables 4.1 and 4.2. (The significance of the rightmost column
["95% C.I."] is explained in **SHB** § 1.3.)

Table 4.1 Spelling of hm/hn

Portion	**hm/hn**	**hmh/hnh**	Total	% Long	95% C.I.
Torah	102	39	141	27.7	20.5–35.8
Former P.	52	56	108	51.9	42.0–61.6
Latter P.	44	154	198	77.8	71.3–83.4
Poetry	10	36	46	78.3	63.6–89.1
Other Wr.	39	37	76	46.7	37.0–60.4

Table 4.2 Spelling of ᵓyk

Portion	**ᵓyk**	**ᵓykh**	Total	% Long	95% C.I.
Torah	6	5	11	45.5	16.7–76.6
Former P.	15	2	17	11.7	1.5–36.4
Latter P.	31	3	34	8.8	1.9–23.7
Poetry	8	7	15	46.7	21.3–73.4
Other Wr.	1	0	1	0.0	0.0–95.0

Their distribution in relation to that of Types 27–29 and the thirty-eight
cases of pseudo-*plene* –kâ (whose locations are listed in Table 4.3) might
be worth studying.

Table 4.3 Locations of –kâ forms

Ge 3:09	Ex 15:11	2S 18:22	Je 29:25
Ge 10:19	Ex 15:11	2S 22:30	Je 40:15
Ge 10:19	Ex 29:35	1K 18:10	Ek 40:04
Ge 10:30	Nu 22:33	1K 18:44	Ps 21:06
Ge 13:10	De 28:22	1K 18:46	Ps 39:05
Ge 25:18	De 28:27	2K 7:02	Ps 41:08
Ge 27:07	De 28:28	Is 3:06	Ps 45:10
Ge 27:37	De 28:35	Is 10:24	Pr 2:11
Ex 7:29	1S 1:26	Je 7:27	Pr 24:10
Ex 13:16	2S 2:22		

ᶜt/ᶜth are another such pair (but see *qere* of Ezekiel 23:43 and Psalm 74:6).

In an otherwise sympathetic review of **SHB**, Pardee (1988: 278), referring to his paper in **JNES 44** (1985), p. 69, continues to maintain that the attestation of two spellings for "the same" suffix "represent inconsistent use of full and defective writing to represent ā," and to ascribe "the -*k*/-*kh* alternation rather to writing convention/inconsistency than to dialectical [*sic*] variation" (p. 279). We are still waiting for scholars who make such statements to explain the expression in the same text of two policies for the spelling of terminal â, one policy accepting *defective* spelling in the case of a few suffix morphemes, the other policy using *he* consistently in all other cases. They must justify two contradictory inferences from the same kind of data, namely that **hmh** and **hm** (Table 4.1) were spelled differently because they were different words but that the three or four pairs which the Masoretes pointed with ā were the same, even though written differently. Pardee speaks of "inconsistent use" in general terms, but does not explain why that inconsistency is allowed in just a few cases. Why is it not equally appropriate to consider any word spelled without terminal *he* as possibly ending in â?

4.2 Suffix *his*

In **SHB** § 11.3.10 we suggested that two other changes which do not come under the rubric of *defective*-versus-*plene* spelling represent a late change of policy that was carried through with amazing thoroughness, namely the use of **w** rather than **h** for word-terminal ō and the spelling of the suffix –āw, *his*, with masculine plural nouns and analogous forms with –**yw** instead of the previous –**w**. Can we track down the history of these developments? There is longstanding dispute over the first appearance of the later form of these spellings. Both are attested in

4QSam^b. (See Chapter 13.) The location in the Masoretic Text of the archaic survivors of this adjustment is accordingly of interest. The cases of *his* on a plural stem spelled –āw rather than –ā(y)w now present in the Masoretic Text must be considered minimal. Because the vocalization, such as ^{c}ēnāw, *his eyes*, is enough to show that it is plural, not singular ^{c}ēnô, *qere* is not needed and does not seem to have been invoked very often for such forms in the best manuscripts. The usual lists (Ginsburg, Gordis) have more examples than found in **A** and its nearest congeners; more even than **L**, which has more than **A**. And **L** has some not in Gordis' lists. In some cases **BHS**, guided by various text-critical considerations, suggests that the *ketib* does, in fact, point to singular. It often could, of course. But by the same token many forms ending in –**w** taken by the Masoretes as singular could be archaic spellings of plural. Similar uncertainty prevails here as with other suffixed nouns which could be either singular or plural, the latter with *defective* spelling of the stem-terminal vowel (**SHB** §§ 5.5.4 [cf. Type 14] and 5.5.5.2 [cf. Type 25]). In the case of prepositions, it is possible that the apparently *defective* form is actually a simple stem which has not developed the pseudo-plural stem-ending vowel of the standard form (cf. Type 13). So we do not know how many nouns with suffix –**w** have been read as singular with ô rather than as plural with –**āw**. Cases of the latter still in the Masoretic Text are found in Genesis (×1), Exodus (×7), Leviticus (×2), Numbers (×2), Deuteronomy (×5) [total for Torah: 17]; Joshua (×3), Samuel (×34!!), Kings (×10) [total for Former Prophets: 47]; Isaiah (×3), Jeremiah (×6), Ezekiel (×51—35 are in chapter 40!!), Minor Prophets (×4) [total for Latter Prophets: 64]; Psalms (×6), Job (×16), Proverbs (×5) [total for Poetry: 27]; Ruth (×1), Song of Songs (×1), Qohelet (×1), Lamentations (×2), Daniel (×1), Ezra (×1) [total for Other Writings: 7—note its absence from Chronicles].

At **SHB** page 325, we noted that Ginsburg's and Gordis' lists have about 180 cases. We find 162. The small number in the latest books, or at least in the last section of the canon (Other Writings), is not surprising if that spelling was obsolete by, say, 400 BCE. (We have seen that its modern replacement was in use by the third century BCE.) The large number in Ezekiel suggests that it was still in vogue in the sixth century, but the concentration in chapter 40 attracts suspicion, especially since this chapter is unusual in other orthographic features. The small number in the Pentateuch, in contrast to the large number in Samuel, is the opposite of what we would have expected and also out of keeping with their orthographic profiles in general. In this particular the Pentateuch has been almost completely updated, while Samuel has retained this archaic feature.

The fifty-five cases of –**h** for *his* are in Genesis (×6), Exodus (×4), Leviticus (×1), Numbers (×1), Deuteronomy (×1) [total for Torah: 13]; Joshua (×1), Judges (×1), Samuel (×1), Kings (×5) [total for Former Prophets: 8]; Isaiah (×3), Jeremiah (×11), Ezekiel (×11), Minor Prophets (×5) [total for Latter Prophets: 30]; Psalms (×3), Daniel (×1) [total for Writings: 4]. The Latter Prophets have the majority of the old forms.

Table 4.4 shows other words ending in ô and possibly spelled either way (Type 31, excluding the frequently occurring invariants).

Table 4.4 Other words ending in ō

Portion	-h	-w	Total	% New	95% C.I.
Torah	52	48	100	48.0	37.9–58.2
Former P.	123	36	159	22.6	16.4–29.9
Latter P.	90	85	175	48.6	41.0–56.2
Poetry	10	11	21	52.4	29.8–74.3
Other Wr.	28*	46†	74	62.2	50.1–73.2

*— 18 in Megillot
†— 44 in Ezra–Nehemiah–Chronicles

The picture is not clear. Both spellings are found in most books. The old spelling of infinitives absolute dominates the Primary History (×34—six "new") and is still strong in the Latter Prophets (×25 and ×21). With other kinds of words, the old spelling is conspicuously lacking only in Ezra–Nehemiah–Chronicles.

The spelling of many such words with terminal –**w** agrees with the tradition that this represents the vowel ō. The Masoretes assumed that this was also the vocalization when such a word ended in –**h**. This assumption was reasonable when the same place was named by words which differed only in this orthographic detail. Example: *Jericho*. But it is not certain that all such names ended in ō from early times. Cuneiform transcriptions suggest that the ending could have been ā in some cases. To the extent that this was so, the Masoretic use of *ḥolem* with such –**h** is a normalization that could have overridden a historical distinction.

4.3   Nouns Ending in –ān and –ōn

Similar leveling seems to have taken place with another class of nouns, both common and proper, ending in –**ān** or –**ōn**. In view of the soundshift *ā → ō, it is surprising that any forms in –**ān** have survived at all, unless the lengthening is secondary and late. The spelling with –**wn** is usually –ōn, and this vocalization is possible also with *defective* spelling in –**n**. When the *defective* spelling is the only one attested, the pronunciation is uncertain, and –**ān** is possible. In some cases the oral tradition sustained –**ān**. In a few cases the *defective* spelling is read as –**ān** even though the vocalization –**ōn** is indicated elsewhere by –**wn**. The result is then a pair of words identical except for the endings –**ān**/–**ōn**. Examples: ᶜênān/ᶜênōn, ʾaddān/ʾaddōn, dîšān/dîšōn, ᶜarnān/ᶜarnōn. In studying this suffix (Type 49) we accepted Masoretic vocalization at face value, not considering that the *defective* spelling, pointed –**ōn**, might have originally recorded –**ān**.

Similar indeterminacy arises with some other words. Thus 2 Kings 19:23 has **mbḥwr**, which can only be pointed **mibḥôr**, whereas the parallel text in Isaiah 37:24 has **mbḥr**, which could have been pointed **mibḥôr** but was pointed **mibḥār**. Likewise with verbs which might contain a secondary ō (Type 36). With *defective* spelling it could be thought that this vowel was not present at all. The matching forms in 2 Kings 19:22 and Isaiah 37:23 are both *plene*, while the matching forms of such verbs in 2 Kings 19:25 and Isaiah 37:26 are both *defective*. But the vowel ō was not supplied to the form in Isaiah 37:26, although it is present in the Kings parallel. 1QIsaᵃ has **hbyʾwty**.

More drastic changes in the pronunciation of certain classes of proper nouns resulted in spellings so different that the Masoretes had to vocalize them differently. As a result, such variants did not fall within our guidelines as *defective*-versus-*plene* spellings of the same word and so were not included in our study. Yet they are part of the history of Hebrew spelling. One set of examples is illustrated by *Abshalom/Abishalom*, the former actually a mispointing of *defective* spelling of the latter. The most abundant cases are names in **yĕhô–/yô–**, and –**yāhû/–yāh**. It would be interesting to see how these alternative forms line up with other spelling differences.

Chapter 5

The Spelling of ō and ē

Francis I. Andersen

5.1 Historical Development

In the Hebrew vowel system expressed in Tiberian pointing ō is only one phoneme, yet the vowel derives from at least five distinct historical changes (**SHB** § 6.4.5). These five sets of ō vowels show different spelling preferences (**SHB** p. 200). The three derivations of ō which concern us here are:

ô ← *aw sometimes *defective*

ô ← *ā sometimes *plene*

ō ← *ú mainly *defective*

Likewise ē is only one phoneme, with two main derivations:

ê ← *ay usually *plene*

ē ← *í rarely *plene*

The histories of ô and ê are not parallel, at least insofar as their spelling reflects their phonetic development. Garr (1985: 35–40) treats the diphthongs **aw** and **ay** together, as if their monophthongization proceeded in step, the changes being analogous; yet their evolution varies from dialect to dialect of Northwest Semitic, and even within Hebrew itself. These phonemes are both secondary; the changes that produced ē are analogous to two of the changes that produced ō. But the schema is skewed by the fact that ō developed also from *ā—the Old South Canaanite sound shift (Garr 1985: 30-32). The diphthongs were originally written by means of the appropriate consonant letter—*waw* or *yod*.

The retention of this spelling after the diphthong has monophthongized (historical spelling) gave *waw* and *yod* the function of vowel letters, so that what are later considered to be *plene* spellings are found at all stages. An early *defective* spelling of a word which originally contained such a diphthong shows that the diphthong had already contracted at a time when the spelling was still consonantal, or at least when it was not usual to represent medial vowels with vowel letters. So far as biblical Hebrew is concerned, the dialects in which this happened have left some, but not much, trace in the orthography of MT.

For the vowel ê ← *ay the spelling is tenaciously historical, i.e., usually *plene*. And ē ← *í is so rarely *plene* in MT that one wonders if the change had even taken place before the spelling of biblical texts was standardized and pretty well frozen. Since the diphthong **ay** contracts when not stressed, but survives when stressed, the Standard Hebrew Spelling (SHS) of the phoneme ē is paradoxical: stressed ē is spelled *defective*; unstressed ē is spelled *plene*. This pattern is perpetuated at Qumran, with practically no change. Leaving aside segholates (**SHB** § 5.4), in which vowels originally short but eventually long under stress are never spelled with vowel letters in SHS, the spelling of the phoneme ō does not reflect its history as clearly as the spelling of ē does. For ō ← *ú is not infrequently *plene* (Types 40–44) (but not ō ← *ú in segholates, **SHB** § 5.4), while ô ← *aw is often *defective*. This contrast is even more striking in Qumran spelling. There vowels derived from *i are almost never spelled *plene*, just as in SHS; but almost all vowels derived from *u are spelled with *waw*.

5.2   Biblical Spelling

If any biblical compositions arose in a northern-dialect area, or passed through channels using such a dialect or following its spelling conventions, the differences would show up in the *defective* spelling of ô ← *aw and ê ← *ay.

In southern and standard Hebrew the apparently *plene* spelling of these diphthongs in pre-exilic times still represented the phonetic spelling of the uncontracted consonant. In due time the contraction of the diphthong transformed this historical spelling into a phonetic spelling of the resultant long vowels. Accordingly one would expect these vowels to be spelled *plene* in all periods. This is more in evidence for ê ← *ay than for ô ← *aw, and that ô ← *aw is often spelled *defective* is thus difficult to explain. While it is possible that some features of Hebrew as spoken in the north have intruded into southern speech, or have infiltrated texts that were transmitted in a northern linguistic environment,

it is important to distinguish cases where ô ← *ā, for here the historical
trend is from *defective* to *plene*, as illustrated by the outliers for Type
39 (**SHB** p. 266). When a word containing ō is frequently spelled defectively in biblical portions which are generally conservative in spelling
practice, notably the Pentateuch, it is likely that that ō derives from *ā.
Such a test might even help to decide between the equivocal claims of
comparative Semitic etymology to determine the primal form of a word
containing ō in Hebrew. The attestation of two spellings for "the same"
word stem might suggest metaplasm, or a mix of dialects. In SHS, *day*
is always םוֹי, *days* םיִמָי, the stem being **yawm** for singular, **yām** for
plural (Garr 1985: 39).

At the end of the biblical period *defective* phonetic spelling of
ô ← *aw became possible in mainstream Hebrew. But then reversion
to a strictly consonantal spelling of words containing this vowel would
have gone against the combined force of historical spelling and the increased use of *waw* as a vowel letter for any and every ō. The *defective*
spelling of ô ← *aw could, of course, have represented a late archaizing
spelling contrary to dominant practice, but it is more likely that such
spellings represented archaic survivals in a text that still bore the marks
of the northern dialect of Hebrew. Freedman (1969) suggested this in
connection with certain orthographic peculiarities in the text of Job.
(Barr's 1985 attempt to discredit Freedman's work fails at crucial points
through elementary statistical lapses, such as ignoring sample size effects
and compounding evidence fallaciously.)

Interpretation of the spelling of ō for the Hebrew Bible as a whole
is complicated by the fact that we do not know the history of the vowel
ō in many words. Only in the case of Type 35 (*hiph^{c}il* forms from
פ"ו roots) can we be sure of the derivation ô ← *aw. The spelling of
ô ← *aw in such verbs is not homogeneous across MT. Unfortunately
the outliers which contribute most to the inhomogeneity of the spelling
of this type of vowel were not correctly reported on page 264 of **SHB**.
The fifth in order should have been Isaiah 40–55 ($G_1^2 = 16.2$; $-D[0]$
$+P[48]$). Jeremiah 45–52 is the sixth outlier in order. The remaining
outliers are much less significant. The second (Psalms 1–41) and fifth
(Isaiah 40–55) outliers for Type 35 use only *plene* spelling (53 and 48,
respectively), which, as we have seen, is standard for all periods. The
other outliers (2 Samuel, Jeremiah 45–52, and Job [only Job 22–42 is
cited as an outlier on page 264; Job 1–21 also behaves suspiciously, and
this supports Freedman's case]) contribute to the inhomogeneity in the
spelling of vowels of Type 35 because of overuse of *defective* spelling,
which is the anomaly we are concerned with here. In 2 Samuel there
are 27 *defective*, 27 *plene* (compare 15.3 percent *defective* for Type 35
in the whole Bible); in Job, 27 *defective*, 49 *plene*; in Jeremiah 45–52,

7 *defective*, 6 *plene*. These outliers thus represent both extremes—non-use of *defective* spelling (Isaiah 40–55, Psalms 1–41) versus overuse of *defective* spelling (the others).

The distribution of the contrasting usage is illustrated by a composition which occurs in two recensions in two of these outliers—2 Samuel 22 and Psalm 18. As is shown in Table 5.1, in Psalm 18 all such vowels are *plene*; in 2 Samuel 22 half of them are *defective*.

Table 5.1 Type 35 in parallel texts

Verse	2 Samuel 22		Psalm 18
	D	P	P
3	מושעי		
3	תושעני		
8		מוסדות	מוסדי
16	מסדות		מוסדות
20	ויצא		ויוציא
28		תושיע	תושיע
42	משיע		מושיע
48		מוריד	
49		מוציא	
50		אודך	אודך

Noun forms are more equivocal. In discussing the spelling of qōl, we noted the remarkable fact that it "is often *defective* in the Bible, specifically in Exodus." (**SHB** p. 46)[1] This would be an archaic spelling in the mainstream only if derived from *qāl. If derived from *qawl, the *defective* spelling would reflect either an archaic usage from a dialect in which the diphthong had contracted, or a late usage in which the *defective* spelling on phonetic grounds overrode the historical spelling. There are difficulties in each explanation. The second is rendered unlikely by the fact that the *defective* spelling occurs mainly in the Pentateuch, in which the earlier spelling of the diphthong would be *plene*, either consonantal spelling of the diphthong or historical spelling of the long vowel derived from it.

---

[1] In his review of **SHB**, Barr (1988: 130) at this point inquires: "Really? How often is often?" At that very place **SHB** gave all the counts, showing that "often" amounts to eleven times out of twelve for plurals (92%), 50 [corrected] times out of 493 [corrected] for singulars (10%), 45 times out of 158 when suffixed (28%). Barr continues: "A/F's statement involves including the affixed forms as part of the same bag as the cases of the word alone, while I think that these are incommensurable and have to be taken separately. This could doubtless be discussed." But we did discuss this point at great length in **SHB** pages 46–48. There we studied the spelling of the suffixed and unsuffixed forms separately, which Barr accuses us of not doing.

Other words present similar patterns. With nouns of shape CōC there are two extremes. First, ṭôb and yôm are always *plene* in MT. Cognates in other Semitic languages suggest *ṭāb; the equivocal evidence for the etymology of yôm is reviewed in **SHB** (pp. 44–46). The uniform spelling in MT points to **ywm** rather than **yām**, but we did not use this logic in the case of ṭôb because its cognates are unequivocal. Second, words like qōl have mixed spelling and comparative evidence allows for derivation from either *qāl (cf. Aramaic, Ethiopic) or *qawl (cf. Arabic), or even from both, with metaplasm in the stem—qawl in singular (because *plene* spelling is preferred), qāl in plural (*defective* preferred). While some allowance should be made for the influence of stress on spelling choice, it is the *distribution* of the variant spellings across MT (**SHB** Table 2.3 [p. 48]) that points to original qāl in Hebrew. The *defective* spellings, predominant in the Torah, are archaic survivals from a time when medial long vowels, and especially ô ← *ā, were not commonly represented by a vowel letter. Third, there are words of shape CōC, such as תֹּם, רֹעַ, רֹךְ, רֹב, עֹז, כֹּל, חֹר, חֹם, חֹק, דֹּב, which continue to reflect their development from *dubb-, etc., in the fact that the spelling of their vowel with *waw* is practically unknown in SHS. So the spelling of these three kinds of nouns in MT is historical, consistently reflecting derivation from *aw (*plene*), *ā (mixed), or *u (*defective*). These distinctions are completely lost in Qumran spelling, where *waw* is used for any and every kind of back vowel o or u, and for nearly all of them, whatever their origin and whatever their position in a word, and whether stressed or otherwise.

The spelling of ō in ʿōlām is mainly *plene* (×414). The twenty-five *defective* spellings are spread across the corpus—Genesis (×2), Exodus (×5), Leviticus (×1), Deuteronomy (×2), Kings (×4), Isaiah (×1), Psalms (×5), Job (×1), Qohelet (×2), Daniel (×1), Chronicles (×1). They represent the survival of archaic spelling in which the long vowel was not represented by a vowel letter. As with the case of the two spellings of qōl, the pattern points to ā, not aw, as the source of ō, and this is confirmed by the cognates. The same applies to the spellings of ʾēpôd (pp. 198–99 in this book), to qômâ (pp. 191–94), and to māqôm. The derivation of māqōm, *place*, is disputed—was it derived from *maqām or *maqawm? The dominant *plene* spelling (×360) has suggested the latter (Freedman 1962). But the vowel is spelled *defective* forty-one times—Genesis (×5), Exodus (×3), Numbers (×1), Deuteronomy (×2), Judges (×5), Samuel (×4), Kings (×1), Jeremiah (×5), Psalms (×1), Job (×8), Ezra–Nehemiah (×3), Chronicles (×3). In forty cases the ō is not stressed, and allowance must be made for the influence of stress on spelling choice. Only in Exodus 29:31 is the stressed vowel spelled *defective*. The orthographic evidence can be interpreted either way. But we are inclined to line these four words up with qôl and account for ō in them as derived from *ā. In this way the history of spelling, and especially the *distribution* of variant spellings over the several portions of the Hebrew Bible, can help to clear up problems of etymology.

5.3   Qumran Spelling

Qumran spelling perpetuates SHS, using the *plene* option in the spelling of long vowels even more. But it goes much further in the case of *waw* than with *yod*. The use of the latter remains more "historical," in that *yod* is still not often used for ē ← *i, let alone for short i as such (Qimron 1986: 19). The generous use in Qumran spelling of *waw* as a vowel letter contrasts completely with that of MT in the case of the so-called segholate nouns, such as קֹדֶשׁ ← *qudš-. In the MT there are over 2300 words with this phonetic shape, and only one of them (קוֹדֶשׁ in Daniel 11:30) uses *waw* to represent the stem vowel. This is in line with general biblical usage and suggests that even late in the biblical period ō ← *u, assuming that the change had taken place, was not perceived as the same phoneme as ō derived from the diphthong **aw** or from **ā**, which are frequently spelled *plene* in MT. The practice at Qumran was quite different. Qimron (1986: 38) studied 232 cases of words like קֹדֶשׁ in non-biblical texts among the Dead Sea Scrolls and found that קוֹדֶשׁ-type spelling predominates (×204), while קְדוֹשׁ and even קוֹדוֹשׁ are found as well. The contrast is typical. The word kōl, *all*, occurs 854 times in the MT. It is spelled כּוֹל only once, otherwise כָּל. In seven Qumran MSS studied by Qimron (1986: 18) כּוֹל occurs about 750 times while כָּל occurs only 28 times. More illustrations could be given. The interpretation of this evidence is problematic. It could be that *waw* is now being used to represent **u**. But whatever its phonological significance, this contrast illustrates the increased use of vowel letters, at least in some circles, at the turn of the era. The MT has almost completely bypassed this development, as if the scribes who copied mainstream proto-Masoretic texts resisted contemporary trends and largely preserved the spellings that came down from earlier times. Qumran spelling thus serves as a reference point which requires standard Hebrew spelling to be dated to the third century BCE at the latest.

Chapter 6

Archaic, Standard, and Late Spelling

Francis I. Andersen

6.1   The Problem of Dating

Another remaining task is to fine-tune the probe into the undocumented channel of transmission between the latest Old Hebrew inscriptions (early sixth century BCE) and the oldest biblical manuscripts (third century BCE, but there is not much evidence before the second century [Cross 1985b]). This issue was raised on page 320 of **SHB**.

In charting the changes in spelling practice between 600 and 300 BCE or, more narrowly, 550–350 BCE, the crucial period, we have fluctuated in our impressions. (They can be no more than that at this stage of research, and we are still a long way from being able to propose absolute dates for the spelling features of any portion of the Hebrew Bible.) In view of the paucity of inscriptional evidence and the complete lack of manuscript evidence, it could be claimed that nothing can be done about locating the main stages of stabilizing the spelling of biblical Hebrew during that uncharted interval.

This lack could be supplied in part, or at least provisionally, by the evidence in Aramaic texts of the Persian period. These are abundant enough. They display remarkable uniformity and stability over a wide geographical area. Many of them come from Jewish communities. It is a reasonable assumption that the spelling of Hebrew would be similar to the contemporary spelling of Aramaic. This can only be an assumption, however. The languages are close, but they are not the same. The available Aramaic documents are almost entirely secular, and sacred Hebrew texts might well have preserved some distinctiveness, most likely on the archaic side.

In any case we cannot yet proceed to use the evidence of Aramaic as a back-up for the missing evidence for Hebrew in the Persian period, because a systematic study of Aramaic orthography for that period is not available. We are therefore obliged for the time being to do our best to get our bearings from the Hebrew inscriptional evidence from before the Persian period and from Hebrew manuscript evidence after the Persian period (**SHB** §§ 11.3.5–11.3.6).

6.2   Phases in Biblical Spelling

In spite of all the differences we have found, the rules of Hebrew spelling in the Masoretic Text are remarkably consistent. On page 327 of **SHB**, we introduced a distinction among:

1. Standard spelling, used everywhere, predominant, and serving as a norm;

2. Archaic spelling, belonging to an earlier norm, as the inscriptions show, and more evident in the Pentateuch but by no means restricted to that part of the Hebrew Bible;

3. Late spelling, as attested by trends in Hebrew manuscripts from post-biblical times, which are already slightly evident in later books of the canon, ones certainly composed after the Exile, but not entirely absent from texts from earlier times.

The differences among these three kinds of spelling are not great; rather it is a question of three kinds of text, in which the spelling options (all legal within biblical spelling) are exercised one way or the other to differing degrees. Hence the need for statistical measures. It has to be emphasized that there are no consistently archaic texts, not even any that preserve the spellings in vogue around 600 BCE, let alone the purely consonantal spelling of 1000 BCE, and none that have been heavily modernized by preferring the *plene* option wherever the opportunity presented itself. Thus the *plene* spelling of ō never rises much above sixty percent for any book, but it is never less than twenty-eight percent (**SHB**, page 162).

We suggest that progress might be achieved by classifying the spelling options for each of the sixty-five types of vowel as "archaic," "standard," or "late." The preferred (statistically predominant) spelling for any type can be considered "standard" and the less-often used alternative classified as either the survival of an outmoded or rarer (archaic) spelling, or as the intrusion of a still rare "modern" spelling which began to appear only in the latest stages of production of the finished corpus (or even only in the post-biblical stages of transmission). We can make these distinctions only vaguely, yet they must be made if we wish to achieve more specific typological inferences from the data.

Each vowel has its own story to tell. In the case of ī and ū, which are nearly always primally long, we can say for all types (Types 1–12, 56–65) that the *plene* spelling is standard, *defective* archaic. The spelling of ε is so unclear that Types 25 and 26 should be left out of the picture. And ā is peculiar, as explained in Chapter 4, since it is doubtful if the apparent *defective* spelling of word-terminal ā, which is restricted to a few morphemes (Types 27–29), should be considered an orthographic variant at all. (See Chapter 4.) If it is included, the *plene* spelling is standard, *defective* possibly archaic (or dialectal).

The vowel ē presents many problems. In view of **SHB** Figure 8.7, it is doubtful if anything can be done with the data. We suspect also that the assignments of nouns to Types 18–20 leave something to be desired, since the etymology of many of them is not clear. We are tempted to say that ê ← *ay is nearly always *plene*, ē ← *í is always *defective*. We cannot be sure about either archaic or modern variants. Perhaps Type 16 could be used. We doubt if Type 17 can be trusted (see the comment on page 174 of **SHB**). And we are even more reluctant to use the nouns (Types 18–22), to say nothing about the residua. In fact we are unhappy about the entire picture for ē, except in the somewhat negative sense that our work shows how different is the orthography of ē from that of ō, in spite of the fact that the phonological histories of these two vowels, both secondary in Hebrew, are parallel in many respects. This leaves the small number of *defective* spellings of Type 14 as possibly archaic and Type 13, whose *defective* variants might not be orthographic at all but specimens retaining archaic morphology.

The vowel ō is the most complicated of all. It presents more opportunities for a spelling choice than any other vowel, and we have distinguished more types (twenty-six) for it than for any other vowel. When ō ← *ā, we can surmise that the *plene* spelling is standard when it is more frequent, *defective* being archaic (Types 30, 36, 38, 45–50, 52). But when *defective* is preferred, *plene* is late (Types 32, 39). When ō ← *u, the picture is the opposite. *Defective* is more frequent and may be taken as standard, *plene* late (Types 40–44). Types in which ô ← *aw are problematic, since *plene* spelling is both archaic (it is still a consonant) and late and the interpretation of *defective* is equivocal (Types 34, 35, possibly 39). Type 31 is unique, with **h** archaic, **w** standard. When the origin of ō is not known, the commoner usage can be taken as standard, the rarer later (Type 33) or earlier (37). The residues (Types 51, 53–55) are too mixed to use. Unfortunately, Type 50 is defined too broadly and could have mixed membership as to the path of evolution. Table 6.1 summarizes matters.

Table 6.1 Archaic/Standard/Late type classification

Archaic D/Standard P	Types 1–14, 30–31, 36–38, 45–50, 52, 56–65
Standard D/Late P	Types 32–33, 39–44
Not used	Types 15–29, 34–35, 51, 53–55

Hebrew Bible portions can be identified as archaic in spelling, perhaps only slightly more archaic than other portions, since the idea is relative, when they are outliers in consequence of a preference for archaic spelling of vowels of the types in the top row of Table 6.1. Restricting attention to the smallest portions (the seventy-six portions shown in Tables 3.4–3.5), the counts of archaic outliers (drawn from Tables 3.11–3.15) are as shown in Table 6.2.

Table 6.2 Outliers due to overuse of archaic spelling

Vowel	Types	Torah	FP	LP	Poetry	Oth. W	Total
ī	1–12	2	12	13	0	1*	28
ē	13–14	6	0	0	0	0	6
ō	30–52	32	4†	1	0	0	37
ū	56–65	8	2	1	0	3‡	14
	Total	48	18	15	0	4	85

*—2 Chronicles 26–36 (Type 9)
†—All in 1 Kings
‡—In Chronicles

Most of the outliers due to archaic spelling are in the Pentateuch, followed by the Former Prophets. Both Former and Latter Prophets are archaic mainly in the spelling of ī, whereas for ī the Pentateuch is not as archaic as the Former and Latter Prophets. Evidently the spelling of this vowel was largely standardized in the Pentateuch but not so completely in the Former and Latter Prophets. It needs to be remembered, however, that much of this effect is due to the retention of the archaic spelling of *David* in Samuel and Kings (**SHB** pages 4–6, 169, and 252).

Hebrew Bible portions can be identified as late in spelling, perhaps only slightly later than other portions, when they are outliers in consequence of a preference for late spelling of vowels of the types in the second row of Table 6.1. Table 6.3 shows the relevant counts.

Table 6.3 Outliers due to overuse of late spelling

Vowel	Types	Torah	FP	LP	Poetry	Oth. W	Total
ō	32–44	0	6	9	4	12	31

The Pentateuch contains no outliers due to late spellings. Most are in the Writings. Connecting these facts with the major moments in the collecting, editing, standardizing, and transmitting of the main body of texts, the possibilities are as follows.

1) Standard spelling is the systematic realization of trends reached by the beginning of the sixth century BCE, except for those discussed in **SHB** § 11.3.10. It is the orthography of the scribes who did the main editorial work during the Exile. Archaic spelling is the result of some resistance to this, survival of pre-exilic spellings from (and in) pre-exilic texts. Recent spellings are found more in texts composed or completed or re-edited after that, say fifth-fourth centuries BCE; but even then and later, new texts (e.g., Daniel) were still written in what must have been for the second century BCE quite old-fashioned spelling. The fact that Daniel turns out to be not significantly different from the rest of the Hebrew Bible in its spelling acquires great significance in the light of our study, and it could be that this fact alone is sufficient to bring everything down by several centuries.

2) Standard spelling is the spelling of a later epoch of intensive work on the text, the traditional time of fixing the canon (or most of it). Conservative opinions on this point tend to be anachronistic (they attribute quite formal and theological ideas about "canon" to Ezra and his circle). But somewhere prior to rabbinic times (as Josephus' famous remark about the attitude of the Jews of his day to the text of Scripture seems to indicate [*Contra Apionem*, VIII, 42]), a strengthened attitude of reverence, whatever the theory behind it, brought increased concern for the text as such, including its spelling. At the same time, the great divergences among the texts actually in circulation in pre-rabbinic times forbid exaggeration of this development. The earliest possible date for this emergent attitude to the sacred writings is late fifth century BCE, or the time of Ezra, whenever we date him. (Freedman [**SHB** page xi] finds this position plausible.) If biblical spelling is Ezra's spelling, as we state rather categorically on page 322 of **SHB**, then the spelling of Ezra–Nehemiah and possibly of Chronicles as well could reflect that usage. Including Chronicles is tricky; some scholars give it a much later date,

but it also apparently used earlier sources besides the Primary History, preserving their old spellings, even though in some details, such as *David*, it updates systematically. If standard spelling is Ezra's spelling, then archaic spelling could represent the standard of exilic times, with very little genuinely pre-exilic spelling surviving at all. And by the same token, the completion of the Pentateuch need not be earlier than the Return (but would have to be prior to Ezra).

3) Perhaps the most archaic spelling in the Hebrew Bible, that of the Pentateuch, is the norm of Ezra's time, and standard spelling is even later, say third century BCE, with "modern" spellings later still.

4) Can the whole thing be slid down even further than that? Possibly to the recovery under the Hasmoneans? Or even to the reconstruction under the early rabbis, associated with the legendary work of the Council of Jamnia?

This is a very wide range of options, and we have no idea at this stage of our work, in spite of the brave words in **SHB** Chapter 11, as to when "standard" spelling became standard. We think that the choice lies between 2) and 3)—Ezra's spelling survives in MT Pentateuch, or Ezra's spelling is standard spelling. Besides a fresh examination of the orthography of **LXX** Vorlage and careful assessment of the earliest manuscripts from Qumran, within the Bible itself the orthographic profile of Ezra–Nehemiah attracts fresh interest. We think that 4) is ruled out by the evidence of the manuscripts from Masada and from Murabbaᶜat, as well as by the fact that two of the earliest Qumran manuscripts, 4QJer^a and 4QEx^f, both third century, already have more vowel letters than standard biblical spelling. But 4QSam^b, the earliest of all, is more archaic than the present Masoretic Text. (See Chapter 13.) Either it represents a specimen of sixth-century spelling that survived unmodernized or, at the latest, a pure sample of standardized fifth-century spelling. But that sample is very small, as, indeed, are all third-century manuscripts from Qumran. So the picture remains very scrappy.

Chapter 7

Aleph as a Vowel Letter in Old Aramaic

Francis I. Andersen & David Noel Freedman

7.1 Introduction

In 1952 F. M. Cross and D. N. Freedman concluded that "there is no evidence for the use of *aleph* as a *mater lectionis*" in any of the Old Aramaic inscriptions which they studied (Cross and Freedman 1952: 28). In 1956 G. Garbini reported a somewhat diffuse use (*uso piuttosto diffuso*) of all four *matres lectionis* in the Zkr inscription, citing אשא (I:11) as evidence for *aleph* as *mater lectionis* in word-final position (Garbini 1956: 252). In 1962 J. J. Koopmans claimed that Cross and Freedman's statement cannot be correct (*kann das doch nicht richtig sein*) (Koopmans 1962: 7). His reason: It has not been proved that the definite article was pronounced –aʾ. In 1975 S. Segert similarly asserted that *aleph* was a *mater lectionis* in the Sefire inscriptions (Segert 1975). In 1967 J. A. Fitzmyer studied the use of *aleph* in the Sefire inscription and concluded: "We find no reason to regard *aleph* in this stele as anything but consonantal, and consequently the emphatic ending as –aʾ" (Fitzmyer 1967: 147). Note the word "consequently." R. Degen recognized only *he, waw,* and *yod* as *matres lectionis* in Old Aramaic inscriptions, stating

Reprinted, with permission, from M. P. Horgan and P. J. Kobelski (eds.), **To Touch the Text: Biblical and Related Studies in Honor of Joseph A. Fitzmyer, S. J.**, (New York: Crossroad, 1989), 1–14.

categorically: " ꜐ ist im Aa. noch keine *Mater lectionis* für –ā꜐." (Degen 1969: 25)

In view of this ongoing debate and discussion of the possible use of *aleph* as a vowel letter in early Aramaic inscriptions, it seemed advisable to consider and evaluate the available evidence and the arguments on both sides of the debate. Our conclusions will not differ appreciably from those previously arrived at, but this discussion may clarify the issues by examining the underlying presuppositions, weighing the methods used, and testing the results.

To begin with, there is the question of definition. What is a vowel letter? And how is it to be distinguished from consonantal letters? Our frame of reference is the so-called Phoenician alphabet and the Northwest Semitic inscriptions of the Iron Age, including the proto-Canaanite inscriptions of the twelfth-eleventh centuries and the major corpus of substantial inscriptions in Phoenician and related dialects of the tenth century and following, as well as the group of Aramaic inscriptions of the same general period. Originally the alphabet was entirely consonantal: every letter had a consonantal value and words were spelled in accordance with their consonantal values. Naturally the words included vowels, but these were not indicated in the orthography. It was, therefore, a form of shorthand or a conventional means for indicating certain sounds (the consonants) while leaving the recognition or reproduction of the vowel sounds to the knowledge, skill, or ingenuity of the reader or speaker. All of the earliest inscriptions (twelfth, eleventh centuries) from Canaan reflect this pattern, and the Phoenician inscriptions for the major part of their history and certainly covering the period of our interest preserve the pattern of purely consonantal spelling. There are no vowel letters in Phoenician inscriptions.

In the related language groups for which the Phoenician alphabet was adopted and adapted, we cannot be sure whether there was an initial period of pure consonantism—and for the purposes of this paper it is not a matter of significance. All of the inscriptions in Old Aramaic (as well as inscriptions in Canaanite dialects such as Moabite and Hebrew) exhibit the use of vowel letters. What this means is that certain letters, originally and regularly representing consonantal sounds, were also used to represent certain vowels, perhaps with corresponding or compatible values. It is universally agreed that three of these letters were so used: *he, waw,* and *yod. Waw* and *yod* were used in both final and medial positions to represent the vowels û and î respectively, whereas *he* was used only in the final position. Its primary and perhaps chief function was to represent the vowel –â, but it also reflects other vowel sounds: ē and ō. Unlike the case of û and î, medial –ā– was not represented in the orthography.

It is immediately clear that the system was neither complete nor flawless, since it handled only certain vowels and used letters that already functioned and would continue to function as consonants. An ambiguity arises, since the same letter cannot be both a consonant letter and a vowel letter in the same occurrence, but it is not always clear which it is in any given instance. In theory at least the three letters listed above can be either consonants or vowel letters wherever they appear, but in most cases the choice can be made without great difficulty or much contention.

In this analysis a question might be raised about diphthongs, e. g., **ay** and **aw**. In principle and in practice these are represented by their consonantal elements, *yod* and *waw* respectively, and therefore diphthongs are treated as consonants. In the case of contracted diphthongs, **ay** → ê, **aw** → ô, the result is a vowel, either ê or ô, and if the *yod* or *waw* is retained in the spelling, then that sign, which remains the same, has nevertheless changed from representing a consonant (the consonantal element in the diphthong) to a vowel letter. Although this apparent sleight of hand actually takes place and can be documented, it nevertheless poses serious problems for scholars. On the basis of orthography alone, it is impossible to tell whether the letter is a consonant or a vowel letter: we need to know whether the contraction of the diphthong has actually taken place.

If the diphthong has been contracted, then we might expect the letter (*yod* or *waw*) reflecting the diphthong to be dropped. Thus, in languages where the contraction has occurred the word for *house*, originally **bayt**, is spelled **bt** (for **bêt**), whereas in those in which it is not contracted the word is spelled **byt** (for **bayt**). In cases where the phonetic shift has occurred after the spelling **byt** has been fixed, this *yod* might be retained in the spelling, producing the equation **byt** = **bêt**, a hybrid form.

This effect or outcome is called "historical spelling," and it results in a new phonemic value for the letter used. Thus *waw* can represent ô and *yod* can represent ê as well as their previously established consonantal (**y** and **w**) and vowel (î and û) indications. Without external evidence (from inscriptions in a writing system using vowels, or a vocalization system such as the Masoretic Text) it is difficult to evaluate historical spelling. In order to establish the new values for a vowel letter derived or developed in this manner, we normally require substantial evidence that the same equivalence or equation occurs apart from historical spelling. In other words, if we are going to maintain that *waw* = ô (along with û or **aw**) and *yod* = ê (along with î and **ay**), then we must be able to demonstrate the utilization of these values in the spelling of words in which the *waw* or *yod* is not part of the root form and does not have a continuous history of use, first for the primal consonant and now for the resultant vowel. In short, the argument from historical spelling is often tainted by these ambiguities and continuities, and so without external supporting data we cannot accept any such cases of historical spelling by themselves as decisive or persuasive.

In the case of *aleph* practically all of the instances for which it is claimed that *aleph* is a vowel letter are cases of historical spelling in which it is claimed that *aleph* has lost its consonantal force and has become a vowel letter representing this or that vowel. What is needed is evidence that *aleph* has been introduced into a word where it had no previous consonantal function and serves purely as a vowel marker. Thus, words derived from the root **rᵓš**, *head*, generally continue to be written with the etymological *aleph*, even after the consonantal sound has ceased to be pronounced (is "quiescent") in such words. The practical outcome of such a change in pronunciation without a corresponding change in spelling is that *aleph* comes to function virtually as a vowel letter in words like **rō(ᵓ)š** or **rē(ᵓ)š** or **rī(ᵓ)š, rā(ᵓ)šîm,** *etc.* But this is only evidence that in later texts the *aleph* is preserved by historical spelling; that is, such an *aleph* has a merely passive association with various vowels because it has lost its consonantal force. To qualify as a vowel letter in the strict sense, however, *aleph* must be used for these or other vowels in words in which it never had consonantal force or an etymological base; e.g., **qāᵓm** (Hosea 10:14). Since the root is **q(w)m**, the *aleph* in such a spelling is a genuine vowel letter, but this is a very rare and late phenomenon in biblical Hebrew. F. I. Andersen and A. D. Forbes report only sixteen specimens (Andersen and Forbes 1986: 83–4). It is even rarer and quite anomalous in Old Aramaic inscriptions.

7.2   Items Excluded

When it comes to the possible use of *aleph* as a vowel letter in early Aramaic inscriptions, we must evaluate the following data, and follow these procedures.

1. Exclude from consideration all instances in which *aleph* is a root or stem consonant or in which it serves as a prefix in verbal and nominal forms. In this category we must likewise include all cases of possible historical spelling, since the most that can be said for such instances is that the *aleph* has quiesced and has been preserved as a passive marker of the accompanying vowel. This at once cancels Garbini's use of **אשא** in Zkr I:11 as evidence of *aleph* as *mater lectionis* in word-final position (Garbini 1956: 252). It is only when such a practice is regularized and extended to cases in which there is no etymological *aleph* in the word and the same vowel or vowels are indicated by *aleph* that we can speak

of *aleph* as a vowel letter in the sense that has been demonstrated for *he*, *waw*, and *yod*.

2. Evaluate the remaining cases in which *aleph* appears as a vowel marker (opposed to vowel bearer, which signifies that it must be a consonant). The issue then is whether the form in question involves *aleph* as a consonant or as a vowel letter. We divide this group into two parts:

(a) The appearance of the *aleph* at the end of nouns (substantives and adjectives) in the emphatic state. Since this is the most frequent and regular usage of *aleph* in a syllable- or word-terminal position and is the form about which much of the dispute has turned, it deserves to be looked at carefully. The suffix $-\bar{a}^{\supset}$ as an indicator of definiteness, while semantically equivalent to the definite article in Hebrew and other Canaanite dialects (**ha**– prefixed to nouns), seems to be unique to Aramaic. Its derivation is unknown. But to say that because the etymology is not known the terminal *aleph* must be only or actually a vowel letter is a *non sequitur*. The natural presumption is that it is a consonant, since all letters are potentially consonantal and it is reasonable to begin at that point with *aleph* as with all other letters. What needs to be shown is that it *is* a vowel letter, and such a conclusion cannot be drawn from the evidence of the inscriptions.

In the first place, there is a perfectly good letter (*he*) available to represent final â, and it is used regularly for all words ending in –â in Aramaic inscriptions, while in those inscriptions in which the noun in the emphatic state occurs, the distinction in spelling is maintained systematically. The final *aleph* is used always in the case of the emphatic state, while *he* is used in all cases in which the word ends in the vowel letter –â. The inference is almost inescapable that the *aleph* is not a vowel letter but a consonant, while *he* is used as a vowel letter. At most we might say that the *aleph* has quiesced and thus serves as a passive vowel marker (regardless of the actual vowel). What still needs to be shown is that *aleph* is used where we would expect *he* to be used, and vice versa. That would show that they were interchangeable vowel letters and that the *aleph* had quiesced. But this phenomenon (use of either *he* or *aleph* to spell the same vowel) is not attested in the early inscriptions at all, and even as late as the most recent of the Samaria Papyri (335 BCE) the complementary distribution between the emphatic ending ($-\bar{a}^{\supset}$) and words ending in –â (just the vowel) is rigorously maintained. That means that in all likelihood the *aleph* was still pronounced as a consonant and the distinction was both phonemic and orthographic. The use of *aleph* with the emphatic state of the noun throughout the whole period of extant inscriptions in turn argues strongly for its being an original and essential part of this enclitic and not simply the result of an arbitrary choice of *aleph* as a vowel letter (instead of *he*) to represent final –â. Alternatively the *aleph* may have been appended to the definite article for reasons unknown to us. There is no basis for doubt that it was pronounced as a consonant, at least in the entire period under consideration, and possibly even beyond it.

(b) What remains for investigation is a handful of anomalous and idiosyncratic cases which may or may not be instances of *aleph* as a vowel letter, but which in any case only serve to demonstrate that *aleph* was an entirely different category from the three standard vowel letters, *he*, *waw*, and *yod*, which are used extensively throughout the whole inscriptional corpus.

One theoretical possibility may be considered before turning to the actual examples. The vowel-letter system is slightly skewed by the fact that *waw* and *yod* are both used at the ends of words and also medially, while *he* appears only in the terminal position. That leaves a gap in the system, i.e., there is no representation of medial $-\bar{a}-$, and theoretically at least this gap could have been filled by *aleph*. This in fact is eventually what did happen, as we have already pointed out in the discussion above. But indubitable specimens of this usage turn up only toward the very end of the period under study, and then only sporadically. The earliest certain attestation of the use of *aleph* as a vowel letter for medial $-\bar{a}-$ (not in historical spelling, which we have excluded as not germane) is in the Dead Sea Scrolls. There is no unambiguous evidence for such usage in the early inscriptions, and hence we can infer that there was no apparent reason to use *aleph* at all as a vowel letter.

We now turn to the examples in the early inscriptions of *aleph* alleged to be a vowel letter. First, we dispose of two cases that are equivocal either from the point of view of decipherment or in terms of morphological interpretation. Garbini adduced **mlkh**, *the king* (which he read in KAI 203), as evidence that the emphatic suffix could be spelled with *he* and therefore was pronounced $-\bar{a}$, even when it was spelled with *aleph*, as it was routinely. But the letter is not clear. Koopmans reads **mlk³**, which is what we would expect. Second, the noun *night* occurs in Hebrew as **lyl** and **lylh**. Both **lyl³** and **lylh** are found in Old Aramaic. One cannot simply declare that these are the same and that therefore *he* and *aleph* can be used interchangeably for the spelling of $-\bar{a}$. The consistent and contrasting use of *he* and *aleph* everywhere else, as well as the distinctive morphology of this word, points to **lylh** as adverbial (*by night*) while **lyl³** is determined (*the night*).

The other cases of the use of *aleph* in Old Aramaic inscriptions allegedly to represent $\bar{a}$ are restricted to particles. This is a most interesting fact, and it raises a number of important methodological considerations. Particles are notoriously difficult to track etymologically or to analyze into ancestral parts. They are also characteristically unruly when it comes to obeying the laws of regular sound changes which are discovered by research in historical-comparative grammar. Regular sound changes, such as the quiescence of *aleph* in certain positions in the syllabic structure of words, take place systematically in words that belong to classes of large membership, notably nouns and verbs. Such changes are fostered and also regulated by paradigmatic analogies. It is otherwise with words that belong to classes of small membership and do not group into paradigms, notably particles. Some of these—for example, the negative lā^ɔ—are the only members of their class. Their evolution is less constrained by analogy; their phonetic development is often erratic. In Northwest Semitic there are several such particles which have only one root consonant—**l, w, z, š, p**—and they are more labile than words with stable roots; they are susceptible to the production of alloforms which use *aleph*, either before or after the primal consonant, so as to yield a closed syllable.

Among these particles the most conspicuous is the negative **la^ɔ**. Whatever the historical status of an alternative form spelled simply with l and presumably pronounced **la**, the form spelled with *aleph* is standard and widespread and stable over the entire period in which we are interested. A typical comment is that of Z. Zevit. He cites **l^ɔ**, *not*, as evidence that *aleph* was used as a vowel letter in pre-exilic Hebrew, "since the ^ɔ *alep* in this word is not etymological." (Zevit 1980: 22) Presumably the same argument would apply to Aramaic, but this begs the whole question, and it does not address the real problem. If *aleph* in **l^ɔ**, *not*, is just another way of writing –ā, why is the negative particle never spelled **lh**?

7.3 Paths of Development

The consistent spelling of both the emphatic suffix and the negative particle points to the existence in Old Aramaic of a word-terminal *aleph* actually pronounced as a consonant. The fact that these particular *alephs* cannot be traced to primal origins does not mean that they could never have emerged in the language; and the fact that in due time they would become quiescent does not mean that they never were pronounced. We conclude that there were four distinct paths along which phonetic and/or orthographic *aleph* developed in Aramaic (see Table 7.1). Some primal *alephs* continue to be pronounced throughout the entire history of the language, and these are written as consonantal *aleph* (column 1). Some *alephs* originally pronounced eventually become quiescent, and when *aleph* is still written at that point, the spelling is historical in the strict sense (column 2). When *aleph* is eventually used to write a vowel in a word that never had a consonantal *aleph* at that point, the *aleph* is a vowel letter (column 4). Column 3 presents an intermediate category; although not demonstrably etymological, it emerged as a real consonant at a certain stage of the language and was written by means of *aleph*, the consonantal letter. When such an *aleph* eventually quiesced but was still shown in the spelling, the result was a vowel marker similar in function to the historical spellings in column 2, but differing from them in ancient historical origins. We need the development shown in column 3 to explain the history of the spelling of the suffix of the emphatic state and of the negative particle. They are not the only cases, although they are the most abundant.

Table 7.1 *Aleph* in Aramaic

	Etymological		Non-etymological	
	1 Stable	2 Quiescing	3 Emerging	4 Never Pronounced
Primal Stage	An original root consonant or stem preformative, pronounced as a consonant.		Not shown to be present in the early language.	No *aleph* was ever pronounced at this point in the word.
Middle Stage Old Aram.	Still pronounced; the written *aleph* is a consonant letter.		A phonetic innovation to close certain syllables at word end or at morpheme juncture; *aleph* represents a consonant.	No certain attestation of the use of *aleph* as a vowel letter.
Late Stage	Consonant is still pronounced and still written *aleph*.	*Aleph* quiesces, written as historical spelling; passive vowel marker.		*Aleph* used to write a vowel as such.

Other examples are **wᵓ**, alternative spelling of **wa–**, *and*; **pᵓ**, alternative spelling of **pa–**, *and*; **zᵓ**, alternative spelling of **z–**, demonstrative/relative. These have been adduced as evidence of the use of *aleph* as a vowel letter in Old Aramaic. These *aleph*s are evidently not etymological. But we contend once more that this does not necessarily prove that

they were never pronounced as a consonant. We consider it significant
that these *alephs* turn up in the writing of particles. It should also be
emphasized that their occurrence is sporadic and very limited.

The spelling of *and* as **wᵓ** occurs apparently twice in Panammu
II (KAI 215). Line 5 has **wᵓgm** (compare with **wgm** in line 16). To
read this as **wāgam** is only one possibility; and this would still require
an explanation of the lengthening of the vowel in this proclitic position.
Giving first preference to reading the *aleph* as a consonant, we have either
waᵓ–gam (the glottal stop is articulated and marks juncture between
the two conjunctions), or **wa–ᵓagam** (ᵓgm being an allomorph of **gm**
with prothetic *aleph*). KAI 215:9 has **wᵓz**, which does not have to be
read as **wā–z(i)**, since it could be **waᵓ–z(i)** or **wa–ᵓaz**.

The word **pᵓ** occurs three times. The simple **p–** occurs ten times
in Old Aramaic. (For the purposes of this paper, the exact dialectal
affiliation of the texts is irrelevant. The conjunction is found in other
Semitic languages, notably Arabic.) The three occurrences of **pᵓ** are **pᵓ**
yᵓmr (KAI 214:17); **pᵓ yšrh** (KAI 214:33); **pᵓ hdd** (KAI 215:22). By
assuming that this is no more than an alternative spelling of simple **p–**,
it is argued that in these three instances the *aleph* has been added as a
vowel letter and that the word should be transcribed as **pā** instead of
paᵓ. But the question arises again: Why didn't they use *he*? Even if
the words are originally of common derivation, the *aleph*, developed secondarily, could still be consonantal, written because it was pronounced.
As with the analogous **wᵓ–**, the secondary form with *aleph* was in free
fluctuation with the prime form and seems to have had a transitory existence in a regional dialect. If it had taken over, or even survived as
an alloform, and then the *aleph* quiesced but was still written, it would
be no more than another example of historical spelling and would not
qualify as a vowel letter in the strict sense.

The demonstrative/relative is variously **z**, **zy**, **zᵓ**. A reading **zh**
has been claimed in line 19 of the Asshur ostracon (KAI 233), but this
is uncertain, and **wg . . .** is preferred.

There is, then, some variety in the spelling of these particles in
Old Aramaic. We wish to be careful not to overstate our argument, but
we think it is more likely that this reflects an accurate spelling of real
fluidity in the pronunciation of these words rather than an inconsistency
in the spelling system. And even if these *alephs* were used as vowel letters
rather than the well established *he*, the practice was restricted to a few
special particles, and very circumscribed in both space and time; that
is, it cannot possibly be recognized as a central and lasting contribution
to Aramaic spelling. On the contrary, by taking these *alephs* at face
value and interpreting them as we do all other *alephs* of the period,
namely as consonant letters, we recover some interesting data about the

phonological and morphological developments of these particles in Old Aramaic.

This interpretation receives further support when we add other evidence from Northwest Semitic to the picture. Some of these particles, and other similar particles, are attested with prothetic as well as following *aleph*. See Table 7.2. The development of energetic *nun* in Canaanite is not understood well enough to connect it with the insistent Hebrew particle nāʾ, not to mention the exclamation ʾānnāʾ.

Table 7.2 Secondary *aleph* in Northwest Semitic

ʾl	l	lʾ
ʾp	p	pʾ
ʾz	z	zʾ
ʾw	w	wʾ
ʾgm	gm	
ʾš (Phoen.)	š	

7.4   Conclusions

For Old Aramaic the orthographic (vowel-letter) system can be explained or described in essentially simple terms: *he, waw, yod* for final long vowels, and *waw, yod* for internal long vowels, in particular û and î respectively. There was no natural or ordinary place for a fourth vowel letter in this system, and it is clear that neither *aleph* nor any other letter had such a function.

Practically every occurrence of *aleph* in the inscriptions is to be explained on the basis of its consonantal value. All cases in which *aleph* is initial in a syllable are to be explained in that fashion, and the same should be maintained for most, if not all, occurrences in which it closes a syllable or word. In these cases *aleph* is either part of the root system or it serves as an indicator of some particle, such as the ending of the emphatic state. The most that can be said of such examples is that the *aleph* may have quiesced and hence, not being pronounced, serves as a vowel marker. Since, however, it can be and is associated with a wide range of vowels, its real value is zero, and hence it does not function in the way that the true vowel letter does. (If any given vowel letter is not dedicated to the representation of one kind of vowel, but can indiscriminately represent any kind of vowel, it does not tell the reader anything. In the classical system *yod* represents front vowels, *waw* represents back vowels, *he* represents central vowels. In complete contrast to this workable system, *aleph* in historical spellings is found associated with any and every kind of vowel.)

There remains a small and anomalous residue of instances of *aleph* which do not yield easily to analysis and interpretation. With respect to the negative particle, it seems easier and more reasonable to recognize in lā⁔ a vocable separate from the preserved negative l, just as the particle ⁔al is recognizably different. Ultimately they may have derived from the same root form = l, which is expanded by a prefixed *aleph* (⁔al), or by one that is affixed at the end (lā⁔). If the *aleph* in the latter case were no more than a vowel letter, then it is not clear why *aleph* was used for this purpose rather than the standard and normative *he*. The case here cannot be proved beyond doubt, but the assumption or assertion that *aleph* is only a vowel letter here is questionable at best.

Out of all the examples of *aleph* in the Old Aramaic inscriptions there remains only the barest handful that still challenge the hypothesis presented here and remain doubtful. These examples are the words **wa⁔** and **p⁔**, which are presumably and apparently equivalent to **w–** and **p–**, well-known particles serving as conjunctions in the Old Aramaic inscriptions. Since the conjunctions are attached directly to the following word, the insertion of the *aleph* makes it appear like an internal *mater lectionis*, not a terminal one. Nevertheless it comes at a juncture point and may have been used to distinguish between or separate the two components of the word or phrase, in pronunciation as well as writing— in pronunciation first, and then, therefore, in writing. It should also be reiterated that the phenomenon is quite rare, **w⁔** and **p⁔** occurring only in the Panammu inscriptions and not used anywhere else in this limited corpus. We would argue that the usage is like that of lā⁔, the negative particle, in relation to l–, and that **w⁔** and **p⁔** are byforms of **w–** and **p–**, and that the differences are phonetic and phonemic and not merely orthographic. Admittedly it is a difficult case, but even if it were agreed that the *aleph* in these circumstances is a vowel letter rather than a consonant, then it should also be noted that this usage of *aleph* was experimental, sporadic, and evanescent, since it was not carried forward in the standard spelling procedure of later Aramaic inscriptions. All that would be left in future centuries would be the fossilized form lā⁔, where *aleph* might once have been a vowel letter. But even so, all these cases can be explained as autonomous byforms or secondary developments resulting from the addition of a genuine consonantal (i.e., glottal stop) *aleph*, either before the root consonant (i.e., ⁔al, ⁔aw, ⁔ap) or after it (la⁔, wa⁔, pa⁔).

There is no convincing evidence that *aleph* was used regularly, systematically, and deliberately as a vowel letter, an assertion that can be made and sustained for the three genuine vowel letters, *he*, *waw*, and *yod*.

The attested uses of *aleph* as a vowel letter in any of the Northwest Semitic languages came much later. Thus, *aleph* is used as a medial vowel letter in the *Genesis Apocryphon* (Freedman and Ritterspach 1967) to represent the vowel **a**, but only after *waw* and *yod*, and then to indicate that the preceding letter is a consonant and not itself a vowel letter. Similar usage may be inferred in forms such as **ky⁾** (= **kiya⁾**) in the Dead Sea Scrolls for Masoretic **ky** (= **kî**). Contrariwise, the *aleph* in the words **hw⁾h** (Dead Sea Scrolls) and **hw⁾** (Masoretic Text) is not a vowel letter at all, but a consonant in both instances: it is clearly meant to be pronounced in the longer form (**hû⁾â**), although it probably had quiesced in the familiar shorter form (**hû⁾**).

Part III

Advances

Chapter 8

Choice of Statistical Methods

A. Dean Forbes

8.1 The Basic Approach

The material in this chapter is quite technical. It discusses our reasons for selecting the statistical techniques used in **SHB**. It also introduces additional ways of exploring the data on spelling.

The exposition builds on and assumes familiarity with **SHB** Chapter 10, the development of which we briefly summarize. For reasons given in **SHB** § 10.1, we opted not to attempt to array the portions of text along a timeline. (This goal is addressed in Chapter 10 of this volume.) Instead we discovered the affinities among portions by clustering them. Our strategy involved first converting the counts in our tables into percentages so as to remove information regarding type incidence. Since this normalization ignored the varying sample sizes for types in portions, we censored those pairs of spelling choices whose total incidence did not exceed a threshold. (Thus, for each portion and for each type, we deleted those cells whose counts summed to less than ten, say.) In accordance with standard practice, we next "standardized attributes." This put each type on an equal footing with the others, preventing any one type from dominating the analysis. Given these censored, normalized, standardized attributes, computation of a Euclidean distance between portions was straightforward. The resulting table of pairwise distances was next supplied to the *furthest-neighbor* clustering algorithm, which produced *dendrograms* showing the affinities among the portions. To allow assessment of the adequacy of the dendrograms, clustering was undertaken using censoring thresholds of ten and twenty and using sets of five, ten, and thirty portions.

On **SHB** page 289, we drew attention to the existence of a less *ad hoc* way of defining the distance between portions. In the *Epilog* (**SHB** page 330), we noted that other distance measures, other clustering algorithms, and other methods of discovering affinities merited investigation in future work. We shall consider each of these matters.

8.2   Distance Measures

In an effort to prevent scant samples from distorting our results, we based our clustering upon various censored Euclidean distances (**SHB** pages 289–290). Because of the huge number of cells with tiny samples for the seventy-six-portion table, we presented dendrograms only for the five-, ten-, and thirty-portion cases (**SHB** Figures 10.2–10.8). With a censoring threshold of ten, a seventy-six-portion dendrogram would have ignored more than sixty percent of the table cells; with a threshold of twenty, almost eighty percent (**SHB** Table 10.1).

There is a distance measure which uses all of the data, the *Mahalanobis distance*. But, as we shall see, it is subject to other limitations. The idea behind the Mahalanobis distance is simple: For each pair of portions, we generate the model of the associated table of counts which assumes that portion and choice of spelling are independent, given vowel type. The goodness-of-fit statistic comparing the observed and model data is then a measure of the squared-distance between the portions, in terms of how they jointly depart from the assumed model.

The statistics literature contains conflicting recommendations regarding whether the Euclidean or the Mahalanobis distance is preferable. On the one hand, Chatfield and Collins (1980: 192) state:

> Euclidean distance is often less than satisfactory, particularly if the variables are measured in different units and have differing variances, and also if the variables are correlated... In order to avoid awkward changes in rankings, Euclidean distance is usually calculated for variables of different types only after each variable has been standardized to have unit variance. But even this metric does not take account of correlation between variables. An alternate possibility, which does take account of correlations, is to use [the Mahalanobis distance].

Against this, Kendall (1980: 36) asserts that the Mahalanobis distance

...is not, in my opinion, suitable as a measure of distance between points in cluster analysis. In fact, for a pair of points
the covariance matrix is degenerate and the distance does not
exist. To use the covariance matrix of the whole group obviously begs the question in clustering... The distance metric
which I prefer is the simple Euclidean distance...[assuming]
all variables have been scaled to unit variance.

Basically, the problems with the censored Euclidean distance are that it
ignores correlations between variables and omits data from the reckoning;
the problem with the Mahalanobis distance is that it makes assumptions
about the data which go counter to its use for finding clusters in those
data. Hartigan (1975: 62) sums up the paradox nicely:

(i) In order to cluster objects, it is necessary to propose a
measure of distance between objects. (ii) In order to define
distance, it is necessary to weight variables. (iii) In order to
weight the variables, it is necessary to know the clusters of
objects so that within-cluster variances can be equalized.

Upon weighing up the various opinions, we conclude: 1) When
there are sufficient data, standardized Euclidean distance seems the best
measure. This is what we did for **SHB** (pages 289–91). Because of
the paucity of data when seventy-six portions were specified, use of this
measure made it unwise to cluster the seventy-six portions. 2) When
one wishes to cluster all seventy-six portions, use of one of the approximate (discrete) Mahalanobis distances seems appropriate, in spite of
their much-noted limitations. As remarked in **SHB** (page 289), an attractive measure is that which gauges the extent of departure of pairs of
portions from the three-dimensional model of contingency which assumes
independence of choice and portion, given type.

8.3 Clustering Algorithms

Clustering algorithms explicitly partition objects into groups. The
groups may be formed by focusing on the *internal cohesion* among the
group members, upon the *external isolation* of groups from each other,
or upon some combination of these defining characteristics. When the
distance between two clusters is defined as the distance between the two
most remote items, the *furthest-neighbor* (*complete-link*) algorithm results. When the distance between two clusters is defined as the distance
between the two closest members, one from each cluster, the *nearest-
neighbor* (*single-link*) algorithm results. These two algorithms emphasize

differing aspects of the data in clustering. "The single-link method concentrates on seeking clusters which are isolated from each other, paying no attention to their internal cohesion; the complete-link method concentrates on the internal cohesion of clusters." (Gordon 1981: 48) These differing focuses result in differing behaviors. The furthest-neighbor algorithm tends to produce compact clusters, as befits its focus on cohesion; the single-link algorithm tends to produce straggly clusters, since a single object between two otherwise isolated clusters can lead to their being joined up. Mardia, Kent, and Bibby (1979: 385) explain:

> In practice single linkage may not provide useful solutions because of its sensitivity to noise present between relatively distinct clusters and the subsequent chaining effect. On the other hand, the complete linkage method gives compact clusters, but it does not necessarily guarantee to find all groups where within-group distances are less than some value. The use of hierarchical methods entails a loss of information... All cluster methods make implicit assumptions about the type of structure present, and when these assumptions are not satisfied spurious solutions are likely to be obtained; that is, each clustering method imposes a certain amount of structure on the data and it should be ensured that the conclusions we reach are not just an artifact of the method used.

For these reasons, in **SHB** Chapter 10 we reported results only for the *furthest-neighbor* algorithm. We varied the data presented so as to allow assessment of the reliability of the resulting clusters. After further study of the clustering literature, this still seems the wisest way to proceed.

We are comfortable using the furthest-neighbor algorithm to cluster our seventy-six portion data but are, for the reasons stated earlier, uneasy in basing the clustering on the Mahalanobis distance. Nonetheless, we present Figure 8.1, the result of furthest-neighbor clustering of the seventy-six-portion Mahalanobis distances. The main value of this figure is heuristic. It identifies affinities among the portions which require interpretation and leads to further investigation by other techniques. It presents three kinds of clustering upon which we shall comment at length: 1) The immediate clustering of canonically adjacent portions suggests that some whole books have similar orthographic patterns throughout. 2) The failure of adjacent portions to cluster, or the clustering of portions widely separated in the Bible, raises the question of why such portions are different from their neighbors but like something further away. 3) The tree as a whole shows some large clusters which embrace whole major portions of the Hebrew Bible, and others again which include miscellaneous portions; why should this be so?

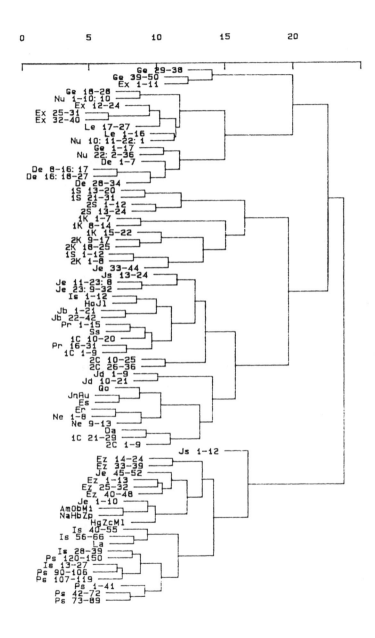

Figure 8.1 Spelling: seventy-six portions (Mahalanobis distance)

1) The immediate clustering of two or more adjacent portions makes intuitive sense. Figure 8.1 shows that the two portions with the smallest distance between them by the measure used (as shown on the scale at the top) are Exodus 25–31 and Exodus 32–40. No surprise! Their distance apart is 6.5. Next closest are Ezra and Nehemiah 1–7 (distance: 7.0), then two adjacent portions of Deuteronomy from chapter 8 through chapter 27 (7.1). At many other places in the dendrogram the first linkages are between portions from the same book, often adjacent.

2) The fourth pair of portions to be linked together (distance: 7.1) are, in contrast to the first three pairs, not adjacent in the Bible. They are Isaiah 13–27 and Psalms 90–106, one from the Latter Prophets, one from the Poetry (Writings). This *is* surprising and raises a natural question: Why are these two portions close together? The methods of **SHB** provide a means of examining this question. In **SHB** §§ 1.9 and 1.11 we introduced the notion of the *standardized residuals* as a means of searching for outliers in our tables of counts, a technique that was used repeatedly in **SHB**. For the present problem, we proceed as follows: Compute the standardized residuals between the counts for the portions of interest and the model which assumes independence of portion and spelling choice, given type. The resulting standardized residuals show, for each attribute of the data (each type), how the portions under consideration compare. By ranking the sub-types in terms of the fraction of the distance between portions they account for and plotting, say, the *bottom* thirty contributors, a picture of the attributes for which the portions are most similar is obtained. Figures 8.2 shows the results of carrying out this procedure for Isaiah 13–27 versus Psalms 90–106.

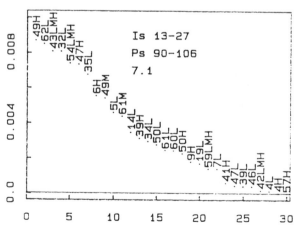

Figure 8.2 Thirty most similar types: Is 13–27 and Ps 90–106

Figure 8.3 shows the results of carrying out this procedure for Isaiah 13–27 versus Isaiah 1–12.

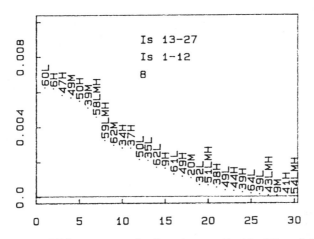

Figure 8.3 Thirty most similar types: Is 13–27 and Is 1–12

The plots show the fraction of portion-to-portion distance (vertical axis) accounted for by each of the bottom thirty sub-types (horizontal axis). (The number given below the portion specification is the Mahalanobis distance between the portions.) The thirty types shown in Figure 8.2 together account for about eleven percent of the distance between Isaiah 13–27 and Psalms 90–106 (7.1). Those shown in Figure 8.3 account for under seven percent of the distance between Isaiah 13–27 and Isaiah 1–12 (8.0). The reasons why Isaiah 13–27 is closer to Psalms 90–106 than to Isaiah 1–12 do not jump out at us from these plots, since the distances are summary numbers which include all spelling behavior. But the plots do show for what types the portions are most similar.

The next pair to be joined are Ruth+Jonah and Esther (7.3), not adjacent, but all "stories," two in the Megillot. The sixth join, at distance 7.5, is not between two of our seventy-six portions, but between Psalms 107–119 and the already-joined portions Isaiah 13–27 and Psalms 90–106 (the fourth join). This makes a cluster of three close portions, two of which are in fact canonically adjacent. The seventh join (7.6) links two adjacent sets of Minor Prophets, the eighth (7.7) the two portions of the book of Job. And so on. Eventually all the portions are joined together so that the completed tree gives an impression of which portions are close to each other in spelling and which distant.

3) The upper branches of the tree, in the right-hand side of Figure 8.1, show that the last join (distance: 23.7) links two large clusters. The topmost of these two was the second-last one to be made. It was made by linking the Pentateuch, which had already been joined into a

single cluster at the top of the figure, with the large cluster in the center, which consists of portions from various parts of the canon. The third large cluster at the bottom was the result of the seventy-first linkage (distance: 16.7) which linked Joshua 1–12 with a cluster which had already been formed out of twenty-one portions (Psalms and various portions of prophetic books). The seventy-second join completed the linkage of the large central cluster (19.7); the seventy-third completed the assembling of the Pentateuch (20.0). Then, at distance 22.6, the Pentateuch was joined to the very large cluster in the middle, and last of all this cluster was joined to the cluster at the bottom (23.7).

These larger clusters make sense, but only in a limited and quite general way. The portions of the Pentateuch come together and stand apart from the rest. This result emerged also in dendrograms made with other measures. The other canonical sections (Former Prophets, Latter Prophets, Poetry, Other Writings) also tend to cluster but not so neatly. Some errant portions do not link with adjacent parts of the same book nor even with portions in the same canonical section.

Close study of Figure 8.1 raises many questions. Some of the clusters of intermediate size are interesting. Thus there is a cluster of twelve portions consisting of Samuel and Kings plus Jeremiah 33–44. All five portions of Ezekiel come together in a cluster of ten portions, the other five being also prophetic, but none from Isaiah. Four of Isaiah's five portions cluster with Psalms rather than with the rest of the Latter Prophets. Why should this be so? What brings Lamentations and Trito-Isaiah together?

The clustering of the Pentateuch shows a distinct set of three portions (Genesis 29–Exodus 11), which suggests continuity of orthographic features from one book to the next. But this cluster does not link with the rest of the Pentateuch until quite late (distance: 19.7).

The distances at which the last four linkages are made are rather close to one another and are different when a different distance measure is used. Thus Figures 10.5–10.8 in **SHB** (censored Euclidean) all show the Pentateuch as the last cluster to be joined to the rest, whereas in Figure 8.1 the Pentateuch first joins the middle cluster, and the bottom cluster of Psalms and Prophets is the last to be joined to the rest. These differences serve as a reminder that the dendrograms present a general picture which invites further study by other means.

As a preventive against unwarranted inferences, it is worth noting that in **SHB** Chapter 9 we engaged in *statistical modeling (SM)*, the model of independence being appropriate if the portions achieved equilibrium in their passage through the copy channel. In *SM*, formal probability models are formulated and tested against the available data. Here (and previously in **SHB** Chapter 10) we are engaged in *exploratory* *data analysis (EDA)*. Many of the methods used in *EDA* apply both to populations and to samples drawn from populations. In particular, hierarchical clustering is a descriptive technique which makes no statistical assumptions about the distances being summarized. The resulting descriptions are the springboard from which further investigations proceed.

Thus, Figure 8.1 discloses that the portions of Joshua are far removed from each other and from the rest of the Former Prophets; Judges coheres but also is isolated from the other Former Prophets. Why?

One place to look for a possible explanation is in the tables of outlier portions, Tables 3.7–3.15. From Tables 3.9–3.10 (30 portions) we see that Joshua underuses *defective* spellings for Type 38H, though not by much; and Judges overuses *defective* spellings for Type 10H and underuses for Type 39M. From Table 3.13 (76 portions) we see that Joshua 1–12 underuses *defective* spellings for Types 33L and 50L and overuses for Types 58 and 64H; Joshua 13–24 overuses *defectives* for Type 25H (not used in the clustering) and underuses for Type 47L. Finally, both Judges portions underuse *defectives* for Type 33L. Recall that these outliers are for the given types across all the portions. Thus, these results disclose aspects of the books in question that differ substantially from other books, but they really do not explain why Joshua and Judges do not cluster with the rest of the Former Prophets.

There is a way to compare the portions with the Former Prophets as a whole. We adapt the technique used to generate Figures 8.2 and 8.3: Compute the standardized residuals of each of the portions of interest (seventy-six-portion division) from the Former Prophets taken as a single portion (five-portion division), using the model which assumes independence of portion and choice of spelling, given type. The resulting standardized residuals show those attributes of the data (those types) for which the portion under consideration differs from the section of the Bible of which it is part. By ranking the sub-types in terms of the fraction of the distance from portion to section they account for and plotting, say, the *top* twenty contributors, a picture of the causes of a portion's behavior is obtained.

For the two portions of Joshua, Figures 8.4 and 8.5 show the fraction of portion-to-section distance (vertical axis) for the top twenty sub-types (horizontal axis). We see that better than a fifth of the Mahalanobis distance between Joshua 1–12 and the Former Prophets is due to Type 64H. Type 50L accounts for a further ten percent of the distance for Joshua 1–12. *Both* of these strong contributions result from the spelling used for the locally-frequent word *Joshua*. The sizable contribution of Type 31H (around six percent) is due to the archaic spelling of *Jericho*. For the second portion of Joshua (chapters 13–24), only sub-types 8H and 9H contribute more than five percent to the distance, neither the result of single forms. In short, the curious behavior of Joshua results, in part, from the concentration of a few words which are locally frequent; but the behavior is not due solely to these few.

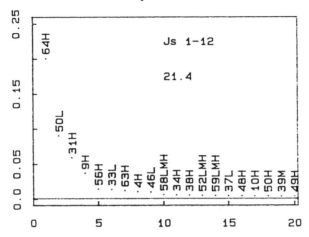

Figure 8.4 Fraction of distance per sub-type: Js 1–12

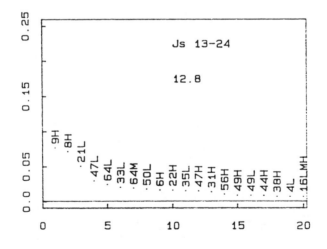

Figure 8.5 Fraction of distance per sub-type: Js 13–24

For the two portions of Judges, Figures 8.6 and 8.7 show the fraction of portion-to-section distance for the top twenty sub-types. We see that better than seventeen percent of the Mahalanobis distance between Judges 1–9 and the Former Prophets is due to Type 9H ("-D +P"). This is due to thirty-nine *plene* ī's in *Abimelek*.

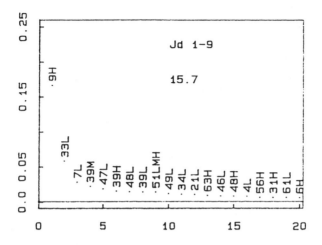

Figure 8.6 Fraction of distance per sub-type: Jd 1–9

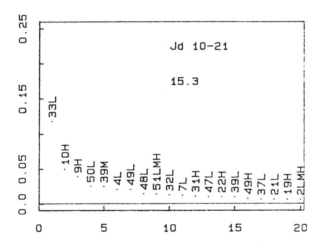

Figure 8.7 Fraction of distance per sub-type: Jd 10–21

Type 33 (*nota accusativi*) accounts for about six percent and twelve percent of the distance for the two halves of Judges, respectively. These portions are outliers for Type 33, as we see from Table 3.13, both halves of Judges being "-D +P." As for Joshua, in Judges an occasional locally-frequent word affects the distance disproportionately, but the positioning of the portions is the sum total of the contributions of all the choices for all the spellings of the sub-types included.

8.4   Multidimensional Scaling

In the **SHB** *Epilog* we remarked that we had checked some of our results via a method quite different from hierarchical clustering, namely, *classical multidimensional scaling (CMDS)*. We suggested that future work might examine this technique and its results in some detail.

The reason for so doing is straightforward: As has previously been noted, the method of hierarchical clustering agglomerates the objects supplied it whether "true" clusters exist or not. As a result, most practitioners suggest supplying the data to other methods to see how the results compare. To quote Dubes and Jain (1979: 252):

> A user of clustering algorithms interested in cluster validity would be well advised to apply several clustering approaches and check for common clusters instead of searching for a technical measure of validity for a single cluster. At present, the application of category information and knowledge from the subject matter area about what "makes sense" is a more fruitful endeavor than applying criteria that depend only on the data.

In **SHB** we varied the data supplied to the clustering algorithm, one approach to cluster validation. But there is an entire class of alternate methods of analysis, the so-called *geometrical* methods. These do not impose a grouping on the data (as does hierarchical clustering). Rather, they transform and project the data so as to show similar items in proximity, leaving the task of forming clusters to the human observer.

Geometrical and clustering methods are complementary. Clustering methods tend to be more reliable in depicting lower-level differences between objects, while geometrical methods generally portray group relationships more reliably (Gordon 1981: 137).

CMDS is a geometrical method. Its goals and rationale can be grasped by considering a hypothetical situation. Suppose one happens upon the mileage table for a set of cities. Question: Is there a way of reconstructing the map, given only the mileage table? Answer: Yes and no... We can reconstruct the map from the distances but have no way to deduce the orientation of the resulting map relative to the points of the compass. Thus, the reconstructed map can show the relationships among the cities, but they may be reflected and/or rotated with respect to a true map. (Going from the map to the distance table involves throwing away the information giving *orientation*.)

The foregoing has ignored an important detail. Suppose the table gives the road distances between pairs of towns in Kansas. Then, since Kansas is flat and the roads tend to be fairly straight, a two-dimensional reconstruction will be an accurate reproduction of the map of Kansas. If we allow the CMDS algorithm to attempt reconstruction in a three-dimensional space, the resulting reconstruction will put the cities in a plane. The third dimension will not be needed. If, however, we supply the CMDS algorithm with a table of distances between pairs of world capitals, the third dimension will be needed, but a fourth dimension would be superfluous. Thus, a given table of distances will have associated with it some number of dimensions in which the distance relations can adequately be represented. If there are n objects in an attribute space of p dimensions, then, if $p > n$, at most $n - 1$ dimensions will be required. (Why this should be is easy to grasp: two points determine a line [a one-dimensional space], three points, a plane [a two-dimensional space], and so on.) As we saw with the example of the cities in Kansas, in practice, far fewer dimensions than $n - 1$ might be required. Given some number of dimensions in which to operate, the CMDS algorithm determines that positioning of objects which maximally accounts for the facts inherent in the distance table. *To a first approximation*, its degree of success is reflected by a set of numbers called the solution *eigenvalues*, one eigenvalue per dimension allowed in the solution produced. To assess how much of the distance information is included in a given positioning of objects, one computes a ratio by dividing the sum of the eigenvalues for the dimensionality of the mapping used by the total of all the eigenvalues calculated by the CMDS algorithm. When some or all of the distances involved are not straight-line distances (as would be the case with road distances for Kansas or "great circle" distances for world capitals), some of the eigenvalues will be negative, a complication discussed in the literature (Mardia, Kent, and Bibby 1979: 408–9). All this will become clearer as we take up a concrete case.

For our first use of CMDS, let us analyze the distance table given by **SHB** Table 10.3 (upon which the dendrogram of **SHB** Figure 10.2 was based). Table 8.1 reproduces **SHB** Table 10.3. The distances are censored Euclidean distances with the threshold set at ten.

Table 8.1 Distances between pairs of portions

	Pent	FP	LP	Poetry	Other
Pent	0.00				
FP	14.00	0.00			
LP	15.25	12.55	0.00		
Poetry	16.36	14.62	10.39	0.00	
Other	16.02	13.04	11.30	11.15	0.00

Because there are five objects, this distance table can be perfectly represented by using CMDS to position the objects in a *four*-dimensional space. When we supply the distances to the CMDS algorithm, the following eigenvalues are calculated: 44.09, 13.36, 4.33, and 0.00; these sum to 61.78. So the first, second, and third dimensions of the CMDS analysis cumulatively account for 71.36%, 92.98%, and 100.00% of the distance information. It follows that the spatial relationships among the five sections can be grasped by plotting the points corresponding to the sections in a three-dimensional space. Figure 8.8 shows the relations among the sections in the first two dimensions.

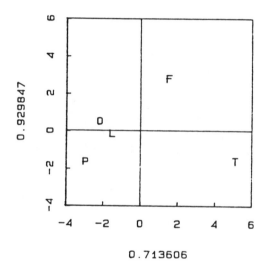

Figure 8.8 First two dimensions of CMDS, Euclidean distance

Almost 93% of the distance information is accounted for by this diagram. (It may assist understanding to observe that if one projected the points onto the horizontal axis [that is, were we to look at the one-dimensional representation of the distances], the resulting positions would account for around 71% of the distance information.) Figure 8.9 shows how the objects are located in the third dimension.

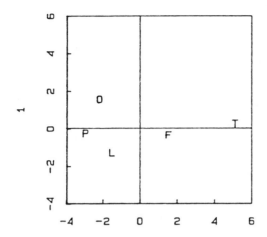

0.713606
**Figure 8.9 First and third dimensions of CMDS, Euclidean
distance**

Thus, in Figure 8.8, the "O" (Other Writings) should be raised above
the plane of the paper about two units and the "L" (Latter Prophets)
should be lowered about two units below the plane of the paper. And so
on. The number labeling each axis indicates the fraction of the distance
information accounted for by using all dimensions up to and including
that axis.

Figures 8.10 and 8.11 show the corresponding results when the
Mahalanobis distance is used rather than the censored Euclidean.

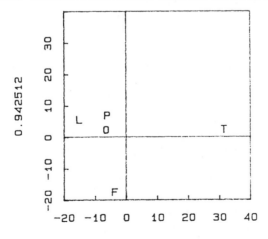

0.722352
**Figure 8.10 First two dimensions of CMDS, Mahalanobis
distance**

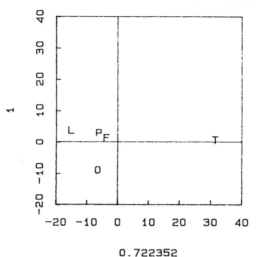

0.722352

**Figure 8.11 First and third dimensions of CMDS,
Mahalanobis distance**

When we supply the distances to the CMDS algorithm, the following
eigenvalues are calculated: 1308, 399, 104, 0. These sum to 1811. So
the first three dimensions of the CMDS analysis cumulatively account
for 72.24%, 94.25%, and 100.00% of the distance information. Again the
spatial relationships among the five sections can be grasped by plotting
the points corresponding to the sections in a three-dimensional space.
Figure 8.10 shows the relations among the sections in the first two dimensions. Better than 94% of the distance information is accounted for
by this diagram. Figure 8.11 shows how the objects are located in the
third dimension. Thus, in Figure 8.10, the "O" (Other Writings) should
be lowered below the plane of the paper about ten units and the "L"
(Latter Prophets) should be raised about three units above the paper.

In comparing Figures 8.8/8.9 and 8.10/8.11, bear in mind that it
is the relative, not the absolute, distances that are of interest and that
the plots are arbitrary as regards orientation. We see that "T" (Torah)
is isolated from the others, that "F" (Former Prophets) is also rather
off by itself, and that the other three portions ("L," Latter Prophets,
"P," Poetry, and "O," Other Writings) tend to cluster. (By reversing
the sense of its second and third axes, Figures 8.10/8.11 can be made to
resemble Figures 8.8/8.9 more obviously.)

When we consider the situation with seventy-six portions, matters
get considerably more complicated. We know that the distance table
for seventy-six portions can be perfectly represented in a seventy-five
dimensional space. Figure 8.12 shows the first two dimensions of the
CMDS analysis.

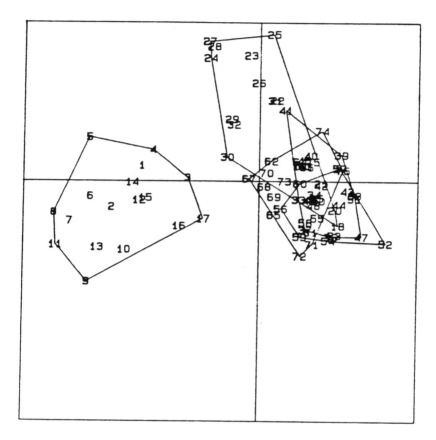

Figure 8.12 First two dimensions of CMDS, Mahalanobis distance

Its two dimensions account for 31.8% of the distance table information. The numbers stand for the various portions and can be decoded by consulting Tables 3.4–3.5 above. The portions making up each of the five sections of the Bible used earlier are enclosed in an irregular polygon so as to allow one to judge how the sections are situated. We see yet again that the Torah and Former Prophets stand aside from the other sections. (Note, however, that Joshua–Judges [Portions 18–21] are down in the midst of the Latter Prophets/Poetry/Other Writings, a behavior we noted when examining the seventy-six-portion dendrogram, Figure 8.1.) Figure 8.13 shows the first and third dimensions. Adding this dimension includes only 38.7% of the distance-table information. Groups of portions which are separated in any CMDS projection are, in fact, isolated. Thus, once again we see that the Torah as well as the Former Prophets are relatively isolated from the other sections.

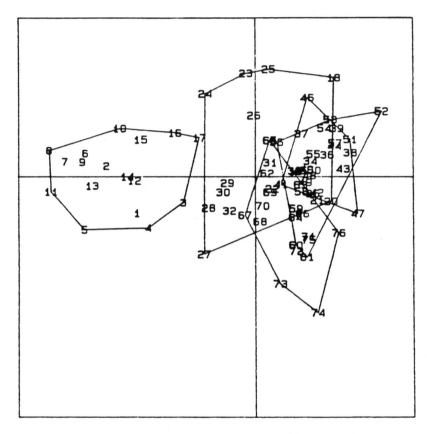

**Figure 8.13 First and third dimensions of CMDS,
Mahalanobis distance**

It should be noted that our criterion for information encompassed
by a CMDS analysis is, for high-dimensional problems, likely very conservative (Lebart, Morineau, and Warwick 1984: 173–6).

Chapter 9

Spelling in Parallel Passages

Francis I. Andersen & A. Dean Forbes

In **SHB** Chapter 4, we used several concepts from information theory to shed light on the process of text transmission. In particular, we viewed the text transmission process in terms of a zeroth-order Markov source and a first-order Markov channel. Under various plausible simplifying assumptions we derived an equation relating the source statistics, the channel statistics, and the decoder statistics. Namely:

$$p^{(0)}(D)[1 - p^{(C)}(P \mid D)] + [1 - p^{(0)}(D)]p^{(C)}(D \mid P) = p^{(C)}(D)$$

There is one such equation for each portion and type, since the source and channel statistics may well have been different for each. (In the equation, each of the probabilities has an implicit subscript pt indicating this fact.) The first factor in the first term is the proportion of *defective* vowels at the source; the second factor (in the first square brackets) is the fraction of *defective* vowels that remain *defective* in passing through the channel. Thus, the first term gives the fraction of vowels originally *defective* that emerge from the channel still *defective*. The first factor following the plus sign (in square brackets) is the fraction of *plene* vowels at the source; the second factor is the fraction of *plene* vowels that become *defective* in passing through the channel. Thus, the second term gives the fraction of vowels originally *plene* that emerge from the channel *defective*. It follows that the left-hand side gives the overall fraction of vowels that emerge from the channel spelled *defective*, which equals the right-hand side. The parallel equation for the fraction of vowels that emerge from the channel spelled *plene* is redundant, as specifying the fraction *defective* also specifies the fraction *plene*, since the fractions must add to unity.

For each portion and type, we have one equation containing four probabilities. We know only $p^{(C)}(D)$. Thus we have one equation in three unknowns, not an enviable situation. In **SHB** we listed three ways of dealing with this situation: 1) Make additional assumptions so as to eliminate the excess unknowns. 2) Put the equation(s) aside and adopt other approaches. 3) Make no attempt to separate encoder and channel effects, clustering the portions as received. In **SHB** we took the third way. Here, we shall examine the first and second ways. In the *Epilog*, we suggested that one might get an independent measure of the rate of increase of the use of *matres lectionis* from inscriptional evidence. We also proposed that one might study parallel biblical texts profitably. We shall here pursue the second of these suggestions, the study of parallel texts.

Figures 9.1 and 9.2 illustrate the two sorts of scenarios that parallel texts might have followed to reach us. We assume that parallel texts either share a common ancestor (Figure 9.1) or that one derives from the other (Figure 9.2). In either case, at some time t_x or t_y an encoder (E_x or E_y) launches the text into its copy channel (X or Y). The encoder may copy the text as presented (subject to the usual error processes) or may systematically adjust its orthography to his dialect and/or epoch ("updater" behavior). To handle the case where both encoders work from precisely the same source, the copyings in the S channel may be taken to be error-free. (This situation might obtain when a court annal is the shared source.) In short, the systems diagramed in Figures 9.1 and 9.2 have sufficient flexibility to describe most any theory of text transmission (including the theory of local-text types). The crucial characteristic of parallel texts is that they, at some point in history, had contact. In both Figure 9.1 and 9.2, the node after which the texts diverged is encircled. The characteristics of the texts at that point in time (t_x for Figure 9.1 and t_y for Figure 9.2) were identical. We can let $p^{(0)}(D)$ in our equation(s) refer to that point of last contact. In both the equation describing the text which passed through the X channel and the equation describing the text which passed through the Y channel, the source statistics will be the same provided they refer to the text as it existed at the "bifurcation time."

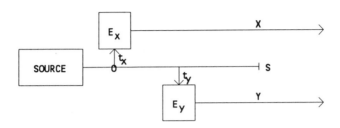

Figure 9.1 Source, encoder, channel model: unrelated channels

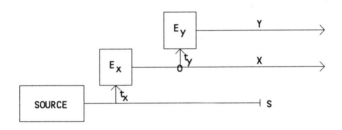

Figure 9.2 Source, encoder, channel model: related channels

9.1 Source–Encoder–Channel Equations

Let us examine the first way out of our situation: Make additional assumptions so as to eliminate the excess unknowns. For each vowel type, for a pair of parallel texts, we have two equations in five rather than six unknowns. Had we a third parallel text, we would obtain three equations in seven unknowns. Each parallel text supplies one additional equation but also supplies *two* additional unknowns (the channel error rates). If we analyze non-parallel texts, each added text supplies one new equation plus *three* new unknowns (the channel error rates plus the source statistic[s]). In order to solve our channel equation(s) we need make fewer assumptions when dealing with parallel texts than when dealing with general texts, since the former involve fewer unknowns than the latter. But in either case, we are left with more unknowns than equations. To proceed, additional assumptions must be made. Suppose we assume that the tendency for the channel to convert *plene* spellings into *defective* spellings is so much less than the tendency to convert *plene* spellings into *defective* spellings as to be negligible. That is, assume $p^{(C)}(D \mid P) \approx 0$. This makes the second term in our equation(s) equal zero. The equations describing a pair of parallel texts under this assumption are thus:

$$p^{(0)}(D) \left[1 - p_x^{(C)}(P \mid D)\right] = p_x^{(C)}(D)$$

$$p^{(0)}(D) \left[1 - p_y^{(C)}(P \mid D)\right] = p_y^{(C)}(D)$$

Two equations in three unknowns. An additional assumption is needed. Setting either of the channel error rates equal to zero involves assuming (relatively) error-free transmission of one of our texts, an uncomfortable assumption. Equating the two channel error rates yields a logical contradiction. (Identical left-hand sides are equated to non-identical right-hand sides.) Specifying the value of one of the channel error rates involves unacceptable arbitrariness, as does specification of a value for the source statistic. When we examine the solutions for the channel error rates as we vary the source statistic over its range of possible values (from zero to one), no fresh insights result. In short, following the first way leads to an uninformative dead end.

9.2 Choice of Parallel Texts

We still have the second way: Put the equation(s) aside and adopt other approaches. Here parallel texts offer a *definite* advantage. With parallel texts, we know the spelling of *corresponding* vowels rather than having only the overall statistics. In examining the texts this allows us, provisionally, to analyze their characteristics as due to the combined effects of gross encoder updating behavior (when certain words appear to have had their spelling standardized) plus, one hopes, less disruptive random copying errors.

It is not easy to decide when two texts should be accepted as "parallels" that fit one of the models shown in Figures 9.1 and 9.2. 2 Samuel 22 and Psalm 18 are clearly the same poem. Word-by-word comparison of the spelling in these two recensions shows differences, but at some places the words themselves differ due to deletions, substitutions, or insertions. A text can be updated by rewriting it more or less extensively, by changing vocabulary, or by recasting the syntax. Exactly the same kinds of changes may take place in the transmission of any text by continual copying.

If the divergence goes far enough, the resulting texts are likely to be called doublets rather than recensions. But this is a matter of degree. Comparison of the respective spelling practices in such divergent texts becomes less and less appropriate the more inappropriate it is to identify them as *copies*, or at most *recensions*, of the same text. Our task is complicated further by the practice of imitation. Similar events are likely to be reported in a conventional manner, using similar literary forms and similar vocabulary. One is in a sense a "copy" of the other, but not in the strictly literary and textual sense illustrated in Figures 9.1 and 9.2. Comparison of the spelling of the same word in two such compositions is not much different from the study of its spelling in all occurrences. Some alleged parallels are similar in theme only. Thus Jeremiah 49:7 and Obadiah 8 both describe the loss of wisdom by Edom, but *Edom* is the only word they possess in common which (theoretically) might have been spelled in more than one way. Hardly worth studying.

There is thus no clear cut-off point between a parallel text which has been copied more or less exactly (such as Isaiah 2:2–4 parallel with Micah 4:1–3), a text which has been copied from another with vocabulary substitution (as often happens when Chronicles re-uses material from the Primary History), doublets which are two divergent (almost independent) accounts of the same incident or speech, "contamination" by the intrusion into one passage of vocabulary from another on the basis of perceived similarity, and the mere use of common vocabulary in passages with similar themes.

The cross-references in the margins of some Bibles draw attention to hundreds of pairs of texts which are "the same" in some respect. Some of these are quotations, which might even be documented. Thus Jeremiah 26:18 quotes Micah 3:12, and the two are identical in every respect. Certain traditional expressions are often repeated and might present spelling variations. Thus Deuteronomy 10:17 uses a title for God, hʾl hgdl hgbr whnwrʾ, which recurs in Nehemiah 9:32 as hʾl hgdwl hgbwr whnwrʾ. In the present investigation we have confined ourselves to parallels or doublets in which two texts run side-by-side for long enough to suggest strongly that both come from the same source by a process that fits Figure 9.1 or 9.2. We do not include quotations of single sentences nor the repeated use of catch phrases or stock expressions. Parallels found in separate books, usually in different divisions of the canon, such as Samuel and Kings in the Former Prophets parallel with Chronicles in the Writings, permit the comparative study of the effects of different transmission channels. Parallels within the same book provide a control, since in such cases both versions likely came down through the same channel. The Hebrew Bible contains many such doublets. Those in Genesis and Jeremiah are well known, and there are some duplicate

Psalms. Comparison of the spelling of any words which such doublets might have in common adds to the picture obtained from similar study of parallel recensions in different books. The parallel passages used for the present study were thus of two kinds. First, we used sets of parallel texts found *within the same book*:

1. Jeremiah 6:12–15 ‖ Jeremiah 8:10–12
   Jeremiah 6:22–24 ‖ Jeremiah 50:41–43
   Jeremiah 16:14–15 ‖ Jeremiah 23:7–8
   Jeremiah 23:19–20 ‖ Jeremiah 30:23–24
   Jeremiah 49:18–21 ‖ Jeremiah 50:40–46
   Parallel opportunities for spelling choice = 89

2. Psalm 14:1–7 ‖ Psalm 52:1–7
   Psalm 40:14–18 ‖ Psalm 70:2–6
   Psalm 57:8–12 ‖ Psalm 108:2–6
   Psalm 60:7–14 ‖ Psalm 108:7–14
   Parallel opportunities for spelling choice = 93

Second, we studied the following parallels between different books. (We shall not supply details of the individual verses which line up side by side. This information can be found in standard handbooks and commentaries. We found Crockett [1951] useful.)

3. Genesis ‖ 1 Chronicles, 143 opportunities

4. Joshua ‖ 1 Chronicles, 34 opportunities

5. 1 Samuel ‖ 1 Chronicles, 59 opportunities

6. 2 Samuel ‖ 1 Chronicles, 630 opportunities

7. 2 Samuel ‖ Psalm 18, 127 opportunities

8. 1 Kings ‖ 2 Chronicles, 909 opportunities

9. 2 Kings ‖ 2 Chronicles, 171 opportunities

10. 2 Kings ‖ Isaiah, 374 opportunities

11. 2 Kings ‖ Jeremiah, 146 opportunities

12. Isaiah ‖ Micah, 36 opportunities

13. Isaiah ‖ Jeremiah, 33 opportunities

14. Jeremiah ‖ Obadiah, 16 opportunities

15. Psalm 105 ‖ 1 Chronicles, 89 opportunities

16. Ruth ‖ 1 Chronicles, 28 opportunities

17. Ezra ‖ 2 Chronicles, 12 opportunities

18. Nehemiah ‖ 1 Chronicles, 22 opportunities

The parallel passages are divided into the thirty portions defined in Table 3.6. Each pair is ordered in canonical sequence. This is simply for convenience and consistency. It does not imply any presupposition as to which text is the source of the other, nor which is older than the other, even though the belief that the Primary History is prior to the work of the Chronicler is not likely to be disputed. Nor can relative chronology be proven by the present research.

Comparisons have been made only between *matching* words in the two texts which presented a scribe with an opportunity to make a spelling choice. We did not include the spelling of any word, however characteristic and revealing it might have been of the orthographic features of a portion as a whole, if that word was not directly matched in the parallel text. The definition of "opportunity" worked out in **SHB** was used; opportunities declared to be statistically invariant (**SHB** Chapter 5) were excluded.

9.3   Behavior of Corresponding Vowels

We shall take an impressionistic rather than a statistical approach. Others may wish to apply statistical methods in an effort to disentangle (systematic) updater effects from (random) copying-error effects.

In analyzing parallel texts, it is important to avoid the trap of believing that the one thought to be earlier was the source for the one thought to be later. In fact, each passed through some encoder plus channel. A difference might be due to a change having occurred in either. Nonetheless, one may usefully characterize the differences between parallels by indicating which sorts of transformations applied to one would result in the other. Loosely, we treat one (for us, the one occurring earlier in the canon) as the source of the other and describe an imaginary channel connecting the two which would account for their behavior.

For the purposes of concise reportage below, we describe the transformation by two 4 × 4 arrays of numbers. The first gives the counts of vowels exhibiting the possible behaviors:

$$\begin{bmatrix} n_z^{(C)}(D \mid D) & n_z^{(C)}(P \mid D) \\ n_z^{(C)}(D \mid P) & n_z^{(C)}(P \mid P) \end{bmatrix}$$

The second shows estimates of the transition probabilities for the imaginary channel, based on the counts:

$$Z = \begin{bmatrix} p_z^{(C)}(D \mid D) & p_z^{(C)}(P \mid D) \\ p_z^{(C)}(D \mid P) & p_z^{(C)}(P \mid P) \end{bmatrix}$$

This array is referred to as the process *transition matrix*. Its elements are just the conditional probabilities of **SHB** § 4.8.

Using matrix algebra, Z can be readily related to the systems in Figures 9.1 and 9.2. Let E_x and E_y be the encoder matrices equal to $\begin{bmatrix} 0 & 1 \\ 0 & 1 \end{bmatrix}$ for complete conversion to *plene* spellings, $\begin{bmatrix} 1 & 0 \\ 1 & 0 \end{bmatrix}$ for complete conversion to *defective* spellings, and $\begin{bmatrix} 1 & 0 \\ 0 & 1 \end{bmatrix}$ for exact encoder copying. (If the encoder updating behavior is not thoroughgoing, other stochastic matrices will be involved.) Let X and Y be the actual channel transition matrices. Finally, as above, let Z be the transition matrix for the notional channel leading from text X to text Y, as though the former were the source for the latter. Then: $Z = X^{-1}(E_x^{-1}E_y)Y$.

9.4   Intra-book Parallels

In analyzing parallel texts, it is important to understand that while differences between the texts may be due to differing encoders and/or channels, they also may have passed through *identical* encoders and channels and yet differ because of random copy errors.

Although book-internal parallels are scant, they provide a useful control. Insofar as each book long existed as a single scroll rather than as part of a large codex, it is likely that each went its own way, systematically different from others. When a passage turns up in two books, differences between the recensions are due to the different copying channels through which the books were transmitted. When both recensions occur in the same book, it is likely that they received the same impressions from the scribes who copied that book. If material was duplicated some time into the transmission process, the recently introduced version might betray its origins by its spelling. Of course, it is also possible that a copy of a book was made with a change of scribe somewhere along the way or that one part was copied from one manuscript and the rest from another manuscript. Such things have often been suspected.

Of the 178 parallel opportunities for spelling choice in the intra-book parallels, fifteen (eight percent) differ from one version to the other. For our entire collection of parallels, 479 of 2962 parallel opportunities differ (sixteen percent). When the effects of *David* are removed, 366 of 2847 parallel opportunities differ (thirteen percent).

The intra-book parallels have count $\begin{bmatrix} 55 & 5 \\ 10 & 112 \end{bmatrix}$ and transition matrix $\begin{bmatrix} .92 & .08 \\ .08 & .92 \end{bmatrix}$. The top row of the transition matrix states that eight percent of the opportunities written *defective* in the first text are written *plene* in the second. The bottom row states that eight percent of the opportunities written *plene* in the first text are written *defective* in the second. Five of the ten opportunities that are *plene* in the first text and *defective* in the second occur in the parallels involving Jeremiah 6 as the first text, about twice as many as we would expect were they distributed uniformly. This *may* be evidence that the Jeremiah 6 parallel derives from the Jeremiah 8 + 50 material. (Due to the small sample size, one should proceed cautiously.)

9.5   Inter-book Parallels

We shall next give an overview of the spelling patterns discernible in the inter-book parallels identified above. And we shall illustrate one method of visualizing the patterns. For the fourteen portions which make up the canonically-prior text of a doublet ("Portion1"), the counts of opportunity pairs are as shown in the rightmost column of Table 9.1.

Table 9.1 Vowel changes by portion

Choice2:	*Defective*		*Plene*		
Choice1:	*Defective*	*Plene*	*Defective*	*Plene*	
Portion1:					Totals
Ge 1–28	14	1	10	46	71
Ge 29–50	12	2	8	50	72
Js	15	1	3	15	34
1S	30	1	4	23	58
2S	174	23	183	371	751
1K	279	26	108	473	886
2K	225	17	54	381	677
Is 1–39	22	4	1	41	68
Je 1–32	16	5	2	35	58
Je 33–52	19	2	0	23	44
Ps 1–72	24	3	3	62	92
Ps 73–150	24	5	2	58	89
Jn/Ru–Da	3	0	3	22	28
Er–Ne	5	3	5	21	34

(In the tabulation, data for vowels $\bar{e}$ and $\bar{a}$ [Types 25–29] have been omitted due to their unrevealing behavior. In this we follow our practice in **SHB**.) Note that 2 Samuel and Kings participate in seventy-eight percent of the pairs. In terms of the first portion of each set of texts ("Portion1"), Table 9.1 lists the counts of vowels in terms of how they are written in Portion1 ("Choice1") and how they are written in Portion2 ("Choice2"). For example, there are 108 vowels written *defective* in 1 Kings whose parallels in 2 Chronicles are written *plene*. And so on.

The breakdown in terms of types is informative. Thirty-three Type 4 vowels that are written *defective* in the canonically-earlier portions are written *plene* in the canonically-later parallel texts. The behavior of Type 9 attracts attention. Of the 120 Type 9 forms which are *defective* in the "earlier" text and *plene* in the "later" text, 113 are contributed by *David*. (All but two of the pairs of this word in our parallels involve a change in its spelling. One *defective-defective* pair is in Psalm 14 ‖ Psalm 53 and the other is in 2 Samuel 22 ‖ Psalm 18.)

The counts and transition matrices for the various vowels are informative. For all parallels and all vowel types considered:

$$\begin{bmatrix} 862 & 386 \\ 93 & 1621 \end{bmatrix} \implies \begin{bmatrix} .69 & .31 \\ .05 & .95 \end{bmatrix}$$

Thirty-one percent of the vowels which are spelled *defective* in a portion that is canonically-earlier are spelled *plene* in the corresponding canonically-later portion. That is, thirty-one percent of the "originally" *defective* vowels undergo a *defective*-to-*plene* transition. Five percent of the vowels undergo a *plene*-to-*defective* transition. Omitting *David*, we obtain:

$$\begin{bmatrix} 860 & 273 \\ 93 & 1621 \end{bmatrix} \implies \begin{bmatrix} .76 & .24 \\ .05 & .95 \end{bmatrix}$$

For ī we find:

$$\begin{bmatrix} 43 & 170 \\ 23 & 698 \end{bmatrix} \implies \begin{bmatrix} .20 & .80 \\ .03 & .97 \end{bmatrix}$$

For ī, omitting *David*, we find:

$$\begin{bmatrix} 41 & 57 \\ 23 & 698 \end{bmatrix} \implies \begin{bmatrix} .42 & .58 \\ .03 & .97 \end{bmatrix}$$

Even after *David* is omitted, the *defective*-to-*plene* transition probability is still quite high. For ē we find:

$$\begin{bmatrix} 350 & 8 \\ 10 & 157 \end{bmatrix} \implies \begin{bmatrix} .98 & .02 \\ .06 & .94 \end{bmatrix}$$

For ō we find:

$$\begin{bmatrix} 434 & 172 \\ 51 & 578 \end{bmatrix} \implies \begin{bmatrix} .72 & .28 \\ .08 & .92 \end{bmatrix}$$

For ū we find:

$$
\begin{bmatrix} 35 & 36 \\ 9 & 188 \end{bmatrix} \Longrightarrow \begin{bmatrix} .49 & .51 \\ .04 & .96 \end{bmatrix}
$$

Note that for these parallels, ē is the most stably transmitted of our vowels. Note also that when the pairs of text are arranged in canonical order, *defective*-to-*plene* transitions are many times more probable than *plene*-to-*defective* transitions.

This raises questions: How are the *plene*-to-*defective* transitions distributed in the texts? Do they clump or are they uniformly distributed? Recall that when studying the intra-book parallels, we speculated that an excess of *plene*-to-*defective* transitions from Jeremiah 6 to Jeremiah 8 + 50 might point to a later encoding for Jeremiah 6.

The graphs in Figures 9.3–9.8 are designed to provide information regarding clumping of D → P and P → D spellings. We lay the canonically-ordered parallels end-to-end and number the vowel pairs consecutively. Each integer value on the horizontal axes in the plots then corresponds to a vowel pair. The short vertical line segments near the top of the plots show the boundaries of the parallels. Thus, for example, the first vowel pair in the parallels involving 1 Kings as the first portion is number 987. At the bottom of each plot runs a swarm of points. In Figure 9.3, a dot at some vowel-pair's position indicates that it involved a D → P transition. Thus, in stretches of text where there are many such transitions, the dots will be densely packed. The curve shows how densely packed are the transitions. For our purposes, its absolute values are unimportant. We simply use it as the basis of statements such as: "2 Samuel has the highest concentration of D → P transitions." Figures 9.3 and 9.4 show the clumping for all vowel types considered.

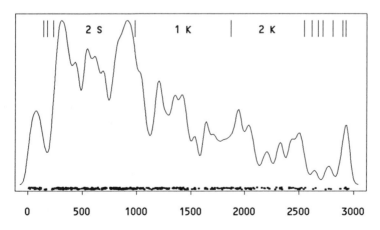

Figure 9.3 Clumping of D→P spellings: all types

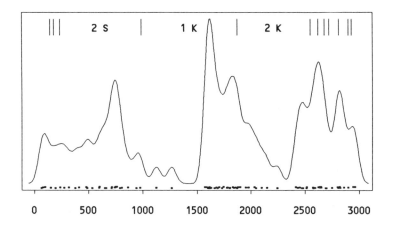

Figure 9.4 Clumping of P→D spellings: all types

By comparing the dot swarms in Figure 9.3 with those in Figure 9.4, we have graphic indication that D → P transitions occur far more frequently than P → D transitions. As we would expect from our earlier results, the D → P plot in Figure 9.3 is dominated by the spelling of *David*. When we remove *all* Type 9 vowels, Figures 9.5 and 9.6 result.

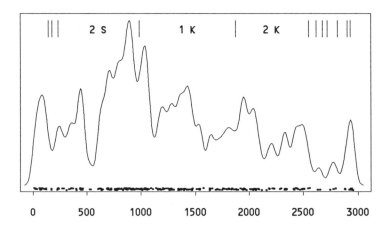

Figure 9.5 Clumping of D→P spellings: Type 9 omitted

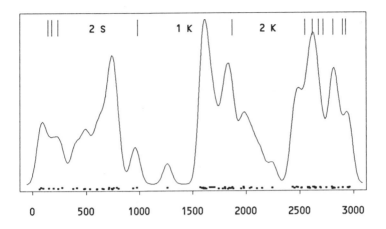

Figure 9.6 Clumping of P→D spellings: Type 9 omitted

Let us focus for a moment on Figure 9.6. We see three intervals of major concentration of P → D transitions. The peak at about 750 corresponds to 2 Samuel 22 || Psalm 18. It suggests that 2 Samuel 22 has more modern spelling than does Psalm 18. The peak at about 1650 corresponds to 1 Kings 12 || 2 Chronicles 10 and suggests that the former is more modern in its spelling than the latter. This parallel contributes three percent of our vowel pairs but twelve percent of our P → D transitions. (Naturally, one must consult the texts to verify that these results are not due to outlier behavior. They appear not to be.)

As a final illustration of the use of this sort of plot, Figures 9.7 and 9.8 show the clumping for Type 4 vowels.

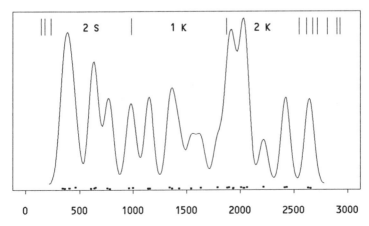

Figure 9.7 Clumping of D→P spellings: Type 4

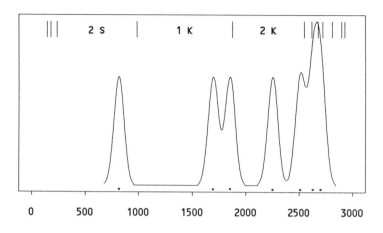

Figure 9.8 Clumping of P→D spellings: Type 4

In Figure 9.7, we see a peak in D → P transitions in the first third of 2 Kings (the part parallel with 2 Chronicles). Examination of the involved parallel discloses that in 2 Kings 8-14, there are ten matched Type 4 vowels, and eight of them involve D → P transitions. Figure 9.8 illustrates what happens when the method is applied to tiny samples of data, there being only seven *plene*-to-*defective* transitions for Type 4 vowels in our parallels.

Chapter 10

The Seriation of Portions

A. Dean Forbes

> ...none of their analyses has permitted them to take a given
> work or portion of a work and to date it by its orthography.
> — Pardee's review of **SHB** in **CBQ**

> It is hoped that further study will touch more directly on the
> questions of textual origins, transmission, etc...
> — Smith's review of **SHB** in **RB**

> In general, the motto for the mathematician trying to work
> in this area [seriation] should be, maximal participation and
> maximal humility.   — D. G. Kendall (1971)

10.1   To Cluster or to Seriate?

Several reviewers of **SHB** expressed disappointment that we made
no direct attempt to *order* the portions of the Hebrew Bible via their
spelling practices, preferring instead to *group* the portions in terms of
their affinities. In **SHB** § 10.1, we suggested a possible method of ordering the portions—log-multiplicative ordinal contingency table analysis—
but gave three reasons for not using the method in our initial foray into
spelling analysis:

1. the method was not yet well understood,
2. its use required a detailed understanding of the effects of stress on
   spelling,

3. extensive spelling updating could easily lead to puzzling results.

For all three reasons, caution as regards log-multiplicative models remains appropriate.

One-dimensional *ordering* of objects (usually along a time line) is referred to as *seriation* or *ordination*. *Grouping* of objects may be accomplished by hierarchical clustering (§ 2.8 and § 8.3) or various geometrical procedures (§ 8.4). The literature of mathematical archaeology supplies two quite distinct methods of seriation: correspondence analysis and multidimensional scaling. For an exposition of the former approach, the interested reader is referred to Greenacre (1984: 291) as well as Ihm and van Groenewoud (1984). We shall consider only seriation by multidimensional scaling.

10.2   Seriation by Multidimensional Scaling

Since seriation involves ordering objects along a time line—a one-dimensional continuum—one naturally wonders why *multi*dimensional scaling is needed. There are two possible phenomena that make a multidimensional approach essential:

1. time may not be the only important variable,
2. the reckoning of distances may be imprecise.

Both of these phenomena are relevant to our situation.

As regards the first phenomenon, Kendall (1971: 120) writes (in an archaeological context):

> Suppose we start with several artifacts or collections of artifacts (such as grave sites), which appear to vary in date of formation. There are many ways in which we can form the distance, or dissimilarity, between objects. ... With the idea in mind that these dissimilarities reflect time intervals between objects (in arbitrary units, and contaminated by random noise, of course), we can reconstruct the underlying values by whichever method we prefer and then hope that we have obtained the dates of formation. ... However, the dissimilarities may reflect other variables in addition to time— for example, social class, wealth, climate, and so forth...One way to allow two variables into the reconstruction is to permit the points to be anywhere in a plane, rather than restricting them to a line.

For the case of spelling behavior, three possible confounding variables were considered in **SHB** Chapter 8: proximity, local frequency, stress. To these should be added *dialect*.

The second phenomenon is less obvious and is best approached by way of two simple, concrete examples. Recall (§ 8.4) that multidimensional scaling involves using the distances among objects to construct the lowest possible dimension map showing the relative positions of the objects. If the objects lie in a straight line or in a plane, this will be revealed in a two-dimensional map resulting from the multidimensional scaling process. Consider a situation which is genuinely one dimensional: the seriation of the integers from one to fifty-one. The distance between integer i and integer j is simply the absolute value of the difference of i and j, written $|i - j|$. (The distance between 10 and 51 is thus 41, and so on.) When the table of distances is supplied to the multidimensional scaling procedure, the map of Figure 10.1 results.

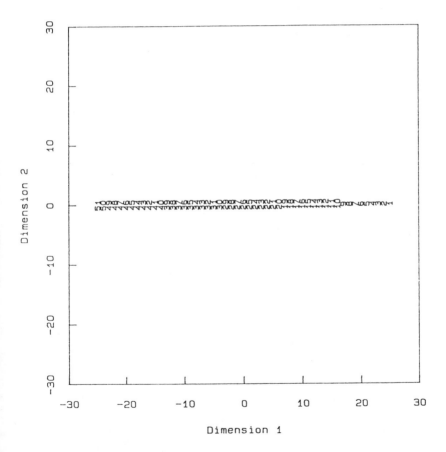

Figure 10.1 **Multidimensional scaling result for the exact distance table of the integers from 1 through 51: One dimension suffices to represent this situation.**

The integers march straight across the plot in their proper order.[1]

The foregoing involved precisely correct distances. What if the distances are not precise? Kendall (1971: 225) has produced a simple example illustrating what may happen. He begins with similarities rather than dissimilarities. The entries in a table of similarity, σ_{ij}, obey two basic conditions (Mardia *et al.* 1979: 402):

1. $\sigma_{ij} = \sigma_{ji}$ (the similarity between i and j equals that between j and i)

2. $\sigma_{ij} \leq \sigma_{ii}$, for all i and j (no object is more similar to another object than it is to itself)

Kendall defines the similarities for his example thus:

$$\sigma_{ij} = \begin{cases} 9 & \text{if } i = j, \\ 8 & \text{if } 1 \leq |\, i - j\, | \leq 3, \\ \cdots & \cdots\cdots\cdots, \\ 1 & \text{if } 22 \leq |\, i - j\, | \leq 24, \\ 0 & \text{if } |\, i - j\, | \geq 25 \end{cases}$$

In words: The similarity of each object to itself is nine. Objects actually separated by one, two, or three units have a similarity of eight. And so on by trios of distances... Objects which are actually separated by 22, 23, or 24 units have a similarity of one. All objects actually separated by 25 units *or more* have a similarity of zero. Assigning objects which actually lie further apart than some threshold (24, in this example) the same value of similarity (zero, in this example) models an actual phenomenon. In the archaeological case, graves close together in time typically have enough artifacts in common to allow fairly precise reckoning of their time separation. But graves far apart in time may have so little in common that gauging their temporal separation becomes inexact.

To see how multidimensional scaling handles this example, we first convert from similarities to distances. Mardia *et al.* (1979: 402) provide a standard method of doing this: If σ_{ij} is the similarity between object i and object j, then the distance between i and j, d_{ij}, is given by

$$d_{ij} = \sqrt{\sigma_{ii} + \sigma_{jj} - 2\sigma_{ij}}.$$

Applying this transformation to the distorted similarities yields a 51-by-51 table of distances. These, when supplied to the multidimensional scaling procedure, result in the two-dimensional map shown in Figure

---

[1]Recall that multidimensional scaling presents the relations among objects in a map but cannot orient the map since the information needed to do that is not present in a table of distances.

10.2. The ordering of the objects (integers) is correct, but they no longer lie in a straight line. Because of this phenomenon (called the "horseshoe effect"), Chatfield and Collins (1980: 205) advise that one

> ...construct suitable measures of dissimilarity, find a two-dimensional solution and then see if the points fall into a comparatively long narrow band, which need not necessarily be straight. If they do, then a one-dimensional solution can be inferred in an obvious way.

We shall follow this scenario.

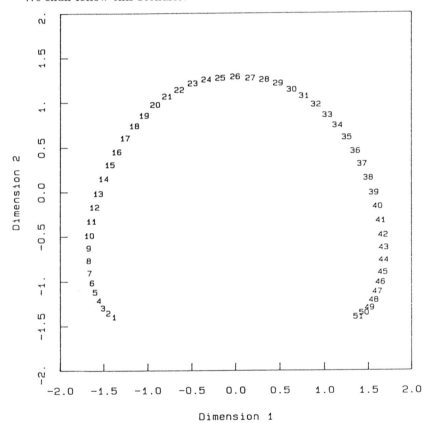

Figure 10.2 Multidimensional scaling result for Kendall's distorted distance table for the integers 1 through 51—*The horseshoe effect*: Two dimensions are required to represent this situation.

10.3   The Abundance Matrix for Spelling

Since our text portions tend to include each and every possible vowel type/spelling choice combination, we work in terms of the *abundance matrix*, a table—in the archaeological case—whose rows represent graves, whose columns represent artifacts, and whose cell ij contains the *proportion* of the ith grave's contents which are of the jth variety (Kendall 1971). To study spelling, we convert our four-dimensional contingency table of counts for vowel type, stress, portion, and spelling choice combinations (a 65-by-3-by-76-by-2 table) into a 30-by-170 abundance matrix whose rows represent portions and whose columns represent the possible type/stress/choice combinations. Note that the method involves *no* assumption that the extent of *plene* spelling increases with time. The relative abundance of an item may increase or decrease over time. It matters not to the method.

The unfortunately tortuous procedure for making the conversion is as follows:

- Select the number of portions appropriate to the problem: too many portions leads to too-small samples with resulting unreliable results. Too few portions leads to too-large samples which may combine texts displaying very disparate spelling practices. The thirty portions used in Chapter 10 of **SHB** are an acceptable compromise between these extremes.

- Follow the practice of **SHB** § 10.2 and collapse the type-stress-portion-choice table, which is 65 by 3 by 30 by 2, into a type/stress-portion-choice table, which is 93 by 30 by 2.

- In addition, remove the six outlier-dominated types (**SHB**, page 297), and incidental sparse types (Type 10 middle stress and Type 22 middle stress), yielding an 85-by-30-by-2 contingency table.

- So that vowel type choice patterns (*but not type incidence*) affect the seriation of portions and so that unrepresentative events do not influence the seriation, adjust the counts for each type/stress and choice so that each type/stress occurs one hundred times in each portion (provided it appears ten times or more).[2] To accomplish this, follow the normalization procedure described on page 289 of **SHB**: for each type/stress and portion, replace each pair of choice counts by the respective percentages (when the total count is ten or more) so that each adequately represented type/stress appears in each portion a hundred times.

---

[2] That is, if a type/stress appears nine or fewer times in a portion, we drop it from further consideration. If it occurs ten or more times, we scale the counts of *plene* and *defective* spellings so they sum to one hundred for that type/stress in that portion.

- Form a 30-by-170 rectangular matrix by laying type/stress-portion-*plene* choice columns alongside type/stress-portion-*defective* choice columns, the portions now being the rows.

- Normalize each row of the 30-by-170 rectangular matrix by dividing each element of a row by the grand total for that row. This creates a rectangular matrix each of whose rows sum to unity, our desired abundance matrix.

10.4   From Abundances to Seriation

To seriate the portions, we must determine the distances among the portions based on the abundance matrix.[3] Kendall (1971) proposes a similarity measure appropriate to this situation. His similarity measure leads to a distance measure which is intimately related to the "city block" metric (Mardia *et al.* 1979: 393, 402).[4] Due to the absence or infrequency of some type/stress entries in some portions, the distances must be adjusted along lines given by Becker and Chambers (1984: 303). The distances form a 30-by-30 matrix. (The distance of each portion from itself is zero; twenty-nine additional numbers specify its distance from each of the other portions.)

Having converted the basic four-dimensional contingency table of spelling counts into the appropriate 30-by-30 distance matrix, we may supply the distances to the multidimensional scaling procedure. Two details must be attended to:

1. We must test our results to reassure ourselves that the particular sort of scaling used is appropriate to the supplied distance matrix. For *classical* multidimensional scaling—which is what we use—to be appropriate, the plot of the original distances against those of the two-dimensional map must disclose "a relationship which is approximately linear and which goes through the origin" (Chatfield and Collins 1980: 204).

2. We must link all those portions positioned within some selected distance of each other so as to disclose the nature of the seriation. As Seber (1984: 250) remarks: "It is important to draw the links..., particularly when the curve is almost closed and when it is more of a wide band rather than a curve; otherwise the one-dimensional structure may be overlooked."

---

[3] This involves several subtle technical issues. Rather than attempt to explain each, we invite interested readers to consult the cited literature.

[4] The "city-block" or "Manhattan" metric measures distances as relevant to a pedestrian in a city, who must move along the sidewalks. The "city-block" distance from the SW-corner to the NE-corner of a block is two blocks, not $\sqrt{2}$ blocks as the crow could fly.

We supply the 30-by-30 distance matrix to the scaling procedure and obtain scaled distances. These allow us to plot Figure 10.3, which shows the original "city-block" distances ("dist.orig") against the scaling map distances ("dist.scaled").[5]

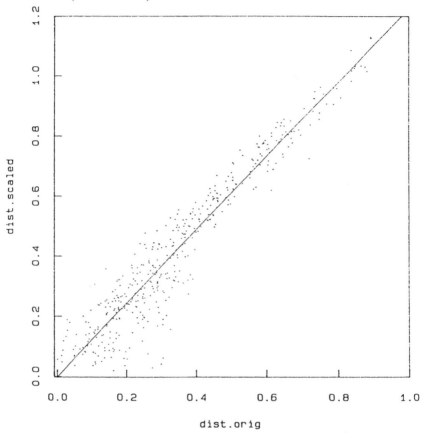

Figure 10.3 City-block versus scaled distances for thirty portions: Though scattered, the two sorts of distance concentrate around a straight line passing through the origin.

The superimposed line is that line which best fits the data points (in a least-squares sense). We note that the adjusted distances approximately obey a linear relation which goes through the origin, providing reassurance that the classical algorithm is adequate.[6]

---

[5] The former have been uniformly reduced by .25 units (as permitted by the classical algorithm which we use [Davison 1983: 76]).

[6] The results of scaling the adjusted distances are the same as those for the unadjusted distances.

Figure 10.4 shows the two-dimensional scaling result based on the "city-block" distances among the portions. Portions separated by .3 units or less on the map are linked by dotted lines, forming a curving band.[7]

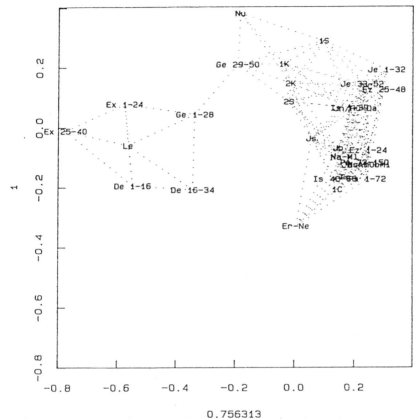

0.756313

Figure 10.4 Seriation of thirty portions with link distance equal to .3: As one sweeps around the arc from the left, one first encounters the Torah, then the Former Prophets, and—finally—the intermixed Latter Prophets, Poetry, and Other Writings. Exodus 25–40 has the earliest spelling, and Ezra–Nehemiah has the latest.

The superiority of the purely descriptive approach taken in **SHB** over an interpretive approach which treats the sequencing of the portions as purely temporal is made manifest when we examine the sequencing. To do so, we must first decide if the sense of time in Figure 10.4 is

---

[7] It is instructive to compare these seriation results with the groupings produced by hierarchical clustering shown in Figures 10.7 and 10.8 of **SHB**, an exercise left to the reader.

clockwise or counterclockwise. Examining the basic pattern of portions
in the band, it seems better to assume time flows clockwise in Figure
10.4.

As we proceed clockwise along the band in the figure, we first en-
counter the portions making up the Torah, which stretch over the first
half of the time interval. The spelling pattern of Exodus 25–40 (82%
P) positions it earliest, while Genesis 29–50 (9% P) and Numbers (73%
P) are latest. Next come most of the portions making up the Former
Prophets. (Kings and Samuel come earliest with Joshua a bit later.
Judges is displaced over into the midst of the Minor Prophets.) The
Latter Prophets, Poetry, and Other Writings come last, thoroughly intermixed. Note that both Isaiah and Ezekiel have experienced "orthographic fission," their halves being separated in time. Note also that 1
Chronicles is dated considerably later than 2 Chronicles. (2 Chronicles
is hidden between Jeremiah 33–52 and Ezekiel 25–48.) Ezra–Nehemiah
is latest.[8] This sequencing of portions raises puzzling questions: Why
is a P-saturated portion (Exodus 25–40) earliest? Why are the halves
of Ezekiel dislocated in time? Why is 1 Chronicles dated considerably
later than 2 Chronicles?

To attribute the ordering of the portions along the band in Figure
10.4 solely to time would be premature. Seriation orders the portions
in time based on the received spelling. Hence, because of the possibility
of extensive spelling updating and/or copying errors, the relative times
associated with portions may bear little relation to the time(s) of their
creation.

---

[8] Jonah/Ruth–Daniel, a conflate of seven disparate books, overlays Isaiah 1–39,
"north-east" of Joshua.

Part IV

Documents

Chapter 11

The Orthography of the Aramaic Portion of the Tell Fekherye Bilingual

Francis I. Andersen & David Noel Freedman

11.1 Introduction

The purpose of this paper is to describe the orthography of the Aramaic section of the recently published bilingual inscription from Tell Fekherye (Abou–Assaf 1981 and Abou–Assaf, Bordreuil, and Millard 1982). On the whole, it is our judgment that the orthography is consistent with the general principles and procedures derived from the study of Northwest Semitic inscriptions, but at the same time there are numerous unusual and novel features which warrant special attention.

In the following study of the text we shall examine all the words in which vowel letters (that is, consonant signs used to represent vowel sounds) or potential vowel letters occur, as well as those in which vowel letters might or should have been used and were not. On the basis of the information we shall then tabulate the results, and summarize the findings in the form of inductive rules or guidelines. In making the selection

Reprinted, with permission, from W. Claassen (ed.), **Text and Context: Old Testament and Semitic Studies for F. C. Fensham**, JSOT Suppl. Series 48, (Sheffield: Sheffield Academic Press, 1988), 9–49.

and in examining the material, the following are our presuppositions, which in turn are confirmed by the data:

1. In the inscription, all final vowels are marked by the appropriate vowel letters, of which there are three: *he, waw,* and *yod. Aleph* is not a vowel letter in this inscription, either in the final or in the medial position. It is either a true consonant (a root phoneme) in medial or in final position; or, in some instances, a marker of the emphatic state in final position, and presumably also consonantal (or at least not demonstrably only a vowel letter), since the purely phonetic spelling of word-terminal long /a/ is regularly *he.* To judge from later Aramaic texts written in syllabic cuneiform, the use of the ꜣA (glottal) sign at the end of emphatic nouns suggests that a distinctive pronunciation was being recorded, although the same device served also to mark some word-terminal long vowels as such.

2. Both *waw* and *yod* are used as medial vowel letters (but not *he*). *Waw* is used for primal /u/ (long or short [?]) and also for the diphthong /aw/. *Yod* is used for primal /i/ (whether long or short [?]) and for the diphthong /ay/.

These premises do not exclude other possibilities, but represent the point of departure for the study. Whether *waw* and *yod* were always used for such vowels remains to be determined.

Since the objective is to establish the governing principles of the spelling in the inscription, we shall avoid areas of controversy concerning readings and interpretations, since it is essential to base the findings on clear cases and consensus readings as much as possible. Fortunately the text is mostly in excellent shape, and the presence of an equally readable Assyrian text makes most of the readings and interpretations secure.

We may now proceed to a word-by-word analysis of the text in terms of its orthography. In order to establish orthographic practice and rules, it is necessary to try to vocalize the text; and while this is all too often a fruitless and thankless job, it has to be attempted. It should be pointed out, however, that we are not concerned about the actual quality of many of the vowels, in particular those short unstressed vowels that are not and would not be represented in the orthography. Thus whether the vowel connecting prepositions to the following words is **a** or **i** or some indistinct sound does not matter in this inquiry. So we have chosen somewhat arbitrarily and trust that our reconstruction of such vowels will not be misunderstood. We make no claim to secret wisdom here, and would be happy to be corrected. In some cases where we think there is a reason for the selection of one vowel over another (the possible survival of old case-endings is a frequent instance), we shall offer explanations of our choices. In matters affecting orthography we shall take up that task in earnest.

11.2 The Basic Data

Table 11.1. The Aramaic portion of the Tell Fekherye bilingual
(Abou–Assaf, Bordreuil, and Millard)

1   dmwtᵓ | zy | hdysᶜy : zy : šm : qdm : hddskn

2   gwgl : šmyn : wᵓrq : mhnḥt : ᶜsr : wntn : rᶜy

3   wmšqy : lmt : kln : wntn : šlh : wᵓdqwr

4   lᵓlhyn : klm : ᵓḥwh : gwgl : nhr : klm : mᶜdn

5   mt : kln : ᵓlh : rḥmn : zy : tṣlwth : ṭbh : ysb

6   skn : mrᵓ : rb : mrᵓ hdysᶜy : mlk : gwzn : br

7   ssnwry : mlk : gwzn : lḥyy : nbšh : wlmᵓrk : ywmwh

8   wlkbr : šnwh : wlšlm : byth : wlšlm : zrᶜh : wlšlm

9   ᵓnšwh : wlmld : mrq : mnh : wlmšmᶜ : tṣlwth : wl

10   mlqḥ : ᵓmrt : pmh : knn : wyhb : lh : wmn : ᵓḥr : kn

11   ybl : lknnh : ḥds : wšmym : lśm : bh : wzy : yld : šmy : mnh

12   wyśym : šmh : hdd : gbr : lhwy : qblh : ṣlm : hdysᶜy

13   mlk : gwzn : wzy : skn : wzy : ᵓzrn : lᵓrm wrdt : krsᵓh

14   wlmᵓrk : ḥywh : wlmᶜn : ᵓmrt : pmh : ᵓl : ᵓlhn : wᵓl ᵓnšn

15   tyṭb : dmwtᵓ : zᵓt : ᶜbd : ᵓl : zy : qdm : hwtr : qdm hdd

16   ysb : skn : mrᵓ : ḥbwr : ṣlmh : šm : mn : yld : šmy : mn : mᵓnyᵓ

17   zy : bt : hdd : mrᵓy : mrᵓy : hdd: lḥmh : wmwh : ᵓl : ylqḥ : mn

18   ydh : swl : mrᵓty : lḥmh : wmwh : ᵓl : tlqḥ : mn : ydh : wl

19   zrᶜ : wᵓl : yḥṣd : wᵓlp : šᶜryn : lzrᶜ wprys : lᵓḥz : mnh

20   wmᵓh : sᵓwn : lhynqn : ᵓmr : wᵓl : yrwy : wmᵓh : swr : lhynqn

21   ᶜgl : wᵓl : yrwy : wmᵓh : nšwn : lhynqn : ᶜlym : wᵓl: yrwy

22   wmᵓh : nšwn : lᵓpn : btnwr : lḥm : wᵓl : ymlᵓnh :
      wmn : qlqltᵓ : llqṭw : ᵓnšwh : šᶜrn : lᵓklw

23   wmwtn : šbṭ : zy : nyrgl : ᵓl : ygtzr mn : mth

Table 11.2. The Aramaic portion of the Tell Fekherye bilingual, vocalized

1 damûta⁾ zî hadyis^{C}î zî śam qudm hadad sikan
2 gugal šamayn wa⁾arq(ḍ) mahanḥat ^{C}usr wanātin ri^{C}î
3 wamašqî lamāt kullan wanātin šilâ wa⁾adaqur
4 la⁾ilāhîn kullam ⁾aḥwih gugal nahar kullam ma^{C}addin
5 māt kullan ⁾ilāh raḥmān zî taṣlûtuh ṭābâ yāsib
6 sikan māri⁾ rab māri⁾ hadyis^{C}î malk guzan bir
7 sasnûrî malk guzan laḥayyay nabšah walama⁾rak yawmwih
8 walakabbar šanwih walašallam baytah walašallam zar^{C}ah walašallam
9 ⁾anāšwih walamallad mariq minnih walamašma^C taṣlûtah wala-
10 malqaḥ ⁾imrat pumih kānin wayahab lih waman ⁾aḥir kan
11 yabil lukāninah ḥadas wašumîm luśam bih wazî yal(l)id šumî minnih
12 wayaśîm šumah hadad gabbār luhawî qābiluh ṣalm hadyis^{C}î
13 malk guzan wazî sikan wazî ⁾azaran l⁾rm wrdt karsi⁾ih
14 walama⁾rak ḥayyawih walama^{C}n ⁾imrat pumih ⁾il ⁾ilāhīn wa⁾il
    ⁾anāšīn
15 tayṭab damûta⁾ za⁾t ^{C}abad ⁾l zî qudm hawtir qudm hadad
16 yāsib sikan māri⁾ ḥabûr ṣalmah śam man yalid šûmî min ma⁾nayya⁾
17 zî bēt(!) hadad mār⁾î mār⁾î hadad laḥmah wamawih ⁾al yilqaḥ min
18 yadih sala mār⁾atî laḥmah wamawih ⁾al tilqaḥ min yadih walu-
19 zara^C wa⁾al yaḥṣud wa⁾alp śi^{C}ārîn luzara^C waparîs lu⁾aḥaz minnah
20 wami⁾â si⁾wān luhayniqān ⁾immir wa⁾al yirway wami⁾â sawr
    luhayniqān
21 ^{C}igl wa⁾al yirway wami⁾â nišwān lahayniqān ^{C}alîm wa⁾al yirway
22 wami⁾â nišwān lu⁾apān batannûr laḥm wa⁾al yamalli⁾ānih
    wamin qalqalāta⁾ lulaqaṭû ⁾anāšwih śi^{C}ārīn lu⁾akalû
23 wamawtān šibṭ zî nîrgal ⁾al yigtizar min mātih

11.3 The Inventory of Words, with Comments on Spelling

1. **dmwt⁾** (line 1), **damûta⁾**, *the image.* The form seems quite
regular, f. s. emphatic of **damût** (Heb. **děmût**).

The older the inscription is, the less confident we can be that a word
such as this one already had the vocalization which we only know from
much later attestation. Arguments from historical-comparative grammar can lead to more than one possibility and their contending claims
cannot be settled. It is only at a later period that the suffix –ût is generally productive for abstract nouns. This one is concrete. The ending
probably arose in the first place from the etymological /w/ in third-
weak roots, as with this word, spreading to nouns with strong roots by

analogy. Hence the possibility exists that in early times, and perhaps
still surviving in the first millennium BCE, a word like this one was
pronounced *dimwut-, or the like. *Damawt- is less likely, because
that diphthong would either hold up or yield /o/. But theoretically
the possibility that the **w** in dmwt‍ᵓ represents a diphthong cannot be
entirely ruled out.

Converging evidence can be brought for this possibility. (i) The survival
of words with primal consonant /w/ in such a position. (ii) The promi-
nence in Aramaic of a consonant /w/ either in this position (ḥaywān,
animals) or as an extension of a strong root (malkĕwān, *kingdoms*).
(iii) The early preference for *plene* spellings of Hebrew infinitives construct of third-*yod*/*waw* verbs in –ōt suggests a possible derivation from
damawatu, or the like. (iv) Some strange spellings in the Hebrew Bible
point to the possible existence of a consonantal *waw* in the third root
position of some derivatives of weak roots. The *ketib* qṣwwtw (Exod
37:8; 39:4) points to a variant plural qiṣwōt-. The word *testimonies*
(ᶜēdōt) is sometimes pointed with *shewa* to yield ᶜēdwōt– (1 Kings
2:3; 2 Kings 17:15; 23:3; Jer 44:23; Psalm 119:14, 31, 36, 99, 111, 129,
144, 157; Neh 9:34; 1 Chron 29:19; 2 Chron 34:31).

The existence of an analogous **w** in other words in this inscription (see
below II. A.) requires that this possibility be taken into account. See also
the discussion of No. 33. Even so, the probability is that the word was
pronounced approximately as we have vocalized it. The reconstruction
of the first stem vowel is admittedly conjectural.

The final *aleph* is a consonant, marking the emphatic state. How it
was pronounced at that time cannot be determined solely from the
inscription (i.e. it may have quiesced in the final position). Such
an *aleph* can be considered to be a vowel letter only when it has no
history as a consonant. There are no such cases in this inscription.
In fact there are only two other cases of the emphatic in the whole
inscription, mᵓnyᵓ (line 16) and qlqltᵓ (line 22). The medial
waw, however, is almost certainly a vowel letter, representing long
/u/, which was evidently considered by the scribe to be the dominant or significant vowel in the word. It may be noted that only
two vowel letters were in use in the middle of words (*he* is never so
used) and so the choice is limited. With a possible exception noted
below (No. 141), a–type vowels are never indicated medially, so
we would expect to find only **u**– and **i**–types represented in the
orthography.

Whether any vowels, considered phonetically, had been deflected to /o/
or /e/ at this stage is not germane. Nor can we prejudge the extent to
which primal diphthongs /aw/ and /ay/ might have monophthongized
in this dialect at this stage. If a vowel is known to be primally long,
all the indications are that it would be stable, particularly in Aramaic.

But the phonology of a previously unattested dialect should not be assumed hastily to be just like the rest of Aramaic. In particular there are two features of the present inscription that dictate caution. First, the letters used for writing certain consonants point to an early, if not archaic stage—typologically speaking. Second, the possible influence of Assyrian has to be kept in mind.

2. **zy** (1), **zî**, *of.* This is the well-known particle used in various ways in Northwest Semitic inscriptions. The vocalization is certain and reflects the use of **y** as a final vowel letter for –î.

3. **hdys^cy** (1), **hadyis^cî**, *Had–yis^ci.* This is the name of the king who erected the statue memorialized in the inscription. Neither the vocalization nor the meaning proposed is certain, but both are plausible. In any case, there seems to be little question about the final vowel sound, î, represented by the vowel letter *yod*. Naturally the initial *he* is a consonant, and so is the medial *yod*. The name, as most suggest, probably means *Hadd (= Hadad) is my salvation*, or the like. The etymology makes it virtually impossible to vocalize the medial *yod* as a vowel letter for î. The second part of the name cannot be a verb, for the **h** of the *hap^cel* would be evident. The other vowels in the name are short and require no comment.

4. **zy** (1), **zî** cf. No. 2. Here the particle is the relative pronoun meaning *who.*

5. **śm** (1), **śam**, *he set.* As expected, the short medial vowel receives no orthographic representation.

6. **qdm** (1), **qudm**, *before.* All Northwest Semitic languages do not follow the same patterns with segholates. Eblaite complicates the picture even more. The vowel or vowels are short, however, and have no significance for this study.

7. **hddskn** (1), **hadad sikan**, *Hadad of Sikan.* On the basis of other instances of personal or place names in the inscription we might have expected, or at least not have been surprised, to see a medial *yod* in the name **skn**, since we find vowel letters in names of persons and places to facilitate identification and pronunciation. It does not seem to matter particularly whether the vowel was originally long or not: it is the quality that counts, and in general only /u/ and /i/ vowels are represented, and then, as this word shows, on a selective basis.

To judge from the rest of the inscription, it is more likely that a vowel written by means of a consonant was long, or at least stressed, rather than short. But that does not mean that all long (or stressed) vowels were so written; nor does it mean that every vowel so written must have been long. While rules are to be expected, and are certainly found, an element of convention operates in all writing systems, some variations are acceptable, and mistakes occur. Insofar as conventions, variants, and mistakes cause a text to fall short of absolute consistency, it is not valid to point to such marginal usage as evidence that there were no rules at all!

In the present text there is no word in which an expected terminal long vowel is not represented by a vowel letter, and there is no word in which such a vowel letter can reasonably be interpreted as a representation of a terminal short vowel. In view of remarks already made, we do not wish to state too dogmatically that this dialect had reached the stage, common throughout Northwest Semitic at this time, when all primal short terminal vowels had been lost, or else lengthened. But all indications are that this was the state of affairs. To assert to the contrary that short terminal vowels were still pronounced, but never written, is to state something which is not only impossible to prove but which flies in the face of both historical-comparative grammar and the orthographic evidence. We are speaking about Aramaic, of course. How far a similar process had gone in Assyrian at this time is another question. But even if this loanword was **Sikanu** in Assyrian at this time, the odds are that it would be pronounced in Aramaic as Aramaic. The spelling of the word here supports this observation. Cf. Nos. 33, 63.

There is no reason to suppose that the place-name was pronounced *Sikanu*. As already remarked, loanwords would conform to Aramaic word patterns. Even if it could be proved that the Assryians were saying *Sikanu*, it would not follow that Arameans did the same. The Assyrian spelling (**si–ka–ni** in line 20) proves nothing, since the final sign could equally represent vowelless terminal –**n**.

8. **gwgl** (2), **gugal**, *water-master*. This is a loanword from Akkadian, so we are not surprised to find it equipped with a medial vowel letter. Again the selection is limited to vowels that can properly be represented by *waw* or *yod*, and we have noted that the scribe limits himself to not more than one vowel letter in the middle of a word. In this case the vowel seems to be short, but it may be under accent. In any case we suggest that the vowel letter was intended to mark quality (and perhaps stress) rather than quantity.

9. **šmyn** (2), **šamayn**, *heavens*. The *yod* here represents the diphthong /ay/. It is important evidence to support the view that the diphthongs /aw/ and /ay/ were preserved in this branch of Aramaic as was true of most of the Aramaic dialects. So far as we are aware, there is only one exception in this inscription to the practice of representing the diphthong by its consonantal element, and that is **bt** in line 17 (see below [No. 130] for discussion).

10. **wᵓrq** (2), **waᵓarq(ḍ)**, *and earth*. No comment is needed, except to note the representation of primal /ḍ/ by means of **q**.

11. **mhnḥt** (2), **mahanḥat**, *the provider*. This form is analyzed as a *hap^cel* participle of the root **nḥt**. The vocalization is not certain, but the vowels are all short, and we would not expect any orthographic representation of any of them.

12. **ᶜsr** (2), **ᶜusr**, *riches*. The vocalization is based on later Aramaic **ᶜutrāᵓ**, but all that matters is that there are no vowels requiring or implying orthographic representation. Syriac **ᶜawtrāᵓ** is secondary. Note that in this dialect primal /ṯ/ is written s (cf. Nos. 3, 159).

13. **wntn** (2), **wanātin**, *and the giver*. Here we seem to have the *pe^cal* participle, m. s. The only point to be made is that long /ā/ here and elsewhere in the inscription is not represented in the orthography in the medial position.

14. **rᶜy** (2), **riᶜî**, *food, provender*. The vocalization is based on the Akkadian cognate, but biblical **rĕᶜî** is also germane. For our purposes the important orthographic element is the representation of final **î** by *yod*. Theoretically the final syllable could be a diphthong; but this is most unlikely, and in any case it would not introduce any departure from standard practice.

15. **wmšqy** (3), **wamašqî**, *and drink*. Here again the orthographically interesting information concerns the final *yod* which represents **î**.

16. **lmt** (3), **lamāt**, *to the countries*. While the form of the noun is apparently singular, it serves as a collective with the following **kullan** (*all of them*). The word is found in Aḥiqar. It is not certain whether **mt** in other Old Aramaic inscriptions (where it often means *man*) might sometimes mean *land(s)*. Whether a loan from Akkadian or not, the stem vowel was probably long, but it is not represented in the orthography.

17. **kln** (3), **kullan**, *all of them*. Here we have the particle **kl** plus the 3rd f. pl. pronominal suffix. Both vowels were probably short.

18. **wntn** (3), **wanātin** (cf. No. 13).

19. **šlh** (3). The form and meaning of this word are obscure. Whether connected with Sefire **šlw** (Sf III 5) or derived from one or other of the roots **šly** (Kaufman 1982: 164), the terminal *he* is hard to explain. If a loan from Akkadian, **silᵓu**, *libation* (*AHw*, p. 1044), is the best candidate. It seems likely that the final *he* is a vowel letter, presumably for –ā, but possibly for another vowel. In view of the availability of *waw* and *yod*, it can hardly be /u/ or /i/, and there is little ground for belief that either /o/ or /e/ yet existed in this dialect. The word was doubtless construed as feminine singular.

20. **wᵓdqwr** (3), **waᵓadaqûr**, *?*. This is another loanword from Akkadian, and therefore we are not surprised at the use of *waw* to indicate the significant medial vowel (the only one eligible for representation in this system). The *waw* represents an original short /u/, but whether it was under accent and possibly lengthened in its Aramaic guise cannot be determined.

21. **lᵓlhyn** (4), **laᵓilāhîn**, *for the gods*. There are two points of orthographic interest: (a) the long î in the final syllable is represented by *yod*; note that this example establishes the use of *yod* as a vowel letter in the medial position for î; the same word, apparently, is spelled without the medial *yod* in line 14 (ᵓlhn). Cf. No. 105. (b) The medial long /a/ (third syllable) is not indicated in the orthography.

22. **klm** (4), **kullam**, *all of them*. Particle with 3rd m. pl. suffix. Cf. No. 17.

23. **ᵓḥwh** (4), **ᵓaḥwih**, *his brothers*. This is a difficult form, and our proposal is admittedly a stab in the dark. The important things to note are as follows. It is the consistent practice in this inscription to include a *waw* before the 3rd m. s. pronominal suffix when it is attached to masculine plural nouns. It also seems clear that this *waw* does not represent a vowel but has consonantal force, or reflects the consonantal element in a diphthong. We therefore regard the *waw* as a part of the plural form of nouns used with pronominal suffixes, in particular with m. pl. nouns with 3rd m. s. suffixes. To interpret this *waw* otherwise, to read it as /u/, for instance, creates problems. How could such a form develop? A consonant in the third root position of a word such as ᵓḥ(w), *brother*, is understandable. Misdivision takes the syllable –wi– as the plural morpheme, extending it by paradigmatic analogy to strong roots. The result is standard in this inscription and in Sefire (convenient inventory in Fitzmyer 1967: 149). Fitzmyer vocalizes ᵓaḥawh, etc. (p. 31), assuming a secondary suffix after the analogy of biblical Aramaic –ôhî. But the loss of the final vowel from a form with that history is a serious obstacle, in our opinion, to say nothing about the consonant cluster /wh/. In any case, whether ᵓaḥwih or ᵓaḥawh (or even ᵓaḥawih), the *waw* is consonantal.

24. **gwgl** (4), **gugal**. Cf. No. 8.

25. **nhr** (4), **nahar**, *rivers*. Another collective, since it is followed by **kullam**.

26. **klm** (4), **kullam**. Cf. No. 22.

27. **mᶜdn** (4), **maᶜaddin**, *?*. We take this to be a *paᶜel* participle m. s. All the vowels are short, and none is represented in the orthography.

28. **mt** (5), **māt**. Cf. No. 16.

29. **kln** (5), **kullan**. Cf. No. 17.

30. **ᵓlh** (5), **ᵓilāh**, *god*. The final *he* here is a consonant; hence the preceding long /a/ vowel is not represented by a vowel letter. Cf. **ᵓlhyn** (4) / **ᵓlhn** (14).

31. **rḥmn** (5), **raḥmān**, *the compassionate*. If the second vowel was actually long /a/, then we have another example of a long medial /a/ not represented in the orthography.

32. **zy** (5), **zî**. Cf. No. 2.

33. **tṣlwth** (5), **taṣlûtuh**, *his prayer*. Apparently a loanword from Akkadian, but adapted to Aramaic usage. The noun is feminine singular with a 3rd m. s. pronominal suffix. Since the noun is in the nominative case, we have supplied the nominative case ending as the connecting vowel between noun and suffix, but this is only a guess. There is a medial vowel letter, *waw*, which represents a long /u/, in the key syllable of the word.

34. **ṭbh** (5), **ṭābâ**, *good*. The word is a predicate adjective f. s. abs., modifying the preceding noun **tṣlwth**. The final vowel, long /a/, is represented by *he*. The medial long /a/ is not represented.

35. **ysb** (5), **yāsib**, *the dweller*, or in this case perhaps *the resident monarch*. We take this form as the *peᶜal* participle m. s., and note the medial long /a/, unrepresented in the orthography.

36. **skn** (6), **sikan**. Cf. No. 7.

37. **mrᵓ** (6), **māriᵓ**, *lord*. To judge from the vocalization eventually attested, this title is probably an original participle. The final *aleph* is a root consonant. The long /a/ in the first syllable is not represented in the orthography.

38. **rb** (6), **rab**, *great*.

39. **mrᵓ** (6), **māriᵓ**. Cf. No. 37.

40. **hdysᶜy** (6), **hadyisᶜî**. Cf. No. 3.

41. **mlk** (6), **malk**, *king*. We take the word in its monosyllabic root form, although there are other possibilities, such as **malik* (which seems to be the Eblaite reading). Cf. No. 6.

42. **gwzn** (6), **guzan**, *Guzan*. Since a foreign place-name is involved, the spelling is enhanced by the use of a vowel letter. The *waw* represents an original short /u/ vowel, but whether it has been modified or lengthened under accent (if it is stressed) cannot be determined. The latter pronunciation *Gozan*, as attested in Hebrew, does not settle the pronunciation here. All that can be said is that a medial vowel letter is used to represent a vowel which was originally short /u/. Cf. the discussion of **gwgl** (No. 8).

43. **br** (6), **bir** (later **bar**), *son*.

44. **ssnwry** (7), **sasnûrî**, *Sas–nuri*. The name seems clear enough, but the vocalization may be partially uncertain. For orthographic purposes, we are concerned with the latter part of the name only:

   (a) The final vowel î of the 1st c. s. suffix is represented by *yod*.

   (b) The medial vowel û is represented by *waw*.

   The name as a whole is doubtless **sas** (for **sams** = *sun*)—**nûrî** = *The sun (god) is my light* (lit. *fire*). Both the suffix and the medial vowel are long.

45. **mlk** (7), **malk**. Cf. No. 41.

46. **gwzn** (7), **guzan**. Cf. No. 42.

47. **lhyy** (7), **lahayyay, lahayyî**, *to give life, to make live*. We take the form to be *pa^cel* infinitive. The first *yod* is consonantal and part of the root. The form is archaic, since the standard form would be **lahayyayâ**. Here the reading may be **hayyay**, but **hayyî** is not ruled out. In either case, the diphthong or vowel reflects a root consonant, so we have an example of historical or etymological spelling.

48. **nbšh** (7), **nabšah**, *his soul/person*. We read this as the noun plus the 3rd m. s. suffix. Since the noun is in the objective case, we supply the accusative vowel –a as the connection between noun and pronominal suffix.

49. **wlm⁾rk** (7), **walama⁾rak**, *and for extension*. We take this as a *pe^cal* infinitive of the root ⁾rk. The *aleph* is etymological.

50. **ywmwh** (7), **yawmwih**, *his days*. The meaning is certain, but the form is difficult. We interpret the form as a m. pl. noun with the 3rd m. s. pronominal suffix. The form of the noun, with medial *waw*, may be unusual, but it is known in Aramaic from Panammu through Elephantine to Qumran. The first *waw* therefore represents the diphthong /aw/. The second *waw* is normal in this inscription for pl. nouns with 3rd m. s. suffixes. We consider it consonantal and vocalize accordingly. Cf. No. 23.

51. **wlkbr** (8), **walakabbar**, *and to multiply*. We take this as a *pa^cel* infinitive of the root **kbr**. No vowels are eligible for consonantal spelling. Short /i/ also is possible, but inconsequential.

52. **šnwh** (8), **šanwih**, *his years*. We have here another example of the m. pl. noun with a 3rd m. s. pronoun suffix connected by a *waw* which marks the stem. We consider the *waw* a consonant and part of the morphology of plural nouns in this dialect. Cf. Nos. 23 and 50.

53. **wlšlm** (8), **walašallam**, *and to give success to*. We take the form to be the *pa^cel* infinitive of the root **šlm**. Cf. No. 51.

54. **byth** (8), **baytah,** *his house.* Since the word is in the objective case, we have supplied the accusative case ending to connect it with the pronoun suffix. The spelling with the medial *yod* shows that the diphthong /ay/ of the original word is still represented. The variant spelling of this word in line 17 (**bt**) poses a problem. See No. 130.

55. **wlšlm** (8), **walašallam.** Cf. No. 53.

56. **zrᶜh** (8), **zarᶜah,** *his seed.* We take the form to be the noun with the 3rd m. s. suffix; the final *he* is a consonant, which is true of all 3rd m. s. suffix forms. Cf. No. 54.

57. **wlšlm** (8), **walašallam.** Cf. No. 53.

58. **ᵓnšwh** (9), **ᵓanāšwih,** *his men.* Another case of a m. pl. noun with a 3rd m. s. pronoun suffix. We take the *waw* to be a consonant and part of the plural form. Cf. Nos. 23, 50, 52.

59. **wlmld** (9), **walamallad,** *and to efface.* We take the form as a *paᶜel* infinitive. See also Nos. 80, 125.

60. **mrq** (9), **mariq,** *plague (?).* This word occurs in Sefire I A 29, and seems to be identical with later Aramaic **mĕraᶜ**, cognate with Akkadian **marṣu,** Arabic **maraḍ,** *illness.* In any case the stem vowels are almost certainly short, so the spelling contains nothing unexpected.

61. **mnh** (9), **minnih,** *from him.* We interpret this form as the preposition **min** plus the 3rd m. s. pronoun suffix. The terminal *he* is consonantal (or historical spelling and hence of no special orthographic significance).

62. **wlmšmᶜ** (9), **walamašmaᶜ,** *and for listening* or *being heard.* We take this form to be the *peᶜal* infinitive of **šmᶜ.** Cf. No. 49.

63. **tṣlwth** (9), **taṣlûtah,** *his prayer.* Except for the hypothetical connecting vowel, the form is the same as No. 33. See comments there.

64. **wlmlqḥ** (9–10), **walamalqaḥ,** *and for receiving* or *accepting.* We take the form as the *peᶜal* infinitive of **lqḥ.**

65. **ᵓmrt** (10), **ᵓimrat,** *the utterance of.* This is the f. s. construct form before the absolute noun **pmh.**

66. **pmh** (10), **pumih,** *his mouth.* We take this form to be the m. s. noun plus the 3rd m. s. suffix. We have supplied the genitive case connecting vowel. The final *he* is consonantal.

67. **knn** (10), **kannan,** or **kānin,** *he built* or *constructed.* We take this to be the *paᶜel* or else the *palil* form, perfect 3rd m. s., like Hebrew **kônēn.** See the discussion under No. 74. The medial long /a/ is not represented in the orthography.

68. **wyhb** (10), **wayahab,** *and he gave.* This form seems to be a *peᶜal* perfect 3rd m. s. from the root **yhb.**

69. **lh** (10), **lih,** *to him.* This form is the preposition **l** with the 3rd m. s. pronoun suffix; the final *he* is consonantal.

70. **wmn** (10), **waman**, *and if (?)*. The form is uncertain, and so
    is the meaning; but in any case it has no particular orthographic
    significance.

71. **ᵓhr** (10), **ᵓaḥir**, *another*. Conceivably it could be read as **ᵓaḥar**,
    afterwards. Assyrian parallels favor this alternative. In either case
    there is nothing to be gained orthographically from the form ex-
    cept that it is consistent with the principles and practices so far
    observed or deduced.

72. **kn** (10), **kan** (?), *if* or *when*. The form and meaning are not clear,
    but the word is not important orthographically.

73. **ybl** (11), **yabil**, *it wears out (?)*. It is hard to say just what this
    form is. The root **bly** (blh in Hebrew, blᵓ in Aramaic) means
    wear out, usually of clothes, but in an Elephantine text it refers
    to a boat in disrepair. If this root were involved, we would expect
    the third consonant to be represented. An apocopated form is not
    out of the question, but would be inconsistent with the morpho-
    phonemics of the rest of the inscription. See however No. 178.
    Derivation of **ybl** from the root **nbl**, *decay* in Hebrew, commonly
    used of foliage, or **npl**, *destroy* in Assyrian, is equally problematic,
    since /n/ does not assimilate in Aramaic. Bordreuil and Millard
    (Abou–Assaf 1982: 32) prefer the root **ybl**, *remove*, extending the
    meaning to *deterioration*. Even then one would expect the first
    syllable to retain a diphthong. The existence of byforms **bl** and
    bll, or at least some measure of semantic overlap between these
    roots, requires us to treat the form with caution. The grammati-
    cal objection that the subject (*image*) is feminine suggests rather
    that the implied subject is *my name*, since it is removal of the name
    on the statue—a vital detail—that is later enjoined. The Assyrian
    parallel uses **anḫūtu**, *dilapidation*. Other usage suggests that a
    general formula, used specifically of temples, is being applied to
    an object not so liable to natural wear and tear but vulnerable,
    nevertheless, to damage, often deliberate.

74. **lknnh** (11), **lukāninah**, perhaps **lukanninah**, *let him build it*.
    We take this form as combination of the precative particle **lu** and
    the 3rd m. s. *palil* perfect of the verb **kn** (cf. No. 67), plus the 3rd
    f. s. suffix. We have supplied connecting vowels in keeping with
    the syntax. It is possible that the **lu-** form had developed into a
    kind of pseudo-preformative verb at this stage. But we think that
    a perfect is not entirely ruled out. The use of the precative particle
    with preformative verbs in Akkadian does not necessarily prove the
    contrary, for they are preterit. Even so, in view of the cultural mix
    exhibited by this inscription, influence of Assyrian on this Aramaic
    dialect is very likely. Nor does the association of this kind of jussive

later on in the text with a negated imperfect prove that it is derived from an imperfect, for part of the contrast lies in the difference in aspect between an act performed and one that does not happen. Precative **lu** is not the only candidate for ancestor of preformative l–. The history of this particle in Semitic is not well understood. Almost any vowel, short or long, is found with it (Huffmon 1965: 78–81; Dion 1974: 166–70). From the present inscription we can infer at least that the connecting vowel was short, especially if it was **lu–**. This is not likely if it came from **luyakannin**, or the like. But to say more than that would be mere speculation in the present state of knowledge. So far as the present investigation is concerned, we are indifferent to the correct identification of the stem of such verbs, whether preformative or afformative; for in each case the stem vowels are short, even if often indeterminate as to quality, and so are not eligible for consideration as potential occasions for the use of vowel letters.

So far as the present word is concerned, the twin consonants of such a root are manifest chiefly in *pa^{c}el*, and later pronunciation consistently (but not quite universally) shows the doubling of the middle radical. So this form is probably **lukanninah**. The final *he* is a consonant and all the vowels are short.

75. ḥds (11), ḥadas, *new*. The syntax is problematical. The matching form in the Assyrian versions is a verb. If this word is an adjective, it cannot refer to the statue. Perhaps it is an adverb—*anew*. In any case there is no reason to suspect that it contains long vowels, so the orthography is normal.

76. **wšmym** (11), **wašumîm**, *and my name*. This form consists of the conjunction plus the noun **šum** with the 1st s. pronoun suffix –î and an enclitic *mem*, which makes the suffix a medial vowel. However, in this inscription some vowels of this kind are represented and here there would be an added reason to do so. Without the enclitic *mem* the word would certainly have been written with the *yod* representing the final vowel, so here it is retained, even though it is no longer final. In the relationship between No. 76 and No. 81 (**šmy**) we can see the mechanism by which the early use of vowel letters for final vowels spread to the interior of words, first to the writing of a vowel which sometimes *is* terminal, then to long medial vowels which are never terminal.

We have adopted the normal Aramaic word for *name*, but there is no indication in the spelling as to how the stem was pronounced.

77. lśm (11), **luśam**, *let him set*. We take this to be the same sort of form as No. 74 with precative **lu–** followed by the *pe^{c}al* form of the

perfect 3rd m. s. Kaufman (1982: 150), however, supposes that l–
is a preformative, as in later Aramaic, and therefore that the stem
is **śim**. Comparing with **yśym** (No. 83) he then infers from the
difference in spelling that the supposed /i/ in No. 77 was reduced,
and so not spelled with a vowel letter. Since we have not found
any certainly short medial /i/ spelled with a vowel letter, the point
remains somewhat moot. But in our opinion, the occurrence of the
normal **yśym** in the same inscription makes it unlikely that **lśm**
is a variant preformative. A diphthong is out of the question.

78. **bh** (11), **bih**, *on it* or *in it*. This form is the preposition **b** plus
the 3rd m. s. suffix. We have supplied a vowel, but we are not
prepared to argue for it. In any case the final *he* is a consonant.

79. **wzy** (11), **wazî**. Cf. No. 2.

80. **yld** (11), **yal(l)id**, *he effaces*. The meaning is certain, since cognate verbs are used in the Sefire inscriptions. There, however, both
peᶜal and *hapᶜel* are attested (Fitzmyer 1967: 76). Here all forms
(Nos. 59, 80, 125) are *peᶜal*. The argument as to whether the
root is **ldd** or **lwd** is inconclusive. The problem is similar to the
one presented by **ybl** (No. 73), and the simplest resolution is to
recognize a simple biconsonantal, rather than a 'hollow' root. *He
will die* is spelled **ymwt** at Sefire, and that *waw* must be a vowel
letter (the attempt of Degen [1969: 28] to explain it as a *Gleitlaut*
is unconvincing). The fact that **yld** is not spelled similarly here
does not necessarily mean that the orthography is inconsistent, as
the root may be different. At Sefire both infinitive and imperative
are spelled simply **ld**. In any event the vowels are short and the
orthography is appropriate.

81. **šmy** (11), **šumî**, *my name*. Here we have the noun plus the 1st
s. pronoun suffix. The final long /i/ is represented by *yod* in the
orthography.

82. **mnh** (11), **minnih**, *from it*. This appears to be the preposition
min plus the 3rd m. s. pronoun suffix. The final *he* is a consonant.
Cf. No. 61.

83. **wyśym** (12), **wayaśîm**, *and he sets*. We take the form to be a
peᶜal imperfect 3rd m. s. from the hollow root **śym**. The first *yod*
is a consonant, of course; but the second one is an internal vowel
letter for long /i/. This is a parade example of the use of the vowel
letter for an internal vowel. We cannot be absolutely certain that
the vowel was long at this time, but the spelling strongly suggests
that it was, and, by the same token, the non-use of a vowel letter
in **yld** (No. 80) suggests that its vowel was not long.

84. **šmh** (12), **šumah**, *his name*. The form consists of the noun plus
3rd m. s. pronoun suffix. The final *he* is consonantal. We have

supplied the connecting vowel –a–, an accusative case ending for the noun.

85. **hdd** (12), **hadad**. Cf. No. 7.
86. **gbr** (12), **gabbār**, *hero, warrior*. The form is no doubt the D–stem for *warrior*, with long /a/ in the second syllable without orthographic representation.
87. **lhwy** (12), **luhawî**, *let him become*. The form combines the precative particle with the *pe^cal* perfect 3rd m. s. of the root **hwy**. Cf. No. 77, and the discussion there. The final *yod* stands as a vowel letter for long /i/, but it also constitutes the third consonant of the root, thus providing an example of the transition from historical to phonetic spelling. Cf. No. 47.
88. **qblh** (12), **qābiluh**, *his enemy*. The form combines the m. s. noun or participle with the 3rd m. s. pronoun suffix. The final *he* is consonantal. We have supplied a connecting vowel reflecting the presumed nominative case of the noun.
89. **ṣlm** (12), **ṣalm**, *the image of*. We assume that the word is the same as Hebrew ṣelem, hence originally monosyllabic. It is the m. s. construct form, and the stem vowel would be short.
90. **hdys^cy** (12), **hadyis^cî**. Cf. No. 3.
91. **mlk** (13), **malk**. Cf. No. 41.
92. **gwzn** (13), **guzan**. Cf. No. 42.
93. **wzy** (13), **wazî**. Cf. No. 2.
94. **skn** (13), **sikan**. Cf. No. 7.
95. **wzy** (13), **wazî**. Cf. No. 2.
96. **ᵓzrn** (13), **ᵓazaran**, *Azaran*. The vocalization of the place-name comes from the Akkadian. Since there are only /a/ vowels in the word, no vowel letters are expected and none are used.
97. **lᵓrm ẇrdt** (13). The reading here is questionable, and while some sense can be made of the phrase in connection with the uncontested following word **krsᵓh**, *his throne*, we prefer to pass over these terms. It is not likely that the *aleph* or the *waw* are candidates for vowel letters.
98. **krsᵓh** (13), **karsiᵓih**, *his throne*. This spelling with *reš* is somewhat surprising, but the form is well attested in Aramaic for the word *throne*. It has the 3rd m. s. suffix. The final *he* is consonantal. There are no vowel letters, and no long vowels.
99. **wlmᵓrk** (14), **walamaᵓrak**. Cf. No. 49.
100. **ḥywh** (14), **ḥayyawih**, *his life*. Again we have an example of a m. pl. noun with 3rd m. s. pronoun suffix. We note the presence of medial *waw*, which we interpret as a consonant representing the plural form of the noun. We have supplied connecting vowels. The final *he* is consonantal. Cf. Nos. 23, 50, 52, 58.

101. **wlm^cn** (14), **walama^cn**, *and so that.* Cf. Hebrew lĕma^can.

102. **ᵓmrt** (14), **ᵓimrat.** Cf. No. 65.

103. **pmh** (14), **pumih.** Cf. No. 66.

104. **ᵓl** (14), **ᵓil**, *to* or *for.*

105. **ᵓlhn** (14), **ᵓilāhīn**, *gods.* Here we have a m. pl. form in the absolute state, but without a vowel letter for the internal long /i/. The form is to be compared with **ᵓlhyn** (No. 21 = **ᵓilāhîn**). It is a little surprising to find the same word spelled in two different ways in a short inscription, and it may reflect the fact that medial vowel letters were a relatively recent innovation and that older spellings persisted even after the more modern system had been introduced. The *defective* four-letter form would naturally be the older original spelling, whereas the five-letter form would be more up-to-date. It is also conceivable that the scribe, having written the word in the fuller, more correct form in its first occurrence, would not feel obligated to give the full spelling the second time (Andersen 1970a). We have another example of this phenomenon in the varying spellings of the word **ś^cryn** (line 19) and **ś^crn** (22), both being the plural form of the word *barley*; and the *defective* form follows the full spelling. Another possibility is that **ᵓlhn** here is part of an old traditional expression (cf. Judges 9:9, 13), and perhaps the phrase was simply copied from an older example or was written out in the older style in which it had originated. Note the two spellings of *earth* in Jer 10:11, one archaic (as in our inscription)—it sounds credal—one current. The parallel term **ᵓnšn** (**ᵓanāšīn**, *men*) also is written defectively. It will be noted that the long /a/ in **ᵓlhn** is not represented in the orthography.

106. **w²l** (14), **wa²il**, *and to* or *for.* Cf. No. 104.

107. **ᵓnšn** (14), **ᵓanāšīn**, *men.* Here we have another m. pl. noun corresponding to **ᵓlhn** (**ᵓilāhīn**, *gods*) in the same line, and, like the earlier word, written defectively, that is, without a vowel letter for the long /i/ in the last syllable of the word. The same reasoning applies here as was proposed in No. 105. It may be observed that in the five examples of m. pl. nouns in the absolute state, two are written out fully or *plene* while three are not. Of all the graphic procedures examined in this inscription the treatment of the m. pl. ending (-īn or -în) is the least consistent.

108. **tyṭb** (15), **tayṭab**, *may be good.* This word is a 3rd f. s. imperfect form of the *pe^cal* stem of the root **yṭb**, a byform of the primal root **ṭb**. The *yod* apparently represents the diphthong /ay/, if we assume that the verb followed the *yaqtal* pattern. Alternatively we could vocalize **tîṭab**, assuming a *yiqtal* formation. Cf. biblical

Aramaic **yêṭab**, apparently derived from **yayṭab** in contrast with Hebrew **yîṭab** (*qal*). We would expect the *yod* to be written in either case, since it is one of the root consonants. The form, however, is new for Old Aramaic. The *hap^cel* is well attested, consistently **hyṭb** in Old Aramaic, **hwṭb** at Elephantine. Ezra 7:18 attests the *qal*. The byform **yṭb** is generally used for derived stems and tenses, so the medial *yod* in the present form is historical spelling in that sense, whether representing the diphthong or long vowel.

109. **dmwt^ᵓ** (15), **damûta^ᵓ**. Cf. No. 1.

110. **z^ᵓt** (15), **za^ᵓt**, *this*. It is the f. demonstrative adjective modifying the preceding noun **damûta^ᵓ**. In this form the *aleph* is a consonant and the /a/ vowel is short. Even if the *aleph* had quiesced at this early period—there is no evidence for this—the preserved *aleph* still could not be regarded as a vowel letter for the (probably) lengthened /a/, but only as an example of historical spelling. Such an *aleph* cannot be regarded as a true or pure vowel letter until it is used in a word where it had no etymological or historical rootage.

111. **^cbd** (15), **^cabad**, *he made*. This is a *pe^cal* perfect 3rd m. s. verb.

112. **^ᵓl** (15), **^ᵓl**, *?*. This is some sort of particle in an idiomatic expression based on an Akkadian cliché, although it does not correspond exactly to the Assyrian parallel here. It was probably accommodated to Aramaic **^ᵓl**. Cf. Nos. 104, 106.

113. **zy** (15), **zî**, *of*. Cf. No. 2.

114. **qdm** (15), **qudm**. Cf. No. 6.

115. **hwtr** (15), **hawtir**, *he has exceeded*, i.e. *done more*. This form is the *hap^cel* perfect 3rd m. s. of the root **ytr** (primal **wtr**). It is noteworthy that the diphthong /aw/ has been preserved and is represented by its consonantal constituent *waw*.

116. **qdm** (15), **qudm**. Cf. No. 6.

117. **hdd** (15), **hadad**. Cf. No. 7.

118. **ysb** (16), **yāsib**. Cf. No. 35.

119. **skn** (16), **sikan**. Cf. No. 7.

120. **mr^ᵓ** (16), **māri^ᵓ**. Cf. No. 37.

121. **ḥbwr** (16), **ḥabûr**, *Habur*. This is the name of the well-known river of Syria // Mesopotamia. Note the use of the vowel letter *waw* for the distinctive /u/ sound in the name. For similar practice in foreign names, cf. **gwzn** (Nos. 42, 46), and in words of foreign origin, cf. **gwgl** (Nos. 8, 24), **^ᵓdqwr** (No. 20) and **tṣlwth** (Nos. 33, 63). We believe that the *waw* is used to identify the quality of the vowel rather than its length or even its position under stress, although neither possibility is ruled out in adaptation to Aramaic word patterns. In time, if not immediately, the effect of the use of a vowel letter might have been to lengthen and accentuate the vowel so represented.

122. ṣlmh (16), ṣalmah, *his image.* The form is the m. s. noun with the 3rd m. s. pronoun suffix. Since it is the direct object we have supplied an accusative connecting vowel /a/. The final *he* is consonantal. Cf. No. 89.

123. šm (16), šam. Cf. No. 5.

124. mn (16), man, *whoever.* We suggest that this pronominal particle serves as the subject of the following verb. The vowel is short.

125. yld (16), yal(l)id, *effaces.* Cf. No. 80.

126. šmy (16), šumî, *my name.* Cf. Nos. 76, 81.

127. mn (16), min, *from.* Cf. Nos. 61, 82.

128. mᵓnyᵓ (16), maᵓnayyaᵓ, *the vessels.* Here we have a m. pl. noun in the emphatic state. We take the *aleph* at the end of the word to be consonantal just as the medial *aleph* is (as part of the root). Cf. No. 1 for discussion of the emphatic state in the inscription and No. 110 for discussion of possible quiescence of *aleph* in different positions. There are apparently no long vowels in this word, and, as we expect, no vowel letters.

129. zy (17), zî. Cf. No. 2.

130. bt (17), bēt, *house.* Here we have the only probable case of diphthong contraction in the whole inscription. The contraction is standard in Phoenician and other Canaanite dialects, including North Israelite and apparently Moabite; but it is not the rule in Aramaic inscriptions where the word is regularly spelled **byt**, showing preservation of the diphthong. Thus in this inscription we have the form **byth** (**baytah**, No. 54), which we would regard as normal for Aramaic in all periods. Elsewhere the diphthongs seem to have been preserved, since they are represented in the spelling. We might try to explain the phenomenon by saying that the diphthongs had contracted, but the consonantal elements **w** and **y** were kept through historical spelling. Then the form here, **bt**, could be explained as an instance of phonetic spelling against the prevailing conservatism of the orthographic system. The main objection to this explanation is that the practice of this dialect would run counter to our whole experience with classical Aramaic, and it is difficult to establish such a revolutionary idea on the basis of one reading, which itself is negated by at least the following examples of diphthongal preservation: **šmyn** (No. 9), **byth** (No. 54), **ywmwh** (No. 50), **tyṭb** (No. 108, probably), **hwtr** (No. 115), **wmwh** (Nos. 136, 144, plausibly), **swr** (No. 166), **lhynqn** (Nos. 160, 166, 172), **yrwy** (Nos. 163, 169, 175, probably), to say nothing about the universal spelling **byt** in Old Aramaic inscriptions, which makes this unique exception all the more remarkable. It is better to seek another explanation. Since at least one other inscription shares

the problem of two different spellings of the same word (in the Mesha Inscription—**bt** [lines 23, 27, 30, 30; some in place names, but always with a word-divider], normal for Moabite; but **wbbth** [line 7] versus **bbyth** [line 25], the exception being the other way around from the Tell Fekherye inscription), we may reasonably suppose that two forms of spelling, if not two different pronunciations, of this word were current, rather than supposing that this word was somehow vulnerable to incorrect spelling. The normal Aramaic pronunciation would be **bayt**, alone and in various combinations. No theory about variations due to differences in stress, or in the construct state, however true for Masoretic Hebrew, has held up with respect to the inscriptional evidence. The efforts of Bange along these lines were not successful. But it is possible that a reference to the temple of Hadad might ultimately derive from Canaanite sources, where Hadad played a central role. Thus *the house of Baal/Hadad* in the Canaanite epics would inevitably be spelled **bt b^cl/hdd** and perhaps that spelling in that combination became a fixed tradition, **bt** serving as a kind of logogram, a hangover of Phoenician spelling. In the Mesha Inscription something similar happened at second remove. Just as the Aramaeans received their writing system from the Phoenicians, with only a trace of Phoenician spelling showing up, as with **bt**, so the South-Canaanite dialects used a writing system already adapted by the Aramaeans, rather than one which they developed along similar lines (but independently) by direct borrowing from the Phoenicians. Aramaean cultural influence is evident in the palaeography, and the one occurrence of the spelling **byt** in the Mesha Inscription could represent a lone intrusion of Aramaic usage.

Beyond such speculation about all we can say is that this is the single exception to diphthongal representation in the inscription, so far as we are aware. Apart from this, the only other deviation from the standard Aramaic spelling of the word *house* (**byt**, corresponding to Southern Judahite, familiar from standard biblical Hebrew) in the entire Aramaic corpus known to us is in a (very late) Hatra text (KAI 249, line 4).

It sould be emphasized that the normal spelling of the same word *is* represented in this inscription, so that any explanation of one spelling must take into account the other, at the same time and in the same place, and carved by the same stone-carver from a cartoon made by the same scribe.

Yet this very circumstance draws attention to the fact that the present inscription consists of two distinct portions which cover much of the same ground. The four words which present archaic (Phoenician) spellings (ʾlhn, ʾnšn, bt, šᶜrn) all occur in the second part and two of them (ʾlhyn, byth) occur with normal spelling in the first part. The second part contains formulaic material of a kind known from other Northwest Semitic inscriptions, such as Sefire. That is, these expressions were not original to the author of the present inscription, and even their spelling reflects derivation from older practice. Andersen (1966) pointed out a similar distribution of contrasting usage in the syntax of the Mesha Inscription.

131. **hdd** (17), **hadad.** Cf. No. 7.

132. **mrʾy** (17), **mārʾî**, or **māriʾî**, *my lord*. Here we have the m. s. noun and the 1st s. pronoun suffix. The final î is represented in the orthography by *yod*. Cf. No. 37 for **mrʾ**.

133. **mrʾy** (17), **mārʾî**. Cf. No. 132.

134. **hdd** (17), **hadad.** Cf. No. 7.

135. **lhmh** (17), **laḥmah**, *his bread*. The form consists of the m. s. noun plus the 3rd m. s. suffix. The final *he* is consonantal.

136. **wmwh** (17), **wamawih**, *and his water*. Here we have an m. pl. (or dual) noun plus the 3rd m. s. suffix. The *waw* represents the plural or dual form and may preserve the diphthong of the dual ending as the *yod* does in Hebrew. We have suggested an appropriate vocalization, although it is also possible that the diphthong has been resolved. The final *he* is consonantal. Cf. Nos. 23, 50, 52, 58, 100 for this construction.

137. **ʾl** (17), **ʾal**, negative particle, *let not*.

138. **ylqh** (17), **yilqah**, *let him [not] receive* or *take*. We read this as a *peᶜal* imperfect 3rd m. s. verb.

139. **mn** (17), **min.** Cf. No. 127.

140. **ydh** (18), **yadih**, *his hand*. Singular noun with 3rd m. s. pronoun suffix. The final *he* is consonantal. We have supplied the connecting vowel reflecting the genitive case of the noun.

141. **swl** (18), **sawl**, *Sala(!)*. Admittedly this is a very difficult form, but we shall attempt an explanation. From the Assyrian version we know that this is a personal name and that it designates the goddess Shala, the consort of Hadad. Apparently it was felt that the key vowel, in fact the only vowel (we do not think that there would be a final vowel in the Aramaized form), should be represented in the spelling of the names, especially exotic names, in the Aramaic version. Since the vowel was **a** (perhaps long **a**), there was no vowel letter available to represent it in a medial position. They might have tried a *he* in the middle of the word, but that

would have violated their rules, since it certainly would have been considered a consonant or pronounced as such.

The only available signs were *waw* and *yod*. *Yod* could represent î or the diphthong **ay**. It would have been possible to write the name **syl** and pronounce it either **sîl** or **sayl**; the latter would have been vaguely similar to **sāl**, but obviously it was rejected. The alternative was not much more promising: use *waw* suggesting û or **aw**. The pronunciation **sûl** would not have met the need, but **sawl** would have been closer to the actual pronunciation; and so the spelling **swl** was adopted. The system did not permit a closer approximation, but the scribe clearly was determined to set the pronunciation, and the readers of the inscription were going to be helped, whether they needed it or wanted it or not.

142. **mr**ᵓ**ty** (18), **mār**ᵓ**atî**, *my lady*. A f. s. noun with the 1st s. pronoun suffix. The final vowel î is represented by *yod*. The medial *aleph* is consonantal and there are no other long vowels or vowel letters.

143. **lḥmh** (18), **laḥmah**. Cf. No. 135.

144. **wmwh** (18), **wamawih**. Cf. No. 136.

145. ᵓ**l** (18), ᵓ**al**. Cf. No. 137.

146. **tlqḥ** (18), **tilqaḥ**, *let her [not] receive* or *take*. 3rd f. s. *peᶜal* imperfect of root **lqḥ**. Cf. No. 138.

147. **mn** (18), **min**. Cf. No. 127.

148. **ydh** (18), **yadih**. Cf. No. 140.

149. **wlzr**ᶜ (18–19), **waluzara**ᶜ, *and let him sow*. The form is a combination of the precative particle **lu** plus the *peᶜal* perfect 3rd m. s. of the root **zr**ᶜ; or possibly a pseudo-preformative jussive **luzra**ᶜ or **lizra**ᶜ.

150. **w**ᵓ**l** (19), **wa**ᵓ**al**. Cf. No. 137.

151. **yḥṣd** (19), **yaḥṣud**, *let him [not] reap* or *harvest*. The vocalization may be uncertain, but, so far as we can see, in this *peᶜal* imperfect 3rd m. s. form of the root **ḥṣd** there are no long vowels.

152. **w**ᵓ**lp** (19), **wa**ᵓ**alp**, *and a thousand (measures)*. The noun is possibly monosyllabic; there are no vowels which might be represented by vowel letters.

153. **ś**ᶜ**ryn** (19), **śi**ᶜ**ārîn**, *barley*. Here we have a m. pl. noun in the absolute state. The final syllable contains the long /i/ vowel marking the plural ending, and this is indicated by a *yod*. Cf. ᵓ**lhyn**, No. 21. Curiously enough, as in the case of ᵓ**lhyn** (No. 21), for which a variant spelling occurs in line 14 (ᵓ**lhn**, No. 105), without the vowel letter, the same is true for this word; the form without the vowel letter occurs in line 22 (**ś**ᶜ**rn**, No. 187). It is difficult to

account for variant spellings of the same word in the same inscription, but these are not the only examples. For previous discussion, see Nos. 21, 105.

154. **lzr^c** (19), **luzara^c** or **luzra^c**. Cf. No. 149.

155. **wprys** (19), **waparîs**, *and a* **parîs** *(measure)*. This is apparently a loanword domesticated in Aramaic. In accordance with the established practice of this inscription or scribal school, the distinctive internal vowel (î) is marked by the appropriate vowel letter (*yod*).

156. **l^ɔḥz** (19), **lu^ɔaḥaz**, *let him grasp* or *collect* or *gather in*. We have a combination of precative particle (**lu**) plus the *pe^cal* perfect 3rd m. s. from the root ^ɔḥz; or else a pseudo-preformative jussive. There are no vowels needing attention.

157. **mnh** (19), **minnah**, *from it (him)*. The antecedent or referent is not entirely clear. The person under the curse is described as going to collect from his plantings some paltry yield. But the final *from it* should refer to his previous efforts or to the person from whom he will gain his reward. In case the suffix is a 3rd f. s., then we would read **minnah**, but if it is 3rd m. s., as are the others, then we would read **minnih**. In either event the final *he* is a consonant. Cf. Nos. 61, 82.

158. **wm^ɔh** (20), **wami^ɔâ**, *and a hundred*. This is the numeral, a feminine noun in the absolute state. The *he* is a vowel letter representing final long /a/.

159. **s^ɔwn** (20), **si^ɔwān**, *sheep* (pl.). Here we have a feminine pl. noun in the absolute state. The vocalization is uncertain, being complicated by the presence of the *waw* which marks the plural form. Since, however, the fem. pl. in all Aramaic has the form –**ān**, there is no reason to think that the *waw* here is a vowel letter for a supposed –**ôn**. It should be regarded as a consonant, in conformity with its use with m. pl. nouns having suffixes. Cf. the comparable f. pl. noun **nšwn** (Nos. 171, 177).

160. **lhynqn** (20), **luhayniqān**, *let them give suck*. Here we have the precative particle (**lu**) along with the *hap^cel* perfect 3rd f. pl. of the root **ynq**; or a pseudo-preformative jussive. Two points should be noted: (a) the preservation of the diphthong /ay/ in the derived conjugation which is represented by the appropriate consonantal *yod*; (b) the vowel in the last syllable is doubtless long /a/, but unrepresented in the orthography. This indicates strongly that the preceding word, **s^ɔwn**, should not be vocalized as **si^ɔôn**, but rather as **si^ɔwān**, or the like. Cf. No. 166.

161. ^ɔ**mr** (20), ^ɔ**immir**, *lamb*. There are no long vowels and no vowel letters, as expected.

162. **w^ɔl** (20), **wa^ɔal**, *and not*. Cf. No. 137.

163. **yrwy** (20), **yirway**, *let it [not] be satiated.* We read this *peᶜal*
imperfect 3rd m. s. form of the root **rwy** as a *yiqtal* form with the
resulting diphthong /ay/ at the end, preserved in the spelling with
the consonantal element *yod*. It could also be read as a *yaqtil* form,
yarwî. In the latter case the final *yod* would be a vowel letter for
long /i/. It would also in all likelihood have been preserved as a
specimen of historical spelling, since the third root consonant was
a *yod*.

164. **wmᵓh** (20), **wamiᵓâ**. Cf. No. 158.

165. **swr** (20), **sawr**, *cattle.* Although the noun is normally masculine
singular, here it is treated as f. collective and the subject of the
verb **lhynqn** which follows. From the orthographic viewpoint, the
important feature of this word is the presence of medial *waw*, which
represents the consonantal element in the diphthong /aw/, itself
part of the primal form of this word. This spelling indicates that
the diphthong has been preserved in this dialect. The formulaic
nature of the language is evident. Similar expressions are used in
Sefire—[šbᶜ] **šwrh yhynqn ᶜgl wᵓl yśbᶜ** (Sf I A 23). The close
similarity to line 20 of our inscription highlights the anomaly of
swr where Sefire has **šwrh**. There are several possible explanations: (a) The words are the same, but Tell Fekherye (for once!)
has not marked the final –â. This is hard to believe in view of the
consistent spelling of *hundred* in the context. (b) Similar to (a),
it is a scribal error, and we should restore the missing *he*. This is
always a possibility, and one mistake would not be unusual in a
text of this size. (c) The term is generic, collective, as often in the
Hebrew Bible, where it includes females (Lev 22:28; Num 18:17;
necessarily so when the verb attributes to them giving birth (as in
the Hebrew text) or giving suck (as here).

166. **lhynqn** (20), **luhayniqān**, *let them give suck.* Cf. No. 160.

167. **ᶜgl** (21), **ᶜigl**, *calf.* There are no long vowels and no vowel letters.

168. **wᵓl** (21), **waᵓal**, *and not.* Cf. Nos. 137, 162.

169. **yrwy** (21), **yirway**, *let it [not] be satiated.* Cf. No. 163.

170. **wmᵓh** (21), **wamiᵓâ**. Cf. Nos. 158, 164.

171. **nšwn** (21), **nišwān**, *women.* This is a f. pl. noun in the absolute
state. We have vocalized the form in accordance with the standard
rules for Old Aramaic and therefore treat the intervening *waw* as
a consonant marking the plural form. Cf. No. 159 **sᵓwn** for a
further discussion of this feature. On affinities of this morphology
with Arabic, see Abou–Assaf, Bordreuil, and Millard (1982: 35f.)
and Kaufman (1982: 169).

172. **lhynqn** (21), **luhayniqān**, *let them give suck.* Cf. Nos. 160, 166.

173. ᶜlym (21), ᶜalîm, *a child*. This is a m. s. noun. Of orthographic interest is the use of a vowel letter *yod* to represent medial long /i/ in the second syllable. The word is attested with the same spelling in Old Aramaic (Sf I A 22) and the vocalization is confirmed by Syriac. (The vocalization ᶜulaym [Cross and Freedman 1952: 28], based on Bauer and Leander, should be abandoned.)

174. wᵓl (21), waᵓal, *and not*. Cf. Nos. 137, 162, 168.

175. yrwy (21), yirway, *let it [not] be satiated*. Cf. Nos. 163, 169.

176. wmᵓh (22), wamiᵓâ. Cf. Nos. 158, 164, 170.

177. nšwn (22), nišwān, *women*. Cf. No. 171.

178. lᵓpn (22), luᵓapān, *let them bake*. To judge from other similar forms in this inscription, this would be a combination of precative **lu** with the *peᶜal* perfect 3rd f. pl.; or a pseudo-preformative jussive. The listing of such forms as apocopated imperfects or jussives (Abou–Assaf, Bordreuil, and Millard 1982: 49f.) is not compelling. A precative perfect is at least a possibility. The expected root here is ᵓpy, *bake*. The absence of a third root consonant requires explanation, whether the form is preformative or afformative. Some other verb forms in this inscription present similar problems (cf. No. 73), but generally III–y/w roots retain the consonant, as such, or as long vowel reflex still evident in historical spelling. Cf. Nos. 15, 47, 87, 163, 169, 175. A biconsonantal byform cannot be entirely ruled out, so it may be better to recognize phonological changes within that family. The Sefire inscriptions, which represent the texts nearest to this one in content and style, present exactly the same mixture, with the expected **y** alongside a terminal *he* which seems to represent, not just the contraction of the diphthong (not represented in the spelling), but possibly a more radical change to long /a/. See Fitzmyer's vigorous statement (1967: 42). What this amounts to, then, is the development of a biconsonantal byform for some items in the paradigm, as in standard Aramaic (ᵓăpô) and Hebrew (ᵓāpû). Whatever the root, the last syllable contains long /a/ which is not represented in the orthography.

179. btnwr (22), batannûr, *in an oven*. We have here a prepositional phrase containing the familiar Northwest Semitic word for *oven*. We note the use of the medial vowel letter *waw* to represent the long /u/ of the second syllable. Several other common nouns in the inscription share this feature. Cf. Nos. 1, 8, 20, 33 and duplicates Nos. 24, 63, 109.

180. lḥm (22), laḥm, *bread*. There are no long vowels and no vowel letters.

181. wᵓl (22), waᵓal, *and not*. Cf. Nos. 137, 162, 168, 174.

182. **yml⁾nh** (22), **yamalli⁾ānih**, *let them [not] fill up*. We take the form to be a *paᶜel* imperfect 3rd f. pl. with a 3rd m. s. suffix. As a connecting vowel we have supplied the old jussive ending of the verbal form –i, but any vowel will do. The final *he* is consonantal.

183. **wmn** (22), **wamin**, *and from*. Cf. No. 127.

184. **qlqlt⁾** (22), **qalqalāta⁾**, *the baskets*. We analyze the form as a feminine plural noun in the emphatic state (cf. Nos. 1, 109, 128 for other examples). The final *aleph* is a consonant. Note also the long /a/ vowel in the penultimate syllable, without representation in the orthography.

185. **llqṭw** (22), **lulaqaṭû**, *let them gather*. We interpret the form as a combination of the precative particle **lu** plus the *peᶜal* perfect 3rd m. pl. of the root **lqṭ**; or a pseudo-preformative jussive. The final vowel –û of the 3rd pl. is represented by *waw*. There are no other long vowels or vowel letters.

186. **⁾nšwh** (22), **⁾anāšwih**, *his men*. Cf. No. 58.

187. **šᶜrn** (22), **šiᶜārīn**, *barley*. This noun is the f. pl. absolute, written defectively, that is, without a vowel letter (*yod*) for the long /i/ in the plural ending. It is to be compared with the full spelling of the same word **šᶜryn** (No. 153). For further discussion see the pair **⁾lhyn** (No. 21) and **⁾lhn** (No. 105). Apparently the use of the medial *yod* in such circumstances was optional. Perhaps the most extraordinary feature of this pair of spellings is that the norm, to judge from actual specimens, is the *defective* spelling. It is the only spelling met at Elephantine, where the word occurs many times. In fact No. 153 represents the only known instance of the *plene* spelling of the plural absolute of this word in the entire Aramaic corpus. Were it not for that fact, one would be tempted to interpret **šᶜrn** as a regular feminine plural (the singular form is feminine). Still it may be further observed that the confusion over the gender and morphology of this word in Northwest Semitic is illustrated by the fact that in Ugaritic the singular is masculine, perhaps also in Hadad (line 5—it is clearly feminine in Bir–rakib lines 6, 9).

The total picture for the spelling of this word suggests another principle, commonly met in the history of spelling. The competition between historical and phonetic spelling goes on all the time. All that matters is that the word be identified unambiguously and that the reader be given as much help as needed. This help is clearly needed in the case of exotic words, less needed in the case of familiar words, for which conventional spellings, not necessarily completely phonetic (not using all the possible vowel letters), serve quite adequately as virtual logograms. The extraordinary tenacity of the archaic spelling of *barley*—for centuries—illustrates the point, with the paradox that the only known case of what would usually be considered a 'modern' spelling occurs in one of the oldest known Aramaic inscriptions.

188. lʾklw (22), luʾakalû, *let them eat.* We interpret the form as a combination of the precative particle lu plus the *peꜤal* perfect 3rd m. pl. of the root ʾkl. The final long –û vowel is represented by *waw* in the orthography (cf. for the other example No. 185). There are no other long vowels or vowel letters.

189. wmwtn (23), wamawtān, *and* mawtān. Apparently this is a proper noun, but it seems to be derived from the root mwt, *death*, and is attested in the literature. We note the use of *waw* to represent the diphthong /aw/, or if the correct vocalization of the word is mûtān, it could stand for the vowel û. We are not sure of the final syllable but it seems to be the classic –ān nominal ending (which becomes –ōn in other dialects).

190. šbṭ (23), šibṭ, *Demon.* This (proper) noun is apparently monosyllabic. There are no long vowels or vowel letters.

191. zy (23), zî. Cf. No. 2.

192. nyrgl (23), nîrgal, *Nergal.* Here we have the name of the well-known Assyrian deity. The medial vowel letter *yod* is supplied to represent the characteristic vowel i in the name. The other vowel is a and would not be represented in the orthography.

193. ʾl (23), ʾal. Cf. No. 137.

194. ygtzr (23), yigtizar, *let him [not] be cut off.* Here we have an infixed *peꜤal* imperfect 3rd m. s. of the root gzr. There are no long vowels or vowel letters.

195. mn (23), min. Cf. No. 127.

196. mth (23), mātih, *his country.* This is the noun f. s., plus the 3rd m. s. suffix. The final *he* is a consonant. We have supplied the connecting vowel, in this instance an i, for the genitive case of the noun.

11.4 Summary

I. Final Letters

A. Consonants

    1. *Aleph* (ʾ) Emphatic state of nouns
        a. dmwtʾ (damûtaʾ): Nos. 1, 109.
        b. mʾnyʾ (maʾnayyaʾ): No. 128.

   c. qlqltᵓ (qalqalātaᵓ): No. 184.

2. *He* (h) as 3rd m. s. pronoun suffix

   a. ᵓḥwh (ᵓaḥwih): No. 23.

   b. tṣlwth (taṣlûtuh): No. 33.

   c. nbšh (nabšah): No. 48.

   d. ywmwh (yawmwih): No. 50.

   e. šnwh (šanwih): No. 52.

   f. byth (baytah): No. 54.

   g. zrᶜh (zarᶜah): No. 56.

   h. ᵓnšwh (ᵓanāšwih): Nos. 58, 186.

   i. mnh (minnih): Nos. 61, 82, 157.

   j. tṣlwth (taṣlûtah): No. 63.

   k. pmh (pumih): Nos. 66, 103.

   l. lh (lih): No. 69.

   m. lknnh (lukāninah): No. 74.

   n. bh (bih): No. 78.

   o. šmh (šumah): No. 84.

   p. qblh (qābiluh): No. 88.

   q. krsᵓh (karsiᵓih): No. 98.

   r. ḥywh (ḥayyawih): No. 100.

   s. ṣlmh (ṣalmah): No. 122.

   t. lḥmh (laḥmah): Nos. 135, 143.

   u. wmwh (wamawih): Nos. 136, 144.

   v. ydh (yadih): Nos. 140, 148.

   w. ymlᵓnh (yamalliᵓānih): No. 182.

   x. mth (mātih): No. 196.

B. Vowels

1. *He* (h) for –â

   a. šlh (šilâ): No. 19.

   b. ṭbh (ṭābâ): No. 34.

   c. wmᵓh (wamiᵓâ): Nos. 158, 164, 170, 176.

2. *Waw* (w) for –û

   a. llqtw (lulaqaṭû): No. 185.

   b. lᵓklw (luᵓakalû): No. 188.

3. *Yod* (y) for –î (or ay)

   a. zy (zî): Nos. 2, 4, 32, 79, 93, 95, 113, 129, 191.

   b. hdysᶜy (hadyisᶜî): Nos. 3, 40, 90.

   c. rᶜy (riᶜî): No. 14.

   d. wmšqy (wamašqî): No. 15.

e. ssnwry (sasnûrî): No. 44.
f. lḥyy (laḥayyay): No. 47.
g. šmy (šumî): Nos. 81, 126.
h. lhwy (luhawî): No. 87.
i. mrᵓy (mārᵓî): Nos. 132, 133.
j. mrᵓty (mārᵓatî): No. 142.
k. yrwy (yirway): Nos. 163, 169, 175.

II. Medial Letters (*waw* and *yod*)

A. Consonants

1. *Waw*

   a. ᵓḥwh (ᵓaḥwih): No. 23.
   b. ywmwh (yawmwih): No. 50.
   c. šnwh (šanwih): No. 52.
   d. ᵓnšwh (ᵓanāšwih): Nos. 58, 186.
   e. lhwy (luhawî): No. 87.
   f. ḥywh (ḥayyawih): No. 100.
   g. wmwh (wamawih): Nos. 136, 144.
   h. sᵓwn (siᵓwān): No. 159.
   i. yrwy (yirway): Nos. 163, 169, 175.
   j. nšwn (nišwān): Nos. 171, 177.

2. *Yod*

   a. hdysᶜy (hadisᶜî): Nos. 3, 40, 90.
   b. lḥyy (laḥayyay): No. 47.
   c. wyhb (wayahab): No. 68.
   d. wyšym (wayaśîm): No. 83.
   e. ḥywh (ḥayyawih): No. 100.
   f. mᵓnyᵓ (maᵓnayyaᵓ): No. 128.

B. Diphthongs

1. *Waw* for **aw**

   a. ywmwh (yawmwih): No. 50.
   b. hwtr (hawtir): No. 115.
   c. swl (sawl or sûl or sôl): No. 141.
   d. swr (sawr): No. 165.
   e. wmwtn (wamawtān or wamûtān): No. 189.

2. *Yod* for **-ay**

   a. šmyn (šamayn): No. 9.
   b. byth (baytah): No. 54. See also bt=bēt—No. 130.

    c. tyṭb (tayṭab): No. 108.

    d. lhynqn (luhayniqān): Nos. 160, 166, 172.

C. Vowels

    1. *Waw* for û

        a. dmwtᵓ (damûtaᵓ): Nos. 1, 109.

        b. gwgl (gugal): Nos. 8, 24.

        c. wᶜdqwr (waᶜadaqûr): No. 20.

        d. tṣlwth (taṣlûtuh): No. 33.

        e. gwzn (guzan): Nos. 42, 46, 92.

        f. tṣlwth (taṣlûtah): No. 63.

        g. ḥbwr (Ḥabûr): No. 121.

        h. btnwr (batannûr): No. 179.

        i. wmwtn (wamûtān or wamawtān): No. 189.

    2. *Yod* for î

        a. lᵓlhyn (laᵓilāhîn): No. 21; but see No. 105 ᵓlhn.

        b. wšmym (wašumîm): No. 76; cf. Nos. 81, 126.

        c. wyśym (wayaśîm): No. 83.

        d. tyṭb (tîṭab): No. 108.

        e. śᶜryn (śiᶜārîn): No. 153; but see No. 187 śᶜrn.

        f. wprys (waparîs): No. 155.

        g. ᶜlym (ᶜalîm): No. 173.

        h. nyrgl (nîrgal): No. 192.

11.5   Conclusions

    The importance and value of the new inscription for orthographic study can hardly be exaggerated. We have here an early text (not later than the ninth century BCE and possibly earlier), well preserved with clearly written signs, and a parallel rendering in readable Akkadian to help with the difficulties of analysis and interpretation. It is written in a language close enough to standard Aramaic and other Northwest Semitic dialects to allow generally for positive analysis and interpretation. And there is considerable information from which spelling practices and underlying principles can be determined.

    We can offer the following by way of summary and evaluation. The orthography of the Aramaic inscription is fairly regular and it is consistent generally with the practices and principles of neighboring states using the Phoenician alphabet and similar Northwest Semitic languages. There are exceptional if not idiosyncratic features, but these for the most part have been incorporated into the system, which may be described as follows.

11.5.1 Final Vowels

Final vowels are regularly represented in the orthography. The system is the same as employed all over the area, except in Phoenicia (or Canaan) proper, where vowel letters were avoided. The system is essentially the same as that used in Moab, Ammon, Israel, and Judah. Final vowels were represented in the following ways:

A. *He* (**h**) represents long –â and possibly other vowels such as ē and ō; but we have no certain examples of the last two.

B. *Waw* (**w**) represents long –û.

C. *Yod* (**y**) represents long –î.

There are several examples of *he* for –â, only two of *waw* for –û, and many of *yod* for –î. There are no known exceptions; that is, every likely word-terminal vowel is so represented. We cannot prove that short final vowels were dropped, but if they were pronounced they were not considered important enough to record. We hold to the position that if final vowels were preserved in the spoken language they would have been indicated in the orthography, and failure to indicate them would mean that they were no longer preserved, or that they were in the process of being lost.

11.5.2 Medial Vowels

Only two vowel letters were used medially, *waw* and *yod*. As with final vowels, they represent û and î respectively. There are enough examples to show that there was an effort to indicate the quality of those vowels which occasionally can be shown to be long and/or under stress, but not always. The usage is clearly not consistent or regular, although it is not merely sporadic. Short vowels are generally not indicated in any way, although there may be, originally, exceptions in the case of foreign and unusual words, especially names. In general the vowel **a** is not indicated at all when medial, whether long or short, stressed or unstressed. There are any number of examples of this non-representation for vowels known to be long. The reason is that no letter of the alphabet has been assigned to this function. *He* could have been tried; after all it was in use for word-terminal –â. But apparently using it as a medial vowel letter would have been too confusing, since it is used so often as a true consonant. But, whatever the reason, it was not so used. And it would be centuries before *aleph* was used as a vowel letter for any vowel in Semitic.

The explanation of the use of three letters for word-terminal vowels but only two for word-medial vowels is probably to be found in the fact that /w/ and /y/ were semi-vowels, and the corresponding consonant letters represented both the diphthongal offglide and the homorganic long

vowel. But etymological /h/ preserved its consonantal pronunciation in
post-vocalic positions, including the ends of words. Morphological factors were at work as well. Many verbs which end with a long vowel can
receive an additional suffix, which then moves that vowel to the interior of the word. So the same vowel can be terminal or medial. Once
the custom is established of spelling such a word in a particular way,
whether suffixed or not, the principle of using a vowel letter for a medial
vowel has taken root. This is illustrated in the present inscription by
comparing **šmy** (Nos. 81, 126) with **šmym** (No. 76). Furthermore,
this circumstance goes a long way to explain the fact that a long vowel
which is always word-medial, such as the long /i/ of the m. pl. ending
of nouns, can be spelled either way. Insofar as the identity of the word
is sufficiently established by the consonantal spelling, its pronunciation
is not likely to be in doubt. But purely consonantal spelling of verbs
would not distinguish plural from singular.

In our inscription the only instances of word-terminal –â, always
spelled with *he*, are f. s. nouns. This vowel does not survive suffixation,
so that it becomes word-medial; the stem ending becomes –at–, so there
is no need or use for any vowel letter. This conventional use of *he* for
word-terminal long /a/ but not for word-medial long /a/ remained fixed
in Northwest Semitic orthography. When, very much later, word-medial
long /a/ was represented by a consonant letter, the one chosen was *aleph*,
particularly in Aramaic.

A certain sensitivity is to be noted in the use of these internal
vowel letters. For the most part they are used in loanwords, foreign or
foreign-sounding names, and certain other terms, where identification of
the vowel might be important. Since in certain cases at least the vowel
is originally short (as in **gugal** and **ᵓadaqur**) we emphasize the use of
these vowel letters to mark quality in preference to quantity. The same
will be true of stress since in some cases the vowel indicated by the vowel
letter will not be in the normally stressed syllable. But by and large the
vowel letters are used for long vowels in stressed syllables, at least if we
follow the generally accepted rules governing long vowels and stressed
syllables for Aramaic and Northwest Semitic in general.

A. *Waw* (**w**) for û.

B. *Yod* (**y**) for î.

A Notable Exception

We know of five cases of the absolute m. pl. noun, the final syllable of which is vocalized –în. In two cases the medial vowel letter *yod*
has been used (full spelling). In three cases the *yod* has been omitted

(defective spelling). Clearly the scribes felt that they had a choice, and it is not clear why they chose one way on one occasion and another way on another, especially in cases where the same words are involved. Thus the word for *gods* is spelled with the *yod* once and without it once: ᵓlhyn // ᵓlhn. There is no detectable difference in grammatical form or force. The same is true of šᶜryn // šᶜrn. We do not observe the same situation with *waw* for û. In all the words in which medial *waw* is used as a vowel letter, the same word is always spelled the same way: dmwtᵓ (Nos. 1, 109), ṭslwth (Nos. 33, 63), gwgl (Nos. 8, 24), gwzn (Nos. 42, 45, 92). The medial *waw* seems to be used more consistently than medial *yod*, but some instances where the former might have been used but was not may have escaped our notice. Our impression is that all vowels we can identify as long /u/ and/or short /u/ under stress have been marked by *waw*. The exceptions in the case of *yod* have been noted.

It is interesting in this connection to note a historical difference between the use of *waw* and *yod* as vowel letters. The use of *yod* to spell long /i/ has a basis in derivation, but the use of *waw* to spell long /u/ seems to have developed by analogy with *yod* on purely phonetic grounds. Does this mean that *waw* for û, being only phonetic, was used more freely, whereas *yod* for î was still constrained by considerations of historical spelling, just as *aleph* was for much longer?

11.5.3 Diphthongs

In general original and etymological diphthongs are preserved in the writing. That would be as true for diphthongs which are ultimately retained in known languages as for those which are ultimately contracted. Without being able to decide between actual and historical spelling we can say that the spelling is more like other Aramaic and Judahite inscriptions in which the diphthongs are preserved in the spelling, than it is like Phoenician and Israelite inscriptions, in which the diphthongs have been contracted and there is no trace of them in the spelling. There are enough examples of both kinds to show that the scribes were consciously representing them in the spelling of the words. The only significant exception to the use of *waw* and *yod* to represent diphthongs is the word bt, *house* (No. 130). The fuller spelling of the same word, representing the diphthong, is byth (No.54). It is difficult to account for the conflicting spellings in the same inscription, and we are inclined to regard the contracted spelling as exceptional and perhaps due to special circumstances which we cannot now reconstruct.

It might seem possible to turn the argument around and say that the spelling bt shows that the diphthong had been contracted and that the survival of *yod* in the other cases such as byth is an instance of historical spelling. The same would be true of *waw*. We would then have to recognize that *yod* represents not **ay** but ê is such cases, and that *waw* represents not **aw** but ô when it marks an internal diphthong. We can consider here the opposite problem of **bt**, which has no consonantal marker (*yod*) where we would expect one. In the word **swl** (No. 144) we have such a marker (*waw*) whether for a vowel or diphthong, when we do not expect one. On the basis of the parallel Akkadian we know that the word is the name of the goddess **šala**, and that the vowel in the Aramaic form should be **a**. According to the system used in our text, this vowel is not marked in medial positions, but we have a marker in this word. The *waw* should represent either **û** or **aw** according to our thesis, but it is suggested that if *waw* represents the contracted diphthong ô ← **aw**, it can represent ô here in this name. It is difficult to imagine the shift from ā to ô in Aramaic of this or any other period; but anything is possible.

Such an hypothesis opens the way for reconsideration of certain remaining problems in the text: e.g., the use of *waw* regularly in all m. pl. nouns which have the 3rd m. s. pronoun suffix. We have interpreted the *waw* as consonantal, but it might be a vowel letter for ô, followed by the 3rd m. s. suffix **h**, which would be pronounced hī, thus giving us a standard form of the suffix attached to plural nouns of later (biblical) Aramaic. This observation would also establish that at least some final vowels are not indicated orthographically.

It would also be possible to explain the f. pl. nouns which are written with internal *waw*: **sꜣwn** and **nšꜣwn**. We have taken the *waw* as consonantal, but these forms could be read as follows: **siꜣôn** (or **saꜣôn**) and **našꜣôn** with a shift from the original long ā. But the assumption that **w** writes ô in such words is not only gratuitious; it cuts across all we know about historical Aramaic phonology. Further it is contradicted within this inscription, where other words containing primal long /a/, notably *peꜥal* active participles, show no sign that this vowel had shifted to ô.

Perhaps it is impossible to decide such issues on the basis of available evidence. We believe that our analysis and conclusions are consistent with the data from this inscription and the whole corpus of related ones, and with our knowledge of the history of the languages of other Northwest Semitic dialects. Problems remain regardless of the hypothesis, and these may be resolved only with further research and more evidence.

[Completed July 1983]

Chapter 12

The Spelling of Samaria Papyrus 1

David Noel Freedman & Francis I. Andersen

12.1 Introduction

The recent publication of the Samaria Papyri is to be welcomed for many reasons. These documents will shed new light on legal customs and practices in that region during the last decades of Persian rule, as well as many related historical, social, and economic matters. The papyri will also provide much useful information about the Aramaic language of this period, its vocabulary, grammar, and syntax. They will also have significant value for the disciplines of epigraphy and orthography. Two key factors make the papyri especially important: they are official documents, and they are dated precisely. For epigraphic research, they provide a fixed point (or points) in the evolutionary charts and thus will be of enormous value in dating the many other written documents from this and adjoining periods. In like fashion, they will enable us to fix the orthographic patterns for official Aramaic documents and establish the prevailing practices for the middle decades of the 4th century BCE. Thus we are in a position to place these documents in the long

We wish to thank Dr. William H. Propp for substantial criticism of and assistance with this paper. Reprinted, with permission, from M. P. Horgan and P. J. Kobelski (eds.), **To Touch the Text: Biblical and Related Studies in Honor of Joseph A. Fitzmyer, S. J.**, (New York: Crossroad, 1989), 15–32.

evolutionary sequence of alphabetic orthography among the Northwest Semitic dialects, especially Aramaic, and at the same time measure and evaluate comparable documents that for the most part lack dates and may not have had official status.

Our purpose in the present study is to examine the orthography of Samaria Papyrus 1 (SP 1), summarize the findings, and present a sketch of spelling practice and principle in the 3rd quarter of the 4th century BCE. According to the editor of the document, its date can be fixed precisely to 19 March 335 BCE, and that is the point from which we will begin (Cross 1985a). In what follows, we will list each readable word of the inscription, transcribe it with appropriate vocalization according to the best information and opinion that we have, and provide an attested or presumed vocalization in Biblical Aramaic. On occasion, we have cited a Hebrew form if an Aramaic parallel is lacking. Since our objective is to determine actual orthographic practice, we restrict ourselves to certain or highly probable readings, although there is no doubt that Frank Cross's reconstruction of the document is correct in all major respects.

12.2   The Evidence

1. (1:1) **b 20**.
2. (1:2) **lᵓdr**—**laᵓadar** (BA **laᵓǎdār**), *of Adar*.
3. (1:3) **šnt 2**—**šanat** (BA **šěnat**), *in the second year*.
4. (1:4) **rᵓš**—**riᵓš** (BA **rēᵓš**), *the first = accession year*. The vocalization in Biblical Aramaic indicates that the *aleph* has quiesced and the vowel therefore changed and lengthened from **i** to **ē**. There is no clear evidence that the change had already occurred by this time, but even if the *aleph* had quiesced it would have been preserved by historical spelling, as is the case in Biblical Aramaic. Only if there were instances in which the word were spelled without *aleph* could we be certain that the *aleph* was no longer pronounced. Even then, the *aleph* should not be regarded as a vowel letter but only as a passive vowel marker (i.e., the result of historical spelling).
5. (1:5) **mlkwt**—**malkût** (BA **malkût**), *of the reign*. The *waw* serves as a vowel letter representing –**û**–.
6. (1:6) **(d)ryhws**—**darayahaweš** or **darayahûš** (BA **dārěyāweš**). The name appears as **darayavaᵓush** in Old Persian; it is transcribed in Elephantine Aramaic as **drywhwš**, which can be vocalized as **darayawahûš**. As can be seen, there are different ways in which to represent this non-Semitic name, and therefore we cannot be certain as to the precise value accorded the letters, which may

be either consonants or vowels. The *he* is certainly to be regarded as a consonant (representing the ᵓ of Old Persian), while the *waw* may be either a consonant (as clearly in BA) or a vowel letter for –û–, reflecting the vocalization of the final syllable of the name in Old Persian.

7. (1:7) mlkᵓ—malkaᵓ (BA malkāᵓ), *the king.* In Biblical Aramaic, the final *aleph* has quiesced and the preceding vowel lengthened. Just when this change took place and whether it had occurred by the time of our document cannot be determined. In any case, we are dealing with an originally consonantal *aleph* which ultimately quiesces and then serves as a passive vowel marker. So it does not qualify as a true vowel letter. If the *aleph* had quiesced and thus had become a vowel letter for final –ā, then we might have expected both confusion and contamination with the letter *he* which is regularly used for that purpose. It so happens that in all clear cases, *he* is a vowel letter for final â, while *aleph* is used only where it had originally consonantal status. The implication is that the distinction between the two letters was still being observed in these papyri.

8. (1:8) bšmry(n)–bišamaray(n) (BA běšāměrāyin), *in Samaria.* In Biblical Aramaic, the diphthong –ay– has been resolved into the bisyllabic –ayi–. That may be the case with the reading in the papyrus, but since the development in question is specific to Biblical Hebrew and Aramaic, it is more likely that the diphthong has simply been preserved in SP 1 (–ayn). It is even less likely that the diphthong has been contracted, –ay– → ê; in that case, the preservation of the *yod* would be an instance of historical spelling.

9. (2:1) lyhwḥnn—liyahawḥanan (BH yěhôḥānān), *Jehohanan.* The analysis and interpretation of this familiar biblical Yahwistic name are difficult. In view of its universal and persistent occurrence, we are convinced that the *waw* in the sequence yhw was originally consonantal, and therefore we question the traditional explanation of the preformative yěhô– as a back-formation from an original yahu → yaw → yô and then with the restoration of the original *he*, yěhô–. We must start further back in the series with the full name yahweh and postulate a combining form such as *yahwi– and then *yahw–. From this basic element, there could be a natural development to yahaw– from which the two biblical forms can easily be derived: yahaw– → yěhô– (for the older form of the name) and yahaw → yaw → yô. In defense of this approach, it should be noted that in all early texts yěhô–names are always spelled yhw–, never yh– (without orthographic indication of the ō). The preservation of the *waw* in all surviving

forms of the name, biblical and otherwise, strengthens the case for its original consonantal character, whether as a root consonant of the divine element or as a diphthong in the development of the form. There is no evidence, therefore, that the diphthong had contracted by the time of this papyrus, or that *he* of the preformative had been lost and was reintroduced at or before this time. We therefore favor the pronunciation **yahaw–ḥanan** in this period as being in harmony with the consistent spelling of the name. The shorter form of the name would have been **yawḥanan**. Whenever the diphthong was contracted, the spelling would have remained the same.

10. (2:2) šmh—**šumih** (BA šĕmēh), *his name*. The *he*, representing the 3rd m. s. suffix, is consonantal, as confirmed by the spelling in Biblical Aramaic.

11. (2:3) br—**bar** or **bir** (BA bar), *the son of*.

12. (2:4) šᵓlh—**šaᵓilâ** (cf. BH šĕᵓēlâ and BA šĕᵓēlĕtāᵓ which is derived from the same basic form) *Shaila*. The root is found in other names such as the familiar šāᵓûl (*Saul*). Closer to the time of the papyrus, the name šĕᵓāl occurs in Ezra 10:29 (K). In addition the masculine name šᵓylᵓ occurs in Palmyrene. The spelling with medial *yod* for **î** may imply that the name in the papyrus is written defectively, but we cannot be sure that the name is precisely the same in both cases. We have assumed that the form of the name in the papyrus is *qatil*, or basically the same as in the biblical common noun, rather than *qatîl* as in the Palmyrene name. The final *aleph* in the Palmyrene name shows that the name belongs to a large class of apparently hypocoristic names ending in *aleph*. There can be little doubt that the *aleph* in all of these cases was originally consonantal (as shown by the occurrence of the same type of name with the same spelling in Phoenician, which has no vowel letters) although in the course of time the *aleph* may have quiesced. After the *aleph* quiesced, it served as a passive vowel marker for the final vowel, presumably –ā. Once that shift had taken place (from aᵓ to ā), then it would be possible to substitute the normal vowel letter for final –ā, namely *he*. It is conceivable, then, that the name šᵓlh in the papyrus is equivalent to the name šᵓ(y)lᵓ attested in Palmyrene and that the original *aleph* has quiesced and been replaced by a pure vowel letter, *he*, but it does not seem likely. Throughout this text, *aleph* is used as consonant, or at most is preserved as historical spelling where it was once a consonant, while *he* is used as a vowel letter when that is appropriate. It seems better to regard the name here as different in form from the one in Pamyrene ending in *aleph*. It may be that the name

here is not that of the father but that of the mother, and the final syllable reflects the feminine ending –â.

13. (2:5) dnh—dinâ (BA děnâ), *this one*. The final *he* is a vowel letter for –â.

14. (2:6) ᶜbd—ᶜabad (BA *ᶜabad or ᶜăbēd), *a slave*.

15. (2:7) zylh—zî lih (BA dî–lēh), *of his* (lit. *who belongs to him*). While the letters are written together to form a single unit we actually have a compound of two terms, so the medial *yod* could be regarded as originally a terminal vowel letter. At this period, the letter *yod* is used both in the final and the medial positions for the vowel î. The *he* retains its consonantal force here, as attested in Biblical Aramaic.

16. (2:8) tmym—tamîm (BH tāmîm), *whole, sound, unblemished*. The medial *yod* is a vowel letter for î. The word does not occur in extant Biblical Aramaic, but is well attested in other Aramaic dialects. In interpreting line 2 of the text, we take the demonstrative dnh as modifying the personal name yhwḥnn and render the passage as follows: *This Jehohanan, whose (sur)name is bar-Shaila, a slave who belongs to him (i.e., Hananyah), unblemished ...*; cf. the phrase lyhwḥnn zk in line 10.

17. (3:1) šḥrṣ—šiḥariṣ, *the exact price* (Cross 1985a: 11*). The editor's analysis of the word combination is undoubtedly correct, but his proposal concerning the vocalization of the resultant form in Aramaic may be questioned. If the development actually was šim → šiw → šû–, then, since there is a consonantal *waw* in the word at a certain point in the sequence, we would expect it to be preserved in the spelling from that time on and even when it became the vowel –û–. Since this vowel is represented elsewhere in the orthography, and always when it is derived from consonantal *waw* (by way of a diphthong), the word should then have been spelled *šwḥrṣ. A defective spelling is always possible, especially with an unusual expression (e.g., we might have expected a *yod* to represent the second vowel of ḥārîṣ). At the same time, there are other possibilities, and these should be explored. Perhaps the m/w at the end of the first syllable was assimilated to the following ḥ.

18. (3:2) dmyn—damîn or perhaps more likely damiyîn. In Talmudic Aramaic, the word is plural and is written dāmîn, with the meaning *payment, equivalent, price*. It seems clear, therefore, that we have a masculine plural ending in –în, and ordinarily we would regard the *yod* as a vowel letter for the final vowel ī. Curiously, however, in this document, and presumably in the other Samaria Papyri, the masculine plural ending (-în) is not indicated by a vowel letter. In all the other occurrences in SP 1, the expected *yod*

does not appear, so it may be questioned whether the *yod* here is a simple vowel letter for î. In view of the fact that the root of this word is **dmy** (i.e., *tertiae yod*), it seems more likely that the *yod* here represents the original consonant of the root. Thus the word would have been written **dmyn** as we have it; then there should have been a time when it was written with two *yods*: **dmyyn**, but with the loss of the consonantal *yod* the spelling would have reverted to **dmyn**. The omission of the vowel letter *yod* to represent the masculine plural in –īn is unusual and apparently reflects archaic usage, frozen into official documents of this sort. The spelling of this form with the vowel letter (*yod*) is attested as early as the Aramaic inscription from Tell Fekherye, but it remains sporadic throughout most of Aramaic inscriptional history, being sparse in the Elephantine papyri and other Persian period documents.[1] By contrast, the use of *yod* as a vowel letter in masculine plural forms in the Hebrew Bible is practically universal and must have been adopted as a general practice quite early in the post-exilic period.

19. (3:3) **gmyrn**—**gamîrīn** (BA **gĕmîr**, *peᶜal* passive participle). In view of the discussion above concerning **dmyn**, there can be little doubt that the form of this adjective is also masculine plural and should be read with the standard –īn ending. It will be noted that the word contains a vowel letter, *yod*, representing î in the second syllable, which shows that this long vowel was regularly represented in the spelling. Its omission before **n** at the end of the word is surprising, but we have pointed out that the omission is regular and consistent in this document, and therefore the reading and the vocalization can be sustained: **damiyīn gamîrīn**.

20. (3:4) **ksp**ᵓ—**kaspa**ᵓ (BA **kaspā**ᵓ), *the silver.* Cf. No. 7.

21. (3:5) **(zn)h**—**zinâ** (BA **dĕnâ**), *this.* The *he* is used here as a vowel letter for final –â, in contrast with the preceding word where *aleph* is used to indicate a consonantal sound at the end of the noun in the emphatic state. Cf. No. 13.

22. (3:6) **š 35**—*35 shekels.*

23. (3:7) **ḥnnyh**—**ḥananyâ** (BA & BH **ḥănanyâ**), *Hananiah.* Note that the *yod* is consonantal while the *he* is a vowel letter for –â at the end of the word.

24. (4:1) **lh**—**lih** (BA **lēh**), *for him.* The *he*, representing the 3rd m. s. suffix, was originally consonantal and has retained its consonantal force according to the Masoretic tradition.

---

[1] We have a detailed study of the orthography of the Tell Fekherye Aramaic inscription in the Fensham *Festschrift* [reprinted as Chapter 11 of this volume].

25. (4:2) **wlbnwhy**—**walibanawhî** (BA **ûbĕnôhî**), *and for his sons.*
In Biblical Aramaic the medial *waw* serves as a vowel letter for
ô, but it is likely that this is historical spelling for an original
consonant or diphthong, as reflected in Syriac. The traditional explanation is that the ô vowel connecting the plural noun with the
suffix (**hî**) is the vestigial remainder of a 3rd m. s. suffix: **-ahu** →
-aw → -ô, to which then another 3rd m. s. suffix was added (**hî**
presumably from **hû** through dissimilation). While such an explanation is barely possible, it does not seem likely, and it would be
advantageous to seek a more plausible and less complicated solution. What we propose, based on a suggestion made by Frank Cross
but for which he should not be held responsible, is that the plural
form **bnw** is an alternate to the normal form represented by **bny**
(reflecting the basic difference between the nominative and oblique
cases of the primitive Semitic noun). According to this analogy the
common form **banay** would become **bĕnê** in Masoretic vocalization, whereas the unusual form **banaw** would become **bĕnô**. The
3rd m. s. suffix would normally be **-hû** but as a result of dissimilation an earlier **banawhû** ends up as **bĕnôhî**. It may be
that the presence of *waw* and *yod* in plural forms originally derives
from III–weak roots with these as third stem consonants, but the
usage spread to other nouns, so that either *waw* or *yod* turns up
in plural forms of nouns generally. We can point to the attested
phenomenon of plural nouns with *waw* in the Tell Fekherye inscription and elsewhere as well as the frequent occurrence of **-wāt** in
feminine plural forms as evidence for the presence of a plural using
waw along with the common *yod*. In this document, therefore, we
would read the plural form of this noun with the suffix as **banawhî**
which can be compared and contrasted with the form used with a
different suffix: **baynayhōn** (BA **bênêhôn**).

26. (4:3) **mn**—**min** (BA **min**), *from.* The preposition is idiomatic
in this context and combines with ᵓ**ḥry** to produce the following
pattern:

bnwhy mn ᵓ**ḥrwhy**		*his sons (from) after him*
bnyk mn ᵓ**ḥryk**		*your sons (from) after you*
bny mn ᵓ**ḥry**		*my sons (from) after me*

27. (4:4) ᵓ**ḥrwhy**—ᵓ**aharawhî** (BA, if the form occurred, would presumably have ᵓ**aḥărôhî**), *after him.* We interpret the form here
on the analogy of **bnwhy**, discussed under No. 25. Instead of the
normal ending of the preposition in **-ay-** → ê, we have an ending
in *waw*, which on the analogy of the regular form would have been

-aw- → ô. The usage seems to be restricted to forms with the 3rd m. s. suffix which itself is modified from a presumably original –hû to –hî. The *yod* at the end of the word is the standard vowel letter for –î (cf. No. 25).

28. (4:5) lᶜlmᵓ—liᶜālamaᵓ (BA lĕᶜālĕmāᵓ), *in perpetuity*. The *aleph* at the end of the word represents the emphatic state of the noun and was originally consonantal. Cf. No. 20.

29. (4:6) šlyṭ—šallîṭ (BA šallîṭ), *having mastery, exercising authority*. The *yod* is an internal vowel letter for î.

30. (4:7) yhwnwr—yahawnûr (the biblical form of the name would be yĕhônûr, if it occurred) *Yehonur: Yahweh is (my) lamp*. For the initial component, **yhw**, we prefer the vocalization **yahaw**, recognizing the originally consonantal force of the *waw* (see the discussion under No. 9). For the last syllable of the word, **nwr**, the *waw* is clearly a vowel letter for –û–.

31. (4:8) lyh(wḥnn)—liyahawḥanan (BH yĕhôḥānān) *Jehohanan*. See the discussion of this name under No. 9.

32. (5:1) hqymw—haqîmû (BA hăqêm and wahăqîm), *they established*. The *yod* surely represents the characteristic –î– of the H–stem in Aramaic as well as other Northwest Semitic languages. The vacillation in MT between –î– and –ê– seems to be a secondary internal development and does not reflect a byform *haqaymû → haqêmû along with haqîmû. The *waw* is a vowel letter for final –û.

33. (5:2) bynyhm—baynayhum (BA bênêhôn), *between them*. In both cases, the *yod* represents an original diphthong –ay–, which in Biblical Aramaic has been contracted to ê, cf. Dan 7:8 **bynyhwn** (*ketib*; the *qere* is bênêhēn, presumably reflecting a different orthography without the *waw* in the last syllable). According to Rosenthal (1974: 20), the suffixes in Biblical Aramaic are: **hm** or **hwn** (3 m. pl.); **km** or **kwn** (2 m. pl.). The spelling in SP 1 coincides with the first form of Biblical Aramaic in this instance and could reflect the older pronunciation –hum before the tone-lengthening to –hōm had occurred.

34. (5:3) zy—zî (BA dî), *that, to wit*. The *yod* represents final –î.

35. (5:4) hn—hin or hēn (BA hēn), *if, whether*. The vowel, originally short, may have been lengthened under the tone but is not represented in the orthography.

36. (5:5) ᵓnh—ᵓanâ (BA ᵓănâ), *I*. The *he* represents final –â.

37. (5:6) ḥnnyh—ḥananyâ (BH and BA ḥănanyâ), *Hananiah*. Once again, the *he* represents final –â. Cf. No. 23.

38. (5:7) br—bir or bar (BA bar), *son of*. In any case, the vowel is short and not represented in the orthography.

39. (5:8) b[y]dʾl—biyadʾēl, *Biyadʾel*. None of the vowels is indicated in the orthography. The first two remain short, while the third, originally i, may have been lengthened to ē under the tone.

40. (6:1) yhwnwr—yahawnûr (or later yĕhônûr), *Yehonur*. In our view the first *waw* represents the diphthong -aw-, while the second is a vowel letter for û. Cf. No. 30.

41. (6:2) wᶜm—waᶜim (BH wĕᶜim), *and with*. Neither vowel is indicated in the orthography.

42. (6:3) bnyk—banayk (BA would probably have been bĕnayik or bĕnêk if the word occurred; i.e., the diphthong might well have been contracted or resolved into two syllables, but in either case the *yod* would be preserved as a consonantal element or by historical spelling) *your sons.*[2] Here the *yod* represents the original diphthong of the construct plural ending, which was later contracted in BH and BA. In our opinion, there is no possibility that the form spelled with final -k could have been pronounced -kā.

43. (6:4) mn—min (BA min), *from*. Cf. No. 26.

44. (6:5) ʾhryk—ʾaharayk (BA ʾaḥărê and ʾaḥărêhôn), *after you*. The *yod* represents the original diphthong, which was probably preserved in SP 1. In Biblical Aramaic, the related forms (given above) reflect contraction of the diphthong but preservation of the *yod* through historical spelling. For the same ending, cf. No. 42, and for a different form of the preposition, cf. No. 27.

45. (6:6) ʾnh—ʾanâ (BA ʾănâ), *I*. Cf. No. 36.

46. (6:7) ḥnnyh—ḥananyâ (BA and BH ḥănanyâ), *Hananiah*. Cf. Nos. 23 and 37.

47. (6:8) wbny—wabanay (BA *ûbĕnay), *and my sons*.

48. (6:9) mn—min (BA min), *from*. Cf. Nos. 26, 43.

49. (6:10) ʾhry—ʾaharay (BA *ʾaḥăray), *after me*. Cf. Nos. 27, 44.

50. (7:1) ᶜmk—ᶜimmak (BA ᶜimmāk), *with you*. Neither of the vowels is represented in the orthography. In Biblical Aramaic tone-lengthening of the second vowel (-ā) has taken place, and this change may also have taken place in SP 1, although we cannot be sure. The orthography is not affected.

51. (7:2) ʾnt—ʾant (BA ʾant as the *qere* consistently, but the anomalous ʾnth, presumably for ʾantâ in the *ketib*) *you*. The spelling of SP 1 supports that of the *qere* in Biblical Aramaic. The *ketib* of BA reflects a longer form, comparable to Biblical Hebrew ʾattâ.

---

[2] In Biblical Aramaic the *ketib* is written -yk while the *qere* is vocalized -āk. It is not clear just how the *ketib* would have been pronounced, but the original form was doubtless a diphthong, pronounced -ayk-. The original diphthong would have been represented in the orthography by *yod*, and even if or when the diphthong was contracted, the *yod* would have remained in place through historical spelling.

52. (7:3) **yhwnwr**—yahawnûr, *Yehonur.* Cf. Nos. 30, 40.

53. (7:4) **bmlyᵓ**—bamillayyaᵓ (BA **millayyā̄ᵓ**), *by, with,* or *in these words.* There are no vowel letters in this word. The final *aleph* was originally consonantal and may have retained that force in SP 1, although it has quiesced in Biblical Aramaic (with attendant lengthening of the preceding vowel ā). For further discussion of the *aleph* representing the emphatic state in nouns, see Nos. 7, 20, and 28.

54. (7:5) **ᵓlh**—ᵓille(h) (BA **ᵓēlleh**), *these.* The final *he* is a vowel letter for –e.

55. (7:6) **[ᵓnt]n**—[ᵓinti]n (BA *ᵓentēn), *I shall give.* There are no vowel letters in this word. Whether the second vowel has been lengthened under the tone, as in Biblical Aramaic, is uncertain.

56. (7:7) **lk**—lak (BA **lāk**), *to you.* Tone-lengthening has occurred in Biblical Aramaic and is possible in SP 1. Since medial **a** (whether long or short) is not represented in the orthography of this document, the spelling is not affected.

57. (7:8) **ᵓnt**—ᵓant (BA *qere* ᵓant), *you.* Cf. No. 51.

58. (7:9) **yhwnwr**—yahawnûr, *Yehonur.* Cf. Nos. 30, 40, 52.

59. (8:1) **lᵓ**—laᵓ (BA **lā̄ᵓ**), *not.* It is our position that the *aleph* in this word (as in other particles) was originally consonantal and later quiesced as in Biblical Aramaic (and also Biblical Hebrew, with a different vocalization). It is difficult to determine whether the *aleph* was still pronounced at the time of SP 1, but the fact that in the manuscript *aleph* is used exclusively in such particles and the emphatic state of nouns indicates that it was pronounced; otherwise, it might easily have been interchanged with the normal vowel letter for final –ā, namely *he.* An example of such an interchange (**lh** for the negative particle **lᵓ**) occurs at Dan 4:32, showing that the *aleph* had quiesced. The consistency and accuracy of the spelling in SP 1 argue against the quiescence of *aleph* in this document.

60. (8:2) **mqbl**—muqabbil (BA *mĕqabbēl), *accept.* There are no vowel letters in this word.

61. (8:3) **ᵓnh**—ᵓanâ (BA **ᵓănâ**), *I.* The *he* represents final –â. Cf. Nos. 36, 45.

62. (8:4) **mnk**—minnak (BA **minnāk**), *from you.* There are no vowel letters in this word. The second vowel has been lengthened under the tone in BA, but whether this change has taken place in SP 1 is not certain. The orthography is not affected. For the same suffix with other prepositions, see Nos. 50, 56.

63. (8:5) ᵓw—ᵓaw (BH ᵓô), *or*. While the original diphthong in this word has been contracted in Biblical Hebrew (which retains the *waw* of the diphthong as historical spelling), there is no reason to suppose that the contraction has occurred in SP 1. In either case, the *waw* represents the original consonant.
64. (8:6) kspᵓ—kaspaᵓ (BA kaspāᵓ), *the silver*. Cf. Nos. 7, 20.
65. (8:7) š 35—*35 shekels*.
66. (8:8) zy—zî (BA dî), *which*. Cf. No. 34.
67. (8:9) yhb[t]—yahabt (BA yĕhabt), *you gave*. There are no vowel letters in this word.
68. (9:1) wᵓḥr—waᵓaḥar (BH wĕᵓaḥar), *and afterwards*. There are no vowel letters in this word.
69. (9:2) ḥyb—ḥayyāb (Talmudic ḥayyāb), *one who is liable, debtor*. A predicate noun is desiderated in combination with the pronoun ᵓnh (*I*). The *yod* is clearly consonantal, and therefore there are no vowel letters present.
70. (9:3) ᵓnh—ᵓanâ (BA ᵓănâ), *I*. Cf. Nos. 36, 45, 61.
71. (9:4) ḥnnyh—ḥananyâ (Biblical ḥănanyâ), *Hananiah*. Cf. Nos. 23, 37, 46.
72. (9:5) ᵓšlm—ᵓašallim (BA has examples of this verb, but not in the paᶜel form; in BH the form would be: ᵓăšallēm), *I will repay*. Tone lengthening occurs in the biblical verbs and is possible in SP 1.
73. (9:6) ᵓntn—ᵓintin (BA *ᵓentēn), *I will give*. Cf. No. 55, which is the same word, reconstructed on the basis of its appearance here.
74. (9:7) lk—lak (BA lāk), *to you*. Cf. No. 56.
75. (9:8) ᵓnt—ᵓant (BA qere ᵓant), *you*. Cf. Nos. 51, 57.
76. (9:9) yhwnwr—yahawnûr, *Yehonur*. Cf. Nos. 30, 40, 52, 58.
77. (10:1) zy—zî (BA di), *which, that*. Cf. Nos. 34, 66.
78. (10:2) lᵓ—laᵓ (BA lāᵓ), *not*. Cf. No. 59.
79. (10:3) dynn—dînîn (BA sing. dîn), *judgments, lawsuits*. The Targum confirms that the vocalization should be dînîn (m. pl. of dîn). The spelling is unusual; we would expect a second *yod* (dynyn) since the second vowel is primitive and "pure-long." We have already observed, however, that in the m. pl. form of nouns the expected vowel letter (which occurs in the Tell Fekherye inscription of the 10th or 9th century) *yod* does not appear (cf. Nos. 18, 19). This idiosyncrasy may reflect archaic usage and highly traditional and conventional language handed down in its original form for centuries. It is also possible that the scribe wished to avoid the use of two *yods* in the same short word (cf. dmyn in line 3, No. 18 and gmyrn in the same line, No. 19). The reasoning would not apply to the word ḥwbn, where the *waw* is presumably not a vowel letter; and note the repeated spelling of yhwnwr, with *waw* written twice.

80. (10:4) wlᵓ—walaᵓ (BA lāᵓ), *and not*. Cf. Nos. 59, 78.
81. (10:5) ḥwbn—ḥawbīn, *obligations, debts*. The word occurs in both a feminine (ḥôbâ) and a masculine (ḥôb) form with generally similar meanings. Here the plural form could be either ḥôbīn (m.) or ḥôbān (f.); in the context, however, and in association with the preceding dînīn, it is more likely to be ḥôbīn. As we have seen, the spelling in this inscription does not offer help in resolving the issue, since the plural in -īn is not indicated by the expected *yod*. The *waw* reflects the original diphthong -aw- in this word, although it has contracted in Biblical Aramaic.
82. (10:6) ksp—kasap (BA kĕsap), *silver*. There are no vowel letters in this word.
83. (10:7) mnn 7—manīn (BH mānîm), *7 minas*. Once again we seem to have a masculine plural form of the noun (in -īn) without the expected orthographic indication (*yod* as a vowel letter for î).
84. (10:8) lyhwḥnn—liyahawḥanan (BH yĕhôḥānān) *Jehohanan*. Cf. Nos. 9, 31.
85. (10:9) zk—zēk (BA dēk), *that (one)*. There are no vowel letters in this word. The word always follows the noun it modifies, in this case the personal name *Jehohanan*.
86. (10:10) lᵓ—laᵓ (BA lāᵓ), *not*. Cf. Nos. 59, 78.
87. (11:1) mn—min (BA min), *from*. Cf. Nos. 26, 43, 48.
88. (11:2) ᵓḥryk—ᵓaḥarayk, *after you*. Cf. No. 44.
89. (11:3) lqbl—laqubil (BA loqŏbēl), *by reason of, on account of*. There are no vowel letters in this word.
90. (11:4) znh—zinâ (BA dĕnâ), *this*. Cf. No. 21, and also 13.
91. (11:5) ᵓsrᵓ—ᵓisaraᵓ (BA ᵓĕsārāᵓ), *covenant, binding agreement*. The *aleph* at the end of the word is the sign of the emphatic state and was originally consonantal. It has quiesced in Biblical Aramaic, but there is no clear evidence that it had quiesced at the time of SP 1. Cf. Nos. 7, 20, 28, 53, 64.
92. (11:6) hqymw—haqîmû (BA *hăqîmû), *they established*. Cf. No. 32.
93. (11:7) bynyhm—baynayhum (baynayhōm?) (BA bênêhôn), *between them*. Cf. No. 33.
94. (12:1) yḥtmwn—yaḥtumûn (BA *yaḥtĕmûn), *they seal, affix seals*. The form seems to be the peᶜal imperfect, 3rd m. pl. The *waw* is a vowel letter for medial û.
95. (12:2) hmw—himmô (BA himmô), *they*. This word is the independent pronoun, 3rd m. pl. Biblical Aramaic also has a byform himmôn. This is the only example of *waw* as a vowel letter for ô in the inscription, unless we suppose that the diphthong -aw- has been contracted in the numerous cases in which it occurs. In

those cases, however, we can explain the presence of the *waw* as an instance of historical spelling and not as a true vowel letter. If the final –ô in this word is explained as deriving from an original –**u**, which seems most likely, then it would be the only example of the use of *waw* as a true vowel letter for final –ô ← **u**. There is no evidence to support an original reading of **himmaw** for this pronoun. This usage may imply that the contraction has already taken place in the diphthong, and we are witnessing the initial stage of the extension of the result of historical spelling to situations in which the *waw* was not originally present in the word. At the same time, we can assert that this practice has not been extended to the interior of words in which an ō vowel derived from **u** has developed (e.g., **bynyhm** for bênêhōm).

96. (12:3) **mhymnn—muhaymanīn** (BA mĕhêmān), *trustworthy*. The form is a *hap^cel* passive participle, m. pl. We note that the *yod* represents the original diphthong in this form of the verb, **ay**, which has been contracted in Biblical Aramaic. We also note that the expected *yod* in the masculine plural form of the participle does not appear. Apparently the *aleph* in the verbal root (ᵓ**mn**) has been lost; this is also true of the surviving forms in Biblical Aramaic.

12.3 Conclusions

Samaria Papyrus 1 contains 96 usable words, which we have numbered serially for ease of reference. Of these, 21 have minimal interest for orthographic studies since they end in a consonant and contain only short vowels originally. (In some cases these are reduced to shewa in Biblical Aramaic, and hence it may not be clear just what the original vowel was.) These are the following: No. 2: lᵓdr; No. 3: šnt; Nos. 11, 38: br; No. 14: ᶜbd; Nos. 26, 43, 48, 87: mn; No. 41: wᶜm; No. 50: ᶜmk; Nos. 51, 57, 75: ᵓnt; Nos. 56, 74: lk; No. 62: mnk; No. 67: yhbt; No. 68: wᵓhr; No. 69: ḥyb; No. 82: ksp. Three numerical expressions are not relevant to our interest: Nos. 1, 22, 65.

1. Before proceeding to a consideration of the three genuine vowel letters in the classical Aramaic spelling system (*he*, *waw*, and *yod*), we can make an observation about the use and distribution of word-terminal *aleph*: in six cases in the inscription, *aleph* serves as the determiner, marking the emphatic state of the noun. The examples are as follows: No. 7: mlkᵓ; Nos. 20, 64: kspᵓ; No. 28: lᶜlmᵓ; No. 53: bmlyᵓ; No. 86: ᵓsrᵓ. The remaining four instances involve the negative particle lᵓ: Nos. 59, 78, 80, 91.

2. In twelve cases, word-terminal *he* is the vowel letter for â.

   - Pronouns: No. 13: **dnh**; Nos. 21, 90: **znh**; Nos. 36, 45, 61, 70: **ᵓnh**.
   - Names: No. 12: **šᵓlh**; Nos. 23, 37, 46, 71: **ḥnnyh**.

   In one instance word-terminal *he* represents the vowel e: No. 54: **ᵓlh**. There are three other words with final *he*: in each of these cases the *he* represents the masculine pronoun suffix, 3rd m. s. and is consonantal.

   In all cases in which a word ends in –â, the vowel letter representing that sound is *he*. As we have pointed out, the case with terminal *aleph* is different, since it is used only for the emphatic state and the negative particle and we believe that it has retained its original consonantal function in both of these sets. Had *aleph* quiesced and been in use as a vowel letter, we would have expected *he* and *aleph* to be used indiscriminately or interchangeably for the same vowel. That is not the case.

3. Word-terminal *yod* represents î: No. 25: **wlbnwhy**; No. 27: **ᵓḥrwhy**; Nos. 34, 66, 77: **zy**; or –**ay**: No. 49: **ᵓḥry**.

4a. Within a word, *yod* may be consonantal: No. 69: **ḥyb**; but is otherwise a vowel letter for î: No. 15: **zylh**; No. 16: **tmym**; No. 19: **gmyrn**; No. 29: **šlyṭ**; Nos. 32, 92: **ḥqymw**; No. 79: **dynn**. The *yod* in No. 84 was originally consonantal and therefore cannot be counted as a vowel letter: **wyhwḥnn**, which in Masoretic vocalization might come out: **wîhôḥānān**. The *yod* in No. 18 is probably consonantal: **damiyīn** rather than **dāmîn** as in later Aramaic (in this inscription that word would probably have been spelled without *yod* at all: **dmn**).

4b. In contrast to this consistent usage of *yod* as a medial vowel letter, we apparently have six masculine plural nouns in all of which the final long vowel (–ī–) is not represented in the orthography: No. 18: **dmyn** (?); No. 19: **gmyrn**; No. 79: **dynn**; No. 81: **ḥwbn**; No. 83: **mnn**; No. 96: **mhymnn**.

5a. In the medial position *yod* represents the original diphthong –ay–, which in Biblical Aramaic regularly is contracted to ê. We cannot tell whether this development has taken place in the Aramaic of the papyri, since there is no difference in the spelling. Alongside the consistent use of *yod* in all cases where there was an original diphthong, which may have been contracted, there is equally consistent omission or non-use of *yod* in cases in which in Biblical Aramaic the original vowel **i** has been changed and lengthened to ē (see 5b). We cannot tell whether this tone-lengthening and qualifying process has taken place in the Aramaic of SP. The point, however, is that this constant complementary distribution corresponds to the derivation of the two vowel sounds and shows either that the phonetic changes described above: –ay– → ê and **i** → ē have not yet taken place, or if they have, then historical spelling has been strictly preserved. Here are the examples: No. 8 **bšmry[n]**; Nos. 33, 93: **bynyhm**; No. 42: **bnyk**; Nos. 44, 88: ꜄**ḥryk**; No. 96: **mhymnn**.

5b. Where Masoretic vocalization indicates the vowel ē from **i**, the spelling in the document is always defective: No. 4: **rē꜄š**; No. 35: **hēn**; No. 85: **zēk**; No. 39: **bĕyad꜄ēl**; Nos. 55, 73: ꜄**intēn**; No. 60: **mĕqabbēl**; No. 72: ꜄**ăšallēm**; No. 89: **loqŏbēl**. This consistent usage indicates that No. 12 is to be pronounced **šĕ꜄ēlâ** or even **ša꜄ilâ**.

6. Word-terminal *waw* represents –û: Nos. 32, 92: **hqymw**; or –aw (–ô): No. 63: ꜄**w**; or –ô presumably from –u: No. 95: **hmw**.

7a. Within a word, *waw* represents û: No. 5: **mlkwt**; Nos. 30, 40, 52, 58, 76: **yhwnwr** (**yahawnûr**); No. 94: **yḥtmwn**. It is also possible that *waw* in No. 6 represents û; the uncertainty arises from the variety of possible spellings of the Persian king's name.

7b. This usage makes it unlikely that the first vowel of No. 17 is û.

8a. Otherwise *waw* within a word is used for the original diphthong –aw–. We prefer to vocalize with the older form (the diphthong) although it is possible that the diphthong has contracted as in Biblical Aramaic. It is the same situation as described for the diphthong –ay– → ê in paragraph 5a. These are the instances: Nos. 9, 31, 84: **yahawḥanan** or **yĕhôhānān**; Nos. 30, 40, 52, 58, 76: **yahawnur** or **yĕhônûr**; No. 81: **ḥawbīn** or **ḥôbīn**; No. 25: **walibnawhî** or **wĕlibnôhî**; No. 27: ꜄**aharawhî** or ꜄**aḫĕrôhî**.

8b. In two cases of a form in which Masoretic pronunciation and comparative grammar point to ō from **u**, the spelling is defective: Nos. 33, 93: **bênêhōm**. But compare No. 95, where in the final position *waw* seems to represent ô from **u**.

The spelling of SP 1 is generally consistent and regular, with only one notable exception. In the final position, *he*, *waw*, and *yod* are used to represent â, û, and î respectively. It is to be noted that in single instances, *he* represents final –e and *waw* apparently represents final -ô as well. *Waw* is used to represent û in medial positions as well as the diphthong –**aw**–, whether or not the latter has been contracted. And in the medial position, *waw* is not used for **o**. *Yod* is used for the diphthong –**ay**–, whether or not it has been contracted, and it is never used for ē derived from **i**. It is also used to represent î internally, but there is a major exception to this practice: while all the cases are not equally decisive, it appears that in the case of all six instances of the masculine plural noun (in –īn), the *yod* representing the final long vowel does not appear.

12.4   Summary of the Orthography of SP 1

The occurrences and functions of *aleph*, *he*, *waw*, and *yod*:

1. *Aleph*

    (a) In the final position (after **a**): Nos. 7, 20, 28, 53, 59, 64, 78, 80, 86, 91.
    (b) In the medial position: Nos. 2, 4, 12, 39, 68.

    Aleph was originally a consonant and is still treated as one in all positions: initial, medial, and final. While it may have quiesced in certain words, it functions only as a passive vowel marker, not as an active vowel letter.

2. *He*

    (a) In the final position
        i. For –â: Nos. 12, 13, 21, 23, 36, 37, 45, 46, 61, 70, 71, 90.
        ii. For –e: No. 54.
        iii. As a consonantal suffix: Nos. 10, 15, 24.
    (b) In the medial position
        i. As a consonant: Nos. 6, 9, 25, 27, 30, 31, 33, 40, 52, 58, 67, 76, 84, 93, 96.

    He is used as a vowel letter in the final position only; it represents â predominantly, but may also represent other vowels, such as ē from **i**. In any other position, initial or medial, it is a consonant.

3. *Waw*

    (a) In the final position
        i. For –û: Nos. 32, 92.

    ii. For –ô (from –u): No. 95.

    iii. As the consonantal element in the diphthong –aw– (which may have been contracted to ô): No. 63.

(b) In the medial position

    i. For û : Nos. 5, 6(?), 30, 40, 52, 58, 76, 94.

    ii. For the diphthong –aw– (which may have been contracted to ô): Nos. 9, 25, 27, 30, 31, 40, 52, 58, 76, 81, 84.

    iii. As a consonant: No. 6 (?).

    iv. Apparently the vowel û from u is not represented in the orthography: Nos. 33, 93.

Waw occurs as a vowel letter in both the final and medial positions. It represents the vowel û in both positions and the vowel ô in the final position only, if that is the correct interpretation of No. 95. It also represents the consonantal element in the diphthong –aw– in both positions. Whether the diphthong was preserved or contracted at the time of the Samaria Papyri, the spelling (with *waw*) was not affected.

4. *Yod*

(a) In the final position

    i. For –î: Nos. 25, 27, 34, 66, 77.

    ii. For –ay– (possibly contracted to ê): Nos. 47, 49.

(b) In the medial position

    i. For î: Nos. 15, 16, 18 (?), 19, 29, 32, 79, 84 (?), 92. In a number of instances, the same vowel is not represented in the orthography: Nos. 18 (?), 19, 79, 81, 83, 96. These are all cases involving the masculine plural –în.[3]

    ii. For –ay– (possibly contracted to ê): Nos. 8, 33 (bis), 42, 44, 88, 93 (bis), 96.

    iii. As a consonant: Nos. 6, 9, 18 (?), 23, 31, 37, 46, 53, 69, 71, 84.

    iv. Apparently the vowel ē from i is not represented in the orthography: Nos. 12, 17 (?), 24, 35, 39, 55, 60, 72, 73, 85, 89.

---

[3] It is possible that No. 17 šḥrṣ belongs on this list. If the expression is derived from Neo-Babylonian šīm ḥarīṣ, as proposed by the editor, then the final vowel would be ī. We might well have expected the long vowel in that position to be represented by *yod* as in a number of instances in the inscription. However, its omission can be justified on the basis of the regular practice in the same inscription of omitting the *yod* in the final syllable where we undoubtedly have a long vowel: –ī in the masculine plural form of nouns. Given the uncertainty of the vocalization of a loan-word, we hesitate to pursue this point or to classify the form.

Yod occurs as a vowel letter in both the final and medial positions. It represents the vowel î in both positions. It also represents the consonantal element in the diphthong –**ay**– or ê ← **ay** in both positions. One important anomaly is to be reported. Contrary to the regular practice of representing ī in the medial position by *yod*, probably all six instances of the masculine plural form of nouns omit the expected *yod*. The exact reason or explanation for this unusual circumstance remains to be determined.

Chapter 13

Another Look at 4QSam^b

Francis I. Andersen & David Noel Freedman

4QSam^b is probably the oldest biblical manuscript found at Qumran. Since its publication by Cross in 1955 interest has focussed on its paleography and on its textual affinities with **LXX**. The importance of its orthography for textual studies was mentioned briefly by Cross in his original publication, but it was Freedman (1962) who pointed out the significance of its distinctive spelling patterns. Yet, in spite of the republication of Freedman's paper in two anthologies (Leiman 1974; Cross and Talmon 1975), the significance of the orthography of 4QSam^b against the larger background of the history of the text of the Hebrew Bible is not generally appreciated.

In two recent papers Tov (1986, 1988) does not give this MS the special attention it deserves. We think that it is appropriate and fitting to raise this question once again.

13.1   The Evidence

The following inventory lists only those parts of the text of 4QSam^b which preserve a whole word or enough of a word to permit something to be said about the orthography. Each item will be identified by (i) an inventory number; (ii) biblical reference; (iii) fragment and line number in 4QSam^b.

Reprinted, with permission, from **Revue de Qumran 14**: 7–29, 1989.

13.1.1   Fragment 1 (1 Sa 16:1–11)

1. 1 Sa 16:1 (1:1): [ᵓšlḥ]k̇ [— Although only one letter is imperfectly
   preserved in this line, Cross's identification is acceptable. The final
   kaph agrees with MT and shows that the variant spelling –kh has
   not intruded.

2. 1 Sa 16:2 (1:2): **bqr**— Standard spelling of **bāqār**.

3. 1 Sa 16:2 (1:2): **q[ḥ**, MT **tqḥ**— The imperative of 4QSam^b is of
   textual interest, since it agrees with **LXX** λαβε. The reading is
   inferior grammatically, however, for imperfect is preferred when
   something precedes the verb, as here, while the imperative is usually clause-initial. It is regrettable that the following text is lost,
   for it would be interesting to know if **qḥ** was used simply, as Cross
   restores, or whether **qḥh** (*hapax leg.*, but used in the similar re-
   quest in Ge 15:9) or **qḥ–lk** or **qḥ–nᵓ** were used. As it is, the
   reading has no orthographic interest.

4. 1 Sa 16:3 (1:3): **ᵓmr** = MT— Standard spelling of **ᵓōmar**, *I will
   say*. The deviant, late, **ᵓwmr** (Ne 2:7, 17, 20) has not intruded.

5. 1 Sa 16:3 (1:3): **ᵓlyk** = MT— Standard and traditional spelling,
   reflecting neither the contraction of the diphthong nor the Qumran-
   type variant –kh.

6. 1 Sa 16:4 (1:4): **hrᵓh**, **hārōᵓeh**, *O seer!*— Not present in MT,
   but agreeing with **LXX** ὁ βλεπων. The *defective* spelling of –ō–
   with the participle is the Masoretic norm although 1040 out of
   5309 specimens in MT are *plene* (**SHB** 193). The only outlier reported by Andersen and Forbes with over-use of *defective* spelling
   and under-use of *plene* is Numbers 22:2–36 (for absolute forms),
   with 2 Kings as an outlier for under-use of *plene* spelling in construct forms. By contrast, Judges is the only portion in the entire
   Primary History plus Latter Prophets that is an outlier due to the
   under-use of *defective* spelling and over-use of *plene*, while there
   are quite a number of outliers in the Writings due to this deviation from the norm. This is what we would expect. Thus **rᵓh** in
   4QSam^b is both archaic and normal, and all one can say of the
   reading is that it is not in line with later post-exilic trends. This is
   a further point in favor of its authenticity, for, had the word been
   added by a post-exilic scribe, one would not have been surprised if
   he had spelled it **rwᵓh**.

7. 1 Sa 16:5 (1:4): **wyᵓmr** = MT— Standard spelling; even MT
   shows no trace of Qumran **ywᵓmr**.

8. 1 Sa 16:6 (1:5): **wyhy** = MT— Standard spelling, no biblical variants.

9. 1 Sa 16:6 (1:5): **bbᵓm**, MT **bbwᵓm**— This contrast is typical and consistent, 4QSam*ᵇ* having the older, MT the later, spelling. The contrast does not, however, point to conspicuous archaism in the one nor modernization of the other; for nearly half such words are spelled *plene* in MT (**SHB** 196), so both are "normal." It remains true, nevertheless, that 4QSam*ᵇ* is consistently "older" in such evenly balanced cases.

10. 1 Sa 16:6 (1:5): **wyrᵓ** = MT— This is the standard form and spelling. The longer **wayyirᵓeh** is a rare alternative. Both occur as *ktyb* / *qry* at Job 42:16. The longer form is in 1 Sa 17:42; 2 Ki 5:21; Ezk 18:14, 28. So here again 4QSam*ᵇ* is unremarkable.

11. 1 Sa 16:6 (1:5): **ᵓt** = MT— No comment.

12. 1 Sa 16:6 (1:5): **ᵓ[**— Only the first letter of the next word, Eliab, is (partly) legible. This loss is regrettable, since it would be helpful to know if the archaic *defective* spelling of this name (**ᵓlᵓb** versus MT **ᵓlyᵓb**) has sustained itself. It does survive in a few names of this kind in MT. Compare the fluctuation of **ᵓbnr** and **ᵓbynr**. Even so, MT might preserve the correct spelling of a shorter form of the name that did exist, not just the artificial vocalization of the *defective* spelling. At least in the case of Abinadab (No. 19 in line 7 below) the standard *plene* spelling is attested.

13. 1 Sa 16:7 (1:6): **qmtw**, MT **qwmtw**— The difference is very significant. **Qōmâ** with derivatives occurs 45 times in MT, of which ten are spelled *defective*. The distribution of the alternative spellings is in accordance with larger general patterns. Only two of the 35 *plene* spellings occur in the Torah (Ge 6:15; Ex 38:18). All but one (Ezk 31:5) of the *defective* spellings occur in the P source of Exodus. Apart from these three specimens (out of 45!) the complementary distribution is clear-cut: Torah *defective* (9 out of 11), the rest *plene* (33 out of 34). The *plene* spelling **qwmtw** in MT 1 Sa 16:7 is thus in line with standard Masoretic practice, while the *defective* spelling in 4QSam*ᵇ* places that MS in the company of the more conservative portions of MT (we are speaking about the orthography), in this instance Exodus.

The evidence of 4QSam*ᵇ* along with the (almost) consistent spelling in Exodus is significant for the history of this word and for the history of the stem vowel in this word. Strictly speaking, the historical nature of that stem vowel is not known. Theoretically the eventually attested pronunciation **qōm-** could have derived from **qawm-*, **qām-*, or **qum-*. Similar considerations apply to the history of the stem vowel in the cognate **māqōm**, which is likewise attested with both *plene* and *defective* spellings, and with a similar distribution. The verb morphology gives little if any support

to the hypothesis of a primal root **qwm**. Most forms, not only the
dominant *qal* but also the *pōlēl*, point to a biconsonantal root **qm**,
rather than a medial **–w–**. In fact the alternative *pi^cel* is based
on **qym**, and is a rare, late, secondary, possibly Aramaizing form.
Furthermore, if the noun in question had been originally ***qaw-
mat(u)**, the *plene* spelling would be the historical spelling, with
the *defective* spelling possible only in a dialect, and at a stage where
the diphthong has monophthongized *and consonantal spelling prevails*. These conditions obtained in two unrelated phases in the
history of Hebrew spelling, widely separated in time. The first
phase is early and is restricted in scope to Samarian inscriptions
within the evidence for Hebrew available at present. The second
phase (when diphthongs had contracted in southern Hebrew) is not
clearly attested, and must be considered no more than a theoretical
possibility in the present state of research. It requires the relinquishment of the historical spelling of a contracted diphthong in
favor of the *defective* option when the spelling has become purely,
or mainly, phonetic. Such a development would have been quite
contrary to all the main trends in Hebrew spelling, which were
not only to maintain historical spelling (think of the uniform *plene*
spelling of such words as *house*, **byt**, and *day*, **ywm**, in MT [SHB
153], even when these words in construct or suffixed states are less
stressed and in spite of the pressure of analogy from the stems of
the plurals—**btym, ymym**, whose imitation would have generated
defective spellings of the singular), but also to spell more and more
long vowels *plene*. To copy the standard **qwmh** as *defective* **qmh**
in post-exilic times could only have been the result of conscious
(and not very well-informed) attempt to imitate archaic consonantal spelling. Against the likelihood of such an interest on the part
of scribes we must emphasize that purely consonantal writing of old
Hebrew texts, if it was ever practiced at all (this question seems to
depend entirely on the identification of the language of the Gezer
Calendar), had gone out of vogue very early in the history of Hebrew literacy, so that later scribes would not have had any models
or specimens of such writing to imitate. The possibility and scope
of such a supposed reaction against dominant trends to more *plene*
rather than more *defective* spellings in post-exilic textual transmission have not yet been investigated systematically. It could be that
the five occurrences of *defective* spelling of gentilic *Moabite*, **m³by**-
(De 2:11; Ezk 9:1; Ru 1:4, 10; Ne 13:1), rather than the standard
(and historical) **mw³by**-, reflect such an archaizing trend. For
the time being we must attribute the *defective* spelling of **qōm**- in
MT to the early phase, and accept it as a genuine archaism. Why

then is this spelling restricted almost exclusively to the P source of Exodus (plus Ezk 31:5, and now 1 Sa 16:7 in 4QSam^b)?

The other possibilities for the history of this vowel, however, present different problems. An original *qāmat(u) would be identical with the f. participle and similar also to the noun qāmâ, *grain*. In these words the long –ā– seems to be primal, since it does not shorten. Yet it did not become –ō– as usual for primal ā, except in qwmym (2 Ki 16:7). If *height* was also originally *qāmat(u), it is hard to see how it would have bifurcated from the participle. It has been suggested by some scholars that there were two distinct epochs in which the change ā → ō took place in Hebrew, the later one mainly affecting ā from primal short a lengthened by stress or pretonic. Another explanation of such inconsistencies (the same rules of historical phonology do not apply to all the vocabulary) is to suppose two early dialects, one in which the Old South Canaanite unconditioned sound shift ā → ō did not take place, as in nouns of type qaṭṭāl. These difficulties do not altogether rule out the possibility that qōmâ was originally qāmatu. This is probably the best hypothesis; and in that case the history of its spelling would be similar to that of *Qal* active participles: qāṭilu → qōṭēl. The *plene* spelling of the ō in the latter set of words has barely begun, if at all, in pre-exilic Hebrew inscriptions (Sarfatti 1982), and the spelling in older portions of MT is largely *defective* (see discussion under No. 6 above). If, on the other hand, we suppose a primal qamatu, which developed pretonic ā and then later ā → ō, the constancy of the long vowel in all variations of the stem would be anomalous.

Finally, can the spelling distribution be explained in terms of primal *qumatu? Hardly, for u → ō normally only under stress. The persistence of qōm– in all forms of this word points to a primal long vowel or diphthong, and if the latter, to an ancient allomorph of the root, so that the *plene* spelling is historical. So we have a paradox. We cannot account for the almost complete absence of the historical spelling in texts otherwise shown to be archaic, notably Exodus. The spelling in 4QSam^b is likewise archaic, no question about that. The one other case outside the Pentateuch (Ezk 31:5) might not be statistically significant, for the word occurs twelve times *plene* in the Latter Prophets. But, for what it is worth, Ezk 31:5 shows that this archaic spelling could still be used in the sixth century BCE when writing a new text, not just copying an old one.

To sum up. The spelling **qmtw** in 4QSam^b is a genuine archaism of enormous significance. But we do not know if it attests an original *qāmatu → qōmâ with *plene* spelling of ō a post-exilic development, or an original *qawmatu, with the earlier *defective* spellings coming from a separate dialect patch in pre-exilic Hebrew in which the diphthong has contracted and consonantal spelling prevailed. The latter presents historical difficulties, for this contrast is attested for north Israel versus south, and the provenience of both the P source and of the sources for the Book of Samuel must be Jerusalem. The suffix **-w** is evidence that the old spelling with *he* has been replaced by the new standard using *waw*.

14. 1 Sa 16:7 (1:6):]**ky** = MT— Standard spelling; Qumran **ky**ᵓ does not intrude into any Masoretic MSS.

15. 1 Sa 16:7 (1:6): **m**ᵓ**styw**, MT **m**ᵓ**styhw** but **m**ᵓ**styw** in v 1 of MT— This alternation is more a matter of morphology than orthography. With two orthographic possibilities for stem-terminal –ī– and two morphological possibilities for the suffix, there are theoretically four possible combinations. But the *defective* spelling of –īw never occurs. The suffix **-w** is preferred (×462) and is found throughout the corpus (Torah ×173; Former Prophets ×120; Latter Prophets ×77; Poetry [Ps, Jb, Pr] ×33; Other Writings ×59). The rarer –īhû occurs 53 times, again in all portions (Torah ×4 [2 with –ī *defective*]; Former Prophets ×11 [2 with –ī *defective*]; Latter Prophets ×12 [2 with –ī *defective*]; Poetry [Ps, Jb, Pr] ×11; Other Writings ×15). It is rarest in Torah (4 out of 177), commonest in the Writings (26 out of 118), presumably because it gained strength towards the end of the biblical period. The –hû variant survives only twice in MT Samuel (1 Sa 16:7 [the present case] and 1 Sa 1:28 [*defective*]), and we cannot say whether they represent the survivors of an old form that has resisted normalization or the intrusion of a form whose use increased after the Exile. Hence we cannot weigh the merits of MT versus 4QSam^b for the reading in 1 Sa 16:7.

16. 1 Sa 16:7 (1:6): **k̇[y** = MT— No comment.

17. 1 Sa 16:8 (1:7): **yšy** = MT— Standard spelling. The late variant ᵓ**yšy** (1 Ch 2:13) does not enter the picture.

18. 1 Sa 16:8 (1:7): ᵓ**l** = MT— No comment.

19. 1 Sa 16:8 (1:7): ᵓ**byndb** = MT— Not infrequently human names with ᵓăbî- as the first element survive in the MT with the old consonantal spelling. Sometimes the vocalization suggests loss of the vowel as in ᵓabšālôm ∼ ᵓăbîšālôm (1 Ki 15:2, 10), ᵓbšy ∼ ᵓbyšy; but *defective* spelling can be recognized as such: ᵓbgyl ∼ ᵓabygyl; ᵓbnr ∼ ᵓabynr. In this instance 4QSam^b has the standard, not the archaic variant.

20. 1 Sa 16:9 (1:8): **yhwh** = MT— Standard; no variations attested.
21. 1 Sa 16:10 (1:8): **wyᶜbr** = MT— *Plene* spelling of the stem vowel would not be unacceptable as a Masoretic option; but it is rare (**SHB** 174), and must be considered equivocal in any case. Here the only point to be made is that the spelling calls for no comment, whereas a *plene* variant would have been astonishing in an otherwise archaic text.
22. 1 Sa 16:10 (1:8): **yš[y** = MT— See No. 17.
23. 1 Sa 16:11 (1:9): **yšy** = MT— See No. 17.
24. 1 Sa 16:11 (1:9): **ḣt[mw** = MT— Of no orthographic interest.

13.1.2 Fragment 2 (1 Sa 19:10–17)

25. 1 Sa 19:10 (2:1): **mpny** = MT— No comment.
26. 1 Sa 19:11 (2:2): **l]hmytw** = MT— The long ī in such *hiphᶜil* forms is spelled defectively in about one in eight cases in MT (**SHB** 166). In this very passage, at the end of verse 15 the *defective* spelling is met in **lhmtw**. It is tantalizing that we do not know how 4QSam*ᵇ* spelled this specimen; but the survival of the archaic form in MT shows that the latter is not consistent, has not been uniformly updated to post-exilic norms. This points up the agreement (more than coincidence) of 4QSam*ᵇ* and MT in the spelling of this same word in verse 11. In fact three of the nine outliers due to over-use of *defective* spelling of this kind of word, as reported by Andersen and Forbes (**SHB** 248) are found in Samuel (two are in Kings, two in Jeremiah, one in Ezekiel; only one [Deuteronomy 1–7] outside the Former and Latter Prophets). It is no surprise that this archaic spelling does not occur with abnormally high frequency in any portion of the Writings, yet even so there are some interesting occurrences in Chronicles (Andersen and Forbes 1985). What is surprising is the rarity of this feature in the Torah. So in this detail the Former Prophets are more archaic than the Pentateuch, a reversal of the pattern found for most other spellings, and especially for those that involve ō. This means that the *plene* spelling found here in 4QSam*ᵇ*, while normal, is a little surprising. From the statistical point of view *defective* spelling *lhmtw would be quite characteristic of Samuel, even in MT. This detail restrains us from saying that 4QSam*ᵇ* is consistently and tenaciously archaic. It is not always as archaic as it might have been, even within Masoretic options.
27. 1 Sa 19:12 (2:3): **d]ẇd** = MT— This *defective* spelling of *David* is very important (Freedman 1983a). In contrast to the point made under No. 26 above, in the case of this word, the history of whose spelling is not matched by that of any other similar word in the

MT, 4QSam*^b* remains in step with MT in retaining the archaic form.

28. 1 Sa 19:12 (2:3): **b^c d** = MT— No other orthographic possibilities.

29. 1 Sa 19:12 (2:3): **hḥln**, MT **hḥlwn**— Here once again we have 4QSam*^b* sustaining the *defective* option for spelling ō, while MT has *plene*. The *plene* spelling is preferred in MT (2542 out of 4413 [**SHB** 198]). The five outliers reported by Andersen and Forbes due to over-use of *defective* spelling for this vowel, when stressed as in 1 Sa 19:12, are *all* in the Torah (**SHB** 274). It is important to emphasize this distribution. Once again 4QSam*^b* lines up with spellings characteristic of the Pentateuch in contrast to the rest of the MT, and in contrast to Samuel in MT, speaking broadly. This is evidence of a stage when the spelling of the entire Primary History was more uniform than it now is in MT. In MT the Pentateuch has not moved as far from this early state as the Former Prophets have done.

30. 1 Sa 19:13 (2:4): **bbgd** = MT— No other possibility.

31. 1 Sa 19:15 (2:5): **d]ẇd** = MT— See No. 27.

32. 1 Sa 19:15 (2:5): **l^ɔmr** = MT— Although it is conceivable that *plene* spelling could have been used, and would have fallen within the range of possibilities for MT (many such infinitives are spelled *plene* in MT), it would have been astonishing and unaccountable for such a spelling to have turned up in such an early MS as 4QSam*^b*. Of 945 occurrences of this word in MT, only three (in Ge 48:20; Je 18:5; 33:19) are *plene*, and they should be ascribed to much later (and very limited) drift in scribal copying. 4QSam*^b* is thus as expected.

33. 1 Sa 19:15 (2:5): **h^c lw** = MT— No other orthographic option. Standard spelling of terminal long –û with *waw*.

34. 1 Sa 19:16 (2:6): **mr^ɔš]tyw** = MT— Enough of this word is preserved to show that the significant part is spelled as in MT, i.e., with the pseudo-*plene yod* marking m. pl. suffixed nouns. The attestation of this spelling in 4QSam*^b* is of special interest in view of other indications that it is generally conservative. Our study will confirm that this is true in respect to the lack of any *plene* spelling of –ō– ← *–ā–, as already pointed out by Cross (1955: 165, n. 38) and highlighted by Freedman (1962: 98). But the same does not hold for the spelling of other vowels, or not so distinctively. The present case is special. The spelling of this suffix with –**w** rather than –**yw** is archaic. As discussed in Chapter 4 and in **SHB** (pp. 324–26), a considerable number of the older spellings survive in MT. So the use of the new spelling in 4QSam*^b* shows that it has moved with the times, at least at this point.

35. 1 Sa 19:17 (2:6): **wy^ɔmr** = MT— Cf. No. 7.

13.1.3   Fragments 3 and 4 (1 Sa 21:3–10)

36. 1 Sa 21:3 (3–4:1): ṣwyt]k̇— The basis of the reconstruction is min-
    imal, since only the tail of the *kaph* is legible. Cross restores from
    MT, but nothing can be said, and the very important question of
    the spelling of the suffix –tī (*defective* in MT!) must remain unan-
    swered, to our great disappointment. The spelling of the object
    suffix is standard; cf. Nos. 1, 5.

37. 1 Sa 21:5 (3–4:2): ẇ[y]ᶜn = MT— Standard.

38. 1 Sa 21:5 (3–4:2): hkhn = MT— This participial form is never
    spelled *plene* in MT. Since this word and derivatives occur 440
    times, it is statistically invariant and the spelling in 4QSam^b tells
    us nothing except that full Qumran spelling has not emerged, not
    a trace, which we would not have expected in any case.

39. 1 Sa 21:5 (3–4:2): ᵓt = MT— No comment.

40. 1 Sa 21:5 (3–4:3):]k = MT— A supralinear correction; the only
    orthographic option.

41. 1 Sa 21:5 (3–4:3): mᵓšh = MT— Standard spelling of terminal
    long –â with *he*.

42. 1 Sa 21:6 (3–4:3): wᵓkltm— Attested by **LXX**, lost from MT; of
    no orthographic interest.

43. 1 Sa 21:6 (3–4:3): mmnw— Not in MT; standard form.

44. 1 Sa 21:6 (3–4:4): wy]hyw = MT— Standard form; final long
    vowel spelled with vowel letter.

45. 1 Sa 21:6 (3–4:4): kl, MT kly— **LXX** shows that kl was under-
    stood as *all* as against MT *weapons, utensils*. We do not enter into
    the strictly textual question as to which of these two readings is
    more likely to be the parent reading of the other. Cross's argu-
    ment against MT is that the first occurrence of kly in it (= kl
    in 4QSam^b) "arose secondarily in anticipation of bkly below" (p.
    168). The second occurrence (and we don't know whether 4QSam^b
    agreed with MT here or with itself by reading kl once more) shows
    that the question is the holiness of the soldiers' equipment. All
    this talk is quite mysterious to us, since we don't know how the
    sacral status of their *weapons* determined their eligibility to eat
    the sacred bread. Both factors are linked with sexual contact with
    women, and this opens the possibility that the soldiers' equipment
    would be desacralized by contagion if that happened. It could be
    precisely the difficulty that we still have in making sense of the
    word kly that prompted its replacement by the quite uncompli-
    cated kl of 4QSam^b. If this is the explanation of the variant, then
    we do not always have to suppose or assume that 4QSam^b is always
    better (more original) than MT when the two are different. In any

case, its reading **kl** agrees with Masoretic usage which shows no trace of the *plene* spelling characteristic of Qumran, except for one *ktyb* (Je 33:8). One could not imagine **kwl** in 4QSam^b.

46. 1 Sa 21:6 (3–4:4): **hn^crym** = MT— Standard spelling of the m. pl. ending, post-exilic, very rare in earlier inscriptions.

47. 1 Sa 21:6 (3–4:4): **qdš** = MT— It is doubtful if the stem vowel (**u**) had lengthened at this point in time. *Plene* spelling of the eventual long –ō– is not to be expected, since only one such spelling of this vowel in such words is found in the received MT (two in **L**).

48. 1 Sa 21:6 (3–4:4): **whwɔ**— Standard.

49. 1 Sa 21:7 (3–4:5): **p]nym** = MT— The long vowel of the m. pl. ending is spelled *plene*, standard in post-exilic orthography. Cf. No. 46.

50. 1 Sa 21:7 (3–4:5): **hmwsr**— MT has **hmwsrym**, which implies a collective meaning for **lhm**. Cf. collective **ɔšh** in this same passage (v 4). MT is not necessarily ungrammatical, as declared by Cross (p. 168), since loaves are clearly implied, and the noun itself is never pluralized. In any case interest focuses on the use of *waw*. Here the recensions agree, and the spelling is standard and historical. Accepting MT as a safe guide, the vowel in question is –û–, which in this MS is always spelled *plene*.

51. 1 Sa 21:7 (3–4:5): **lpny** = MT— Standard.

52. 1 Sa 21:7 (3–4:5): **yhẇ[h** = MT— No comment.

53. 1 Sa 21:8 (3–4:6): **ɔšr** = MT— No comment.

54. 1 Sa 21:9 (3–4:7): **byd]y** = MT— No comment.

55. 1 Sa 21:9 (3–4:7): **ky** = MT— Cf. No. 14.

56. 1 Sa 21:9 (3–4:7): **hyh** = MT— Standard spelling of terminal long –â with *he*.

57. 1 Sa 21:10 (3–4:8): **ɔhr**, MT **ɔhry**— Here it is a matter of different words, not different spellings of the same word. The shorter form of the preposition is acceptable, although rare in MT. A mild suggestion arises as to whether a different meaning is intended, since it is not clear why the trophy should be stored *behind* the ephod. In any case it is out of the question that in 4QSam^b **ɔhr** is intended as an alternative spelling of **ɔahărê**, since it would be unparalleled (in a text otherwise so impeccable in its spelling) to have a word with a terminal long vowel (let alone diphthong) undeclared by the appropriate vowel letter.

58. 1 Sa 21:9 (3–4:8): **ɔpd**, MT **hɔpwd**— There are two differences here. 4QSam^b is textually inferior in the lack of the article, orthographically more archaic in its lack of the vowel letter. The word *ephod* occurs 49 times in MT and the balance between *defective* (×25) and *plene* (×24) is almost even for the whole corpus. We

are using **L** (B19^a) as our witness to MT in this exercise, and it needs to be remembered that the orthographic fidelity of this MS is open to some doubt. In the present case it happens that the great Rabbinic Bible also presents eight *plene* spellings of ꜣēpōd in the Torah, but they are not the same as those in **L**! See Ex 28:27 (last occurrence) and Ex 28:28 (first occurrence). Yet even when we allow for indeterminacy of this kind, the overall distribution is not at all even.

Portion	*Defective*	*Plene*	Total
Torah	23	8	31
Former Prophets	2	14	16
Remainder	0	2	2
Total	25	24	49

Nothing could be clearer. The trend to *plene* spelling has made some headway in the Pentateuch, but the older *defective* spelling has held out strongly against it. The opposite has happened in the rest of the MT. Only two of the occurrences (both *plene*) occur outside the Primary History, in Ho 3:4 and 1 Ch 15:27. Clearly there was no interest in ephod traditions after the Exile; no new texts containing this word were composed. In the Former Prophets the *defective* spelling has survived only in 1 Sa 30:7, in a fragment of an early source. If we had only MT, we might have inferred from the use of *plene* spelling in the rest of the Primary History (Judges and Samuel) that the later spelling reflects late composition or at least editing. The evidence of 4QSam^b rules out any such hypothesis. It attests a recension or text-type of Samuel in which the *defective* spelling was used. And since, as we shall see when this march-past is complete, 4QSam^b never spells ō ← ā *plene*, we can assume that every occurrence of ꜣēpōd in the complete MS of which 4QSam^b is the sad remains was *defective*. This is the original spelling in the archetypical Samuel. 4QSam^b contains a survival of that spelling, not an archaizing correction from a text which was like the prototype of MT in this detail.

13.1.4 Fragments 5, 6, 7 (1 Sa 23:9–17)

59. 1 Sa 23:9 (5–7:1): š꜓wl = MT— Standard spelling, never *defective*. This word is the result of erasure and insertion, perhaps due to a later attempt to "correct" 4QSam^b nearer to MT. If that were all, its evidence could not be used with confidence for the orthographic character of the original 4QSam^b. But in any case the word occurs a few more times in this fragment (first hand), so the *plene* spelling is assured.

60. 1 Sa 23:10 (5–7:1): ^{c}**lyw** = MT— Standard spelling; note the use of the redundant marker *yod*.

61. 1 Sa 23:10 (5–7:2): **mḥryš** = MT— Full (post-exilic) spelling of word-medial long –ī–. See No. 26.

62. 1 Sa 23:10 (5–7:2): **hr̊[^{c}h** = MT—As far as the word can be read, it agrees with MT. It is of no orthographic consequence.

63. 1 Sa 23:10 (5–7:2): **š]ṁ^c** = MT— It is a pity that the preceding infinitive absolute has not been preserved, for it would be of great interest to know how this word was spelled in 4QSam^b, since MT is *defective*. This happens to be the preferred spelling, but not strongly so (245 out of 424 [**SHB** 193]). It is worth noting that 1 Samuel is one of only two outliers reported by Andersen and Forbes for over-use of the historically earlier *defective* spelling of *qal* infinitive absolute (the other is Jeremiah 33–52) (**SHB** 266). Note also that Joshua is the only portion reported as an outlier for over-use of *plene* spellings of such words. This means that 1 Samuel and Jeremiah 33–52 stand aside from the rest of MT as the most archaic in respect to this orthographic feature. Even the Torah has been adjusted to the general mix of *defective* and *plene*. As a token that each book can go its own way in the spelling of particular classes of words or vowel types, as well as individual words, we note that Joshua and 1 Samuel have gone in opposite directions in their treatment of *qal* infinitive absolute. All nine are *plene* in Joshua, only six of the 21 in 1 Samuel. The spelling **šm^c** in MT 1 Sa 23:10 is thus characteristic of that tradition. So, even if the word had been available in 4QSam^b, a *defective* spelling would have been a salutary reminder that we should not exaggerate the orthographic differences between 4QSam^b and MT, since the latter can also be quite conservative in some details, while 4QSam^b comes from a MS tradition that has undergone a considerable amount of updating of spelling to post-exilic standards. So we cannot assume from the absence of *waw* to spell –ō– in what remains of 4QSam^b that this MS never used *waw* in this way. Here the evidence of 4QJer^a (ca. 200 BCE) is important, for it is consistently *plene* in the spelling of –ō– in *qal* infinitives absolute (×3—no corresponding evidence from 4QSam^b) and consistently *defective* in spelling the –ō– in *qal* active participles (×6—like the two in 4QSam^b, Nos. 6, 38).

64. 1 Sa 23:10 (5–7:2): ^{c}**bdk** = MT— Once more the standard spelling of the suffix –**ak**, not –**kā**.

65. 1 Sa 23:10 (5–7:2): **ky** = MT— Cf. No. 14.

66. 1 Sa 23:10 (5–7:2): **mbqš** = MT— No comment.

67. 1 Sa 23:10 (5–7:2): **š^{ɔ}wl** = MT— Cf. No. 59.

68. 1 Sa 23:11 (5–7:3): ^{ɔ}**lhy** = MT— Standard spelling; *plene* spelling of –ō– as found at Qumran never intrudes into Masoretic MSS.

69. 1 Sa 23:11 (5–7:3): **yśr‌ᵓl** = MT— Standard, no orthographic options.

70. 1 Sa 23:11 (5–7:3): **hgydh**, MT **hgd-nᵓ**— Now here is something really interesting from the textual point of view. The Masoretes have, of course, punctuated the *defective* imperative of MT as proclitic—**hagged**. Cross has shown that the variant in 4QSam*ᵇ* lies behind **LXX**; but the decision as to which of the variants represents the original is more nuanced. This same passage contains **hgyš̌h** (v 9). Note the standard spelling of the long terminal vowel. But MT is quite mixed in its spelling of –ī– in *hiph‌ᶜil* stems.

Verse	MT	4QSam*ᵇ*
9	**m̧hryš̌** (*p.*)	= **m̧hryš̌**
9	**hgyš̌h** (*p.*)	missing
11	**hysgrny** (*d.*)	missing
12	**hysgrw** (*d.*)	missing
12	**ysgyrw** (*p.*)	**ys[**

MT has clearly been arrested in mid-flight between pre-exilic *defective* spelling and standard post-exilic *plene* spelling of this vowel. So far as the evidence of 4QSam*ᵇ* goes (it is meager), 4QSam*ᵇ* is more modernized, or at least not more archaic, than MT in this particular, since it does not present a single instance of *defective* spelling of long ī.

71. 1 Sa 23:11 (5–7:3): **l‌ᶜbd[k** = MT— We assume, in light of all other extant specimens, that the missing suffix was –k, not –kh.

72. 1 Sa 23:12 (5–7:4): **š‌ᵓ]wl** = MT— Standard; cf. No. 59.

73. 1 Sa 23:12 (5–7:4): **wy‌ᵓmr** = MT— Standard; cf. No. 7.

74. 1 Sa 23:12 (5–7:4): **yhwh** = MT— Standard; cf. No. 20.

75. 1 Sa 23:12 (5–7:4): **ys[** = MT(?)— The vital question of the spelling of the stem vowel cannot be settled. Perhaps it is unwise to restore from MT, as Cross does, even though all the indications are that the spelling would have been *plene*.

76. 1 Sa 23:13 (5–7:5): **n]mlt̩** = MT— No comment.

77. 1 Sa 23:13 (5–7:5): **d[wd** = MT— We may take it as certain that the old *defective* spelling was consistently used.

78. 1 Sa 23:13 (5–7:5): **mq̇‌ᶜylh** = MT— Cross reports that the vital *yod* is legible. The spelling of this toponym in MT fluctuates between *defective* and *plene*, and the allocations vary from MS to MS. Thus **L** has two *defective* in this chapter (vv 3, 13), and even has a Masoretic note to that effect (Mm 1656). The Rabbinic Bible has **q‌ᶜlh** at the end of verse 5, with a masora to confirm that there are three such cases. In verse 13, however, both specimens are spelled

plene in the Rabbinic Bible, *contra* **L**. The point to be made is that
it was difficult for a minority of surviving archaic spellings to hold
out against leveling all to standard spelling. 4QSam^b shows that
the *plene* spelling is already in place in the third century BCE,
but with only one specimen surviving in the fragments of 4QSam^b
we cannot say whether any of the others were still *defective* or
whether they were the same ones that survived more than one
thousand years of further copying into the MSS on which modern
editions are based. In view of that survival, we must register mild
surprise that 4QSam^b is modern in this detail.

79. 1 Sa 23:14 (5–7:6): **wl³** = MT— *Plene* spelling is standard at
    Qumran; possible, but rare in MT. Details in **SHB** (pp. 186–88).
    1 Samuel 21–31 is reported by Andersen and Forbes (**SHB** 262) as
    an outlier with abnormal over-use of the *plene* spelling option (even
    though the one we are studying here is *defective* in MT), along
    with other portions of both Former and Latter Prophets. While
    it is no surprise that Torah prefers *defective* spelling (Mm 681 has
    only two instances of *plene* in Torah), it is a little unexpected that
    plene spelling of this word is rather rare in the Writings. At the
    same time it should be emphasized that there is probably no other
    word whose spelling in individual cases varies between MS and MS
    as much as this word. Even so, the *defective* spelling in 4QSam^b is
    expected, whereas a *plene* spelling at this point would have dras-
    tically altered our whole assessment of the orthographic character
    of this MS.

80. 1 Sa 23:14 (5–7:6): **ntnẇ** = MT— If the incomplete letter is cor-
    rectly read as *waw*, we have further evidence, along with Nos. 13,
    26, 84, that the old spelling of word-terminal –ō with *he* has been
    abandoned by this time. Of the 55 cases which survive in MT of
    –ōh, only one (2 Sa 2:9) occurs in Samuel (Torah ×13; Former
    Prophets ×8; Latter Prophets ×30!!; Writings ×3).

81. 1 Sa 23:14 (5–7:6): **yh[wh**— MT ³**lhym**, here and in v 16. 4QSam^b
    agrees with **LXX**. Of no orthographic consequence.

82. 1 Sa 23:15 (5–7:7): **lb]q̇š** = MT— No comment.

83. 1 Sa 23:15 (5–7:7): ³**t** = MT— Cf. No. 11.

84. 1 Sa 23:15 (5–7:7): **npšw** = MT— Post-exilic standard spelling of
    the suffix pronoun; cf. Nos. 13, 26, 43, 80.

85. 1 Sa 23:15 (5–7:7): **wd[wd** = MT— No comment.

86. 1 Sa 23:16 (5–7:7): **wẏlk** = MT— No comment.

87. 1 Sa 23:16 (5–7:7): ³**l** = MT— No comment.

88. 1 Sa 23:17 (5–7:8): **wy³mr** = MT— Cf. Nos. 7, 35.

89. 1 Sa 23:17 (5–7:8): ³**lyw** = MT— Cf. No. 5.

90. 1 Sa 23:17 (5–7:8): ³**ỉ** = MT— No comment.

13.2 Summary

13.2.1 Invariant Spellings

Of the ninety words or word fragments studied, twenty-eight (Nos. 2, 3, 10, 11, 12, 15, 18, 37, 39, 40, 42, 52, 53, 54, 57, 62, 63, 66, 69, 71, 76, 79, 81, 82, 83, 86, 87, 90) contribute nothing to this study, either because they presented the scribe with no spelling options or because the portions of such words which would have disclosed the scribes' choice have not been preserved. Such words, of course, match MT exactly and could hardly have been otherwise.

13.2.2 Standard Spellings

Interest focuses rather on those words which presented a scribe with an opportunity to make a choice within the range of options attested by MT and known to be in vogue when this MS was produced. Here the first point to be made is an important one, albeit a negative one. All of the optional spellings found in 4QSam^b lie within the range of Masoretic usage. In fact it contains no spellings which are not found somewhere or other in MT. And we can even say that it contains no spellings which are rare in MT. So a superficial reading would suggest that the orthography of this MS is of no great interest and cannot be made the basis of arguments or inferences. Yet, insofar as there is nothing un-Masoretic about the spellings in 4QSam^b, we can infer that the Masoretic system and set of spelling rules were firmly in place in all principles and particulars by the third century BCE. This tells against the claim, often made, that the spelling system was not finalized and stabilized until the Masoretic Text as such was fixed in the first or even the second century CE.

13.2.3 Spellings in 4QSam^b

4QSam^b follows standard practice in writing all terminal vowels with a vowel letter.

1. Note, however, that any letter can sustain its primal function of representing a consonant sound at the end of a word. In the present instance *yod* (Nos. 17, 23) and *waw* (Nos. 34, 60, 89).

2. Word-terminal *waw* is a vowel letter for –û (Nos. 33, 43, 44), and –û is always written that way.

3. Word-terminal *waw* is now used consistently for the suffix –ô, *his*, previously written with *he* (Nos. 26, 80, 84). We know from the book of Ezekiel that this practice remained in vogue in the sixth

century. The evidence of 4QSam*b* is therefore important for showing that the changeover was complete by the third century BCE.
We cannot do any better than this in dating this important development more precisely within the fifth-fourth centuries, for this
period is void of the needed documentation for Hebrew.

4. Word-terminal *yod* represents –î and –î is always written that way:
Nos. 8, 14, 55, 65.

5. Word-terminal *yod* also represents –ê, contracted from –ay: Nos. 5,
25, 51, 68.

6. Word-terminal *he* represents –â, and –â is always so written: Nos.
41, 56, 70, 78. Note that *aleph* is never so used.

7. Word-terminal *he* can also represent the vowel –e, at least in the later
traditional vocalization of the Masoretes: Nos. 6, 20, 74.

8. Note that the traditional pronunciation of the 2nd. m. sg. suffix
as –kā finds no support in 4QSam*b*. In every case the spelling is
–k, not –kh: Nos. 1, 5, 36, 64. The same option dominates MT,
where only 38 out of 7073 occurrences of this suffix are spelled
–kh. It is true that the Masoretes uniformly read both these
spellings as –kā, overriding the information preserved in the traditional spelling without *he*. It is invalid to impose their decision on
ancient texts, and to suppose the same pronunciation for 4QSam*b*
and then to use this spelling without *he* as evidence that all word-
terminal vowels were not necessarily written with vowel letters. If
word-terminal –â as such could be written either way, i.e., with or
without *he*, we have to explain why *he* is never used with –k, *thee,
thy,* and always used with every known –â–. See 6 above.

9. Turning now to the writing of word-medial vowels, we note first the
fact that no short vowel is ever represented by a vowel letter while
vowel letters *may* be used to represent internal long vowels.

10. Long –û– is spelled with *waw* in every instance in 4QSam*b*: Nos.
48, 50, 59, 67, 72. The specimens are not impressive, since three
are š^ɔwl, which has invariant spelling in all attestations, and one
is hw^ɔ, likewise invariant in all biblical occurrences. The fifth is
No. 50, **hmwsr**, likewise invariant in MT, although some words of
this phonetic shape do have *defective* spelling of –û–. Here then
4QSam*b* is not archaic, and its use of standard Masoretic *plene*
spelling of this vowel shows that this policy was in place by 200
BCE at the latest.

11. Long –î– is routinely spelled with *yod* in 4QSam*b*, with one significant exception, to be discussed in the next paragraph. Examples:
Nos. 26, 61 (*hiph^cils*), 46, 49 (m. pl.), 19, 78 (proper noun). In MT
the *defective* spelling of such words is less common, but common

enough to be accepted as within the range of "normal" biblical options. The *defective* spelling of –ī– in such words is always archaic, and so the absence of such spellings from 4QSam*ᵇ* is another sign that the spelling of this vowel in the stream of text transmission represented by this MS has been fully adjusted to post-exilic preferences.

12. The one exception is *David*, fully preserved only once (No. 27), but there is no reason to doubt that it was **dwd** in all occurrences (Nos. 31, 77, 85), since even MT Samuel preserves this old spelling in every case (Freedman 1983a).

13. A special note is required for the spelling of the suffix –āw, *his*, on m. pl. nouns and on prepositions with –**yw**: Nos. 34, 60, 89. On first sight this spelling is a commonplace, and calls for no remarks. The orthography is standard, and over two thousand specimens are found in MT.

Even so, the uniform attestation of this spelling in 4QSam*ᵇ* is very revealing for the history of Hebrew spelling and for the scribal history of Old Testament texts.

i. The spelling of the suffix –āw with **yw** is unique within the system and quite out of line with all other rules and usages. Phonetically the *yod* is a cipher, representing no sound at all if the Masoretic vocalization is correct; and there is no explanation for its introduction in terms of historical phonology. If *his words* is d*ᵉ*bārāw, then **dbrw** is correct consonantal representation, indistinguishable from the spelling of singular d*ᵉ*bārô, *his word.*

ii. Such a spelling is the only one attested in pre-exilic sources; but this did not then cause confusion or ambiguity with the singular, for d*ᵉ*bārô was then spelled **dbrh**.

iii. The changeovers from **dbrh** to **dbrw** for sg. and from **dbrw** to **dbryw** for pl. are different in principle from all the other developments which brought about such a great difference between pre-exilic and post-exilic Hebrew spelling. In all other cases there was nothing really new about the rules; it was just that they were applied more widely and on an ever-increasing scale. The end result would have been the spelling of *all* long vowels by means of vowel letters. The MT never arrived at this saturation point. In a sense, the new spelling of *his word* as **dbrw** rather than **dbrh** was no more than an extension of the use of *waw*, which was already in use to spell word-medial –ō–, to the spelling of word-terminal –ô. But in doing so the former practice, using *he*, was abandoned. The

introduction of *yod* into the spelling of **d^{e}bārāw**, *his words*,
was also an innovation, based on neither phonetic principle
nor on historical spelling (at least not directly—it arose from
paradigmatic analogy from other m. pl. forms in which the
yod was historical spelling of a diphthong). We suspect that
these two innovations were closely related, that the use of the
yod with plural nouns was introduced precisely to resolve the
ambiguity otherwise created when **dbrw** made singular and
plural graphically indistinguishable. As already hinted, we
suspect further that the *yod* was introduced by analogy with
other plural forms in which it functions either as a vowel letter
(representing –î– in the absolute) or as a consonant (in the
diphthong ending of construct and suffixed forms). Yet it is
silent in **dbryw**, *his words*, a function unique in the system.
It is simply a marker of the plural stem as such.

iv. This double changeover is one of the most complete and thor-
ough of all the revisions of Hebrew spelling made after the
Exile. Our suspicion that the two changes were concomitant
is supported by the distribution—**dbrh** and **dbrw** in early
inscriptions, **dbrw** and **dbryw** in standard spelling. The
question could be settled otherwise if we found texts from the
transition period (fifth-fourth centuries BCE) which had one
of the new spellings, but not the other. We know of no such
evidence. When we begin to get Hebrew texts with 4QSam^b,
it has both new spellings, and only those. At the same time
we should recognize that there are a few survivors in MT—55
cases of *his* spelled with *he*, and about 180 with only *waw* for
plural or preposition. In both instances the provision of *qry*
with the more modern option seeks to complete the modernization, but MSS vary widely in their resort to this device.

v. We don't know when this double switch of –**h** to –**w** and of –**w**
to –**yw** took place, but the evidence of the book of Ezekiel
shows that the old spellings were still in vogue in the sixth
century BCE. 4QSam^b contains the earliest specimens of these
new spellings known to us, and it uses them consistently. We
can infer, therefore, that the reform was complete by the third
century, and took place sometime during the fifth or fourth
centuries. This is only one of many indicators of major over-
haul of biblical texts during that period, and tradition asso-
ciates this with the career of Ezra, and with the adoption of
the square (Aramaic) character. It should be pointed out,
however, that Aramaic orthography does not provide models
for these two changes, which are peculiar to Hebrew.

vi. It is a little surprising to find this change complete in such an old MS as 4QSam^b, and the more so in a MS of Samuel, which even in MT preserves a remarkable number of specimens of pre-exilic orthography, and notably the old spelling of suffixed m. pl. nouns with –**w**, not –**yw**. About twenty such spellings in 1 Samuel alone evoke marginal *qry* in **L**. The exact number of such survivors for the entire MT is not known, and cannot be known. First, because words like **dbrw** are ambiguous; and, while many if not most can be resolved by grammatical connections in context (most commonly by agreement with singular or plural verb, adjective, pronoun nearby), many remain ambiguous, unless arbitrarily resolved by decisions of scribes, first by adding *yod* to those thought to be plural and eventually by supplying the appropriate differentiating vowel points. It is therefore possible, and indeed likely, that many singulars have been wrongly marked by *yod* as plural, and that many plurals are still masquerading in MT as wrongly identified singulars. At this late hour we have little choice but to accept the decisions of early scribes and later Masoretes, since in most dubious cases either reading makes perfectly good sense. There is no reason, however, to be cynical. 4QSam^b shows that this was all over and done with by the third century, and we must grant that the scribes who did this were still so close to the living tradition of oral knowledge of the true readings that there was not much guesswork in their decisions.

vii. Keeping these limitations in mind we may none the less trace the parallel history of the spelling of such word pairs as *his word* and *his words* through five stages, each of which has contributed a stratum of readings to MT. (a) Up through the sixth century BCE and possibly into the fifth, the spellings were **dbrh** and **dbrw**, respectively, consistently and with no known exceptions. (b) Massive revision of these spellings with almost complete replacement of **dbrh** by **dbrw** and of **dbrw** by **dbryw** took place some time in the fifth century, or in the fourth at the latest. (c) The changeover was complete by the third century, and the older spellings were no longer considered to be scribal options, unless by deliberate archaizing. At the same time the text was fixed, so that any survivors (**dbrh** and **dbrw**, respectively for sg. and pl.) were copied faithfully from then on, and so preserved until this day. (d) With a fixed consonantal text, all that could be done with such survivors is to resolve their ambiguity (the suffix on **dbrh** could be taken

as feminine; the stem of **dbrw** could be sg. or pl.) by means
of marginal *qry*, **dbrw** for **dbrh** to show that the suffix is
masculine, not feminine; **dbryw** for **dbrw** to show that the
stem is plural, not singular. We find 97 cases of the latter
in **L**, and five cases of the ending $-\bar{\text{a}}$**w** without *qry*. They
are **mdlyw** (Nu 24:7), **hyw** (2 Ki 25:30; Je 52:33; Qo 5:17),
w^cnyw (Is 49:13). See Mm 1811. **L** has *qry* at Qo 5:17 and
a spurious one at 2 Sa 18:18. When we observe that **hyyw**
of 2 Ki 25:19 matches **hyw** of Je 52:33 and that **hyw** of 2
Ki 25:30 matches **hyyw** of Je 52:34 (neither with *qry*), there
can be no doubt that both words were **hyw** originally. In all
these instances adoption of the later spelling could have been
restrained by avoidance of **-yy-**, but the restraint was not absolute, and the texts remained in flux. (e) This kind of touching up seems to have been done casually, for the MSS and editions are in wide disagreement at these points. For example,
the Rabbinic Bible spells *his tent* **ᵓhlh** at Ge 26:25, where **L**
has **ᵓhlw**. Most MSS have *ktyb/qry* for **bᵓlpw/bᵓlpyw** in
1 Sa 29:6, but **L** has only the latter; i.e., the traditional *qry*
has supplanted the archaic and textually superior *ktyb* in this
instance.

viii. As a result of this long and complex history, a word like **dbrw**
has five possible significations in MT:

a. correctly identified and vocalized sg.;

b. plural wrongly identified as sg.;

c. singular wrongly vocalized as (defectively spelled) pl.;

d. defectively spelled pl. correctly vocalized, but without *qry*;

e. the same, but with *qry*.

Thus there remains a considerable amount of uncertainty in
the reading of such words, and this uncertainty is reflected in
MSS. One should also note a backlash from the perfection of
the Tiberian vocalization, which rendered the supply of the
full spelling as *qry* unnecessary in a vocalized text, since, unlike most other *ktyb*'s, the vowels fit either set of consonants
equally well, with no difference in meaning.

ix. Keeping in mind all the differences among Masoretic MSS in
this matter, it is still possible to say something about the
general distribution of the surviving older spellings. They are
rare in the Torah, as if that section has been carefully and
thoroughly revised, updated, and maintained. Samuel has
more than its share, and its high score is a conspicuous survival of an archaic feature in a text which otherwise, at least

in MT, has been handled carelessly by scribes and suffered severe textual injuries somewhere along the way. Most important for our purpose is the relatively large number of such spellings still to be found in Ezekiel. This shows, or at least suggests, that the old spellings continued in use well into the sixth century. Their rarity in Chronicle–Ezra–Nehemiah and in the Writings generally points to the fifth century as the time of revision. 4QSam^b shows no trace of the old spellings. When we try to locate its spelling in this historical development, in so far as we have been able to reconstruct it, we can conclude that 4QSam^b, while old and doubtless deriving from some earlier exemplar (since it represents an authoritative text type which served as *Vorlage* for **LXX**), does not permit the existence of its distinctive text type to be projected very far back in time. The differences in readings between 4QSam^b and MT are more substantial and spectacular than the differences in spelling. The latter, in fact, are quite few. From the point of view of orthography, 4QSam^b is in the same tradition as MT and proves the early existence of that spelling tradition. It bears the same marks of the great revision that took place in the fifth century.

x. An additional inference can be made from this conclusion. The catastrophe that made the ancestral text of Samuel in MT textually inferior to the type of text which survives in **LXX** and whose Hebrew *Vorlage* is now attested in 4QSam^b must have happened after the normalization of orthography which they share, i.e., after the fifth century BCE, but before the third century BCE, the date of 4QSam^b.

14. The inconsistency of MT in the spelling of word-internal long $-\bar{o}-$ either *defective* or *plene* is *not* found in 4QSam^b, which has not one case of *plene* spelling of this vowel. In one instance (No. 6) the word does not occur in MT. In five cases the *plene* option for $-\bar{o}-$ is not a Masoretic option (Nos. 4, 7, 38, 47, 73). In three instances 4QSam^b agrees with MT in *defective* spelling, but the *plene* option is rarely used for such words in MT in any case (Nos. 21, 32, 79). There are four cases in which MT has *plene* against *defective* of 4QSam^b (Nos. 9, 13, 29, 58). (Freedman [1962] adds ṯhr, not attested in the fragment published by Cross.) These, in fact, are the only words which 4QSam^b spells differently from MT. The number is small, but the picture is consistent. 4QSam^b shows no trace of the influence of the trend to *plene* spelling of $-\bar{o}-$ which has left its mark in varying degrees across MT, which has taken only partial hold on MT, and which comes to full expression in the consistently *plene* spelling of this vowel in Qumran texts, especially those produced by the Covenanters themselves (Tov 1986).

13.3 Conclusions

1. 4QSam^b does not preserve a single instance of *distinctively* pre-exilic spelling.
2. In its spelling of all long vowels, except for –ō–, the practice in 4QSam^b is identical with that of MT. We see this solidarity as the result of the revisions in spelling made to biblical texts in the fifth century BCE.
3. That revision did not include the provision of a vowel letter for –ō–, since 4QSam^b has not one example.
4. Since 4QSam^b resembles MT in *plene* spelling of ū and ī, and in the –yw spelling of –āw, but stands aside from MT in the spelling of –ō– (4QSam^b *defective*, MT *plene*), we conclude that the latter practice came in after the former. In every instance the vowel in question is primally long, whether from *ā or *aw, so this feature is different from the delay in the use of the vowel letter to spell ō ← *u, which has made the least headway of all in MT (**SHB** 200). It is precisely in the use or nonuse of *waw* for ō that MT itself shows the widest variation and instability (**SHB** 162), in contrast to its almost uniform use of *waw* for û and even more of *yod* for î. It seems as if this use of *waw* for û and of *yod* for î was imposed by authority (it was also of long standing), while the use of *waw* for ō remained more open. 4QSam^b bears the impress of the former, but totally lacks the latter. 4QSam^b thus marks the watershed, and suggests that whereas the changeover from pre-exilic to post-exilic spelling of û and î was deliberate, systematic, and official, and took place before the third century, the spelling of –ō– with *waw* remained arbitrary, and did not manifest itself fully until after the third century.

Chapter 14

The Orthography of 4QTestimonia

Francis I. Andersen & David Noel Freedman

14.1   Introduction

A recent study by Tov (1986) has drawn attention in detail to the peculiarities of the spellings in certain MSS found at Qumran in contrast to the orthography used in mainstream biblical MSS. As for Hebrew spelling in the Masoretic tradition, Andersen and Forbes (1986) have provided systematic information which assists us in determining whether and how much a MS of a biblical text departs from the normal patterns in its spellings. One of the issues is whether spelling "rules" were already in place, at least for prestigious texts, even before rabbinic times, possibly as a result of the standardization of orthographic practice in association with the publication of definitive editions under influential patronage.

In this study we shall look at the spelling of each word in one Qumran MS (4QTestim = 4Q175) to find out how it matches the general biblical practice. For the sake of control we shall confine our study to those portions of lines 1–20 of 4QTestim which are transcriptions of canonical texts, that is Deut 5:28–29; 18:18–19; Num 24:15–17; Deut 33:8–11. The remainder (lines 21–30) is a midrash on Josh 6:26 and precise comparison with biblical sources is not possible. The text chosen (4QTestim) offers the possibility of comparing its spelling with standard Hebrew spelling (SHS) on the one hand and with sectarian Qumran spelling (SQS) on the other, for it consists of biblical passages arranged in a catena, presumably to serve some special purpose. It is not possible for us to assess the "canonical" status of such a derivative text in the minds of its producers. Did they still think that these quotations were part of "the Bible," or did separating them from their contexts, threading them together in a new composition, and especially associating them with a non-biblical midrash diminish the influence of authority and so give scope for some freedom, particularly in spelling? The possible messianic interests of the compiler were considered by Allegro in the *editio princeps* (1956) and have been discussed by Amusin (1971) and Fitzmyer (1971) among others. Textual deviations from MT which might be attributed to such motivation are not of direct concern in the present study, as our purpose is to locate the orthographic profile of 4QTestim in the larger picture. At the conclusion of his study, Tov (1986: 49) labels 4QTestim a "sectarian composition," with some of its most distinctive peculiarities summarized in his Table 1 (p. 50). The document is unique, so we do not know whether the scribe of this MS was also the author of the composition or merely its copyist; we do not know whether the changes from MT in both wording and spelling were made at the time of compilation or during subsequent transmission. Such questions are rendered even more intriguing in light of an observation made by Allegro that the same scribe wrote 4QTestim and 1QS (DJD V, p. 58, n.).

14.2   Procedure

In the following discussion we identify each word by a number as well as its location (line and position) in the MS. Its orthographic features are indicated by the following code:

A. The word is identical with MT.

B. Spelled differently from MT but evidently the same.

C. Spelled differently from MT but similar enough to be taken as a variant of the same word.

D. Spelled so differently from MT that a quite different word must be identified.

E. Not present in the source MT.

In some cases we need to differentiate further:

a. Words with biblical spelling.

b. Non-biblical spelling of a word that is nevertheless the same as the matching biblical word.

c. Words with no biblical counterpart.

14.3   Inventory: Deuteronomy 5:28–29

1. וידבר (1:1). Da. MT ויאמר. While 4QTestim diverges from MT at this point, the reading וידבר is SHS: **waydabbēr** ← *wayadabbir. In this instance we can point to three different kinds of short vowels: a) short vowel that is reduced to shewa in open, unaccented syllable and then to zero by special rule, –**ya**– → –**yĕ**– → –**y**–; b) short vowel that is preserved in closed, unaccented syllable, **way**–, –**dab**–; c) short vowel that is lengthened under the tone in a closed, accented syllable, –**bēr** ← –**bir**. The shift from –i– → –ē– may involve only a change of vowel position without lengthening, or the lengthening may be intermediate. Whether the changes reflected in Tiberian vocalization had already taken place by the time the Qumran MSS were written or whether the primal vowels as postulated by phonological theory still remained, the important point is that in normal Qumran spelling, no vowel letters are used to represent any of the vowels in this word. The importance of this word for Qumran orthography can hardly be exaggerated. It is precisely because no vowel letters are used, here or elsewhere, for **a**, or **ē** from **i**, that we can affirm the essential congruity of Qumran spelling with SHS in the spelling of such vowels.

2. ‥‥ (1:2). B. MT יהוה. A writing of the Tetragram found in other Qumran texts. Cf. No. 157.

3. אל (1:3). Da. MT אלי. The change is due to the paraphrase, which transposes from first to third person. 4QTestim has אל מושה . The short vowel is preserved in the closed (unaccented) syllable and is not indicated in the orthography.

4. מושה (1:4). Eb. MT משה is always *defective; plene* is standard in Qumran sectarian texts (details in Tov 1986: Table 1). The four-letter spelling reflects the representation of –ō– in the first syllable. Such spelling of the vowel –ō– with *waw* is in line with biblical practice, the more so in the case of this word, since it resembles the *qal* participle, in which –ō– is often spelled with *waw*,

especially at Qumran. In the case of this word, whatever the true history of its derivation, the spelling in MT should be regarded as archaic (pre-exilic and perhaps early post-exilic) spelling preserved as the standard spelling throughout the Scriptures. While the Qumran spelling of this word could be regarded as a normal development in later Hebrew spelling, the Qumran community seems to have been the only group that adopted it systematically. Contrast the spelling of the name *David* (Freedman 1983a). In MT two different spellings are preserved: דוד (three-letter spelling) is found in Samuel and Kings primarily, while the later four-letter spelling דויד is found in the Chronicler's work and routinely at Qumran. The two names have been handled differently; in the case of *David* we find the optional use of the vowel letter for the medial long vowel in later portions of the Bible and at Qumran; in the case of *Moses* the fuller spelling was used only at Qumran. In later practice the archaic form for *Moses* remained standard, while the later form for *David* became standard.

5. לאמור (1:5). Eb. The addition is required by the change of initial ויאמר to וידבר. In MT לאמר is standard for this word (×945 out of ×948). *Plene* spelling of this vowel, however, is quite common in MT for other infinitives of this type (19%—**SHB**, p. 195), with Qohelet and 2 Chronicles as the extreme outliers (Type 43 on page 58 of this volume). The *plene* spelling is predominant at Qumran. The *waw* represents –ō–, probably from an original –u–. The tone-lengthened vowel is reflected in the orthography. The frequent occurrence of the *plene* spelling of this vowel in other infinitives in MT shows that the development at Qumran is part of the mainstream evolution of Hebrew spelling and not eccentric. MT spelling generally reflects an earlier state of orthography, while SQS reflects a later stage for the most part. The development is לאמור ← לאמר and is perfectly regular.

6. שמעת (1:6). Ca. MT שמעתי. The change from *I heard* to *you heard* is the result of a shift in focus, due most probably to grammatical pressure from the following אליך rather than theological motivation. Again it will be observed that no vowel letters occur in this verb form, a practice entirely consistent with SHS. The spelling of the suffix –t follows SHS (×1785 out of ×1934 in MT), rather than SQS –th. Qimron (1986: 23, 42) reported over 250 cases of the latter at Qumran, only five of the former; with –kh about 900 times, –k 160 times. So, while both spellings are attested in both corpora, the proportions have been inverted. Tov does not record the retention of biblical usage in this case when he lists 4QTestim as

"sectarian" (1986: 50). Strictly speaking, these are not instances of the alternative spellings of the same suffix; rather the pairs of spellings attest variant or alternative pronunciations—šāmaᶜt or perhaps šāmaᶜat, reflected in the preferred MT spelling, versus šāmaᶜtā, reflected in the preferred Qumran spelling but supplying the standard Tiberian vocalization. There is thus a curious reversal of forms here, as we would expect 4QTestim to have the long form, whereas MT, which preserves the shorter spelling in the text, nevertheless vocalizes the form as though it had the long pronominal suffix. In our view, the two forms are different, alternate morphemes which existed side by side for centuries. The longer form of the suffix is authentic and is preserved in SQS, whereas the short form predominates in the orthography of MT. This datum has been obscured by the MT insistence on spreading the long pronunciation through vocalization, against the orthographic indications of the traditional text. See No. 14.

7. אֵת (1:7). A. The short vowel—whether ᵓēt ← ᵓit or ᵓet—is not indicated in the orthography, in accord with SHS.

8. קוֹל (1:8). A. SHS prefers *plene* spelling of singular (×443 out of ×494), but prefers *defective* spelling of the stem vowel in the plural. This could indicate metaplasm or a byform. Full details and discussion are found in **SHB** (pp. 46-48). A study of the spelling of this and related words in chapter 5 of this book points to *qāl as the more likely primal form. In SQS all such ō vowels are spelled *plene*.

9. דברי (1:9)—**dibrê** in MT. A. SHS and SQS represent word terminal –ê by *yod*. The final vowel is presumably a contraction from the original diphthong –ay. The short vowel in the first, closed syllable is not represented in the orthography.

10. העם (2:1). A. MT hāᶜām, הָעָם. Neither –ā– is spelled with a vowel letter, whether *aleph* or *he*. The use of *aleph* for spelling word-medial –ā– (when *aleph* is not etymological) occurs a few times in MT (**SHB** § 3.3.1.2 lists twelve instances) and enjoyed some vogue at Qumran, at least in Aramaic (Freedman and Ritterspach 1967); see Nos. 33, 40. Regardless of the vocalization, whether the vowels are short or long, accented or not, the vowel **a** in the medial position is normally not indicated in the orthography. Here SHS and SQS conform completely.

11. הזה (2:2). A (**hazzeh**). The Qumran spelling is the same as MT and SHS. The use of *he* to represent the final vowel –e is standard.

The internal short vowel is not represented in the orthography by SHS or SQS.

12. אשר (2:3). A (ʾăšer in MT). Cf. Nos. 17, 51, 119. As in MT, so in 4QTestim, there is no orthographic indication of either internal short vowel, regardless of vocalization and accentuation.

13. דברו (2:4). A (dibběrû). Both SHS and SQS represent final –û by *waw*. There is no indication in the orthography of the internal short vowels.

14. אליכה (ʾēleykâ) (2:5). B. MT אליך, which is SHS. The spelling of this suffix as –kh is highly diagnostic of SQS, but relatively rare in MT (×38 out of ×7073, ×26 in the Primary History); see Table 4.3. The dominant Masoretic spelling –k represents a form of the suffix with no terminal vowel—not an alternative *defective* spelling of –kâ. The latter variant is paramount at Qumran, as the preferred spelling with *he* shows, and the variant pronunciation that it documents becomes the standard Masoretic pronunciation as the anomalous Tiberian vocalization shows. In this MS, however, there are eleven without, seven with *he*. See the related discussion under No. 6 above. Even though the short spelling is dominant in MT, there are examples of the long spelling, showing that both pronunciations existed side by side in the language. MT vocalization supports this position, since the short form is vocalized without the final vowel in the pausal form, i.e., –āk. While the issue of the coexistence of alternate forms of the same morpheme is somewhat confusing, certain points can be made: a) In spite of Masoretic vocalization, the short form is not simply a defectively written long form. b) The Masoretes apparently preferred MSS in which the short spelling predominated but at the same time thought that the long pronunciation was superior or literarily more attractive and so leveled it through the language. c) In SQS the long form is preferred.

15. היטיבו (hêṭîbû) (2:6). A. Standard *plene* spelling of all three long vowels. The first was originally a diphthong represented by the consonantal element, which was retained in the spelling after the diphthong had contracted (historical spelling). The second vowel is –î– represented by *yod*. Such *plene* spelling of the hiphᶜil form of the verb goes back to pre-exilic times, as evidenced by the Arad ostraca. Final –û is regularly represented by *waw* in all pre-exilic Hebrew inscriptions. This usage is the same in SHS and SQS.

16. כֹּל (2:7). B or C. MT כֹּל is SHS for all forms of this word—
pausal and normal (**kōl** in Masoretic pronunciation) as well as
construct **kol** and suffixed **kull**–. It is spelled *plene* only twice in
MT (Jer 31:34; 33:8—adjusted by *qry*, and actually construct, so
doubly anomalous). The *plene* spelling used here in 4QTestim is
dominant at Qumran for all forms, including construct and suffixed (which have short stem vowels in Masoretic vocalization).
This usage poses a major problem for Qumran phonology, since
the vowel letter can be read either as a non-Masoretic representation of a short vowel (–o– or –u–) or as an indication that at
Qumran this vowel was long. There does not seem to be any way
of deciding between these two possible explanations without beg-
ging the question. Some researchers, expecting Qumran Hebrew
to lie in the mainstream of the historical evolution of the Hebrew
sound system, have preferred to try out Masoretic pronunciation
first, so that Qumran construct כוֹל, **kol**, and כוֹלוֹ, **kullô**, show
that *waw* was used to represent short vowels, contrary to SHS.
Other researchers, beginning with the assumption that vowel letters were used *only* to spell long vowels, come to the conclusion
that in Qumran Hebrew all vowels derived from primal short **u**
had become long, even those which in mainstream Hebrew had
become *shewa*. Andersen and Forbes' study of the relationships
between grammatical functions and spelling patterns (**SHB** § 8.4)
has brought to light unexpected evidence that construct forms in
MT use more *plene* spellings than would be anticipated given a
correlation of stress, length, and full spelling. So a spelling such as
כוֹל, while anomalous by Masoretic rules, could have been valid
for a scribe who gave the vowel stress and heard it as long, in spite
of the construct state. The same could apply to at least some of
the numerous similar spellings found at Qumran which use *waw*
to spell a vowel which, by all the evidence of historical phonology,
should be short. While it might be possible to suppose that for
some reason the stem vowel in **kwl**, *all*, was always stressed in
Qumran Hebrew, so that the vowel was lengthened (**kōl**), even in
construct, it would be going too far from the known patterns of
stress in Hebrew words to maintain that the *stem* in the suffixed
forms of this word was stressed and its vowel lengthened, so that
כוֹלוֹ represented **kûl(l)ô**. And it is asking too much to claim
that קוֹדָשִׁים represents a pronunciation **qôdāšîm** or **qûdāšîm**,
for nowhere in the history of Semitic languages does such a primal
short vowel become long *in that position*. We know, from the conventional vocalization of this word in both Hebrew and Aramaic,
that the back position of the first vowel was sustained (doubtless

under the influence of the velar consonant), since not only קָדְשִׁים
but even קָדָשִׁים is found. The Qumran practice shows that they
too safeguarded this peculiarity, using *waw* to spell the back vowel
as such, regardless of its length and/or stress status.

This phenomenon is well-known in the case of the Qumran spellings
of certain verbs, and in some cases—not all!—it is possible to suppose that the spelling documents an otherwise unattested stress
pattern, a supposition based in its turn on the expectation that
primal short **u** becomes long only under stress. But this explanation is hardly plausible in the case of nouns (Qimron [1986: 35]
reports 42 cases) in which there are no grounds for supposing that
the primal short **u** could be stressed or had become long, for it
corresponds to MT *shewa* or *ḥatuf*. While no possibility should be
excluded *a priori*, it is simplest to assume that the original use of
waw to spell all word-terminal –û's, and then to spell (optionally)
word medial –û–'s, has been extended to safeguard the distinctive
pronunciation of primal short **u** surviving in unstressed syllables.
If that is the correct reading of the evidence, this Qumran practice
was not the logical extension of SHS to the spelling of unusual, but
long, vowels; it was the beginning of the extension of the use of
vowel letters to represent some short vowels, a trend which continued to develop through medieval times.

The Masoretes were very strict in not recognizing a long vowel
in a closed, unstressed syllable. Yet even MT has words where
waw is present but the vowel is *qameṣ qaṭan*; thirty-six cases are
listed in **SHB** § 3.4.3. All are corrected in *qry*. MT contains
even more specimens of the occurrence of *waw* as vowel letter in
the consonantal text where the vowel was understood to be –**u**–
and where the punctators were content to point the *waw* as *shureq*,
while securing the closed syllable by means of *dagesh*. **SHB** § 3.4.2
lists sixty cases. In spite of the anomaly of an apparently long
vowel in a closed unaccented syllable, there was no attempt to
relieve the strain by supplying a more appropriate *defective qry*,
as was the procedure when *waw* represented short –**o**–. Ninety-six
specimens in MT might not seem to be many, but the frequency
of the same phenomenon at Qumran enhances its significance and
invites search for explanation in both settings along similar lines.
The inconsistency of a word like גְּדוּלָה within Masoretic practice
has been explained by the theory that it is a mixed reading allowing
for either גְּדוּלָה or גְּדֻלָּה, each legal. In any case the doubling
of the final consonant is a secondary development which creates a
closed syllable for the short vowel to survive in.

It is very important, however, to distinguish between vowels derived from primal short –i–, which hardly ever evoke *yod* when –i– survives, and only rarely when (according to Tiberian vocalization at least) –i– becomes –ē– under stress, and vowels derived from primal –u–, whose representation at Qumran by means of *waw* is "almost universal" (Qimron 1986: 17). This contrast in spelling patterns for vowels derived from –i– and –u– respectively is found in MT also. In contrast to the 96 examples of *waw* for –o– or –u– which the Masoretes took to be short, it is practically impossible to find cases of *yod* used for –i– or for –ē– ← *–i–. None of Tov's diagnostic spellings involve *yod*. Restricting discussion at this point to the word now under study, *all* is usually spelled *plene* (exclusively so in some quite long texts), as here, in striking contrast to the uniform *defective* spelling in the MT.

17. אשר (2:8). A. Cf. Nos. 12, 51, 119.

18. דברו (2:9). A. Cf. No. 13.

19. מי (3:1). A. Not the fuller Qumran מיא. *Yod* represents final –î. Cf. No. 38.

20. יתן (yintēn) (3:2). Ca. MT יתן. While the form reflects Aramaizing influence (against MT normal Hebrew **yittēn**) the orthography is consistent with SHS. Neither of the two originally short vowels is represented in the orthography: a) **yin**–: short vowel in closed, unaccented syllable; b) –**tēn**: originally short vowel in closed, accented syllable (so-called tone-lengthening). Whether the change postulated in Masoretic pointing had already occurred or not, there is no change in the spelling between SHS and 4QTestim.

21. ויהיה (wayihyeh) (3:3). Da. MT ויהי. The Qumran variant reflects the retreat of late biblical Hebrew from the use of *waw*-consecutive constructions, particularly in precative discourse, as in this case. The form itself conforms exactly to SHS. Final *he* represents the vowel e, while the short vowel in a closed syllable is not indicated in the orthography.

22. לבבם (lĕbābām) (3:4). A. Note the absence of vowel letters for all vowels in internal positions, whether in open or closed syllables, accented or unaccented, short or lengthened.

23. [זה] (zeh) (3:5). A. Added above the line by a corrector. Qumran texts consistently spell this pronoun in the biblical manner. The final vowel is represented by *he* as in SHS. Cf. No. 11.

24. להם (lāhem) (3:6). A. The Qumran copy remains with the biblical source although elsewhere the longer and more typical המה–variant may be adopted (see Nos. 40, 42, 48). Neither internal vowel is represented in the orthography, confirming that originally short vowels (apart from **u**) are not so represented, conforming with SHS.

25. לירא (3:7). Ca. MT ליראה. How did they pronounce this word? Possibly lîrōʔ or lîrāʔ. In view of the Qumran preference to represent every –ō– with *waw* (cf. Nos. 5, 27), the latter is more likely. 4QTestim has the infinitive construct rather than MT's verbal noun, which is standard usage in MT. The long form with apparent feminine ending is preserved in the Bible, but the shorter, "normal" form is found in Josh 22:25 (and an apparently elliptical form in 1 Sam 18:29). 4QTestim here uses the short form. The *aleph*, of course, is not a vowel letter but a case of historical spelling, since the *aleph* is one of the root consonants of the word. Regarding the initial vowel, whatever its development to lîrāʔ, the *yod* represents the long –î– resulting from the merging of the first two syllables. Thus the originally consonantal *yod* becomes a vowel letter representing the congruent vowel –î–.

26. אותי (3:8). B. MT אתי. The long –ō– in an open, pre-tonic syllable is represented by *waw* in 4QTestim; the addition of the vowel letter is characteristic of Qumran and an option already taken in 26% of cases in MT (**SHB** p. 189). In this case SQS does not differ significantly from SHS, except in the scale of use.

27. ולשמור (wališmôr) (3:9). B. MT ולשמר. Excluding לאמר as a statistically invariant *defective* spelling (**SHB** p. 153), 202 out of 1076 such infinitives in MT have *plene* spelling (**SHB** p. 195). The main outliers due to overuse of *plene* spelling are found in the Writings (**SHB** p. 269). This contrasts strikingly with the almost complete absence of this kind of spelling in the Torah—only two cases, עבור (Num 22:26), לרגום (Num 14:10). The *waw* is used in 4QTestim to represent the long –ō– vowel in the final, accented syllable. SQS represents a still later development of earlier usage with consistent preference for *waw* as the vowel letter for long –ō– in medial positions.

28. את (ʔet) (3:10). A. Short front vowels are not represented in the orthography of 4QTestim or SQS, as is also the case with MT and SHS.

29. כול (3:11). B or C. MT כל. See No. 16.

30. מצוותי (miṣwōtay) (4:1). A. Overall 68.2% of such –o– vowels
in the feminine plural suffix –ōt– are *plene* in MT (**SHB** p. 11),
but in Torah only 31.4%. The word here is a special case, with
waw in the root, for *plene* spelling would result in two successive
*waw*s. This pattern was avoided in SHS (**SHB** § 4.7). Here SHS
seems to have survived against Qumran trends. But this inference
is by no means certain. Qumran scribes had no compunction about
using two *waw*s to spell –wō–; ᶜăwōn is routinely spelled עוון in
1QIsaᵃ. And feminine plurals of the type מצות have the part of
the word corresponding to MT –wōt– spelled variously ות, וות, or
אות. This word is even spelled מצאת in CD 6:19. This evidence
has been interpreted to mean that it is the same vowel, namely
–ō–, that is being spelled in these several ways, –wōt– having lost
the **w**. If that is the case with 4QTestim, then the *waw* which is a
consonant in MT, with *defective* spelling of –ō–, is a vowel letter
in 4QTestim *plene* spelling of –ō–.

31. כול (4:2). B or C. MT כל. See Nos. 16, 29.

32. היומים (hayyômîm) (4:3). Ca. MT הימים (hayyāmîm). Here
the Qumran spelling clearly represents a distinct dialectal variant
(יומים) against standard יָמִים. The attestation of this variant
plural stem is reviewed in **SHB** § 2.3.6. Here is clear evidence that
Qumran spelling was phonetic. Certainly, *waw* does not represent
–ā– as in the vocalization of MT, but –ô– i.e., the stem vowel of a
plural form consistent with and based directly on singular יום. It is
conceivable that the spelling ימים (as in SHS) could be pronounced
either yōmîm or yāmîm, and that 4QTestim reflects a normal
orthographic development from yômîm spelled defectively. The
second vowel, –î–, is naturally represented by *yod* in both SHS and
SQS.

33. למעאן (4:4). Cb. MT למען: *lamaᶜn(i) → lĕmaᶜan. The
use of *aleph* in a medial position apparently as a vowel letter is unusual in SQS (and even more so in SHS). It is not etymologic and
it plays no role in the structure of the word, so it must be regarded
as a vowel letter, although the short **a** in MT vocalization is secondary as part of a segholate formation. Presumably, the *aleph* is
used to represent short **a** as is also the case in 1QapGen, where it is
used mainly after *yod* and *waw* to preserve their consonantal status
in medial positions (Freedman and Ritterspach 1967). This factor
does not operate here, however. Furthermore, non-etymological
aleph is rarely used as a vowel letter for short **a** in non-biblical *Hebrew* texts at Qumran. As examples of its rare use in biblical texts

we may cite יאכה for MT יָכֶּה (1QIsa[a] 30:31). Non–etymological *aleph* as a vowel letter occurs very rarely in MT, where it usually represents an original short **a**, tone lengthened (**SHB** § 3.3.1.2). Examples from Qumran are גמאלם for MT גמלם (1QIsa[a] 63:7) and יאתום for MT יתום (1QIsa[a] 1:17, 23). Even at Qumran non-etymological *aleph* did not establish itself as a vowel letter with clearly defined, let alone peculiar functions; rather it is used sporadically in a variety of situations. Besides its occasional use as a vowel letter for vowels other than **a**, as in the spelling of MT עֲוֺר as עואר, there are places where it is hard to associate it with any vowel at all, as in כלאיות for MT כִּלְיוֹת (1QIsa[a] 34:6) or קצאוות for MT קְצוֹת (1QIsa[a] 41:5). It occurs also in various digraphs, in some of which it could represent the secondary development of a non-etymological glottal stop or perhaps *Vokalträger*. There is no need to review all the evidence here, nor to debate the several explanations that have been advanced. Non-etymological *aleph* can represent short **a**, and that is the best suggestion here. The Qumran spelling would then show that the epenthetic vowel was already in place, and spelled with *aleph* in spite of the likelihood that it was only short –**a**–. One other case of *aleph* for word-internal –ā– is found in this text (see No. 40).

34. יטב (4:5). B. MT ייטב. Cf. No. 15. If the pronunciation is the same, we have a case that is the opposite of the usual Qumran trends—*defective* spelling of a long vowel. But, given the other indications that SQS was consciously phonetic and preferred full spelling for long vowels, it is possible (we think it likely) that this spelling reports a form with a short vowel in the first syllable. Roots with *yod* as the first consonant are generally unstable, with loss of this consonant in "imperfect" derivatives. The root טב ~ יטב is metaplastic in biblical Hebrew, and the second form is derivative. יטב could be derived from the biconsonantal root rather than from the triconsonantal byform; or it could result from analogical imitation of such familiar models as ישב, *sit*, thus **yēṭēb** or **yiṭab** rather than MT **yîṭab**. This word cannot be used uncritically as evidence for *defective* spelling of long vowels at Qumran. The same fluctuation persisted long in the transmission of biblical texts. The many variants in D62 are reported in Chapter 15 of this book.

35. להמ (4:6). A. Cf. No. 24. The form of *mem* is medial, as if the scribe began to write להמה by habit, but then was restrained by his *Vorlage*. The option is not a question of orthography (choice between two acceptable spellings of the same word) but rather

of two distinct forms of the pronoun. Both occur frequently in the Hebrew Bible (all portions—the short form is preferred in the Torah, the long form elsewhere—details in Table 4.1 in this book) and at Qumran. Qimron (1986) reports 70 long, 17 short free forms (p. 58) and 250 long, 650 short suffixed forms (p. 62) in the non–biblical texts he studied; this continues the biblical preference for the long free form and for the short suffixed form.

36. ולבניהם (MT wĕlibnêhem) (4:7). A. SHS is retained. The *plene* spelling of stem –ê– (a contracted diphthong) is normal (historical spelling of the original consonant). The long form of the suffix is not invoked. Cf. No. 35. All the other internal vowels are short and left unrepresented in the orthography (whether under accent or not).

37. לעולם (laᶜôlām) (4:8). B. MT לעלם. The *defective* spelling of this word occurs ×25 out of ×438 in **L**; the tally for other MSS varies. The distribution of the two spellings in MT is discussed on page 71. 4QTestim has *plene* spelling of long –ō– in a medial position, while Deut 5:29 in MT does not represent the vowel in the orthography. So 4QTestim is squarely in the mainstream of Hebrew orthography, but overlapping with later phases of SHS, whereas the *defective* spelling would preserve an earlier orthographic pattern. The position just taken reflects the view that the word ᶜôlām derives from (as in Aramaic) an earlier *ᶜālam rather than a diphthongal form *ᶜawlam. The original spelling would have been עלם, as in MT, but when long ā became ō, then in due course the vowel would have been represented by *waw*.

14.4 Inventory: Deuteronomy 18:18–19

38. נבי (5:1). Cb. MT נביא. The *aleph* in MT is etymological, i.e., part of the root of the word, and although it had long since quiesced (as *aleph* generally did at the end of syllables), it was preserved in MT (and SHS) by historical spelling. Even so, loss of word-terminal *aleph*, particularly after –î–, is found several times in MT, usually corrected in *qry*. Gordis (1937: 95, List 7) draws attention to the fact that in such cases the next word begins with *aleph*, as here. The writing of *aleph* only once in such an environment could be a purely graphic *scripta continua*; or omission by oversight (haplography); or it could have a phonetic explanation in the difficulty of articulating juncture between two successive glottal stops. This MS is consistent, in the spelling of *prophet*, even

when the next consonant is not *aleph* (No. 62). So the spelling documents the loss of this word-terminal *aleph*. The question here is why the scribe did not retain the historical spelling. There are several possibilities. 1) With the quiescence of the *aleph*, the omission follows naturally, especially in the case of SQS with its penchant for phonetic writing unless there are pressures to retain the letter. 2) An influential factor for Qumran scribes may well have been the sequence יא in the word. From the use of *aleph* as a vowel letter in 1QapGen in association with consonantal *yod* and *waw*, and the use of digraphs including *aleph* generally at Qumran, a case can be made that the function of the *aleph* is to preserve those letters as consonants, where otherwise they might have been misread as vowel letters. The very common particles כי and מי are often spelled with final *aleph*: כיא, מיא, and we read **kiyaʾ** and **miyaʾ**. It should be emphasized that the final *aleph* in such words has no consonantal force, never did, and is strictly a vowel letter. In the word נביא the normal spelling in SQS might prompt a pronunciation **nābiyaʾ**, and we suggest that the aleph was omitted so as to avoid a wrong pronunciation. The writing נבי would represent the current pronunciation: **nābî**.

39. אקים (**ʾāqîm**) (5:2). A. Normal spelling of –î– for SHS and SQS. The *aleph* here is clearly consonantal, and the initial vowel is not represented in the orthography, whether it is short or an example of pre-tonic lengthening. The second vowel is so-called pure long, and under the tone it is consistently represented by *yod* in SHS and SQS. There are numerous cases of *defective* spelling of such *hiphʿil* forms in MT, and these reflect a much earlier phase of Hebrew spelling—early pre-exilic (outliers in Chapter 3 of this book).

40. לאהמה (**lāhēmmâ**) (5:3). Cc. MT להם. The apparatus of BHS reads לאהם, but the photograph in DJD V Plate XXI confirms the longer form. The medial vowel **e** in a closed, accented syllable (Tiberian style) is not represented in the orthography, while the final long –**â** is indicated by *he*, all in accord with standard spelling rules. This word presents three distinct spelling features of interest:

1) It is a noteworthy case of *aleph* for word-medial **ā**. Normally such vowels are not represented in SHS or SQS. Even so there are about a dozen cases in MT, some doubtful, and some varying in MSS (list in **SHB** § 3.3.1.2). In any case this preposition is never so spelled in MT. The usage in 4QTestim reflects the belated introduction of *aleph* as a fourth vowel letter in Hebrew orthography.

2) In contrast to No. 24, the scribe has used the longer form of
the pronoun suffix. Cf. Nos. 42, 48. As argued previously, the two
forms existed side by side in the language and survived in both
SHS and SQS. Here it is not a question of different spellings of
the same form but different forms of the same pronoun. Very few
examples of the long form survive in MT, but enough to show that
the form existed and is part of the larger repertoire of Hebrew and
not simply an eccentricity of Qumran Hebrew.

3) Even so, this decision must have been an afterthought, for the
mem has its terminal form. Here, as in No. 35, we can see the
scribe's mind at work. There it was the other way; he began to
write the long form and then changed his mind, sticking to the
biblical original.

41. מקרב (**miqqereb**–Masoretic vocalization, possibly **miqqirb** at
this time) (5:4). A. Correction written over מתוך. The word contains no vowel letters, showing that SQS conforms to SHS and that
short front vowels are regularly not represented in the orthography,
regardless of other factors: accent, closure, and the like.

42. אחיהמה (ʾăhêhēmmâ) (5:5). Ca. MT אחיהם. The word
has moved to the preferred Qumran form, with standard spelling
of terminal –â. As with Nos. 40 and 48, the scribe copied from a
MS resembling MT and added the *he* after reproducing the original
terminal *mem*. Both words are spelled in accordance with the rules
of SHS—short vowels are not represented, long vowels are. The
contracted diphthong ê is represented by its consonantal element
yod, even after the contraction, through historical spelling.

43. כמוכה (kāmôkâ) (5:6). B. MT כמוך. The *plene* spelling of ō
in the prepositional stem in this form is preferred in MT (×51 out
of ×84). Seventeen of the thirty-three *defective* spellings occur in
the Torah and only eight of the *plene* (**SHB** Table 6.4). The proportions are the other way in the rest of the Hebrew Bible. So the
plene spelling now attested in MT Deut 18:18 is slightly atypical,
and hence we cannot be sure that the scribe's original presented
this feature. The fact that MT here in Deuteronomy uses the fuller
spelling only means that the surviving MSS do not provide an absolute guide to the history of any given vowel type. One could
have expected most of the differences to be leveled through constant copying. The surprising thing is that the differences between
archaic and standard spelling are still markedly preserved and visible in the text we now have. In any case the Qumran scribe used
the standard spelling, as expected.

The longer pronunciation of the pronoun suffix is reflected in SQS, although not always adopted in this MS (see No. 14).

44. וגתתי (5:7). A. It does not have the Aramaizing dissimilation (reconstruction) of etymological *nun* as in No. 20. All interior vowels, whether short or long, in closed or open syllables, remain unrepresented in the orthography. This is standard spelling of such vowels. The final –î is represented by *yod*, also standard.

45. דברי (děbāray) (5:8). A. The internal vowels are not represented in the orthography. The final diphthong is indicated by its consonantal element, *yod*. All this is normal for SHS and SQS.

46. בפיהו (běpîhû) (6:1). Ca. MT בפיו (běpîw). The only difference is the lack of medial *he* in MT. The Qumran form is more original in this case and might well have stood in the Vorlage. The short vowel after the preposition is not represented in the spelling. The second vowel, î, is represented by *yod*, which may reflect the original root consonant preserved through historical spelling. The final vowel, û, is represented by *waw*, as usual. In MT the elision of the *he* results in the merging of the vowels î and û into a diphthong îw. The spelling conventions are the same in both words.

47. וידבר (6:2). Da. MT ודבר. For the spelling see No. 1. 4QTestim has made the same grammatical adjustment as in No. 21. Contrast No. 53. 4QTestim has substituted the imperfect for the perfect form of the verb, avoiding the *waw*-consecutive construction but preserving the intended tense.

48. אליהמה (ʾălêhēmmâ) (6:3). Ca. MT אליהם. As with No. 42 this word was first written after the source with *mem sophith*, and then the characteristic Qumran *he* was added. See No. 42.

49. את (6:4). A. Cf. No. 7.

50. כול (6:5). B or C. MT כל. See No. 16.

51. אשר (6:6). A. Cf. No. 12.

52. אצונו (ʾăṣawwennû) (6:7). A. All short vowels (in medial positions) remain unrepresented in the orthography. The final long û is represented by *waw*. Spelling is standard for both SHS and SQS.

53. והיה (wahāyâ) (6:8). A. The scribe retained the *waw*-consecutive clause; contrast Nos. 21, 47. There are no internal vowel letters; the final long –â is indicated by *he*.

54. ‏שׁיא[ה]‏ (hā'îš) (6:9). A. Spelling is standard. The first vowel is not represented in the orthography, while the î in the noun is represented by *yod*.

55. ‏אשׁר‏ (7:1). A. Cf. No. 12.

56. ‏לוא‏ (lô') (7:2). B. MT ‏לא‏. A characteristic Qumran adjustment, and an important diagnostic in Tov's list. On the distribution of the 187 *plene* spellings of this word in MT (out of 5184) (small compared with the Qumran preference for *plene*) see **SHB** pp. 186–188; but note that MSS vary considerably in this detail.

57. ‏ישׁמע‏ (7:3). A. Once again we emphasize that SQS, just as SHS, does not use vowel letters for the short vowels in this word.

58. ‏אל‏ (7:4). A. Cf. No. 3.

59. ‏דברי‏ (7:5). A. Cf. No. 9.

60. ‏אשׁר‏ (7:6). A. Cf. No. 12.

61. ‏ידבר‏ (7:7). A. Cf. Nos. 1, 47.

62. ‏הנבי‏ (7:8). Eb. Agrees with LXX. On the absence of *aleph*, see discussion at No. 38.

63. ‏בשׁמי‏ (bišmî) (7:9). A. Normal spelling of terminal –î. The internal vowel is not represented in the orthography. The spelling is standard.

64. ‏אנוכי‏ ('ānôkî) (7:10). B. MT ‏אנכי‏. The *plene* spelling of –ō– never occurs in this word in MT. It is characteristic of SQS, although not on Tov's list. The use of *waw* here is a later development.

65. ‏אדרושׁ‏ (8:1). B. MT ‏אדרשׁ‏. The *plene* spelling of this kind of –ō– is rare in MT (×125 out of ×1481). It occurs only once in Torah (Lev 25:5—safeguarded by a masora), and only four times in the Former Prophets. Leading outliers (they are not conspicuous, for the trend is only slight in MT) due to overuse of *plene* spelling of such a vowel are Job 1–21; Hosea-Joel, and Isaiah 40–66 (**SHB** p. 267). This slight trend in later biblical books comes to full flood in SQS. As expected, 4QTestim uses *waw* to represent long ō in the medial position (here under the accent). The *plene* spelling of this word happens to occur in Ezek 20:40. Once again we argue that SQS is in the mainstream of orthographic development and that it overlaps with later developments in SHS while increasing the number of *plene* spellings.

66. מֵעִמּוֹ (mēᶜimmô) (8:2). A. 4QTestim does not represent medial short (or tone lengthened) vowels derived from **i**. The final vowel long ô is represented by *waw*. All this is SHS.

14.5   Inventory: Numbers 24:15–17

67. וַיִּשָּׂא (9:1). A. Etymological *aleph* is retained, even though it is likely that it was no longer pronounced in that position. Contrary to the treatment of נְבִי (No. 38), 4QTestim here retains etymological *aleph*, as there was no danger of confusion with the convention of using *aleph* as a vowel letter after *yod* and *waw*.

68. מְשָׁלוֹ (mĕšālô) (9:2). A. 4QTestim follows standard spelling practice: no representation of medial short (or lengthened) vowels (based on **a**) and normal representation of final ô by *waw*.

69. וַיֹּאמַר (9:3). A. The characteristic SQS variants וַיֹּאמֵר, וַיוֹאמֵר, וַיוֹמֵר do not intrude. Contrast No. 70. These Qumran spellings represent long ō by *waw* (either before or after the *aleph*, which is silent, or with the omission of *aleph* altogether). The influence of a standard Hebrew text can be seen here.

70. נְאֻם (9:4). Cc. MT נְאֻם, always so spelled (×376) in MT. The characteristic SQS (נואם also, cf. Nos. 73, 77) points to a simplified monosyllabic pronunciation **nûm**. Although it retains *aleph* and never uses *waw*, MT pointing could be an artificial attempt to secure the historical pronunciation. As with זוֹת, זוֹאת, זוֹאות for MT זֹאת, it is *waw* that is the vowel letter at Qumran. This shows that they did not accept such a historical *aleph* as a vowel letter. Its frequent omission shows that it was now quiescent, but it was generally kept as a historical spelling.

71. בִּלְעָם (bilᶜām) (9:5). A. The internal vowels are not represented in the orthography of 4QTestim or MT.

72. בנבעור (9:6). Ca. MT בְּנוֹ בְעֹר. There are three orthographic differences between MT and 4QTestim. 1) The editor transcribed the patronymic as one word. There can be no doubt about this, since the MS usually has clear spaces between words, and moreover its *nun sophith* is quite distinctive (see No. 20). 2) The archaic bĕnô has been replaced by standard **ben**. 3) The name bĕᶜōr is spelled *plene*, a later spelling. 4QTestim reflects later developments in the transmission of the text, but its spelling is consistent with later SHS.

73. וכאם (wanūm) (9:7). A. Contrast Nos. 70, 77, each within sight of the others. We do not interpret this variety as indiscriminate use of arbitrary spellings, but rather as a point of instability of spellings in flux. All variants point to the same pronunciation (nūm), the *aleph* being silent and *waw* representing the vowel or not used at all when SHS was perpetuated, as in this case. As in other instances, it seems that the biblical texts could exert a restraining or conservative influence, if we assume that the original text (as preserved to a large extent in MT) was written defectively, and if the MS from which the Qumran scribe was copying preserved these features at least to some extent. We can hardly expect complete consistency when a spelling system is undergoing changes.

The representation in MT ûně˒ūm of initial *waw* as û in numerous places in certain environments is pure affectation and is entirely out of line with the historical grammar of the language. The basic usage requires an initial consonant **w**, and the following vowel is either short or lengthened under the influence of the tone (tonic or pretonic).

74. הגבר (9:8). A. The spelling suggests that they still knew the cognate **haggabr** or **haggeber** and did not read **haggibbōr**, which would have evoked הגבור. The internal vowels are not represented in the orthography.

75. שׂהתם (10:1). Cc. MT שׂתם (šětūm). This is a remarkable variant. First, it does not use a vowel letter for the long –ū– in the passive participle of MT. Secondly, the use of *he* makes it doubtful that the scribe read the word as in MT. Allegro draws attention to LXX and Targum, both of which read š as the relative rather than as part of the root štm, *open*. This leaves תם to be read as *perfect*, and each version has handled it in its own way, although neither is literal—*beautiful* (Targum), *true* (LXX). Moreover they translate *the eye* as a verb, and adjust the syntax to fit. The instinct of the versions was sound, up to a point. In analyzing these words, we must also attempt to interpret and therefore to restore the text to an original and reasonable form. Long ago Wellhausen (followed by others), partly on the basis of the versions, provided a basic solution that has withstood the test of time and repeated reexamination (Albright 1944). In an interesting way 4QTestim confirms the essential correctness of the reconstruction, although not all of it.

Undoubtedly 4QTestim reflects the relative pronoun š of biblical Hebrew, writing the morpheme with a vowel letter šh. William

Propp (written communication) pointed out the similarity of שׁד,
relative, to מה, ma(h), interrogative, which doubles the next consonant and may be written **mh** or **m–**. We must read the remainder
as תמה עין, shifting the definite article attached to ᶜyn to the
end of the predicate adjective **tm** to produce the required feminine form. The result is excellent but archaic Hebrew poetry—šeh
tammâ ᶜayn, *whose eye is perfect*; in prose it would have been
ᶜênô. 4QTestim agrees with MT in העין. The spelling of the
relative pronoun is unusual, doubly so because while the scribe
supplied the vowel letter that would be needed to treat the particle as a *separatum*, he nevertheless ran the word into the next one.
In spite of that slip, the reading is correct—the *he* is a standard
vowel letter but a final, not a medial one—and the rest of the colon
makes sense as analyzed.

76. העין (10:2). A. For this word the *yod* is clearly consonantal and
originally part of the diphthong in ᶜayn, which is later resolved
into ᶜayin in Masoretic vocalization.

77. נואם (nûm) (10:3). Cc. MT נאם. The third distinct spelling of
this word in two lines. See Nos. 70, 73. The spelling in 4QTestim
implies that the *aleph* has quiesced with the *waw* representing û.

78. שומע (šômēᶜ) (10:4). B. MT שמע. The usual SQS of the –ô–
in *qal* active participles. In the entire Hebrew Bible about 20% of
such participles are spelled *plene* (**SHB** p. 193). It is only in late
books (Lamentations, Qohelet, 2 Chronicles) that there are more
plene than *defective* spellings of this class of words. Once again we
can place SQS at the *plene* end of the spectrum, but already in
sequence with SHS and for the most part a normal development
from the former. The *defective* spelling of the other stem vowel (ē
or perhaps still i) is common to SHS and SQS.

79. אמרי (ʾimrê) (10:5). A. In 4QTestim, as also in MT, the initial
short vowel is not represented in the orthography while the final
long ê (derived from the diphthong **ay**) is represented by *yod*.

80. אל (ʾēl) (10:6). A. The *defective* spelling of the stem vowel (ē or
perhaps still i) in a closed syllable under stress is common to SHS
and SQS.

81. וידע (10:7). A (?). Here the *qal* active participle, if that is how
they read it, has not been moved from the *defective* spelling of MT,
which is more usual in MT in any case, to the *plene* standard for
SQS, as in No. 78. But did they read it as a participle? While

ידע can be vocalized in several ways, the odds are that it was read as the participle, not only because of the oral tradition that accompanied the written text, but also because of the pressure of parallelism from the preceding colon. But this very factor underscores the inconsistency—in the same line!—with biblical spelling holding out against the trend to rewrite even sacred texts into the orthography prevailing at Qumran. There are other possibilities, however. It could be read as the imperfect וַיֵּדַע, which would be more likely at Qumran given the spelling without medial *waw*. Then the verb forms of v 16 would be in chiastic parallelism with the participle followed by the imperfect in v 16a and the imperfect יחזה followed by the participle נפל in v 16b. The shift back and forth between participle and imperfect is quite acceptable in Hebrew grammar, especially in (archaic) poetry.

82. דעת (daᶜt) (10:8). A. 4QTestim has no internal vowel letter, agreeing with MT. Contrast No. 33.

83. עליון (10:9). A. 4QTestim has no vowel letter for the initial short vowel, but represents the long ô under accent with *waw*, in agreement with MT. In MT 58% of words with this ending are spelled *plene* (**SHB** p. 198). We would expect this to be higher at Qumran. All the outliers due to overuse of *defective* spelling are in the Torah (**SHB** p. 274); in Leviticus 1–16, for instance, ×71 out of ×78 are *defective*. All the outliers due to overuse of *plene* are in the Writings (**SHB** p. 273). MT overall shows a typical evolution from Torah to Writings with *defective* spellings preferred in Torah and *plene* spellings preferred in the later books. 4QTestim and SQS belong to the later phases.

84. אשר (10:10). Ea. Not in MT. The relative pronoun has been copied into the text under the influence of the same reading in Num 24:4. It was introduced secondarily there and has crept into the text here. The scribe simply copied what was in front of him. Contamination of this kind is very common in the transmission of parallel passages.

85. מחזה (mah[ă]zēh) (11:1). A. In 4QTestim the internal vowel is not represented in the orthography, while the final vowel is indicated by *he*. The spelling is the same in MT, reflecting consistency and continuity between SHS and SQS.

86. שדי (11:2). A. In 4QTestim the initial short vowel is not indicated, while the final diphthong is represented by its consonantal element.

87. יחזה (yeḥ[ĕ]zeh) (11:3). A. The occurrence of an imperfect verb in a sequence of participles shows that ידע (No. 81) could be vocalized as an imperfect instead of a participle. Here the internal short vowel is not represented in the orthography, while the final vowel e is indicated by *he*. 4QTestim and MT agree throughout; the orthography is standard.

88. נופל (nôpēl) (11:4). B. MT נפל. Typical SQS of *qal* active participle. Cf. Nos. 78, 81. 4QTestim represents the long ô of the participle with *waw*, while MT is *defective*. This pattern supports the view that וידע (No. 81) in 4QTestim is not the *qal* active participle but the imperfect form of the verb. The *defective* spelling of the final stem vowel is standard for both MT and Qumran.

89. וגלו (11:5). Cc. MT וגלוי. The third consonant of the root, which survives in classical Hebrew only in *qal* passive participle, as in MT, has now been lost. The orthography of the other vowels is not affected, as 4QTestim retains the *waw* for long û, while the interior vowels are both short and not represented.

90. עין (11:6). Da. MT עינים, dual. The change to singular could be the result of leveling to the preceding עין (No. 76). The difference in the form is of textual interest only. MT dual form is doubtless more original. The spelling in 4QTestim is the same as No. 76.

91. אראנו (11:7). A. 4QTestim has no internal vowel letters (the vowels are short) while the final long û is indicated by *waw*. All is standard spelling, whether SHS or SQS.

92. ולוא (11:8). B. MT ולא. The usual adjustment. Cf. No. 56.

93. עתהא (11:9). B. MT עתה, which is standard. It is not likely that the Qumran spelling represents *ᶜattahā(ᵓ), which would require a consonantal reading of *he* without foundation in the history of this word. More likely the two vowel letters represent final –â. Kutscher (1959: 139) adduced forms like הירא, found in 1QIsaᵃ, equivalent to MT הָיָה, as evidence that the digraph was another way of spelling word-terminal –â. A reading hāyĕhâ seems out of the question. See § 14.8, below.

94. אשורנו (ᵓăšûrennû) (12:1). A. *Plene* spelling of internal –û– is retained. The short vowels are not represented in the orthography, The spelling is standard throughout.

95. ולוא (12:2). B. MT ולא. Cf. Nos. 56, 92.

96. קָרוֹב (qārôb) (12:3). A. The first vowel is not represented in the orthography, although it is a long, pretonic ā. The second vowel, long ō, is represented by *waw*. All is standard for SHS and SQS.

97. דָּרַךְ (dārak) (12:4). A. No vowel letters.

98. כּוֹכָב (kôkāb) (12:5). A. The *waw* of the original diphthong has been preserved through historical spelling and now represents the resulting long ô. The spelling is standard.

99. מִיעֲקֹב (12:6). B. MT מִיעֲקֹב. The full spelling of this word is very rare in MT (×5 out of ×349), not uncommon at Qumran. Once again 4QTestim is at the latter end of the scale but carries on in the same tradition as MT.

100. [וַיָּקֻם] (12:7). Da. MT וָקָם. A supralinear correction. MT, with perfect verb, is a better formal parallel to דָּרַךְ, but וָקָם, if *waw*-consecutive, is better as prophetic future. 4QTestim resolves the ambiguity. The question is whether 4QTestim has the *waw*-consecutive with the imperfect or the simple conjunction. In view of the fact that the parallel verb is perfect, we would expect the *waw*-consecutive here. In that case the Qumran *plene* spelling has moved beyond MT, in which this form is always (×107!) *defective*. If Qumran is still close to SHS, then **wĕyāqûm** is indicated, clearly future. The first two vowels in the word do not appear in the orthography.

101. שִׁבְט (šibṭ) (12:8). A. No vowel letters are used even though the principal vowel, i, is lengthened under the accent. The spelling is standard.

102. מִישְׂרָאֵל (12:9). A. There are no vowel letters. Standard spelling.

103. וּמָחַץ (wamāḥaṣ) (12:10). A. Here the classical *waw*-consecutive, for future, is retained in spite of its relinquishment in Nos. 53, 100. For the vocalization of the conjunction see No. 73 above. There are no vowel letters in 4QTestim or MT.

104. פְּאָתִי (13:1). A. Qumran and biblical spelling are identical. There are no internal vowel letters; *aleph* is a root consonant. Final ê (from diphthong **ay**) is represented by *yod*.

105. מוֹאָב (13:2). A. At Qumran, as in SHS, diphthongs are regularly represented by their consonantal elements, which are then preserved through historical spelling to represent the resulting long vowel. The second stem vowel, ā, is not represented in either tradition by a vowel letter.

106. וקרקר (13:3). A. Supports MT against recommended emendation to וקדקד. There are no internal vowel letters.

107. את (13:4). Ea. Prose particle added. This fixes the grammar, making קרקר a verb parallel to מחץ, not a noun parallel to פאתי. This weakens further the suggestions that קרקר is an error for קדקד, *skull.*

108. כול (13:5). B or C. MT כל. Cf. Nos. 16, 29.

109. בני (13:6). A. The final vowel ê is represented by *yod.* Standard spelling.

110. שית (13:7). B. MT שֵׁת. If MT vocalization is correct, then 4QTestim represents ē by *yod* in the medial position. Since such usage is otherwise very rare or unattested in this text and elsewhere in SQS, we may consider other possibilities. Normally the spelling šyt would represent either šît with long î or šêt from *šayt. Given the spelling in MT, the leading possibilities would be šit or šēt, with šīt a less likely *defective* spelling. Had the original form been *šayt, then we would expect the *yod* to be preserved throughout all the transmission history. So we are left with the alternatives of šit or šēt. Similarly, if the vowel had originally been long î, we would expect the spelling to be šyt, even in MT. The logical inference is that the original form was šit, and that MT reflects the normal development under stress to šēt. The spelling in 4QTestim would be a rare instance of *plene* spelling of ē. The fact that it is a proper noun may help to explain the full spelling (to ensure the correct pronunciation).

14.6   Inventory: Deuteronomy 33:8–11

111. וללוי (walĕlēwî) (14:1). A. The only vowel letter is at the end of the word: *yod* for final long –î. Spelling is standard. Long ē is not represented in the orthography.

112. אמר (14:2). A. No vowel letters. Cf. No. 97.

113. הבו (hābû) (14:3). Ea. Not in MT. In 4QTestim the final long û is represented by *waw.* Standard spelling.

114. ללוי (14:4). Ea. Cf. No. 111. Agreement with LXX confirms the authenticity of this reading. MT lost Nos. 113 and 114 by homoioteleuton.

115. תמיך (**tummeyk**) (14:5). A. MT has the same text: **tmyk**, but vocalized **tummeykā**, which would fit better a text with the long form of the suffix –**kā**. Curiously, 4QTestim has the short spelling of the suffix, although SQS is characterized by the long form. It would, however, be a mistake to vocalize 4QTestim as MT. Rather, we must vocalize as above and recognize that MT has mixed the two forms, combining in effect a *ktyb* representing the short form and a *qry* with the long form. 4QTestim here supports the short form. There are no vowel letters, the *yod* being diphthongal.

116. ואורך (14:6). B. MT ואוריך. In view of pressure from the preceding plural, and the propensity of Qumran for full spelling, this singular may be taken as a textual variant, rather than a totally unexpected *defective* spelling of a plural form, especially in Judahite, because the *yod* represents the consonantal element in a primitive diphthong and therefore is least likely to be omitted in the spelling. Nevertheless, the singular would be an inferior reading and probably indicates interpretation as *light* rather than *Urim*. MT vocalizes the suffix –**k** as though it were –**kh**, but there is no basis for supposing this was the actual pronunciation of the same spelling in 4QTestim. 4QTestim has the short form of the suffix here, against its common practice, but clearly reflecting a scribal choice to retain the usage which its source shared with MT.

117. לאיש (14:7). A. Standard spelling; *yod* is used internally as a vowel letter for long î.

118. חסידך (**hăsîdak**) (14:8). A. The agreement with MT singular weakens the case for plural, in spite of MS support. The occurrence of *yod* as a vowel letter for medial long î shows that the word is **hāsîd** in MT and 4QTestim, and not **hesed** as in the emendation to **hasdekā** suggested by various scholars, unless it is an error in transmission based on misunderstanding of the word, which is not very likely. If the word were plural, we would expect the vowel before the suffix to be represented in the orthography by *yod*. This omission in both MT and 4QTestim supports the interpretation as singular.

The scribe did not bring in the usual SQS suffix כה–. The usage of this MS is mixed. It is hard to imagine that the scribe substituted selectively, but it is more likely that both forms occurred in the tradition and in the transmission of the text and that MSS varied in the proportion of long and short forms. See discussion under Nos. 6, 14, 35, 40. There is no reason to suppose that SQS systematically changed all short forms to long forms, but rather that these were two traditions about the use of the pronouns and pronoun suffixes which existed in two allomorphs, both of which occurred in the language. In a text such as this both forms occur side by side. The difference, in short, is not dialectal nor is it purely orthographic.

119. אשר (14:9). A. Cf. Nos 12, 17.

120. נסיתו (nissîtô) (15:1). A. Medial long î is represented by *yod*, which might also be a survival of the original third stem consonant by historical spelling. The final long ô is represented by *waw*, standard in biblical spelling and at Qumran.

121. במסה (15:2). A. Final long â is represented by *he* in SHS and SQS.

122. ותרבדהו (15:3). B. MT תריבדהו. BHS wrongly reports this variant as ותריבדהו. 4QTestim differs from MT in two respects. It shares the initial *and* with LXX while MT lacks the conjunction, showing that 4QTestim was not copied from a standard proto-MT MS. In addition and orthographically more important, 4QTestim lacks the vowel letter *yod* in the medial position between r and b, where MT has it. For 4QTestim to be more defective than MT at any point is unusual but not inexplicable. The lack of *yod* is certainly puzzling, the more so in view of assonance with the following מריבה. The earlier (pre-exilic) spelling of such a form would have been תרבדו and only later would the *yod* have been introduced, primarily in syllables bearing the accent. Still later the usage was extended by paradigmatic analogy to unaccented syllables like this one. In this marginal case, either spelling would have been appropriate. By the end of the biblical period the spelling of this kind of vowel would present a scribe with virtually no choice. All of the outliers in MT are due to an overuse of the archaic *defective* option. There are no outliers in the Writings, and even the Pentateuch has been almost completely normalized to *plene* spelling of this kind of vowel (**SHB** pp. 247-48). For once things are the opposite of what we have learned to expect, and it is hard to believe that a Qumran scribe would change a *plene* spelling to *defective*, if his *Vorlage* resembled the present MT. It is possible (and we think more likely) that the scribe correctly copied his original, which still had the older spelling, and that his action was legitimized by reading the word as a derivative of רבה רבד or רבב.

123. על (15:4). A. SHS. The short vowel is not represented. Cf. No. 154.

124. מִי (mê) (15:5). A. SHS.

125. מְרִיבָה (15:6). A. SHS: both long vowels represented by vowel letters.

126. [ה]אֹמֵר (15:7). A. Supralinear correction. The older spelling of the participle is retained. See No. 81. Does the spelling in 4QTestim (without *he*) mean that the form was originally intended to represent the 3rd m. sg. perfect form? That might explain the absence of the *waw* in the form in 4QTestim. Originally written as אמר, later it was corrected in the direction of MT.

127. לְאָבִיו (lĕᵓābîw) (15:8). A. Standard.

128. לוא (15:9). Ea. An error, erased.

129. /// (16:1). Ec. Illegible erasure.

130. וּלְאִמּוֹ (walĕᵓimmô) (16:2). A. Standard.

131. ליד[ע]תי[ע]כהו (16:3). Dc. MT לֹא רָאִיתִיו. The word evidently caused the scribe difficulty, since it now presents at least one overwrite and a supralinear correction. It seems that he began with לא, which matches MT. But the problem here is that that word is usually spelled with *waw* (Nos. 56, 92, 95, 128, 134, 138). The MT is admittedly difficult: 1) because it is hard to accept –w, *him*, as a distributive singular object referring to both father and mother;[1] 2) because of the idiom *I did not see him* (the verb is confirmed by the versions), when *respect* would make more sense. It is possible that MT results from the use of רא as a biconsonantal byform of ירא, of which there are many instances in the Hebrew Bible (Andersen 1970), which is then read as the verb *to see*. The scribe might originally have written ירתיכה, *I feared thee*, omitting the second *aleph* and placing *yod* over the original *aleph* of לא. The hypothecated form already lacks two letters of MT (–אי–). But the form was unintelligible, and ידע probably suggested itself as a better parallel to the following הכיר under the influence of ידע later in the verse. ידע was produced by touching up the –ר– and the *ayin* was supplied supralinearly. Amusin (1971: 358) has drawn attention to the Vulgate *nescio vos*, which at least supports ידע. He also links the reading with other occurrences of ידע in Qumran texts with similar connotation and even pursues the idea

---

[1] A similar grammatical pattern in this same passage involves the relation of plural *hābû* to the singular 2nd person pronouns (Propp 1987). Samaritan seems to have dropped it, and LXX has the easier *thee*.

into the New Testament. But he was unable to make any progress in explaining the letters at the beginning and end of the word, any more than we can. Accepting יָדַעְתִּי as *I knew* leaves כְדֹ-, which is hard to explain, since the *waw* seems to be original, so that יִרְתִּיכְדֹהוּ or יִדְתִּיכְדֹהוּ looks like a *hiphᶜil* with root רתך or דתך, object הֹו-. But there are no such roots; the second violates the rule that a triradical root cannot have the first two consonants at the same point of articulation. If the final *waw* is a careless dittograph of the following *and*, it escaped the eye of the corrector. Until we can decipher the word we cannot infer anything from it concerning Qumran orthographic practice.

132. וָאֵת (wĕᵓet) (16:4). A. Cf. No. 7.

133. אֶחָיו (ᵓāḥîw or ᵓeḥāyw) (16:5). A. Cf. No. 42.

134. לוֹא (16:6). B. MT לֹא. See Nos. 56, 92, 95, 128.

135. הִכִּיר (hikkîr) (16:7). A. The short i is not represented; the long î is represented by *yod*. Normal spelling.

136. וָאֵת (16:8). A. Cf. No. 7.

137. בְנוֹ (bĕnô) (16:9). A. The Masoretic reading of the noun is plural (bānāw—with *yod* supplied in *qry*), which makes the best sense in context, although the parallel אֶחָיו could be singular or plural. See No. 133. LXX agrees with MT. The spelling in 4QTestim, however, suggests that that scribe read בְנוֹ (possibly אֶחָיו as well) as singular. The singular (understood as collective or representative) would be the more difficult reading and hence to be preferred. It is easier to understand a shift from singular to plural than the other way around. We think, therefore, that the scribe of 4QTestim read singular in both cases and that the text underlying MT did likewise. The changeover from the pre-exilic spelling of this suffix (Masoretic -āw) from -w to -yw (this -y- is purely graphic) is one of the most curious innovations in the spelling reforms of the Persian period. Qumran texts (even 4QSam*b* [Andersen and Freedman, Chapter 13]) suggest that this spelling was already in place by the third century BCE. Its status in MT remains equivocal in many instances, since even the best MSS show numerous variations (e.g. L differs from A in this detail), and MSS also vary widely in the supply of corrective *qry* for the pseudo-*defective* spelling of plural without *yod*, so that the aggregate remains indeterminate. We find 162 cases, with a very uneven distribution—Torah ×17, Former Prophets ×47 (×34 in Samuel), Latter Prophets ×64 (×51

in Ezekiel, which is very important, for it shows that the earlier usage was still in vogue in the sixth century, or even later), ×27 in the three poetry books (×16 in Job), but only ×7 in the rest of the Writings (none in Chronicles!). Its survival in this Qumran text which elsewhere moves freely to late spellings can accordingly be taken as as indication that the scribe probably read it as singular, not that in this case he preserved and understood the archaic spelling. See the similar problem with Nos. 160, 164, 165.

138. לוא (16:10). B. MT לא. See Nos. 56, 92, 95, 128, 134.

139. ידע (17:1). A. Standard; no medial vowels indicated.

140. כי (17:2). A. Not Qumran כיא.

141. שמר (šāmar) (17:3). Ca. MT שמרו (šāměrû). There is no chance that 4QTestim spelled the plural defectively. This is a variant with some claim to authenticity, since it is in accord with all the preceding singular verbs. LXX agrees. MT is anomalous, but as the subject is certainly collective the plural forms are acceptable. It is difficult to say which tradition is more original, but it may be easier to explain a shift from plural to singular in the course of transmission than the other way around. Perhaps the readings belong to alternate traditions which have been conflated in MT, whereas 4QTestim and LXX preserve one of them intact.

142. אמרתכה (ʾimrātekâ) (17:4). B. MT אמרתך. The usual Qumran variant of the suffix; but note that the scribe did not use this form with the very next word. Cf. Nos. 14, 43, 116, 118, 143, 146. So far as the stem is concerned, the agreement of 4QTestim with MT (both singular) is textually important, for versions read plural; cf. the following משפטיך. The plural of this word is rare in MT (only twice, both in Ps 12:7), but if the scribe had read it here, he would most likely have supplied the vowel letters—אמרותיכה*.

143. ובריתך (17:5). A. The long Qumran form of the suffix is not expressed. Cf. No. 142. MT uses the long vocalization, even when it has the short spelling, leveling the allomorphs. 4QTestim has both spellings, hence both forms, which must have been pronounced differently to reflect different spellings. The point is that final vowels are always represented orthographically everywhere— the Masoretes created the illusion that some vowels could be added without vowel letters.

144. ינצר (17:6). Ca. MT ינצרו (yinṣōrû—pausal). Cf. No. 141. 4QTestim reads the singular as with שמר above, while MT has

plural. The Qumran scribe did not supply *waw* (ינצור), which is surprising if he read the stem-vowel as –ō–, which is routinely spelled *plene* at Qumran. Perhaps he vocalized the word differently, **yinṣar?**

145. [ויאירו] (17:7). Da. MT יורו. After two singular verbs for plurals of MT (Nos. 141, 144), 4QTestim here follows MT plural. But the word is quite different and added later, "by the same hand" according to Allegro. The orthography is standard.

146. משפטיך (mišpāṭeyk) (17:8). A. Once more the longer suffix preferred at Qumran is not expressed. Cf. No. 143.

147. ליעקוב (17:9). B. MT ליעקב. Cf. No. 99.

148. תורתכה (tôrātěkâ) (18:1). B. MT ותורתך. 1) 4QTestim lacks *and.* 2) Qumran כה–. 4QTestim and MT have different forms of the suffix. The final vowel is written in 4QTestim but missing in MT. Use of *waw* for ô in the stem is standard.

149. לישראל (18:2). A. Cf. No. 102.

150. יש[י][מ]ו(ו) (18:3). B. MT ישימו. Without perusal of the original we are obliged meanwhile to work with Allegro's reported impressions. It seems that the first copy followed plural of MT, but lacked *yod* (which could have been missing in his *Vorlage*; cf. No. 153). This letter was then added supralinearly. But the word was changed to singular (cf. Nos. 141, 144) by touching up the *mem.* The final *waw* was not erased. The result either way is standard spelling.

151. קטורה (qěṭôrâ) (18:4). A. Standard spelling of long vowels.

152. באפך (18:5). A. Both spellings expressed the shorter suffix.

153. וכל[י]ל (18:6). B. The addition of supralinear *yod* was probably part of the correction that replaced a previous letter with *kaph.* The final result is standard.

154. על (18:7). A. Cf. No. 123.

155. מזבחך (18:8). A. Both spellings expressed the shorter suffix.

156. ברך (19:1). A. No vowel letters. Standard.

157. ⁙ (19:2) B. MT יהוה. Cf. No. 2.

158. חילו (ḥêlô) (19:3). A. ê ← *ay is *plene.*

159. וּפֹעַל (19:4). A. The eventual Masoretic vocalization ûpōᶜal should not be assumed. SQS *plene* preferred spelling of such words does not emerge; but the status of this vowel at Qumran and generally in Hebrew at this time is not clear.

160. יָדוֹ (yādô) (19:5). B. MT יָדָיו (yādāyw), Sam. ידו. It quite possible that 4QTestim faithfully reproduces an original reading that survived in its *Vorlage*, and that the ambiguous reading was resolved to plural in the Masoretic channel. Cf. Nos. 137, 164, which show that the scribe read all these words as singular in keeping with settled orthographic practice, even if this involved misreading an archaic text. In these variants we have before our eyes what must have happened in numerous cases.

161. תרצה (19:6). A. Standard.

162. מחץ (19:7). A. See No. 103.

163. [מתנים] (19:8). A. Correction. Supports MT against Sam.

164. קמו (qāmô) (19:9). B. MT קמיו (qāmāyw) . Cf. Nos. 137, 160, 165. While קמו might have been taken as singular by the scribe, like the other nouns in this passage, qām with this meaning is always plural in MT, and the verb shows that the parallel משנאו is plural.

165. ומשנאו (19:10). B. MT ומשנאיו is again plural against Qumran apparent singular. Cf. Nos. 137, 160, 164, all of which would be read as singular at Qumran; and this misreading accounts for the surprising survival of the authentic archaic spellings. If we assume that the original reading was plural, then MT reflects normal evolution, while 4QTestim preserves archaic spelling. It is also possible to see a double tradition—one singular, one plural—reflected in the two texts. The final plural verb reflects the double subject: whether each is singular or plural, the combination is plural.

166. בל (20:1). Da. MT מן. Of no orthographic interest (except for the obvious non-use of a vowel letter for the short vowel), but very significant philologically. 4QTestim has doubtless got the meaning right, but whether MT is privative *min* or a variant of interrogative with negative force (which is certainly the case with מי in Gen 49:9) is indeterminate. Since the scribe usually respected his *Vorlage* it is possible that this emendation existed in his source.

167. יקומו (20:2). B. MT יקומון. The archaic nunation has been abandoned. Otherwise the spelling is standard.

14.7   Discussion

Of the 167 words studied, 127 are graded A or B. The five cases of כול are graded "B or C" because of the marginal status of the *plene* spelling in biblical practice. This high correspondence to MT is enough to show that the document is presented as a copy of canonical texts, even though it is a catena. We can assume that the scribe believed he was reproducing the sacred text faithfully, and not writing a paraphrase or commentary. At the same time the continuation of the document with a midrash restrains us from overstating this point. Words of classification B are merely orthographic variants within the options of SHS; the 17 C words are textual variants with minimal departure from the original. This means that only 18 of the words (×9 D, ×9 E) are not in MT. In other words, the texts from which this catena was derived are proto-Masoretic in recensional character. This general agreement with MT enhances the claims that some textual variants might be superior to MT. Of the nine readings rated E, two are scribal errors corrected (Nos. 128, 129), two are "corrections" in the grammar (Nos. 84, 107), two are interpretive shifts (Nos. 4, 5), and three have claims to textual authenticity by agreement with **LXX** (Nos. 62, 113, 114). Of the substantial departures from MT graded D, two are interpretive (paraphrastic) (Nos. 1, 3); five are grammatical, three of these due to changes in the grammar of the verb (Nos. 21, 47, 100—the others are 90, 166); and only two represent quite different words from the original (Nos. 131, 145). Nos. 129 and 131 are unusable. Of the 165 usable words, 159 point to a *Vorlage* of proto-Masoretic text type. The six excluded are Nos. 1, 3, 4, 5, 75, and 145. It is accordingly appropriate to compare the orthography of 4QTestim with that of MT. Twenty-three of the words which differ from or are absent from MT nevertheless are spelled within the bounds of SHS, so that 150 of the 165 usable words have standard spellings. The scribal procedure discloses an obligation to preserve the words of the *Vorlage*, combined with liberty to move some of those words to characteristic Qumran spellings and pronunciations. At the same time the scribe did not systematically standardize the orthography to SQS. The result is a mixed picture, whose inconsistencies should not be misinterpreted as indifference of the scribe to spelling rules. Rather the occurrence of SHS and SQS in the same document, and sometimes in the spelling of the same word or word type in a mix of both, shows that biblical norms continued to exercise restraints on trends to modernization or on scribal preference for spellings peculiar to Qumran and more in evidence in purely sectarian compositions. The spelling decisions made by the scribe may be classified as follows:

1. No decisions needed to be made in the case of words (or parts of

words) which were spelled the same way in the Bible and at Qumran. All word-terminal long vowels are represented by appropriate vowel letters. There is no case where it can be seriously entertained that such a vowel is not so represented. Thus we do not consider that verbs like Nos. 141, 144 might be plural in spite of their spelling as if singular. In all, 80 of the words in 4QTestim (nearly half the text) are ones which have only one spelling everywhere in Hebrew, ancient or modern. This fact is not as trivial as it might seem. It permits us to emphasize the feature that there are few really deviant spellings in this text, even though, as we shall see, it is a mixture of archaic Hebrew spelling (AHS), standard Hebrew spelling (SHS), late Hebrew spelling (LHS) and sectarian Qumran spelling (SQS). It is important to emphasize that much SHS was also part of the Qumran orthographic repertoire.

2. Besides these 80 words with stable Hebrew spellings, there are 40 words with SHS which already use a vowel letter for an internal long vowel, and the same spelling is used in 4QTestim:

(i) *Yod* for –î–: Nos. 15, 32, 38, 39, 42, 46, 54, 62, 117, 118, 120, 125, 127, 133, 135, 143, 145. In Nos. 150, 153 such a *yod* has been added by a corrector. In Nos. 38 and 62 such a *yod* has become terminal by loss of etymological *aleph*.

(ii) *Yod* for –ê–: Nos. 14, 15, 36, 48, 115, 146, 158.

(iii) *Waw* for –ô–: Nos. 8, 43, 83, 96, 98, 100 [not MT], 105, 116, 148, 151.

(iv) *Waw* for –û–: Nos. 89 (final consonant lost), 94, 167.
Total ×40.

The only option for a Qumran scribe, when copying such a word, would be to revert to the *defective* AHS. Under 6. below we shall consider this possibility. So 120 of the words are spelled as in MT.

3. When SHS still prefers *defective* spelling of internal long vowels of particular types, the few *plene* spellings of such vowels in MT are a sign of LHS. See Chapter 6. This trend comes to fuller expression at Qumran. Even so, 4QTestim retains *defective* SHS in Nos. 30, 81, 126, 159. More often, however, it moves *defective* SHS to *plene* LHS (Nos. 5, 26, 27, 37, 65, 72, 78, 88, 99, 147—all involving –ō–). Two cases deserve special listing—לוא, *not*, rare in MT, dominant at Qumran, uniform in 4QTestim (56, 92, 95, 128, 134, 138); and כול, *all*, only once in MT, so really a post-biblical spelling, preferred at Qumran, and uniform in 4QTestim (16, 29, 31, 50, 108).

4. The Qumran community used forms of pronouns that occur rarely in MT and that cannot be characterized as archaic or late. They are not orthographic variants, since different pronunciations are involved. We list them here because they are part of the total picture and because they have been widely misinterpreted as no more than orthographic

variants: retaining MT −t, not −th (No. 6), retaining MT −k, not −kh (Nos. 115, 116, 118, 143, 146, 152, 155); changing to −kh (Nos. 14, 43, 142, 148); retaining −hm (Nos. 24, 35, 36); changing to −hmh (Nos. 40, 42, 48). The trend is one way, towards the Qumran preference. Tradition also holds out in the case of מי and כי (Nos. 19, 140); the characteristic Qumran מיא and כיא are not used.

5. 4QTestim contains some spellings peculiar to Qumran, which are not spelling options in the Masoretic tradition. There may be one or two intruders in the whole Bible, but they do not change the larger picture. The five cases of כול, *all*, could come here, although in principle it would not offend biblical practice (examples already listed), along with the abnormal spelling in No. 5. It is quite otherwise with spellings that are never used in MT, namely מושׁדה (No. 4—an interpretive addition!), אנוכי (No. 64), שׁית (No. 110), and the variants נאום (No. 70), נאם (No. 77), alongside normal נאם (No. 73). הייומים (No. 32) is phonetic spelling of a dialectal variant. כבי (Nos. 38, 62) and וגלו (No. 89) are the result of loss of word-terminal consonant. למעיאן (No. 33) remains problematical. In addition 4QTestim contains a few curious spellings which could represent the extension of *he* (No. 75) and *aleph* (No. 40) to spelling −a−. Finally עדהא (No. 93) seems to use both these letters to spell terminal −â. We can make nothing of No. 131.

6. So far we have identified 80 spellings common to all traditions, 66 biblical spellings, and 25 nonbiblical spellings, most of the last group characteristic of Qumran. (The tally is more than the number of words because some words contain more than one spelling feature of interest.) Against this picture we set the remarkable fact that 4QTestim contains no fewer than seven words that differ from MT in being more archaic in spelling, assuming, that is, that they are supposed to be writing the same word. These words involve (i) *defective* spelling of −î− (Nos. 34, 122, corrected in Nos. 150, 153); (ii) *defective* spelling of −ey− (No. 116?); (iii) archaic −w for plural −yw (Nos. 137, 160, 164, 165; but we believe that these were read as singulars at Qumran). Choices were available for the 87 words which are not bound by common Hebrew spelling. While it is conceivable that the scribe copied these words from his originals in three distinct ways—retaining the standard spelling of MT, moving to Qumran spelling, reverting to archaic spelling—this is too complicated. In about 11 cases his changes seem to be due to differences between the Hebrew in vogue at Qumran and the standard Hebrew of MT. Apart from these there seem to be about 14 nonbiblical spellings of distinctively Qumran type, and the seven apparently archaic spellings sit rather oddly with them.

The several corrections of the text disclose a concern to be accurate, and two originally archaic spellings have been adjusted to SHS. We think,

accordingly, that the seven surviving archaic spellings are more likely to
be accurate reproductions of the *Vorlage* than conscious archaizing. So
there are only two kinds of spelling—biblical originals (including the
archaic spellings) and Qumran spellings (orthographic and dialectal). It
is worth noting also that there is a complementary distribution between
4QTestim *defective* spellings where MT is *plene* (all involve *yod*) and
4QTestim *plene* spellings where MT is *defective* (all involve *waw* for –ô–).
We do not think that the *yod*s were left out in copying. Rather the scribe
had a *Vorlage* that was more conservative than MT in this detail. We
mention also its occasional agreement with versions against MT. On the
other hand, it does not follow that the additional *waw*s now in 4QTestim
and not in MT (there are 25 in all) were present in the *Vorlage*. If, then,
the scribe's *Vorlage* resembled the present MT in lacking these additional
*waw*s, now present in 4QTestim, but lacked also the *yod*s still missing
in 4QTestim, we may infer that MT represents a later stage of textual
transmission than the *Vorlage* of 4QTestim (in orthographic typology,
that is) and that in that transmission there was restraint in the use of
more *waw*s to spell internal –ō– (our scribe was not so restrained), while
the situation was still open to normalizing the spelling of –î– and of
plural –ā(y)w, a change our scribe was reluctant to make.

14.8 Excursus: עתהא in 4QTestim

This spelling, with הא– at the end of the word, is unique in 4QTes-
tim, but known elsewhere. Its interpretation raises methodological issues
which have to be faced again and again when comparing the linguistic
features found at Qumran with the rest of Hebrew. There are two possible ways of proceeding. 1) Beginning with the expectation that spelling
reflects pronunciation, so that an unusual spelling of a familiar word such
as עתה was the result of conscious and deliberate choice, the departure
from the traditional orthography was intended to secure and express a
different pronunciation of this particular word, namely, ᶜattāhâ. 2) If
this word was pronounced the same at Qumran as everywhere else, so
far as our knowledge goes, namely, ᶜattâ, then הא– is another way of
writing –â, used in this word alone in 4QTestim, all other occurrences
of –â being spelled with ה–, the standard practice. The first alternative
conforms to everything we have observed so far about Qumran spelling,
but the use of the same combination of letters with one form of the verb
to be from 1QIsaᵃ raises some doubt:

MT היה → 1QIsaᵃ היהא (5:1)
MT ויהי → 1QIsaᵃ היהא (12:2)
MT והיה → 1QIsaᵃ והיהא (*aleph* superscript) (65:10)

To interpret these spellings as a representation of **hāyĕhâ** would be to
invoke a verb form otherwise unknown, just as **ᶜattāhâ** would be unique.
In 1QS 7:4 בדעדהא presents similar problems.

The well-known הואהא, *he* (?), in 1QS 8:13 has aroused much
debate, since it occurs at a place where one would expect a divine name.
The suggestion that it is an abbreviation of הוא האלוהים does not
seem to have won support. Rüger (1969) reviewed the problem and
concluded that הא– in הואהא and in עתהא is just a variant spelling
of –â. This was already the conclusion of Kutscher (1959: 139). The
dilemma remains, all the same, and in the final analysis can only be
resolved if we could resurrect those people and hear their living speech.
Either הא– in some occurrences spells –â, or, if it always spells –hâ,
we have at Qumran some forms of Hebrew words—**hāyĕhâ**, *he was*,
daᶜhâ, *knowledge*, **hûᵓāhâ**, *he*, **ᶜattāhâ**, *now*—unknown in the rest
of Hebrew. One way or the other, at Qumran either the spelling or the
pronunciation of some Hebrew words is off the beaten track.

In SHS (and in standard Aramaic as well) the 3rd f. sg. suffix
is always simply ה–. Since SHS always represents a terminal vowel
by a vowel letter, the orthography shows that no vowel followed this
consonant. The suffix was either –**āh**, as in בָּה, *in her*, or simply –**h**, as
in אליה, ᵓ**ēleyh**, not ᵓ**ēleyhā**, as in MT. If the form of this suffix now
found in MT were in use in biblical times, this would be the only case of
a commonly used word-terminal long vowel that was not systematically
represented by a vowel letter, which would normally be *he*. Out of more
than 1300 occurrences of –**hā**, *her*, in MT, only one is spelled הָא– (Ezek
41:15). According to Blau (1976: 8) this apparently *defective* spelling of
a word-terminal long vowel is explained by the "trend against using a
vowel letter after the same letter serving as a consonant." This assertion
is true for *waw* and *yod*, but not for *he*. In all instances where it is
certain that a word ends in –**hā**, the spelling is הה–, whereas *her* is
never הה–. The explanation of the unique spelling of this suffix without
a vowel letter is historical (Blau 1982). The suffix developed from a
primal Northwest Semitic ∗–**ha**, and the short vowel was either dropped
or lengthened. The SHS ה– reflects a speech pattern in which the final
short vowel was dropped; the Masoretic pointing הָ– reflects a speech
pattern in which the original vowel survived in some environments by
being lengthened.

What we can say for certain, however, is that at Qumran הא–
ordinarily represents –**hâ**. This is most evident in the 3rd f. sg. personal
pronoun *her*, where the Qumran MSS variously employ ה (–**āh** or –**h**),
הא (–**hâ**), הה (–**hâ**), or הנ (–**nâ**). This case is analogous to that of the
2nd m. sg. suffixes, and their history is somewhat parallel. There is an

important difference, however. Whereas the long and short forms of the 2nd person pronouns are both attested in the orthography of MT and evidently always existed side by side in the language, the consonantal text of MT attests only the vowelless form of the 3rd f. sg. pronoun suffix (the sole exception is Ezekiel 41:15).

The evidence for הא- is almost completely restricted to two Qumran MSS. They are 1QIsaᵃ (Hebrew) and 1QapGen (Aramaic). The 3rd f. sg. pronoun suffix occurs 221 times in MT of Isaiah. Table 14.1 shows the correspondences with 1QIsaᵃ.

Table 14.1 The suffix "her" in MT and 1QIsaᵃ

MT Form/Count		Matches	1QIsaᵃ Form/Count		
הָ-[1]	128	113	ה-	-āh	104+1[2]
			ה-	-h[3]	1
			אה-	-āh[4]	1
			הא-	-hâ	5
			נה-	-nâ	2
הָ-	72	67	ה-	-h	52
			הא-	-hâ	13
			הה־	-hâ	2+1[2]
נה-	21	19	נה-	-nâ	19

[1]– Sometimes **L** lacks *mappiq*.
[2]– 1QIsaᵃ has one instance not in MT.
[3]– The stem is different from MT.
[4]– The spelling of MT בה as באה in 37:34 is a case of *aleph* as vowel letter for medial ā.

Of the 221 occurrences of 3rd f. sg. pr. suffix in MT, 199 are matched in 1QIsaᵃ. The decrement is due to change or loss of text or damage to the MS. Of these, 178 and one addition follow SHS. The remaining 20 plus one addition in 1QIsaᵃ are deviants from SHS and consist of: 1) MT הָ- → 1QIsaᵃ הא- (×13); 2) MT הָ- → 1QIsaᵃ הא- (×5). 3) MT הָ- → 1QIsaᵃ הה- (×3); Note that the spelling א- for הָ- is not found, showing that *he* was still a consonant. The departures from SHS are not spread at random through 1QIsaᵃ. They are found mainly in a few clumps: 30 (×1); 34:10–13 (×5) 40–45 (×7); 61 (×1); 66:8–12 (×7).

1) 1QIsaᵃ has הא- for MT הָ- (×13):

אליה → אליהא (40:2; 66:12)
עליה → עליהא (34:11; 42:5; 45:12; 66:10)

במבצרייה ← במבצרידא (34:13)
ויושביה ← ויושבידא (40:22)
ומאצליה ← ומאצלידא (41:9)
כליה ← כלידא (61:10)
בניה ← בנידא (66:8)
אהביה ← אודבידא (66:10)
תנחמיה ← תנוחמידא (66:11)

2) 1QIsa*ᵃ* has דא- for MT הָ- (×5):

בָּהּ ← בדא (34:10, 11; 62:4; 66:10)
כָּתְבָהּ ← כותבדא (30:8)

3) 1QIsa*ᵃ* has דה- for MT הָ- (×3):

וירשׁוה ← וירשׁודה (34:11)
ויאדיר ← ויאדרדה (42:21)
ויערכה ← ויערוכדה (44:7)

In 1QIsa*ᵃ*, then, SHS –h, *her*, when MT has –hā, is retained in the
majority of cases (× 52); in 13 cases it is spelled דא–, in two דה–. In
1QIsa*ᵃ* SHS –h, *her*, when MT has –āh, is retained in the majority of
cases (× 104); in one case באה (37:34) *aleph* represents a medial vowel.
In five cases we find דא–. In all these cases the *he* is consonantal. If the
spelling דא– has the same phonetic value in בדא as it has in אלידא,
unto her, we must pronounce bāhā as a variant of bāh, *in her*.

A similar picture emerges from 1QapGen. The famous description
of Sarah's beauty in col. 20 uses the pronoun suffix *her*, many times.
Sometimes it is simply ה–: with a preposition לה, *to her* (20:3, 3, 3, 4,
4, 6, 31); with a noun ראישׁה, *her head* (20:3), חדיה, *her breast* (20:4),
כפיה, *her hands* (20:5); a verb רחמה, *he desired her* (20:8). The suffix
attached to a stem ending with a vowel (prepositions or plural nouns) is
commonly דהא–: עלידא, *upon her* (7:1), אנפידא, *her face* (20:2, 4),
עינידא, *her eyes* (20:3), דרעידא, *her arms* (20:4), ידידא, *her hands*
(20:4, 5, 5, 7), רגלידא, *her feet* (20:5), שׁקידא, *her thighs* (20:6),
קודמידא, *before her* (20:32). Note also בלחודידה, *by itself* (19:15).
In these words the pronunciation –hā is surely intended. The spelling
דא– is also used for the suffix when the traditional form is –ah: with
preposition בדא, *in her* (20:17), מנדהא, *from her* (20:6), בדילדא,
because of her (20:10, 10); noun נדנהא, *her sheath* (2:10), רוחהא, *her
spirit* (2:13), כולדהא, *all of her* (10:13; 16:11—Beyer [1984: 172] reads
this word [uncertainly] at 19:10; Fitzmyer reads kwlʔ), אנפהא, *her*

nose (20:3), לבנהא, *her whiteness* (20:4); ארכהא, *its length* (21:14), כתידא, *its width* (21:14); verb וחזהא, *and he saw her* (20:9), ונסבהא, *and he took her* (20:9), ונסבתהא, *I took her* (20:27), ידעהא, *he knew her* (20:17), ואן[ש]למהא, *he gave her back* (29:32). In reporting these data Beyer (1984: 424, 450, 474-80, 495-497) does not discuss the variant orthography, but gives –(á)hā as the only form for them all. The spelling הא–, however, is hardly known outside 1QapGen and 1QIsa*a*, apart from the two in 1QS, the one in 4QTestim, and also אחוהא (RES 1300:4), אחתהה (Hermop. 7:4). In a classical essay, Kutscher (1957: 11) argued that 1QIsa*a* was under Aramaic influence in this matter and that "the only other source for this suffix with the singular noun ending in a consonant (or feminine plural) seems to be the Targum Pseudo-Jonathan." This observation is important for the dialectal affinities of the language of 1QapGen, a dialect in which allomorph –hā has moved into the terrain of the traditional –h. Strikingly, just as 1QIsa*a* uses both בה and בהא, so does 1QapGen employ, even within a single line, alternate spellings of the 3rd f. sg. suffix with the same word: with preposition עמה (20:17), עמהא (20:7) *with her*; noun שפרה (20:7), שפרהא (20:7, 9) *her beauty*; בעלה (20:25), בעלהא (20:23) *her husband*; verb דברה (20:27), דברהא (20:9) *bring her*. Either we suppose that *her husband*, baᶜlah, could be spelled in two ways, or else we invoke a form baᶜlahâ, maintaining that הא– was always read as –hā. If the former alternative, that הא– = –āh, could be demonstrated, it might be used to support the argument that in the word עדהא the final letters represent –â rather than –hâ, although, despite their graphic identity –â and –āh are distinct in pronunciation. Since, however, SQS is generally phonetic, it seems best to leave the vocalization of this peculiar word in 4QTestim open until new data or arguments can be brought to bear.

14.9   Final Comment

The conclusions reached in this part (*Documents*), placed alongside the large picture of biblical spelling found in **SHB** together with the *Extensions* and *Advances* found in the present volume, permit some fine tuning of results. It is generally recognized that the edition or recension of the Hebrew Bible which came down to modern times through rabbinic channels already existed in definitive form at the beginning of the Common Era. Whether this source existed then as a set of model scrolls or as authoritative MSS of the same text type is of less concern to us here. The open question is the relation of this primal rabbinic Hebrew Bible to MSS which existed before that turning point. Was this definitive Bible the result of deliberate scholarly work of a text-critical kind, or did the scribes simply recognize and foster a recension that already existed, a recension that enjoyed some prestige, a recension that might have come down in that form from much earlier times? We believe that our work on the history of Hebrew and Aramaic spelling points more strongly to the latter alternative. This research shows that the spelling in the present MT is essentially that of standard Hebrew spelling of the Persian period. The orthography is not uniform. There are archaic features which are best understood as the survival of spelling practices from the early stages of fixing the biblical corpus during the sixth century BCE rather than as a late archaizing revision, as suggested by Cross (Cross and Talmon 1975: 185). Cross (1964: 288) discussed the production of "an archetypal recension as the ancestor of all Medieval biblical manuscripts." He described the procedure (Cross 1964: 289) thus:

> The rabbinic scholars and scribes proceeded neither by wholesale revision and emendation nor by eclectic or conflating recensional procedures. They selected a single local textual tradition, which may be called the Proto-Massoretic text, a text which had been in existence in rough homogeneity for some time.

At the same time he recognized that "some recensional activity was involved. *A single orthographic tradition, in part archaizing to pre- or non-Maccabaean spelling practices, was systematically imposed*" (p. 289, italics ours). In this book we suggest rather that the spellings now found in MT are a perpetuation and preservation of norms that were put in place during the Persian Period, even though we range from the fifth (p. 15) to the fourth (p. 35) to the third (p. 72) century in dating this achievement. To be sure, there is a limited incidence of later spelling preferences, limited in range (some later spellings do not appear at all), in scale (later spellings are few in number) and in location (they are mainly in the latest books). We know, for instance, that by the first century BCE the Qumran scribes were freely spelling the ō in segholates of type **qudš** or **qōdeš** with *waw*. The total absence of this orthography in MT (**SHB** § 5.4) is not the result of an archaizing restoration of **qwdš** to **qdš** at the turn of the era; it is the result of using MSS in which the standard spelling had never been modernized, as it had been at Qumran. Numerous illustrations of this pattern can be gathered from the data systematically presented in our research (p. 72).

Our present Hebrew Bible, minus Daniel, is an old text preserved from Persian times, not a new text created by scholars at the turn of the era. In **SHB** we suggested, somewhat light-heartedly, that biblical spelling is Ezra's spelling. Here we would say, a little more cautiously, that SHS is the reformed spelling of the Persian period, and that biblical texts were normalized to it. Just when the system was put in place we are not yet able to say; it could be as early as the first Return or as late as the fourth century. Five factors converge on the same result: the adoption of the Aramaic square character, the fuller use of old spelling rules (e.g., the *plene* spelling of medial long vowels) and the adoption of new spelling rules (notably the use of *waw* to spell ‑ō, *his*), the revision of texts to the new orthographic practices, the publication of definitive editions of the sacred texts, and the career of Ezra. It would be too long a shot to say that the Rabbinic Bible is Ezra's Bible, but in light of the history of Hebrew and Aramaic spelling as we are now recovering it, that is not altogether a shot in the dark.

Chapter 15

The Orthography of D62

Francis I. Andersen

The Library of the Leningrad Branch of the Institute of Oriental Studies of the Academy of Sciences of the U.S.S.R. has a rich collection of Hebrew manuscripts, with pride of place for a codex of the Latter Prophets, sometimes known as the Karasu–Bazar Codex. A full catalogue of the Hebrew MSS in the Institute Library has been prepared by Dr. Igor F. Naftul'eff, and will be published shortly. In the meanwhile some codicographical details are available in the report of Starkova (1974). I have not been able to track down a report allegedly given by Kahle.

15.1   The Codex from Karasu–Bazar

When the codex was complete, it consisted of the Latter Prophets in the canonical order. Annotations in the MS itself identify it as follows: ס(פר) ישעיה ירמיה יחזקאל ותרי עשר. Compare this formulation with the identification of the Cairo Codex (**C**) (p. 581) as: זה הספר הנביאים. It is written on parchment, 34 x 29 cm., each

---

In January 1989, it was the author's privilege to be the guest of the Academy of Sciences of the U.S.S.R. under an exchange agreement with the University of Queensland. I wish to record my gratitude to each of these institutions for facilitating my research. I would like also to express my appreciation to the Leningrad branch of the Institute of Oriental Studies for its hospitality and to its scholars for their collegiality, particularly for providing means for hands-on study of this magnificent manuscript. I am grateful to the Institute for permission to discuss some of its textual features.

page having two columns with 18–20 lines. It was originally (or at some stage) bound between two massive slabs of wood; but only the back cover survives. The front cover was most likely lost as a consequence of severe injury to the codex which resulted in the loss of many folios. What survived was crudely bound with twine, but some of the surviving portions of Isaiah were jumbled up, so far as their sequence is concerned, and some were placed within Jeremiah, some within Ezekiel. There are now 191 folios, numbered 1 to 190, with f. 32 repeated. The contents are as follows:

1–32	Isaiah 60:20–Jeremiah 20:17
32(*bis*)–33	Isaiah 37:20–38:17
34	Isaiah 42:13–43:7
35–38	Isaiah 38:17–42:13
39–69	Jeremiah 32:12–52:21
70–126	Ezekiel 1:1–43:21
127–128	Isaiah 51:13–54:2
129	Isaiah 46:4–47:11
130–134	Isaiah 54:3–60:1
135–190	Ezekiel 43:21–Minor Prophets

This means that Isaiah 1:1–37:19, 43:8–46:3, 47:12–51:12, 60:2–19, and Jeremiah 20:18–32:11 are missing. In addition the folio originally between 156 and 157, containing Amos 5:26–7:8, has been lost. This loss occurred after the folios had been numbered using Hebrew numerals (which have a gap at this point) and before the numbering with Arabic numerals. Folio 173 has been torn out, except for a small strip, so that Zephaniah 3:12–Haggai 1:15 is almost all lost.

The original codex was written with the consonants as square characters of an archaic kind, but so far there has been no detailed palaeographical analysis that might assist in dating the time when this work was done. Starkova (1974) pointed out a few of the archaic features that could be observed in five of the letters. The MS was provided with vocalization, accentuation, and masora, as well as other kinds of miscellaneous marginal annotations. It has been extensively "corrected," apparently by more than one subsequent scribe or user.

On f. 44b there is an inscription: כתבתי אני יצחק הסופר. There is no way of determining how many of the scribal tasks this covers. The inscription resembles the Masoretic notes in being written in an oriental cursive hand (which Beit-Arié [1977] has declared to be later than the consonantal text). On f. 190a there is a report that the number of verses in the "book" of the Latter Prophets is 9290. (The Leningrad Codex reports 9285 [actually 9286].) An intriguing inscription occurs on f. 190b. It reads (Harkavy 1876: 233):

וזה הספר ישעיה ירמיה יחזקאל
ותרי עשר נפל בידו של סעיד בן עיבט
הגדול מנחלת אביו בחלק ונחלקו המקומות
אשר לקחו כל האחים מנחלת אבידהם
כאשר לקחו איש חלקו ונתפשרו הם
באהבה ובחבה איש לאחיו באין (שום)
מחלוקת וסכסוך כי אם בשלום לעולם
ולא לערער דבר (איש) .....
שלמה בן ר אליקים (יְשִׁיֹּם)
נתן בן אלישע נֹ כלב בן אלי .....
.....בֹ שלחיה נֹ.....

Some parts of the note are unclear, but evidently it records and
certifies the settlement of a dispute over a legacy in which this volume
became the property of Saʿid ben ʿEybaṭ, an arrangement agreed to
amicably by his brothers.

Even more intriguing is a further note of seven lines (Harkavy 1876:
233):

והרשימה השניה אחריה וזל
מכרתי את סֹ ישעיה
ירמיה יחזקאל ותרי עשר
אני סעיד בן (עיבט).....לאל.....
בן רֹ יעקב ביום (אֹ לשבוע)
בחדש מרחשון בכֹה יום בו
.....שנת דֹ אלפים תֹרֹוֹ

.....

This records the subsequent sale of the codex to one ben R(abbi)
Jacob on 24 Marheshwan, in the year 4608.

Controversy over this MS has surfaced from time to time, but only
partial and confused reports are available. The most recent reference in
Yeivin (1980: 26) seems to have been based on Kahle's 1927 report. The
MS is L[15] in Kahle's list. I have not been able to confirm all the details
supplied by Yeivin.

The MS seems to have first come to the attention of modern scholars in 1839, when the notorious Abraham Firkowitch saw it in the synagogue at Karasu–Bazar in the Crimea. In reporting the content of the
certificates at the end of the codex, Firkowitch alleged that the names of
the three witnesses to the legal settlement of the will of ʿEybaṭ were followed by the words בקהל הקראים, "in the assembly of the Karaites."
This part was pure fabrication, characteristic of Firkowitch's chicanery.

It is clumsy in any case: the colophons of **C** refer to the Karaite community as ארקמ בני עדת. And, although suspicion of taint remains
on anything that passed through Firkowitch's hands, it is doubtful if
he ever had a chance to meddle with this document. The transcriptions of the two certificates cited above were published by Harkavy in
1876. He claimed to have copied them in Karasu–Bazar in 1874. He
recorded his doubts concerning the date, and reported also that someone
in Karasu–Bazar had told him that Firkowitch had deliberately damaged
the inscriptions, wishing to smuggle in his supposed Karaite community.
(Even as late as 1908 Kahle [1959: 8] was told similar stories by the
Samaritan High Priest.) But in this case Chwolson (1882) claimed to
have himself checked out this rumor and was assured by two elders of
the synagogue that Firkowitch had never been left alone with the MS.
Starkova (1974: 39) draws attention to the presence of a marginal note
on f. 188b by Police-chief Zhinevsky, possibly nineteenth century, and
wonders if this might have something to do with Firkowitch's attempts
to obtain the MS. I do not know how the MS eventually made its way
to Leningrad and ended up in the Library of the Oriental Institute.

Debate focuses on the alleged date of the MS as ninth-century. This
claim is based on the two certificates reproduced above about the legal
disposal of the codex, which was apparently sold in 847 CE and so must
have been produced some time before that (Shifmann 1987: 19). The
information quoted above suggests that there is no foundation for the
statement made by Yeivin that the MS originally contained a colophon
recording details of its *production* in 847 CE, which colophon is now lost.
The annotation of Isaac the Scribe has no date; and, as already noted,
it is not clear what he claims to have written and it is not clear why the
annotation occurs on f. 44b. It could be the signature of the punctuator,
since the ascription is written in the same eastern cursive script as the
Masoretic notes at that place. If the record of sale is authentic, and if the
date proves correct, then the significance of this codex for textual studies
of the Hebrew Bible can hardly be exaggerated, for it would be the oldest
dated MS of a portion of the Hebrew Bible known. It invites comparison
with the Cairo Codex (**C**) of the Prophets (895 CE), with the Codex
Petropolitanus (**P**) (Prophets with Babylonian pointing) (916 CE), as
well as with the magisterial Aleppo Codex (**A**) (early tenth century) and
the well-known Leningrad Codex (**L**) (1008/9 CE).

The fullest discussions of this MS are those of Chwolson (1882) and
Starkova (1974). Chwolson seriously contested the accuracy of Harkavy's
readings of the annotations. He insisted that the date was genuine, was
part of the original inscription. (Whether the inscription as a whole is
authentic and whether, given that, the date is correct, are quite distinct questions, which cannot be settled merely by debating the intrinsic

credibility of the certificates.) Objections to the evidence of the two inscriptions have been raised. Starkova points out the oddity of a person disposing of such a sacred heirloom. According to *T. Bikkurim* 2:15 one who sells his books will gain no benefit from the proceeds. But Kahle (1959) reports other evidence which suggests that it was quite acceptable to buy and sell such items. And who would invent such a story as a means of giving a MS a false certificate of antiquity? Nor is it likely that an endorsement giving legal ownership to the buyer would contain an erroneous date. Chwolson pointed out that Harkavy had not given his reasons for doubting the date 847 CE as such. Chwolson dismisses the claim of Harkavy and Strack than an original ה had been altered to ד, thus lowering the date by one thousand years. Chwolson polemicized at length against Harkavy, but confined his attention to the two certificates, and mainly to the date. The various philological difficulties in the inscriptions, such as the name ʿEybaṭ, cannot be used as evidence of authenticity one way or the other. Chwolson (1882: 189) could not believe that Firkowitch would have been capable of thinking up the numerous unfamiliar names like this one which are found in the Hebrew MSS from the Crimea, even though it is known that he interfered with grave inscriptions to further his aims. There does not seem to have been any independent attempt to date the text of the codex itself by appropriate internal tests—codicology, palaeography, textual affiliation, etc.

Even so, the apparent date of 847 CE will put a strain on anyone's credence. Kahle's research has established the history of the various systems of vocalization which preceded the triumph of the Tiberian system. This outcome was the achievement of the ben-Asher family, who worked at the project for five generations. There is a treatise on the *Shewa* (in Arabic) which supplies the chain of succession:

> Asher
> Nehemiah ben Asher
> Asher ben Nehemiah
> Mosheh ben Asher
> Aharon ben Asher

Now we know from the colophon that Moses ben Asher produced the Cairo Codex of the Prophets in 895 CE, and his son Aaron is almost certainly the person responsible for the Aleppo Codex (some time in the first part of the tenth century). Furthermore, Codex Petropolitanus (916 CE) shows that Babylonian vocalization was still in vogue in the early tenth century, but had already given way to the Tiberian masora (Kahle 1959: 63). The Tiberian system was therefore in place by the end of the ninth century; but, if the codex **D62** was sold in 847 CE and had previously been held by Saʿid ben ʿEybaṭ and before that owned by his father (for who knows how long?), then it must have been made about a hundred years before the Aleppo Codex. It is hard to believe that a text which exhibits the standardized Tiberian system (consonants, points, masora, *ktyb/qry*—as we shall see) was already in circulation and in use for purposes of private study as early as that. At the same time this difficulty should not be pressed. There was a remarkable revival of Bible study as an exercise for pious Jews during the ninth century, a movement attested both by the establishment of the Masoretic Text and by the emergence of the Karaites. After all, the Cairo Codex, prepared personally by no less a notable than Moses ben Asher himself—the greatest biblical scholar of the time—was requisitioned by a Karaite called Ya^cbes ben Shelomo for his own use. The quality of the Cairo Codex shows a Masoretic text if not yet the finally firmed up ben Asher text. To judge from Misha^el ben ^cUzzi^el's treatise on the *hillufim* the Cairo Codex contains some ben-Naphtali variants, and so does **D62**, as we shall see. There is enough agreement among **C**, **P**, **A** and other early and good MSS (Breuer 1976) to suggest that what would eventually be accepted as the Masoretic Text was already firm and authoritative by the end of the ninth century, and not only in Karaite circles. The work of the ben-Asher family had eventually carried the day throughout all Jewry, gaining a universal acceptance (the differences from the ben-Naphtali group do not amount to material dissent, since they concern only a few details that did not gain consensus). Not even the bitter polemics of Sa^cadya Gaon, which came to a climax in the third decade of the tenth century, could discredit the achievement of the ben-Asher family with the biblical text, which was not itself the object of the Gaon's attacks (Dotan 1977). Remembering too that the Petrograd Codex is only twenty years later than **C**, it is not impossible than another codex of the (Latter) Prophets already existed in the ninth century. Yet things were moving so fast during that century that the stabilization that can be perceived in the chain from **C** to **P** to **A** to **L** should not be extrapolated back very far. To locate **D62** earlier than any of these other MSS we need to get a bead on its textual affiliation by collating its details with these prime bench marks. Already I can report some striking agreements of **D62** with **P** (against **L**). **D62** also shares with **C** and **P** the use of a special fustiform symbol (it looks like a large heavy *zayin*) to flag its marginal *ktyb/qry* annotations.

I do not know whether the date Starkova reported (747 CE!) was due to a misreading or miscalculation or typographical error. The claims made by Starkova were questioned by Beit-Arié (1977). My own examination, however, suggests that neither she nor anyone else for that matter had even looked at the whole text very carefully. For example, it had always been said that the MS conserved Isa 37:20–43:7; Isa 60:20–Jer 20:17; Jer 32:12–52:21, with Ezekiel and the Twelve complete (Starkova

1974: 38). But when I reached Ezekiel 43:21, there was a lot more of
Isaiah which apparently had not been noticed before!

15.2 The Text

In spite of the calamities suffered by the MS, what survives is in
good condition. The text is perfectly legible; at least the consonants
are. The punctuation and marginal annotations are often very faint,
and their proper study must await the assistance of technological aids.
The MS gives all the appearance of having been made with the greatest
of care, and, for the most part, agrees with the best Masoretic Texts,
even in tiny details and in various oddities. In this report we shall
use **L** as our reference point, not through any prejudgment as to its
superiority as an exemplar of the ben-Asher text type (indeed we have
some reservations on this point), but more for convenience because of its
widespread use and availability and because it is the oldest complete MS
of the Hebrew Bible. We shall report all **D62**'s observed deviations from
L, however slight. This implies that any peculiarity of **L** not mentioned
is found in **D62** as well, so far as we noticed. In fact it was uncanny to
observe the numerous coincidences in trivial details, which conveyed the
impression that **D62** was a quality MS in the ben-Asher tradition. To
illustrate: In Jer 33:26 **D62** agrees with **L** and other mainstream MSS in
the peculiar spellings of *Jacob* and *Isaac*, both protected by the masora
(Mm 822, 2659); in Ezek 46:22 **D62** has מדהקצעות with the *puncta
extraordinaria*.

Side by side with such indications of textual respectability, however, there are some oddities or idiosyncrasies. Examples: 1) There are
some places where *Jeremiah* is pointed ירמידו rather than ירמִידו;
2) There are places where word-terminal *shewa* (normal for verbs like
קָטַלְתְּ) is used with derivatives of ל״י roots, such as בָּנִיתְ (Ezek 16:22,
24, 27), normally בָּנִית; 3) *ktyb* which has *yod* where *qry* has *waw* for
qibbuṣ is written יָ, not the usual יֻ; 4) When marginal notes report differences between Eastern and Western readings, the symbols are בבל מ͏ע,
not the usual מדינחאי in whatever abbreviations. **D62** presents cases
of the familiar alternation of *ḥateph* with simple *shewa*. Someday the MS
should be collated carefully with the *ḥillufim* of Misha²el ben ᶜUzzi²el.
I saw no trace of the pointing לִישׂרָאל, a ben-Naphtali feature in C. I
am not sufficiently knowledgeable in such mysteries to appreciate their
possible value as clues to the textual orientation of **D62**. I report them
for the use of scholars who know what to make of them.

The high measure of agreement of **D62** with prime witnesses needs
to be emphasized at the outset, because during the course of this study

we shall point out hundreds of features in which **D62** differs from received Masoretic Texts and editions. In this it is no different, of course, from any other medieval manuscript; but the important issue is the *kind* and *scale* of these differences.

In studying a MS of a portion of the Hebrew Bible, the data fall into several distinct registers, each of which constitutes an almost autonomous domain. Solutions to the problems of one register do not necessarily help in the resolution of problems in another register. Each domain, in fact, has its own methodology and specialty.

15.3   Codicology

The arrangement of the signatures obeys Gregory's Law. It has quires of four sheets, which could indicate North African origin (Beit-Arié 1976: 48, n. 90). The fact that the text is laid out in two columns could indicate that it is late rather than early, since the oldest known codices have three columns (Ben-Zvi 1960: 2). But note that **P** has two columns. I did not observe any trace of Mp "within the text" (a Babylonian practice) as claimed by Yeivin (1970: 76).

15.4   Palaeography

The consonantal script is archaic, consistent with a ninth-century origin, but not enough to prove such a date, because of the rarity of dated controls. So far as I know, the only facsimile ever published is Plate VIII in Starkova (1974).

15.5   Orthography: Spelling Variants

The spellings in **D62** compared with those of **L** are listed here, using the classification worked out by Andersen and Forbes (1986). **SHB** utilized sixty-five types of word or word class to discuss the spellings in the Hebrew Bible (in that case **L**). Here we shall use the same categories for the most part.

The agreement of **D62** with **L** in consonantal spelling is uncanny, and includes many peculiarities in the use of vowel letters (*matres lectionis*). The great majority of words are identical in their spelling, but there is a significant number which differ in the use of vowel letters in the spelling of words otherwise identical in both consonants and vowels. In fact **D62** shares with other medieval manuscripts the paradox of deviating less in vowel points than in consonantal letters, even though the latter are more venerable. We shall accordingly not discuss here differences between **L** and **D62**, admittedly few, when the use or nonuse of a particular vowel letter indicates a difference in the vowel being written. At first we shall restrict our observations to the original text of **D62** as it came from the first hand (the third column of Table 15.2, at the end of this chapter). This can usually be distinguished from later "corrections," first because changes made by the punctuator use the same red ink for consonants as for the points, and secondly because changes made to consonants even later than the punctuation are usually crude and inferior in penmanship.

Type 1. Suffix –ī– on finite verb— **D62** *plene* where **L** is *defective*: 0. **D62** *defective* where **L** is *plene*: 3. Total: 3.

L *def.* ⟺ **D62** *pl.*: none.
L *pl.* ⟺ **D62** *def.*: Isa 43:4; Jer 6:15; 33:6.

> The *defective* spelling is archaic. Outlier portions due to overuse of *defective* are Exodus 25–40 and 1 Samuel; Ezekiel 1–24 is an outlier due to nonuse of *defective* spelling. The thirty-five cases for the whole Hebrew Bible are listed in **SHB** (pp. 163–64). Twelve of sixty-one opportunities are *defective* in the Pentateuch, only eleven of 265 opportunities in the Latter Prophets are *defective*. The three additional cases of *defective* spelling of this type of vowel in **D62** are thus quite striking, and one has to ask whether they represent a survival of archaic usage or a reversion, against the prevailing trends to more *plene* spellings. Note that **P** and **S**[1] (Sasoon MS 1053) have *defective* against **L**'s הראיתים in Isa 39:4.

Type 2. Stem –ī– in *qal* **of hollow root—** **D62** *plene* where **L** is *defective*: 0. **D62** *defective* where **L** is *plene*: 1. Total: 1.

L *def.* ⟺ **D62** *pl.*: none.
L *pl.* ⟺ **D62** *def.*: Isa 51:16.

> The *defective* spelling is archaic. In this case **D62** agrees with **A, C, S**[1], and **R** against **L, P, 240** (Diez-Macho 1960), but Mm 2528 confirms the *defective* spelling against **L**!

Type 3. Stem –ī– in perfect of ל״ה root— No deviations.

> The *defective* spelling is archaic, but it survives abundantly in Jeremiah (**SHB** 165, 247). **D62** showed no deviations, that is no preference for the modern spelling of this type of vowel.

Type 4. Long –ī– second vowel in *hiphᶜil* **verb stem—** **D62** *plene* where **L** is *defective*: 25. **D62** *defective* where **L** is *plene*: 15. Total: 40.

L *def.* ⟺ **D62** *pl.*: Isa 37:25; 42:23; Jer 1:8; 2:19; 11:7; 17:26; 34:13; 50:44; Ezek 3:2; 5:13; 16:60; 21:22; 28:18; 33:32; 34:23[I]; 39:2;

47:2^I; Hosea 6:2; 7:12; Amos 3:11; Jonah 3:6; Micah 1:16; Hab 3:19; Zeph 2:10; Mal 3:11.

L *pl.* ⇔ **D62** *def.*: Isa 42:2; Jer 2:17 ^{II} (**D62** agrees with **A**, **C**, **S**^{1}, **R**); 4:19 (**D62** agrees with **A**, **C**, **S**^{1}, **R**); 8:9 (**D62** agrees with **A**, **C**, **S**^{1}, but **R** agrees with **L**, while **L** has the *defective* spelling of this word in Jer 8:12, as does **D62**); 38:26; 49:8 (**D62** agrees with **C**, **S**^{1}, **R**, but **A** agrees with **L**); Ezek 11:24 (**D62** agrees with **A**, **S**^{1}, **R**, but **C** agrees with **L**); 16:10; 27:26; 43:5 (**D62** agrees with **A**, **S**^{1}, **R**, but **C** agrees with **L**); 46:21; Hosea 2:7; Micah 2:6, 11; Zech 12:7.

> The *defective* spelling is archaic, but over seven hundred cases are met in **L** (**SHB** 166). All the outlier portions reported in **SHB** (248) are due to overuse of *defective*, underuse of *plene*, with only one in the Pentateuch and none in the Writings, showing that the Prophets have conformed least to the standard spelling. One might have included in this set proper nouns based on *hiph^{c}il* verbs, adding יהויקים which is *plene* in both **D62** and **L** at Isaiah 52:2, where **A**, **C**, **S**^{1}, **R** are defective. The continued indeterminacy of the spelling of this type of vowel is shown by the considerable number of variants exhibited by **D62**. In this it resembles other MSS. The line-up of **D62** with other MSS noted above is not exhaustive, but the patterns are typical. While **D62** prefers *plene* spelling of this type of vowel against *defective* of **L** more times than the reverse, there is nonetheless a significant number of *defective* spellings, which could be survivals of a tradition in which this archaic spelling was still quite abundant. In other words, when these fifteen cases are added to the many more in which **D62** agrees with **L** in *defective* spelling (we have not listed these), **D62** appears to be quite conservative.

Type 5. Long –ī– first vowel in imperfect verbs, פ"י root— **D62** *plene* where **L** is *defective*: 0. **D62** *defective* where **L** is *plene*: 5. Total: 5.

L *def.* ⇔ **D62** *pl.*: none.
L *pl.* ⇔ **D62** *def.*: Isa 41:5; 59:19; Jonah 1:10^I; 4:7; Hab 2:13.

> The *defective* spelling is archaic, and **D62**'s preference for it is another conservative trait. The spelling of w^{e}yīrā$^{\textup{ɔ}}$û in Isa 41:5 varies, with וייראו (**L**, **C**, **S**^{1}, **P**, **R**), ויראו (**A**, 240, **D62**, but with pointing וַיִּרְאוּ). Mm 1180 lists six occurrences of this word, but in **L** three are *plene*. In Isa 59:19 **D62** agrees with **A** against the rest. In Jonah 4:7 and Hab 2:13 **D62**'s *defective* spellings contradict the masora in **L** which indicates *plene*.

Type 6. Long –ī– in suffix –īm of plural nouns— D62 *plene* where **L** is *defective*: 1. **D62** *defective* where **L** is *plene*: 6. Total: 7.
L *def.* ⇔ **D62** *pl.*: Ezek 46:6.

L *pl.* ⇔ D62 *def.*: Isa 41:18[I]; Jer 4:11 (D62 agrees with A, C, S[1], P, and R against L); Ezek 40:14; 47:2[II]; Hosea 8:6; Obad 21.

The *defective* spelling is archaic and the Prophets contain several outlier portions (SHB 249). The evidence suggests that L has tended to modernize the spelling of this vowel, in contrast to other prime manuscripts.

Type 7. Stem –ī– first vowel in a noun— D62 *plene* where L is *defective*: 5. D62 *defective* where L is *plene*: 2. Total: 7.

L *def.* ⇔ D62 *pl.*: Jer 36:13; Ezek 40:22[II] (D62=A), 31; 42:5 and 7.

L *pl.* ⇔ D62 *def.*: Jonah 4:6[I,II] (in the other three occurrences of this word [vv 7, 9, 10] D62 agrees with L in *plene* spelling).

Type 8. Stem –ī– a noun with hollow root— D62 *plene* where L is *defective*: 1. D62 *defective* where L is *plene*: 1. Total: 2.

L *def.* ⇔ D62 *pl.*: Micah 6:10.

L *pl.* ⇔ D62 *def.*: Amos 8:10.

Type 9. Long –ī– second vowel in noun stem— D62 *plene* where L is *defective*: 24. D62 *defective* where L is *plene*: 16. Total: 40.

L *def.* ⇔ D62 *pl.*: Isa 38:20; 55:3; Jer 2:15; 10:13; 17:25; 34:18; 36:9; 50:38; Ezek 1:13[II]; 19:2; 20:1; 32:6; 34:24; 37:24[I]; 38:13; 48:23; Hosea 3:5; 14:10[II]; Amos 2:11, 12; Jonah 2:7; Zech 6:3; 7:3; 11:2[II].

L *pl.* ⇔ D62 *def.*: Isa 65:3[I] (D62 agrees with A, C, S[1], and R against L and P); Jer 2:8 (D62 agrees with A, C, S[1] against L, P, and R); 4:9 (D62 agrees with A, C, S[1], P against L, and R); 5:31 (D62 agrees with A, C, S[1], P, R against L); 13:13 (D62 agrees with A, S[1], against L, C, P, R); 36:1 (D62 agrees with A, C, S[1], P, and R against L); 48:36; Ezek 6:9; 7:7; 11:1[III]; 29:1; Nahum 2:5[II]; 3:18; Zech 1:4[II], 5[II]; 11:15.

D62 shows a slight preference for the *plene* spelling, but in many cases its *defective* against L's *plene* lines up with the other prime manuscripts in various combinations, enough to show that the readings in D62 are good, if not superior to those of L. A more complete and rigorous analysis is needed in order to achieve quantitative estimates of the "distances" between these manuscripts in this feature.

Type 10. Long –ī– in miscellaneous proper nouns— D62 *plene* where L is *defective*: 4. D62 *defective* where L is *plene*: 0. Total: 4.

L *def.* ⇔ D62 *pl.*: Jer 46:2[II]; Ezek 14:14, 20; 28:3. The last three involve *ktyb/qry* of *Daniel*.

L *pl.* ⇔ D62 *def.*: none.

Type 11. Long –ī– in suffix –ît of feminine nouns—   **D62** *plene* where **L** is *defective*: 1. **D62** *defective* where **L** is *plene*: 1. Total: 2.

     L *def.* ⇔ **D62** *pl.*: Jer 36:1 (**D62** agrees with **A**, **C**, **S**¹, **P**, and **R** against **L**).

     L *pl.* ⇔ **D62** *def.*: Ezek 5:10.

Type 12. Miscellaneous use of *yod* **for -i-** —   **D62** *plene* where **L** is *defective*: 4. **D62** *defective* where **L** is *plene*: 0. Total: 4.

     L *def.* ⇔ **D62** *pl.*: Ezek 12:27 (nonstandard *plene* spelling of short vowel); Hosea 10:1 (use of double *yod* for –î–); Jonah 4:10^{II} (*bis*—the vowel letter for short -i- secures the unusual pronunciation of **bin**). All these cases are outside the bounds of acceptable biblical practice.

Type 13. Stem-terminal –ē– in prepositions—   **D62** *plene* where **L** is *defective*: 2. **D62** *defective* where **L** is *plene*: 8. Total: 10.

     L *def.* ⇔ **D62** *pl.*: Ezek 33:27; Zech 1:3.

     L *pl.* ⇔ **D62** *def.*: Jer 1:17; 14:17; Ezek 2:7; 12:10; 13:12; 14:4; 16:37; 33:25^I.

> All these cases involve אֶל, not עַל. The *defective* spelling is found mainly in the Pentateuch (**SHB** Tables 6.2, 6.3), rarely in the Latter Prophets. Here **D62** not only agrees with **L** (Ezek 20:3, 7, 29; 37:19), but has no fewer than eight *defective* spellings not in **L**. Mm 1954 attests twenty-nine cases of *defective* spelling of אֲלֵהֶם in the Prophets, and even has it against Ezek 33:25^I. In this detail, then, **D62** is superior to **L**; in fact **A**, **C**, **S**¹, **R** agree with **L**'s masora against **L**! **P** agrees with **L**, however.

Type 14. Stem-terminal –ē– in nouns—   **D62** *plene* where **L** is *defective*: 10. **D62** *defective* where **L** is *plene*: 4. Total: 14.

     L *def.* ⇔ **D62** *pl.*: Isa 51:23; 53:5; 63:17; 64:7; Ezek 5:10; 16:25, 29; 33:25^{II}; Nahum 2:8; Zech 12:3. In the case of Isa 51:23, 63:17, 64:7 the *plene* spelling is incorrect for a singular noun.

     L *pl.* ⇔ **D62** *def.*: Isa 53:4; 64:10; Jer 14:7; 44:8^{II}. The *defective* spelling is acceptable for the plural noun.

Type 15. Stem-initial –ē– in verbs—   **D62** *plene* where **L** is *defective*: 2. **D62** *defective* where **L** is *plene*: 12. Total: 14.

     L *def.* ⇔ **D62** *pl.*: Ezek 36:11; Joel 1:5.

     L *pl.* ⇔ **D62** *def.*: Isa 41:23; 52:5; 65:14; Jer 2:11; 4:22; 7:5; 18:11; 32:40; 35:15^{II}; Micah 1:8; 7:3; Zech 8:15.

> These cases all involve *hiph^cil* forms with roots beginning with a secondary *yod*, nine of them יטב. **D62**'s preference for the spelling without this *yod* is so consistent that one suspects the scribe (or his source) of having a different perception of the morphology of these verbs.

Type 16. Stem –ē– in verb, ל״י root— **D62** *plene* where **L** is *defective*: 2. **D62** *defective* where **L** is *plene*: 2. Total: 4.

L *def.* ⇔ **D62** *pl.*: Isa 38:16; Hosea 7:6.

L *pl.* ⇔ **D62** *def.*: Amos 3:1; Nahum 3:5.

Type 17. Stem –ē– in verbs, miscellaneous— **D62** *plene* where **L** is *defective*: 5. **D62** *defective* where **L** is *plene*: 2. Total: 7.

L *def.* ⇔ **D62** *pl.*: Ezek 14:16 (un-Masoretic); Hosea 14:10^I (against the masora of **L**); Zech 9:15^I; 11:2^I; 12:8.

L *pl.* ⇔ **D62** *def.*: Jer 35:15^I (**D62** agrees with **A**, **C**, **S**^{1}, **P**, and **R** against **L**); 36:16.

The uncertain status of the vocalization was discussed in **SHB** (p. 174). MSS reflect uncertainty over the spelling. In Jer 3:15 **D62** agrees with **L** in והשכיל, but Mp says that *yod* is "not to be read." In Jer 44:4 **S**^{1} and **P** have השכם against השכים of **L**.

Type 18. Stem –ē– in noun with two-consonant root— **D62** *plene* where **L** is *defective*: 1. **D62** *defective* where **L** is *plene*: 7. Total: 8.

L *def.* ⇔ **D62** *pl.*: Zech 6:14.

L *pl.* ⇔ **D62** *def.*: Ezek 1:13^{III}; 13:10; 31:11; 39:18; 40:29; 45:23; Jonah 4:11.

The *plene* spelling is appropriate when the root is C^1yC^2, but not for C^1C^2 nor for $C^1C^2C^2$. The notorious problem of אל versus איל accounts for several of these cases; but the *defective* spelling of bên, *between* (Ezek 1:13^{III}; Jonah 4:11) is exceptional—it occurs only once in **L** (Hosea 13:15), but here the other prime MSS are *plene*.

Type 19. Long –ē– first stem vowel in nouns— **D62** *plene* where **L** is *defective*: 2. **D62** *defective* where **L** is *plene*: 1. Total: 3.

L *def.* ⇔ **D62** *pl.*: Ezek 6:3; 40:22^I.

L *pl.* ⇔ **D62** *def.*: Ezek 46:14.

Here we report also the nonstandard spelling חילם (Zech 6:14).

Type 20. Long –ē– second stem vowel in noun— **D62** *plene* where **L** is *defective*: 3. **D62** *defective* where **L** is *plene*: 0. Total: 3.

L *def.* ⇔ **D62** *pl.*: Jer 50:29 (**D62** agrees with **A**, **C**, **S**^{1}, **P**, and **R** against **L**); Ezek 4:1; 14:22^I (here, but not at Jer 50:29, the *defective* spelling is protected by Mm 434). The not infrequent spelling פליטה could be due to influence from pālît.

L *pl.* ⇔ **D62** *def.*: none.

Type 25. Stem-terminal -ē̆- in plural nouns— **D62** *plene* where **L** is *defective*: 5. **D62** *defective* where **L** is *plene*: 7. Total: 12.

The *defective* spelling of this vowel is relatively rare in the Bible (78 out of 2466), but the vowel is difficult to identify with certainty because of ambiguities in morphology (**SHB**: 141–47). In the case of **D62** it is sometimes difficult to decide whether an abnormal *plene* spelling is a misreading of a form as plural or an illegal spelling of the pausal form of a singular noun with a vowel letter. The several cases of the latter show that in this matter **D62** has gone beyond the limits in its use of modern *plene* spelling.

L *def.* ⇔ **D62** *pl.*: Isa 58:7[II] (illegal spelling of sg.); Ezek 3:11 (illegal spelling of sg.); Hos 13:9 (illegal); Joel 2:17 (illegal); Micah 5:13 (illegal).

L *pl.* ⇔ **D62** *def.*: Isa 64:4; Jer 15:16[I,II]; 17:3[II]; Ezek 2:1; 28:9; Joel 1:7.

Type 26. Stem-terminal -ē̆- in verb— **D62** *plene* where **L** is *defective*: 3. **D62** *defective* where **L** is *plene*: 1. Total: 4.

L *def.* ⇔ **D62** *pl.*: Isa 54:10 (**D62** agrees with **A**, **S**[1], **P**, and **R** against **L**, **C**, **240**; since the word is unique, the Mp לֹ in both **A** and **L** does not secure any spelling); Ezek 34:16; Zech 5:9 (here *yod* supplements *aleph*, a spelling in which **L** agrees with **D62** and other MSS at Ezek 23:49– תשׁאינה).

L *pl.* ⇔ **D62** *def.*: Zech 1:17 (other MSS agree with **D62**).

In Jer 18:21 **L** and **D62** both read ותהיינה, but **D62** Mp reads ק̇ ותהיינה, using the *ktyb/qry* apparatus to adjust a spelling discrepancy.

Types 27–28. Suffix –â on various verbs— **D62** *plene* where **L** is *defective*: 1. **D62** *defective* where **L** is *plene*: 2. Total: 3.

L *def.* ⇔ **D62** *pl.*: Ezek 34:10.

L *pl.* ⇔ **D62** *def.*: Ezek 4:2; 35:11.

Type 31. Suffix –ô spelled with *he* or *waw*— **D62** *he* where **L** has *waw*: 0. **D62** *waw* where **L** has *he*: 2. Total: 2.

L *waw* ⇔ **D62** *he*: none.

L *he* ⇔ **D62** *waw*: Isa 59:11; Ezek 18:9.

This alternative is often supplied as **qry**, which is really a pseudo-use of that device since the identity and pronunciation of the word are not in question.

Type 32. The negative particle lō[ɔ]**,** *not*— **D62** *plene* where **L** is *defective*: 7. **D62** *defective* where **L** is *plene*: 20. Total: 27.

L *def.* ⇔ **D62** *pl.*: Jer 5:9, 12, 24[I]; 13:17; Ezek 18:25; 24:17; 26:15.

L *pl.* ⇔ **D62** *def.*: Isa 40:21[I]; 42:24; 55:1[I,II], 2[I,II]; 58:7[I]; Jer 3:1, 3, 12; 8:6; 10:4; 15:7, 11; 35:14; 44:21; Ezek 16:56; 24:16; Zech 4:5; Mal 2:10.

Type 33. *Nota accusativi* ᴐōt-—— **D62** *plene* where **L** is *defective*: 8. **D62** *defective* where **L** is *plene*: 11. Total: 19.

L *def.* ⟺ **D62** *pl.*: Jer 33:9 (**D62** agrees with **A**, **C**, **S**[1], and **R** against **L**, **P**; **P** protects the *defective* with Mp); 39:5 (**D62** agrees with **A**, **C**, **S**[1], against **L**, **P** and **R**); Ezek 16:4 (**D62** agrees with **L**'s masora against **L**'s text), 5; 20:23; 34:14; Zech 6:8; Mal 3:22.

L *pl.* ⟺ **D62** *def.*: Isa 65:3[II] (**D62** agrees with **A**, **C**, **S**[1], **P**, and **R** against **L**); Jer 12:1 (**D62** agrees with **A**, **C**, **S**[1], and **R** against **L**, **P**; **P** protects the *plene* with Mp, but Mm 2565 does not list this case, so **L** is wrong); Ezek 7:27 (**D62** agrees with **A**, **C**, **S**[1], **P**, and **R** against **L**, which contradicts its own masora); 16:39 (**D62** agrees with **A**, **C**, **S**[1], against **L**, **P** and **R**); 20:22, 28; 23:35; 43:20[II]; Hosea 4:19; 10:6; Mal 1:12.

Type 34. Long –ō– as stem vowel in monosyllabic nouns, prepositions, adverbs— **D62** *plene* where **L** is *defective*: 4. **D62** *defective* where **L** is *plene*: 6. Total: 10.

L *def.* ⟺ **D62** *pl.*: Jer 50:39[I]; Hosea 13:8; Joel 2:20; 4:5.

L *pl.* ⟺ **D62** *def.*: Jer 4:3 (**D62** agrees with **A**, **C**, **S**[1], **P**, and **R** against **L**, which contradicts Mm 3402); 33:8 (at least originally); 36:32; 50:39[II]; 51:55; Ezek 14:11.

Type 35. Stem –ō– in *hiphᶜil* **of** ᵞ″ꟼ **root and analogous nouns—** **D62** *plene* where **L** is *defective*: 13. **D62** *defective* where **L** is *plene*: 10. Total: 23.

L *def.* ⟺ **D62** *pl.*: Jer 32:20; 51:16[I] (Mm 2194 confirms **D62** against **L**), 44; Ezek 16:3; Hosea 2:7; 10:12; 11:6; Joel 1:12, 17[III]; Obad 21; Micah 6:2, 16; Zeph 3:1.

L *pl.* ⟺ **D62** *def.*: Isa 63:6; 66:14; Ezek 2:3; 12:11; 18:12; 31:18; Hosea 6:3 (**D62** agrees with **A**, **C**, **S**[1], **P**, and **R** against **L**, which contradicts Mm 3011); Micah 7:7; Nahum 3:17[II]; Zech 9:5.

Type 36. Stem-terminal –ō– in *hiphᶜil*— **D62** *plene* where **L** is *defective*: 4. **D62** *defective* where **L** is *plene*: 4. Total: 8.

L *def.* ⟺ **D62** *pl.*: Isa 40:21[II] (**D62** agrees with **A**, **P**, and **R** against **L**, **C**, **S**[1]); Ezek 34:13 (**D62** agrees with **A**, **C**, **S**[1], **P**, and **R** against **L**; Mm 3933 does not deal with spelling), 23[I]; Mal 3:10.

L *pl.* ⟺ **D62** *def.*: Jer 10:18; Ezek 11:17; Zech 10:6, 10.

Type 37. Stem –ō– in infinitive, ᵞ″ꟻ **root—** **D62** *plene* where **L** is *defective*: 1. **D62** *defective* where **L** is *plene*: 1. Total: 2.

L *def.* ⟺ **D62** *pl.*: Jer 18:9.

L *pl.* ⟺ **D62** *def.*: Mal 3:2[I].

Type 38. Stem $-\bar{o}-$ **infinitive absolute—** **D62** *plene* where **L** is *defective*: 0. **D62** *defective* where **L** is *plene*: 1. Total: 1.

L *pl.* ⇔ **D62** *def.*: Jer 19:1 (**D62** agrees with **A**, **C**, **S**[1], **P**, and Mm 1408 against **L** and **R**).

Type 39. Stem $-\bar{o}-$ **in** *qal* **active participles—** **D62** *plene* where **L** is *defective*: 39. **D62** *defective* where **L** is *plene*: 20. Total: 59.

> In **L** 1040 of 5309 are *plene*, or 19.6%. Both spellings are well represented in the Hebrew Bible, and either would be acceptable in any manuscript. In **D62**[1] there are twenty more *plene* spellings than in the corresponding parts of **L**.

L *def.* ⇔ **D62** *pl.*: Isa 40:6; 66:12 (**D62** agrees with **S**[1], **P**, **R** against **L**, **A**, **C**); Jer 2:21 (**D62** agrees with **A**, **C**, **S**[1], **P**, and **R** against **L**); 4:30; 5:24[II]; 6:28; 14:12; 20:6; 32:36; 33:11; 34:22[II]; 36:30; Ezek 13:13; 28:16; 32:29; 34:23[II]; 43:24; 44:1, 11 (**D62** agrees with **A**, **C**, **S**[1], **P**, and **R** against **L**); 45:17; Hosea 9:13, 15; 10:12; 13:3; Amos 4:13; 9:4, 5; Micah 6:6; Nahum 1:5 (**D62** agrees with **A**, **S**[1], and **R** against **L** [which contradicts its masora], **C**, **P** [corrected later]); 2:6; 3:10; Zeph 2:5; 3:1; Zech 7:7; 9:8; 11:5[I]; 13:1; 14:12; Mal 2:12.

L *pl.* ⇔ **D62** *def.*: Isa 57:13 (**D62** = **P**); 59:20; Jer 36:30; 50:6; Ezek 3:15; 7:12, 13 (in both cases **D62** agrees with **A**, **C**, **S**[1] against **L**, **P**, **R**); 11:1[II]; 22:25; 32:15; 37:24[II]; 40:42; Hosea 4:1, 3; Amos 2:3; 5:8; Jonah 1:11; Micah 2:7; Zeph 1:9; Zech 5:5.

Type 40. Stem $-\bar{o}-$ **in** *qal* **imperfect of regular verbs—** **D62** *plene* where **L** is *defective*: 8. **D62** *defective* where **L** is *plene*: 5. Total: 13.

> For the whole Bible the *plene* spelling is rather rare, only 125 out of 1481. Three of the outliers reported in **SHB** (p. 267) are in the Prophets, and many of these "modern" spellings evoke Masoretic notes. It is a token of the stability of the mainstream tradition, and of the affinity of **D62** with that tradition, that it mostly agrees with **L** in these atypical *plene* spellings (Isa 57:17, 17; 61:8; 62:1; Hos 2:20; 4:14; 5:10; 7:4, 12; 9:9, 9; 10:11; Joel 1:20; 3:1, 2; Amos 2:3; 3:5; Micah 6:15; 7:19; Hab 3:2). The agreement of **D62** in the *plene* spelling of *Jacob* also belongs here. This measure of agreement in the peculiarities of **L** makes the thirteen disagreements all the more interesting.

L *def.* ⇔ **D62** *pl.*: Jer 2:20[II] (**D62** agrees with **A**, **C**, **S**[1], **P**, **R** against **L**); Ezek 8:18 (adjusted later); 9:10 (adjusted later); 18:23 (adjusted later); 20:4 (adjusted later); 33:11 (adjusted later); Micah 7:19 (=**P**); Zeph 3:9 (adjusted later); Mal 3:17[II].

L *pl.* ⇔ **D62** *def.*: Isa 57:15 (adjusted later); Ezek 7:8 (adjusted later); 11:10 (adjusted later); Nahum 1:6 (adjusted later); Hab 3:18 (adjusted later).

Type 42. Stem –ō– in *qal* **imperfect of verb with hollow root—** **D62** *plene* where **L** is *defective*: 3. **D62** *defective* where **L** is *plene*: 10. Total: 13.

Both spellings of this vowel in verbs of this type are well represented in the Bible—874 *defective*, 202 *plene*—so it is not surprising that it manifests disagreements between manuscript and manuscript. **D62**'s marked preference for *defective* spellings is conservative.

L *def.* ⇔ **D62** *pl.*: Ezek 9:5 (Mm 2804); Joel 2:26, 27.

L *pl.* ⇔ **D62** *def.*: Isa 38:1 (**D62** agrees with **P** against **L** and the others; in Isa 37:34 **S**[1] and **240** have the *defective* spelling of this word, which, unlike וַיָּבֹא [Mm 1552] is not protected by masora; in 37:33 **240** alone has it; in Jer 36:29 **C**; and so on); Jer 2:36 (**D62** agrees with **A**, **C**, **S**[1], **P**, **R** against **L**); Ezek 14:1; 38:9; Hosea 7:1; Joel 1:15; Zeph 2:1, 2; Zech 4:1; 9:9.

Type 43. Stem –ō– in *qal* **imperative or infinitive of three-consonant root—** **D62** *plene* where **L** is *defective*: 2. **D62** *defective* where **L** is *plene*: 4. Total: 6.

L *def.* ⇔ **D62** *pl.*: Jer 15:3; Ezek 3:21.

L *pl.* ⇔ **D62** *def.*: Jer 11:10; 33:19; Joel 1:15; Zech 7:11.

Type 44. Stem –ō– in *qal* **imperative or infinitive, hollow root—** **D62** *plene* where **L** is *defective*: 2. **D62** *defective* where **L** is *plene*: 2. Total: 4.

L *def.* ⇔ **D62** *pl.*: Ezek 8:9[I]; 26:10 (**D62** agrees with **C**, **R** against **L**, **A**, **S**[1], **P**).

L *pl.* ⇔ **D62** *def.*: Mal 3:2[II], 23 (against Mm 169).

Type 45. Stem –ō– in *pōlēl*— **D62** *plene* where **L** is *defective*: 3. **D62** *defective* where **L** is *plene*: 2. Total: 5.

L *def.* ⇔ **D62** *pl.*: Jer 5:7; Hosea 10:2; Jonah 2:6.

L *pl.* ⇔ **D62** *def.*: Hosea 7:14[II]; Nahum 3:17[I] (**D62** agrees with **A**).

Type 46. Long –ō– as first stem vowel in nouns— **D62** *plene* where **L** is *defective*: 7. **D62** *defective* where **L** is *plene*: 8. Total: 15.

L *def.* ⇔ **D62** *pl.*: Isa 59:4[I] (תִהוּ is not traditional); Jer 7:19 (un-Masoretic spelling of segholate); 32:20; 51:16[II]; Hosea 8:1; Joel 1:17[II]; Zeph 1:15[I].

L *pl.* ⇔ **D62** *def.*: Isa 41:18[II]; Ezek 17:7[I]; 22:18, 20; 32:10; 38:5 Jonah 1:7[I,II].

Type 47. Plural suffix −ōt of nouns, two-consonant roots—
D62 *plene* where **L** is *defective*: 11. **D62** *defective* where **L** is *plene*: 17.
Total: 28.

    L *def.* ⇔ **D62** *pl.*: Isa 64:10; Jer 16:3; 18:9; 19:8; 35:8; Ezek 37:24^{III}; 43:11; Joel 1:2; Zech 1:4^I; 8:14; Mal 3:7.

    L *pl.* ⇔ **D62** *def.*: Isa 43:6; Jer 14:16; Ezek 1:9; 16:20^I, 55; 20:11, 19, 21; 24:25; 26:12; 27:11; 28:23; 43:11; 46:23; Hab 2:2; Zech 1:2, 5^I.

Type 48. Plural suffix −ōt of nouns, three-consonant roots—
D62 *plene* where **L** is *defective*: 35. **D62** *defective* where **L** is *plene*: 32.
Total: 67.

    L *def.* ⇔ **D62** *pl.*: Isa 55:9; 63:7; Jer 2:20^I (**D62** agrees with **A**, **C**, **S**^{1}, **P**, **R** against **L**); 15:8 (**D62** agrees with **A**, **C**, **S**^{1}, **R** against **L**, **P**); 19:8; 35:8; 49:11; Ezek 5:9; 6:3; 7:20; 14:6; 16:22^I, 38, 43, 51; 17:7^{II}; 20:31; 22:8; 27:16; 29:4; 30:4; 32:22; 38:12; 40:16^{II}; Hosea 8:11, 14; Joel 1:17^I; 4:10; Amos 1:7; Micah 5:4; 7:17; Hab 3:8; Zeph 3:11; Zech 12:14^{I,II}.

    L *pl.* ⇔ **D62** *def.*: Isa 59:2 (**D62** contradicts Mm 1383, but agrees with **C**, **P**), 3 (as in **P**), 12; Jer 5:24^{III} (**D62** agrees with **A**, **C**, **S**^{1}, **P**, **R** against **L**); 25; 7:10 (**R**); 17:3^I; 38:22 (**D62** agrees with **A**, **C**, **R** against **L**, **S**^{1}, **P**); 42:20; 50:45; Ezek 5:2, 5, 6, 9; 8:9^{II}; 11:18; 17:6, 22; 18:24; 20:21^{I,II}; 22:26^{II}; 27:11; 28:23; 36:33; 37:12; 46:23; 47:19; Joel 4:4^I; Micah 6:16; Nahum 2:4^I; Zech 9:15.

Type 49. Suffix −ōn on nouns— **D62** *plene* where **L** is *defective*:
10. **D62** *defective* where **L** is *plene*: 1. Total: 11.

    L *def.* ⇔ **D62** *pl.*: Isa 58:5; Jer 2:25^I; Ezek 10:5; 40:16^I, 44; 41:16; 42:5, 6; Amos 3:4; Hab 3:1. **D62** tends to the modern spelling.

    L *pl.* ⇔ **D62** *def.*: Ezek 11:1^I.

Type 50. Long −ō− second vowel in noun stem— **D62** *plene*
where **L** is *defective*: 24. **D62** *defective* where **L** is *plene*: 21. Total: 45.

    L *def.* ⇔ **D62** *pl.*: Isa 37:36; 54:7 (**D62** agrees with **A**, **S**^{1}, **P**, **R** against **L**, **C**); 63:5 (**P**); 66:3; Jer 4:7; Ezek 4:7; 8:6; 13:14, 16^{I,II}; 16:22^{III}; 20:28, 41; 29:18; 30:4; 40:9^I, 34, 37; Amos 3:4; 4:8; Nahum 2:4^{II}, 5^I; Zeph 2:14; Zech 10:5.

    L *pl.* ⇔ **D62** *def.*: Jer 8:16; 20:10; 44:7; 51:5; Ezek 1:10; 3:25; 16:31; 23:5; 34:14; 40:11, 21; 41:6; Hosea 7:14^I; 9:2; Joel 2:7^I; Micah 1:3; Hab 1:8; Zeph 1:15^{II}; Zech 4:2, 11; Mal 1:11.

Type 54. Miscellaneous verbs— **D62** *plene* where **L** is *defective*:
0. **D62** *defective* where **L** is *plene*: 1. Total: 1.

    L *pl.* ⇔ **D62** *def.*: Zeph 2:1.

Type 56. Suffix –ū– on finite verb with object suffix— **D62** *plene* where **L** is *defective*: 3. **D62** *defective* where **L** is *plene*: 2. Total: 5.

    L *def.* ⇔ **D62** *pl.*: Zeph 1:6; Zech 7:5; 13:3.

    L *pl.* ⇔ **D62** *def.*: Jer 20:5 (against Mm 2569); 34:22^I.

Type 57. Suffix –ūn on finite verb— **D62** *plene* where **L** is *defective*: 1. **D62** *defective* where **L** is *plene*: 0. Total: 1.

    L *def.* ⇔ **D62** *pl.*: Zech 11:5^{II}.

Type 58. Stem –ū– in *qal* **imperfect verb—** **D62** *plene* where **L** is *defective*: 2. **D62** *defective* where **L** is *plene*: 2. Total: 4.

    L *def.* ⇔ **D62** *pl.*: Ezek 18:31; Joel 2:7^{II}.

    L *pl.* ⇔ **D62** *def.*: Ezek 18:26; Zech 1:6.

Type 59. Stem –ū– in *qal* **imperative verb—** **D62** *plene* where **L** is *defective*: 1. **D62** *defective* where **L** is *plene*: 0. Total: 1.

    L *def.* ⇔ **D62** *pl.*: Joel 2:12.

Type 60. Stem –ū– in *hoph^{c}al* **verb—** **D62** *plene* where **L** is *defective*: 2. **D62** *defective* where **L** is *plene*: 0. Total: 2.

    L *def.* ⇔ **D62** *pl.*: Hosea 12:5; Zech 11:11.

Type 61. Stem –ū– in *qal* **passive participle —** **D62** *plene* where **L** is *defective*: 1. **D62** *defective* where **L** is *plene*: 1. Total: 2.

    L *def.* ⇔ **D62** *pl.*: Jer 32:19.

    L *pl.* ⇔ **D62** *def.*: Nahum 1:10.

Type 62. Stem –ū– in monosyllabic noun— **D62** *plene* where **L** is *defective*: 2. **D62** *defective* where **L** is *plene*: 2. Total: 4.

    L *def.* ⇔ **D62** *pl.*: Jer 14:16; Zech 6:5.

    L *pl.* ⇔ **D62** *def.*: Isa 63:19; Ezek 24:21.

Type 63. Stem –ū– first in bisyllabic noun— **D62** *plene* where **L** is *defective*: 7. **D62** *defective* where **L** is *plene*: 0. Total: 7.

    L *def.* ⇔ **D62** *pl.*: Isa 66:19; Ezek 27:13; 34:27; 40:7, 9^{II}; 44:3 (**D62** agrees with **A**, **S^1**, **P**, **R** against **L**, **C**); Amos 9:7.

Type 64. Stem –ū– second in miscellaneous bisyllabic nouns— **D62** *plene* where **L** is *defective*: 20. **D62** *defective* where **L** is *plene*: 12. Total: 32.

    L *def.* ⇔ **D62** *pl.*: Isa 55:4^{II}; 57:9 (**P**); 58:8; 63:15; Ezek 10:7^{I,II}; 16:20^{II}, 22^{II}, 25, 26; Joel 4:4^{II}; Nahum 2:2 (**D62** agrees with **A**, **C**, **S^1**, **P**, **R** against **L**), 11; 3:6; Hab 3:14; Zech 1:8, 13; 3:9; 5:11; Mal 3:17^I.

    L *pl.* ⇔ **D62** *def.*: Isa 55:4^I; 58:8; Jer 1:18; 9:22; Ezek 10:19, 20; 28:16; Micah 2:8; 5:5; Zeph 2:8; Zech 8:22; Mal 2:15.

15.6　Orthography: Interpretation

Table 15.1 reports our observation of 615 vowels in **D62**[1] which are spelled differently from the matching, identical vowels in **L**. More than two-thirds (418) involve the use of *waw* to represent ō or ū, mainly the former (360). Use or nonuse of *yod* to represent ī or ē yields 194 cases, while only three involve the use of *he* to represent word-terminal –ā. The impression that the deviations of **D62**[1] from **L** show no marked tendency in any direction is confirmed by quantitative analysis.

Table 15.1. Counts of variant spellings in D62[1] by Type

Type	*plene*	*def.*	Type	*plene*	*def.*
Type 1	0	3	Type 34	4	6
Type 2	0	1	Type 35	13	10
Type 4	25	15	Type 36	4	4
Type 5	0	5	Type 37	1	1
Type 6	1	6	Type 38	0	1
Type 7	5	2	Type 39	39	20
Type 8	1	1	Type 40	9	5
Type 9	24	16	Type 42	3	10
Type 10	4	0	Type 43	2	4
Type 11	1	1	Type 44	2	2
Type 12	4	0	Type 45	3	2
Types 1–12	**65**	**50**	Type 46	7	8
Type 13	2	8	Type 47	11	17
Type 14	10	4	Type 48	35	32
Type 15	2	12	Type 49	10	1
Type 16	2	2	Type 50	24	21
Type 17	5	2	Type 54	0	1
Type 18	1	7	**Types 31–54**	**182**	**178**
Type 19	2	1	Type 56	3	2
Type 20	3	0	Type 57	1	0
Types 13–20	**27**	**36**	Type 58	2	2
Type 25	5	7	Type 59	1	0
Type 26	3	1	Type 60	2	0
Types 25–26	**8**	**8**	Type 61	1	1
Types 27–28	**1**	**2**	Type 62	2	2
Type 31	0	2	Type 63	7	0
Type 32	7	20	Type 64	20	12
Type 33	8	11	**Types 56–64**	**39**	**19**

Nearly all of the hundreds of differences from **L** in spelling in the original text of **D62** involve the use or nonuse of *waw* or *yod* to spell word-medial long vowels. It must be emphasized that in nearly every case both the *plene* and *defective* spellings of such vowels are quite legal options within Masoretic practice. Theoretically, any scribe confronted by such a vowel had a choice; he could spell the vowel either way, and no harm done. In practice, however, the scribe was under three powerful constraints. First, the task of a scribe was not simply to replicate a text, but to copy a manuscript, reproducing every detail, however slight, with complete precision. Quite apart from the professional standards of his guild, reinforced by reverence for the sacred text and set out in great detail in the Talmudic tractate *Sopherim*, the scribe was restrained secondly by numerous marginal notes, which drew attention to peculiarities in individual words and served as warnings not to alter them in any way. Such warnings were needed, not only when the scribe might feel that the word he had to copy looked so abnormal it was incorrect, but even when the form was unremarkable and quite acceptable, but simply rare. Numerous notes of the latter kind came to be attached to individual words which had a dominant or normal spelling (the spelling of the great majority of its occurrences) but which occurred a few times with another spelling. This could be occasional *plene* spelling of a word usually *defective*, or the other way around. For example, the word **malkût** occurs 136 times; the three cases when û is spelled *defective* (Num 24:7; 1 Kgs 2:12; Jer 52:31) are flagged with a marginal masora (Mm 971). In the other way, the form **wayyābōᵓ**, which occurs 261 times, occurs *plene* nineteen times. Mm 1552 is based on a count of fifteen, which excludes Megillot, because there the majority spelling is *plene* (four cases in Esther). The minority two cases of *defective* spelling of this word in Megillot (both in Esther) evoke a masora. These examples illustrate the system. Only the rarer deviant is noted; the score of the majority is not recorded and the occurrences are not flagged. Because the *defective* spelling of **wayyābōᵓ** occurs 242 times, it might seem to be more "correct" than the rare *plene* variant. If it were not for the flag attached to all cases of ויבוא (except in Esther), the dominant ויבא might be preferred. This kind of constraint, however, could be offset by the general trend in the history of Hebrew spelling towards more *plene* spellings, since even the rules of the scribes could be relaxed for this one kind of "error" (*Menaḥot* 29b). Even so the marginal masora was intended to prevent this trend from getting out of hand. Its success, however, is often exaggerated: all manuscripts and editions do not present the fifteen *plene* spellings of **wayyābōᵓ** listed in Mm 1552. L agrees with A and C that **wayyābōᵓ** in Isa 38:1 is *plene*, but in D62 it is *defective*, as in P. One could, of course, set such variants aside as random fluctuations or even as evidence that manuscripts such as P or D62 are thereby shown to be inferior to, say, L. This is too easy. Every manuscript has its blemishes, and each variant has to be evaluated on its own merits while assessing each reading of a given manuscript in the light of its overall characteristics. This is where the overwhelming agreement of **D62** with manuscripts of acknowledged quality is important; since it is generally good, its variant readings should be taken seriously, especially in a case like this where the deviant is confirmed by another early manuscript (**P** in this instance) and even more when it agrees with several, as the annotations given above frequently show. This example illustrates the need for safeguards in the text-transmission process. So far as the identity of the word **wayyābō꞊** is concerned, the use of *plene* or *defective* spelling makes not the slightest difference; but the anxiety of the scribes to preserve such meaningless trivia is very revealing of their mentality and of their approach to their work. As a hedge around the text, the innumerable marginal notes could not provide a description of every word; they were confined for the most part to protecting rare deviants which were in danger of being absorbed by the dominant normal spelling. Normal spellings did not need flags.

15.7   Corrections in D62

Table 15.2 shows that of the more than six hundred words in which **D62**[1] differs from **L** in consonantal spelling, over three hundred have been subsequently adjusted. The proportion is higher in Ezekiel than in the other books. These "corrections" have been made by more than one scribe or user, but for convenience we have labeled them all **D62**[2] (the rightmost column of Table 15.2). At least three stages can be discerned. First, corrections were made in black ink and with letter shapes resembling those of the first hand (example at Ezek 1:10). Later, corrections were made using red ink, apparently by the punctuator, since you can often tell from the position of the points that the punctuator was guided by the position of the corrected consonants. Corrections made even later are very few. They can be detected by the facts that they are in black ink, crudely done, and the points sometimes do not fit the consonantal pattern.

So far as the consonantal orthography is concerned, the corrections move in both directions, deleting or adding vowel letters almost to the same extent. As can be seen from Table 15.2, all types of spelling which deviate from **L** with any frequency are adjusted in both directions; decisions have not been guided by belief that there is a correct way to spell individual words such as lō꞊, *not*, or types of vowels such as the –ō– in feminine plural. Rather do these adjustments, which do not make the slightest difference to the identity of the word, suggest "correction" down to such tiny details against some authoritative standard, so that each word is spelled the same way at the same place in each, even when both ways occur abundantly overall.

All the indications are that most of these corrections were made at the same time (most likely by the punctuator himself), and the standard used was a text considerably closer to **L** than the original source of **D62**, assuming that the scribe who made the consonantal text in the first place was conscientious in copying his source exactly, replicating *plene* and *defective* spellings as he found them. To the degree that the corrector worked deliberately and systematically, his control text was not identical with **L**, for many of **D62**[1]'s deviations from **L** were left uncorrected (blanks in the rightmost column of Table 15.2). Furthermore, many of the words which were not changed agree with other prime manuscripts against **L**, and there are a few cases in which a word, originally the same as in **L**, was "corrected" away from agreement with **L** (Isa 59:4[II]; Jer 35:14; 46:28; Ezek 17:10; 22:26[I]; 40:7, 21; 41:6; 43:20[I]; Jonah 1:11; Micah 2:6; Zech 1:5; 9:5; 11:15, 17). There are even a few cases where more than two spellings of a word are permitted and neither **D62**[1] nor **D62**[2] agrees with **L** (Jer 32:19; Ezek 16:22).

In contrast to these indications of assiduity in those who handled the manuscript, the ways in which the corrections were made creates an untidy effect. A number of different remedies were used to add a needed vowel letter or to remove a superfluous one. According to *Sopherim* 8:2, an omitted letter must be hung above the line. The corrector(s) of **D62** did not always follow this rule. The technique used in each case is shown in Table 15.2 by means of a code with the key at the foot of the page. Besides the approved supralinear addition (category 3), a vowel letter might be squeezed in between two consonants (category 4). Usually it was quite thin, but legible because in red. If there was no space, a tiny *waw* or *yod* might be put inside another consonant, such as *lamed*. Or an adjacent letter might be remodeled (category 5). To insert a *waw* before a *taw*, say, the right leg of the *taw* would be made into the *waw* (black) and a new down-stroke (red) provided for *taw*, which became quite narrow. When this could not be easily achieved, an adjacent letter would be partly or wholly erased and replaced along with the new vowel letter. This last measure corresponds to the latest stages, since the work is usually badly done, and in black ink.

The "correctors" got rid of unwanted vowel letters in three ways. Sometimes the whole letter was erased (category 0), leaving an unsightly gap in the word. In the case of *waw* for −ū−, *qibbuṣ* might be put into this space. A more common way of avoiding a gap was to leave the top knob of *waw* or *yod* (category 1). It is not likely that this expedient showed that the scribe was leaving his spelling options open, for the same procedure was followed when other letters were canceled, as when a whole word, erroneously present by dittography, was erased, leaving all the top portions to fill the space. Another way of taking up the slack was to merge the doomed letter with either of its neighbors—the reverse of category 5—for instance making a *waw* into the right leg of a following *taw* and scratching out the original right leg, so that the *taw* was stretched out (category 2). I did not notice any instance of a device used in **P** to cancel an unwanted letter by writing a small circle over it.

Sometimes none of these devices was used. Instead the error was noted with a circule and the correction was supplied in the margin using the machinery of *qry*. This practice deserves a full study, since it promises to give us insights into what some scribes thought the *qry* marginal annotations could be used for. **D62** has its own story to tell about *ktyb/qry* in general. Again it presents every possible relationship to other manuscripts. Compared with **L**, it often agrees; but sometimes it lacks a common *ktyb/qry*, sometimes it has one not in **L**, sometimes it has **L**'s *qry* as its *ktyb*, with or without **L**'s *ktyb* as its *qry* (in such cases the margin often labels the variants as Western and Eastern, in various patterns). A full listing will be reserved for a study of the *qry* marginal notes of **D62** which will be published (*deo volente* in due time). It should be noted that some *ktyb/qry* pairs involve purely orthographic differences and could have been included in the present study. The line is hard to draw, and indicates that there was not clear demarcation between *ktyb/qry* notes and other textual details; the scribe evidently felt free to use the device to record textual variants and to make corrections.

Table 15.2. Variant spellings in D62

Citation	L	D^1	D^2
Isa 37:25	ואחרב	ואחריב	ואחר¹ב
Isa 37:36	ושמנים	ושמונים	ושמ¹נים
Isa 38:1	ויבוא	ויבא	
Isa 38:16	והחיני	והחייני	
Isa 38:20	ונגנותי	ונגינותי	ונג⁰נותי
Isa 40:6	אמר	אומר	
Isa 40:21^I	הלוא³rd	הלא	הלו⁴א
Isa 40:21^{II}	הבינתם	הבינותם	
Isa 41:5	יראו	וייראו	
Isa 41:18^I	שפיים	שפים	
Isa 41:18^{II}	למוצאי	למצאי	
Isa 41:19	ברוש	בראש	
Isa 41:23	תיטיבו	תטיבו	
Isa 42:2	ישמיע	ישמע	
Isa 42:23	יקשב	יקשיב	יקש¹ב
Isa 42:24	הלוא	הלא	הלו⁴א
Isa 43:4	אהבתיך	אהבתך	
Isa 43:6	ובנותי	ובנתי	ובנו⁴תי
Isa 51:16	ואשים	ואשם	
Isa 51:23	גוך	גויך	
Isa 52:5	יהילילו	יהללו	יהי³לילו
Isa 53:4	ומכאבינו	ומכאבנו	
Isa 53:5	מפשענו	מפשעינו	מפשע⁰נו
Isa 54:7	גדלים	גדולים	
Isa 54:10	תמוטנה	תמוטינה	
Isa 55:1^I	בלוא	בלא	בלו⁴א
Isa 55:1^{II}	ובלוא	ובלא	ובלו⁴א
Isa 55:2^I	בלוא	בלא	בלו⁴א
Isa 55:2^{II}	בלוא	בלא	בלו⁴א
Isa 55:3	דוד	דויד	
Isa 55:4^I	לאומים	לאמים	לאו⁴מים
Isa 55:4^{II}	לאמים	לאומים	
Isa 55:9	ממחשבתיכם	ממחשבותיכם	ממחשבת²יכם
Isa 56:3	אל	על	
Isa 56:7	אל	על	
Isa 57:9	רקחיך	רקוחיך	רקח²יך
Isa 57:13	והחוסה	והחסה	

D^2 Deletions:		D^2 Insertions:	
	0: complete erasure		3: supralinear
	1: bar residue		4: squeezed in
	2: stretched		5: remodeled

Citation	L	D¹	D²
Isa 57:15	אשכון	אשכן	אשכו⁴ן
Isa 58:5	כאגמן	כאגמון	כאגמ¹ן
Isa 58:7ᴵ	הלוא	הלא	הלו⁴א
Isa 58:7ᴵᴵ	לחמך	לחמיך	
Isa 58:8	וארכתך	וארוכתך	ואר⁰כתך
Isa 59:2	וחטאותיכם	וחטאתיכם	
Isa 59:3	ואצבעותיכם	ואצבעתיכם	
Isa 59:4ᴵ	תהו	תוהו	
Isa 59:4ᴵᴵ	והוליד	והוליד	והול¹יד
Isa 59:7	מחשבותיהם	מחשבותיהם	מחשבת²יהם
Isa 59:11	הגה	הגו	
Isa 59:12	וחטאותינו	וחטאתינו	
Isa 59:19	וייראו	ויראו	ויי⁴ראו
Isa 59:20	גואל	גאל	גו⁴אל
Isa 61:1	פקח־קוח	פקחקוח	
Isa 62:4	חפצי־בה	חפציבה	
Isa 63:5	זרעי	זרועי	
Isa 63:6	ואוריד	ואריד	ואו⁴ריד
Isa 63:7	תהלת	תהלות	
Isa 63:15	מזבל	מזבול	מזב¹ל
Isa 63:17	לבנו	לבינו	
Isa 63:19	לוא	לא	לו⁴א
Isa 64:4	בדרכיך	בדרכך	
Isa 64:7	יצרנו	יצרינו	
Isa 64:10	אבתינו	אבותנו	אבת²י⁴נו
Isa 65:3ᴵ	המכעיסים	המכעסים	
Isa 65:3ᴵᴵ	אותי	אתי	
Isa 65:14	תילילו	תלילו	תי⁴לילו
Isa 66:2	על	אל	
Isa 66:3	לבנה	לבונה	לב¹נה
Isa 66:12	נטה	נוטה	
Isa 66:14	ונודעה	ונדעה	ונו⁴דעה
Isa 66:19	תבל	תובל	ת⁰בל
Jer 1:8	להצלך	להצילך	להצ¹ל⁴ך
Jer 1:17	אליהם	אלהם	אלי⁴הם
Jer 1:18	ולעמוד	ולעמד	
Jer 2:8	והנביאים	והנבאים	
Jer 2:11	ההימיר	ההמיר	

D² Deletions: D² Insertions:

     0: complete erasure   3: supralinear

     1: bar residue   4: squeezed in

     2: stretched   5: remodeled

Citation	L	D¹	D²
Jer 2:15	כפרים	כפירים	
Jer 2:17[I]	תעשׂה	תעשׂו	תעשׂה
Jer 2:17[II]	מוליכך	מולכך	
Jer 2:19	תוכחך	תוכיחך	תוכ²חך
Jer 2:20[I]	מוסרתיך	מוסרותיך	
Jer 2:20[II]	אעבד	אעבוד	
Jer 2:21	שׂרק	שׂורק	
Jer 2:25[I]	וגורנך	וגרונך	וגורנך
Jer 2:25[II]	לוא	לו	לוא
Jer 2:36	תבושׂי	תבשׂי	
Jer 3:1	הלוא	הלא	
Jer 3:3	לוא	לא	לוא
Jer 3:12	לוא	לא	לו⁴א
Jer 4:3	קוצים	קצים	
Jer 4:7	ממקמו	ממקומו	ממק⁰מו
Jer 4:9	והנביאים	והנבאים	
Jer 4:11	שׂפיים	שׂפים	
Jer 4:19	אחריש	אחרש	
Jer 4:22	ולהיטיב	ולהטיב	ולה⁵יטיב
Jer 4:30	עגבים	עוגבים	ע⁰גבים
Jer 5:7	יתגדדו	יתגודדו	
Jer 5:9	לוא	לוא	ל⁰א
Jer 5:12	לא	לוא	
Jer 5:24[I]	ולא	ולוא	ול¹א
Jer 5:24[II]	הנתן	הותן	הנ⁵תן
Jer 5:24[III]	שׂבעות	שׂבעת	
Jer 5:25	עונותיכם	עונתיכם	עונו⁴תיכם
Jer 5:31	הנביאים	הנבאים	
Jer 6:15	פקדתים	פקדתם	
Jer 6:28	הלכי	הולכי	
Jer 7:5	תיטיבו	תטיבו	
Jer 7:10	התועבות	התועבת	
Jer 7:19	בשׂת	בושׂת	
Jer 8:6	לוא	לא	לו⁴א
Jer 8:9	הבישׂו	הבשׂו	
Jer 8:16	ומלואה	ומלאה	ומלו⁴אה
Jer 9:22	בגבורתו	בגברתו	
Jer 10:4	ולוא	ולא	ולו⁴א

D² Deletions:		D² Insertions:
	0: complete erasure	3: supralinear
	1: bar residue	4: squeezed in
	2: stretched	5: remodeled

Citation	L	D¹	D²
Jer 10:13	נשׂאים	נשׂיאים	
Jer 10:18	והצרותי	והצרתי	
Jer 11:7	העדתי	העידתי	
Jer 11:10	לשׁמוע	לשׁמע	
Jer 12:1	אותך	אתך	
Jer 13:13	הנביאים	הנבאים	
Jer 13:17	לא	לוא	
Jer 14:7	עונינו	עוננו	עוני⁴נו
Jer 14:12	עלה	עולה	
Jer 14:16	בחצות	בחוצת	
Jer 14:17	אליהם	אלהם	אלי⁴הם
Jer 15:3	לאכל	לאכול	
Jer 15:7	לוא	לא	לו⁴א
Jer 15:8	אלמנתו	אלמנותי	
Jer 15:11	לוא	לא	לו⁴א
Jer 15:16ᴵ	דבריך	דברך	דברי⁴ך
Jer 15:16ᴵᴵ	דבריך	דברך	
Jer 16:3	אמתם	אמותם	
Jer 17:3ᴵ	אוצרותיך	אוצרתיך	
Jer 17:3ᴵᴵ	גבוליך	גבולך	
Jer 17:25	דוד	דויד	
Jer 17:26	מבאים	מביאים	
Jer 18:9	לבנת	לבנות	
Jer 18:11	והיטיבו	והטיבו	
Jer 19:1	הלוך	הלך	
Jer 19:8	מכתה	מכותה	מכת²ה
Jer 20:5	ולקחום	ולקחם	
Jer 20:6	ישׁבי	יושׁבי	
Jer 20:10	שׁלומי	שׁלמי	
Jer 32:19	פקחות	פקוחות	פק¹חת²
Jer 32:20	ומפתים	ומופתים	ומ¹פתים
Jer 32:36	אמרים	אומרים	א⁵מרים
Jer 32:40	להיטיבי	להטיבי	
Jer 33:6	ורפאתים	ורפאתם	
Jer 33:7	שׁבות	שׁבית	
Jer 33:8	עונותיהם	עוונתיהם	עונת²ידהם
Jer 33:9	אתם	אותם	
Jer 33:11	אמרים	אומרים	

D² Deletions:		D² Insertions:	
	0: complete erasure		3: supralinear
	1: bar residue		4: squeezed in
	2: stretched		5: remodeled

Citation	L	D¹	D²
Jer 33:19	לאמור	לאמר	לאמ
Jer 34:2	צדקידו	צדקיה	צדקידו
Jer 34:13	הוצאי	הוציאי	הוצ¹אי
Jer 34:18	ברתי	בריתי	בר²תי
Jer 34:22[I]	ולכדוה	ולכדה	ולכדו⁴ה
Jer 34:22[II]	ישב	יושב	י¹שב
Jer 35:8	ובנתינו	ובנותינו	
Jer 35:14	ולא	ולא	ולו⁴א
Jer 35:15[I]	השכים	השכם	
Jer 35:15[II]	והיטיבו	והטיבו	
Jer 36:1	הרביעת	הרבעית	
Jer 36:9	התשיעי	התשיעי	התש¹עי
Jer 36:13	מכידו	מיכידו	מ¹כידו
Jer 36:16	הגיד	הגד	
Jer 36:28	על	אל	
Jer 36:30	יושב	ושב	י⁴ושב
Jer 36:32	ועוד	ועד	
Jer 38:22	אמרות	אמרת	
Jer 38:25	אל	את	
Jer 38:26	השיבני	השבני	
Jer 39:3[I]	שר־אצר	שראצר	
Jer 39:3[II]	שר־אצר	שראצר	
Jer 39:5	אתו	אותו	
Jer 39:11	על	אל	
Jer 39:13	שר־אצר	שראצר	
Jer 40:8	ויזנידו	ויזניה	
Jer 42:20	בנפשותיכם	בנפשתיכם	
Jer 43:13	בתי	בית	
Jer 44:7	גדולה	גדלה	
Jer 44:8[I]	במעשי	במעשה	
Jer 44:8[II]	גויי	גוי	
Jer 44:21	הלוא	הלא	הלו⁴א
Jer 46:2[I]	על	אל	
Jer 46:2[II]	בכרכמש	בכרכמיש	בכרכמ⁰ש
Jer 46:28	שמה	שמה	שם²
Jer 48:36	כחלילים	כחלילים	כחלי⁴לים
Jer 49:8	העמיקו	העמקו	
Jer 49:11	ואלמנתיך	ואלמנותיך	

D² Deletions:	D² Insertions:
0: complete erasure	3: supralinear
1: bar residue	4: squeezed in
2: stretched	5: remodeled

Citation	L	D¹	D²
Jer 49:16	בחגוי	בחגיו	
Jer 50:4	יחדו	יחדיו	
Jer 50:6	שׁובבים	שבבום	שׁו⁴בבום
Jer 50:9	על	אל	
Jer 50:29	פליטה	פליטה	
Jer 50:38	פסלים	פסילים	פס¹לים
Jer 50:39ᴵ	דור	דור	דר
Jer 50:39ᴵᴵ	ודור	ודר	
Jer 50:44	יועדני	יועידני	יוע⁵דני
Jer 50:45	ומחשׁבותיו	ומחשבתיו	ומחשבו⁴תיו
Jer 51:5	מקדושׁ	מקדש	מקדו⁴שׁ
Jer 51:15	נטה	נוטה	ניטה
Jer 51:16ᴵ	ויצא	ויוצא	
Jer 51:16ᴵᴵ	מאצרתיו	מאוצרתיו	
Jer 51:44	והצאתי	והוצאתי	וה¹צאתי
Jer 51:55	קולם	קלם	קו⁴לם
Ezek 1:9	אחותה	אחתה	
Ezek 1:10	מהשׁמאול	מהשמאל	מהשמאו⁴ל
Ezek 1:13ᴵ	מראיהם	מראידן	
Ezek 1:13ᴵᴵ	הלפדים	הלפידים	
Ezek 1:13ᴵᴵᴵ	בין	בן	
Ezek 2:1	רגליך	רגלך	
Ezek 2:3	המורדים	המרדים	המור⁵דים
Ezek 2:7	אליהם	אלהם	אלי⁴הם
Ezek 3:2	ויאכלני	ויאכילני	
Ezek 3:11	עמך	עמיך	עמ¹ך
Ezek 3:15	יושׁבים	ישבים	
Ezek 3:21	חטא	חטוא	חט¹א
Ezek 3:25	עבותים	עבתים	עבו⁴תים
Ezek 4:1	לבנה	לבינה	לב²נה
Ezek 4:2	ונתתה	ונתת	ונתתה³
Ezek 4:7	וזרעך	וזרועך	
Ezek 5:2	סביבותיה	סביבתיה	סביבו⁴תיה
Ezek 5:5	וסביבותיה	וסביבתיה	וסביבו⁴תיה
Ezek 5:6	סביבותיה	סביבתיה	סביבו⁴תיה
Ezek 5:9	תועבתיך	תועבותיך	תועבת²יך
Ezek 5:10	שׁאריתך	שארתיך	שארי⁴ת⁰ך
Ezek 5:13	והנחותי	והניחותי	והני⁰חותי

D² Deletions:		D² Insertions:
	0: complete erasure	3: supralinear
	1: bar residue	4: squeezed in
	2: stretched	5: remodeled

Citation	L	D[1]	D[2]
Ezek 6:3	ולגאית	ולגיאות	ולג[1]אות
Ezek 6:9	פליטיכם	פלטיכם	פלי[4]טיכם
Ezek 7:7	הצפירה	הצפרה	הצפי[4]רה
Ezek 7:8	אשפוך	אשפך	אשפו[4]ך
Ezek 7:12	והמוכר	והמכר	
Ezek 7:13	המוכר	המכר	
Ezek 7:20	תועבתם	תועבותם	תועבת[2]ם
Ezek 7:27	אותם	אתם	
Ezek 8:6	גדלות	גדולות	גד[0]לות
Ezek 8:9[I]	בא	בוא	
Ezek 8:9[II]	התועבות	התועבת	התועבו[4]ת
Ezek 8:18	אחמל	אחמול	אחמ[1]ל
Ezek 9:5	תחס	תחוס	
Ezek 9:10	אחמל	אחמול	אחמ[1]ל
Ezek 10:5	החיצנה	החיצונה	
Ezek 10:7[I]	הכרבים	הכרובים	
Ezek 10:7[II]	לבש	לבוש	לב[1]ש
Ezek 10:19	הכרובים	הכרבים	הכרו[4]בים
Ezek 10:20	כרובים	כרבים	כרו[4]בים
Ezek 11:1[I]	הקדמוני	הקדמני	הקדמו[3]ני
Ezek 11:1[II]	הפונה	הפנה	הפו[3]נה
Ezek 11:1[III]	קדימה	קדמה	קדי[4]מה
Ezek 11:10	אשפוט	אשפט	אשפו[4]ט
Ezek 11:13	בניה	בניהו	בניה
Ezek 11:17	נפצותם	נפצתם	נפצות[5]ם
Ezek 11:18	תועבותיה	תועבתיה	תועבו[3]תיה
Ezek 11:24	ותביאני	ותבאני	
Ezek 12:10	אליהם	אלהם	אלי[4]הם
Ezek 12:11	מופתכם	מפתכם	מו[4]פתכם
Ezek 12:24	בית	בני	בית
Ezek 12:27	ולעתים	ולעיתים	
Ezek 13:10	חיץ	חץ	חי[4]ץ
Ezek 13:12	אליכם	לכם	א[5]ליכם
Ezek 13:13	שטף	שוטף	ש[1]טף
Ezek 13:14	יסדו	יסודו	יס[1]דו
Ezek 13:16[I]	שלם	שלום	שלם[2]
Ezek 13:16[II]	שלם	שלום	שלם[2]
Ezek 13:17	אל	על	

D[2] Deletions:

    0: complete erasure
    1: bar residue
    2: stretched

D[2] Insertions:

    3: supralinear
    4: squeezed in
    5: remodeled

Citation	L	D[1]	D[2]
Ezek 14:1	ויבוא	ויבא	ויבו[4]א
Ezek 14:4	אליהם	אלהם	אלי[4]הם
Ezek 14:5	בית	בני	בית
Ezek 14:6	תועבתיכם	תועבותיכם	תועב[1]תיכם
Ezek 14:11	עוד	עד	עו[4]ד
Ezek 14:14	דנאל	דניאל	דנ[1]אל
Ezek 14:16	ינצלו	ינצילו	ינצ[1]לו
Ezek 14:20	דנאל	דניאל	דנ[1]אל
Ezek 14:22[I]	פלטה	פליטה	פל[1]טה
Ezek 14:22[II]	על	אל	
Ezek 16:3	ומלדתיך	ומולדתיך	
Ezek 16:4	אתך	אותך	
Ezek 16:5	אתך	אותך	את[2]ך
Ezek 16:6[I]	בדמיך	בדמייך	בדמי[0]ך
Ezek 16:6[II]	בדמיך	בדמייך	בדמי[0]ך
Ezek 16:10	ואלבישך	ואלבשך	
Ezek 16:20[I]	בנותיך	בנתיך	בנו[3]תיך
Ezek 16:20[II]	מתזנותך	מתזנותיך	מתזנות[0]ך
Ezek 16:22[I]	תועבתיך	תועבותיך	תועב[1]תיך
Ezek 16:22[II]	ותזנתיך	ותזנותיך	ותזנת[2]יך
Ezek 16:22[III]	ערם	ערום	עי[4]רם[5]
Ezek 16:25	תזנתך	תזנותיך	תזנת[02]ך
Ezek 16:26	תזנתך	תזנותיך	תזנת[02]ך
Ezek 16:29	תזנותך	תזנותיך	תזנות[0]ך
Ezek 16:31	רחוב	רחב	רחו[4]ב
Ezek 16:37	אלהם	אליהם	אל[1]הם
Ezek 16:38	ושפכת	ושפכות	ושפכת[2]
Ezek 16:39	אותך	אתך	
Ezek 16:43	תועבתיך	תועבותיך	תועבת[2]יך
Ezek 16:51	תועבותיך	תועבותיך	תועבת[2]יך
Ezek 16:55	ובנותיה	ובנתיה	ובנו[3]תיה
Ezek 16:56	ולוא	ולא	
Ezek 16:60	והקמותי	והקימותי	
Ezek 17:6	פארות	פארת	
Ezek 17:7[I]	נוצה	נצה	נו[4]צה
Ezek 17:7[II]	מערגות	מערגת	מערגות[5]
Ezek 17:10	הלוא	הלוא	הל[1]א
Ezek 17:22	ינקותיו	ינקתיו	ינקות[5]יו

D[2] Deletions:

0: complete erasure
1: bar residue
2: stretched

D[2] Insertions:

3: supralinear
4: squeezed in
5: remodeled

Citation	L	D¹	D²
Ezek 18:9	חיה	חיו	
Ezek 18:12	תועבה	תעבה	תו⁴עבה
Ezek 18:23	אחפץ	אחפוץ	אחפ¹ץ
Ezek 18:24	התועבות	התועבת	התועבות⁵
Ezek 18:25	הלא	הלוא	הל¹א
Ezek 18:26	ימות	ימת	ימות⁵
Ezek 18:31	תמתו	תמותו	תמת²ו
Ezek 19:2	כפרים	כפירים	כפר²ים
Ezek 20:1	בחמשי	בחמישי	בחמ¹שי
Ezek 20:4	התשפט¹ˢᵗ	התשפוט	התשפ¹ט
Ezek 20:11	חקותי	חקתי	חקות⁵י
Ezek 20:19	בחקותי	בחקתי	בחקות⁵י
Ezek 20:21ᴵ	בחקותי	בחקתי	בחקות⁵י
Ezek 20:21ᴵᴵ	שבתותי	שבתתי	שבתות⁵י
Ezek 20:22	אותם	אתם	א⁵ותם
Ezek 20:23	אתם	אותם	את²ם
Ezek 20:28	אותה	אתה	א⁵ותה
Ezek 20:31	מתנתיכם	מתנותיכם	מתנת⁵יכם
Ezek 20:41	ניחח	ניחוח	ניחח⁵
Ezek 21:14	אדני	יהוה	
Ezek 21:19	אל	על	אל
Ezek 21:22	והנחתי	והניחתי	ּ
Ezek 22:8	שבתתי	שבתותי	שבתת⁵י
Ezek 22:18	ועופרת	ועפרת	וע⁵ופרת
Ezek 22:20	ועופרת	ועפרת	וע⁵ופרת
Ezek 22:25	שואג	שאג	
Ezek 22:26ᴵ	לחל	לחל	לחול
Ezek 22:26ᴵᴵ	ומשבתותי	ומשבתתי	ומשבתות⁵י
Ezek 23:5	קרובים	קרבים	קרו⁴בים
Ezek 23:35	אותי	אתי	א⁵ותי
Ezek 24:16	ולוא	ולא	ולו⁴א
Ezek 24:17	הלא	הלוא	הל¹א
Ezek 24:21	עזכם	עוזכם	ע⁰זכם
Ezek 24:25	ובנותידם	ובנתידם	ובנו⁴תידם
Ezek 25:8	יהודה	ישראל	יהודה
Ezek 26:10	בבאו	בבואו	בב¹או
Ezek 26:12	חומותיך	חומתיך	חומות⁵יך
Ezek 26:15	הלא	הלוא	הל¹א

D² Deletions: D² Insertions:

0: complete erasure	3: supralinear
1: bar residue	4: squeezed in
2: stretched	5: remodeled

Citation	L	D¹	D²
Ezek 27:11	חומותיך	חומתיך	
Ezek 27:13	תבל	תובל	
Ezek 27:26	הביאוך	הבאוך	
Ezek 28:3	מדנאל	מדניאל	מדנ^{1}אל
Ezek 28:9	מחלליך	מחללך	
Ezek 28:16	הסכך	הסוכך	הס^{1}כך
Ezek 28:18	ואוצא	ואוציא	ואוצ^{1}א
Ezek 28:23	בחוצותיה	בחוצתיה	
Ezek 29:1	העשירית	העשרית	
Ezek 29:4	בקשקשתיך	בקשקשותיך	בקשקשׂת^{2}יך
Ezek 29:18	גדלה	גדולה	
Ezek 30:4	יסודתיה	יסודותיה	יסד^{2}ותיה
Ezek 31:11	איל	אל	
Ezek 31:18	והורדת	והרדת	והו^{4}רדת
Ezek 32:6	ואפקים	ואפיקים	ואפ^{0}קים
Ezek 32:10	בעופפי	בעפפי	בעו^{3}פפי
Ezek 32:15	יושבי	ישבי	יו^{4}שבי
Ezek 32:22	קברתיו	קברותיו	קברת^{2}יו
Ezek 32:29	ירדי	יורדי	יר^{5}די
Ezek 33:10	בית	בני	בית
Ezek 33:11	אחפץ	אחפוץ	אחפ^{1}ץ
Ezek 33:25^I	אליהם	אלהם	
Ezek 33:25^{II}	ועיניכם	ועיניכם	ועינ^{0}כם
Ezek 33:27	אלהם	אליהם	אל^{1}הם
Ezek 33:32	ומטב	ומטיב	ומט^{1}ב
Ezek 34:10	תדיין	תדיינה	
Ezek 34:13	והביאתים	והביאותים	
Ezek 34:14	אתם	אותם	את^{2}ם
Ezek 34:16	ארענה	ארעינה	
Ezek 34:23^I	והקמתי	והקימותי	והק^{0}מותי
Ezek 34:23^{II}	רעה	רועה	
Ezek 34:24	דוד	דויד	
Ezek 34:27	עלם	עולם	ע^{0}לם
Ezek 35:11	עשיתה	עשית	עשׂיתה^3
Ezek 36:11	והטבתי	והיטבתי	
Ezek 36:33	עונותיכם	עונתיכם	עונות^{5}יכם
Ezek 37:12	קברותיכם	קברתיכם	קברו^{4}תיכם
Ezek 37:24^I	דוד	דויד	דו^{1}ד

D² Deletions:		D² Insertions:
	0: complete erasure	3: supralinear
	1: bar residue	4: squeezed in
	2: stretched	5: remodeled

Citation	L	D¹	D²
Ezek 37:24[II]	ורועה	ורעה	ורו⁴עה
Ezek 37:24[III]	וחקתי	וחקותי	
Ezek 38:5	וכובע	וכבע	וכו⁴בע
Ezek 38:9	תבוא	תבא	תבו³א
Ezek 38:12	נושבת	נושבות	
Ezek 38:13	כפריה	כפיריה	
Ezek 39:1	על	אל	על
Ezek 39:2	והבאותך	והביאותיך	והב⁰אותיך
Ezek 39:18	אילים	אלים	א⁵ילים
Ezek 40:7	אולם	אולם	א⁴לם
Ezek 40:9[I]	שמנה	שמונה	שמ¹נה
Ezek 40:9[II]	ואלם	ואולם	וא¹לם
Ezek 40:11	שלוש	שלש	שלו⁴ש
Ezek 40:14	אילים	אילם	איליֿ⁴ם
Ezek 40:16[I]	חלנות	חלונות	
Ezek 40:16[II]	אטמות	אטומות	אט⁰מת²
Ezek 40:21	ושלשה	ושלשה	ושלו⁴שה
Ezek 40:22[I]	ואלמו	ואילמו	
Ezek 40:22[II]	ותמרו	ותימרו	
Ezek 40:29	ואילו	ואלו	ואי⁴לו
Ezek 40:31	החצונה	החיצונה	
Ezek 40:34	ושמנה	ושמונה	ושמ¹נה
Ezek 40:37	ושמנה	ושמונה	ושמ¹נה
Ezek 40:42	לעולה	לעלה	לעו³לה
Ezek 40:44	הצפן	הצפון	הצפ¹ן
Ezek 41:6	שלוש	שלוש	שלש
Ezek 41:16	והחלנות	והחלונות	
Ezek 42:5	ומהתכנות	ומהתיכונות	ומהת⁰כונות
Ezek 42:6	ומהתיכנות	ומהתיכונות	ומהתיכ¹נות
Ezek 42:7	החצונה	החיצונה	הח⁰צונה
Ezek 43:5	ותביאני	ותבאני	
Ezek 43:11	חקתיו	חקותיו	
Ezek 43:20[I]	על	על	אל
Ezek 43:20[II]	אותו	אתו	א⁵ותו
Ezek 43:24	עלה	עולה	
Ezek 44:1	הפנה	הפונה	
Ezek 44:3	אלם	אולם	
Ezek 44:11	העלה	העולה	

D² Deletions:		D² Insertions:
	0: complete erasure	3: supralinear
	1: bar residue	4: squeezed in
	2: stretched	5: remodeled

Citation	L	D¹	D²
Ezek 45:17	העולות	העלות	הע[5]ולות
Ezek 45:23	אילים	אלים	א[5]ילים
Ezek 46:6	כבשׂם	כבשׂים	
Ezek 46:14	האיפה	האפה	הא[5]יפה
Ezek 46:21	ויעבירני	ויעברני	
Ezek 46:23	הטירות	הטירת	
Ezek 47:2¹	ויוצאני	ויוציאני	ויוצ[0]אני
Ezek 47:2¹¹	מפכים	מפכם	מפכים[5]
Ezek 47:19	מריבות	מריבת	מריבו[4]ת
Ezek 48:23	קדמה	קדימה	קד[2]מה
Hosea 2:7	הבישׁה	הובשׁה	
Hosea 3:5	דוד	דויד	
Hosea 4:1	יושׁבי	ישׁבי	
Hosea 4:3	יושׁב	ישׁב	
Hosea 4:12	ומקלו	ומקולו	
Hosea 4:19	אותה	אתה	אות[5]ה
Hosea 6:2	יקמנו	יקימנו	יק[0]מנו
Hosea 6:3	מוצאו	מצאו	
Hosea 7:1	יבוא	יבא	יבו[4]א
Hosea 7:6	אפדם	אפידם	
Hosea 7:12	איסרם	איסירם	
Hosea 7:14¹	ותירושׁ	ותירשׁ	ותירו[4]שׁ
Hosea 7:14¹¹	יתגוררו	יתגררו	
Hosea 8:1	שׁפר	שׁופר	שׁ[1]פר
Hosea 8:6	שׁבבים	שׁבבם	שׁבבי[4]ם
Hosea 8:11	מזבחת	מזבחות	
Hosea 8:14	ארמנתיה	ארמנותיה	
Hosea 9:2	ותירושׁ	ותירשׁ	
Hosea 9:13	הרג	הורג	
Hosea 9:15	סררים	סוררים	סר[2]רים
Hosea 10:1	היטיבו	היטיבו	
Hosea 10:2	ישׁדד	ישׁודד	ישׁד[2]ד
Hosea 10:6	אותו	אתו	
Hosea 10:12	וירה	ויורה	
Hosea 11:6	ממעצותידם	ממועצותידם	
Hosea 12:5	ויכל	ויוכל	וי[0]כל
Hosea 13:3	הלך	הולך	ה[1]לך
Hosea 13:8	כדב	כדוב	כד[1]ב

D² Deletions:

0: complete erasure
1: bar residue
2: stretched

D² Insertions:

3: supralinear
4: squeezed in
5: remodeled

Citation	L	D¹	D²
Hosea 13:9	בעזרך	בעזריך	
Hosea 14:10[I]	ויבן	ויבין	
Hosea 14:10[II]	וצדקים	וצדיקים	
Joel 1:2	אבתיכם	אבותיכם	אבת[2]יכם
Joel 1:5	והילילו	והלילו	והי[4]ללו
Joel 1:7	שריגיה	שריגה	
Joel 1:12	הביש	הוביש	ה[1]ביש
Joel 1:15	יבוא	יבא	יבו[4]א
Joel 1:17[I]	מגרפתידם	מגרפותידם	מגרפת[2]ידם
Joel 1:17[II]	אצרות	אוצרות	
Joel 1:17[III]	הביש	הוביש	ה[1]ביש
Joel 2:2	שני	שנית	שני
Joel 2:7[I]	כגבורים	כגברים	
Joel 2:7[II]	ירצון	ירוצון	יר[1]צון
Joel 2:12	שבו	שובו	
Joel 2:17	עמך	עמיך	
Joel 2:20	באשו	באושו	בא[1]שו
Joel 2:26	יבשו	יבושו	יב[1]שו
Joel 2:27	יבשו	יבושו	יב[1]שו
Joel 4:4[I]	גלילות	גלילת	
Joel 4:4[II]	גמולכם	גמולכם	גמ[0]לכם
Joel 4:5	הטבים	הטובים	
Joel 4:10	ומזמרתיכם	ומזמרותיכם	ומזמרת[2]יכם
Amos 1:7	ארמנתיה	ארמנותיה	
Amos 2:3	שופט	שפט	
Amos 2:11	לנזרים	לנזירים	לנז[0]רים
Amos 2:12	הנזרים	הנזירים	
Amos 3:1	העליתי	העלתי	
Amos 3:4	ממענתו	ממעונתו	ממע[1]נתו
Amos 3:11	והורד	והוריד	והור[1]ד
Amos 4:8	שלש	שלוש	של[1]ש
Amos 4:13	ובורא	ובורא	
Amos 5:8	הקורא	הקרא	
Amos 8:10	שיריכם	שריכם	
Amos 9:4	איבידם	אויבידם	א[1]יבידם
Amos 9:5	יושבי	יושבי	י[0]שבי
Amos 9:7	כשיים	כושיים	
Obad 1:7	שלחוך	שליחוך	של[0]יחוך

D² Deletions:		D² Insertions:
0: complete erasure		3: supralinear
1: bar residue		4: squeezed in
2: stretched		5: remodeled

Citation	L	D¹	D²
Obad 1:21	מושעים	מושעם	
Jonah 1:7[I]	גורלות	גרלות	גו³רלות
Jonah 1:7[II]	גורלות	גרלות	
Jonah 1:10[I]	וייראו	ויראו	
Jonah 1:10[II]	ויאמרו	ויאמר	
Jonah 1:11	וסער	וסער	וסו³ער
Jonah 1:14	נקיא	נקי	נקיא³
Jonah 2:6	יסבבני	יסובבני	
Jonah 2:7	בריחיה	בריחיה	
Jonah 3:6	ויגע	ויגיע	ויג¹ע
Jonah 4:6[I]	קיקיון	קקיון	
Jonah 4:6[II]	הקיקיון	הקקיון	
Jonah 4:7	וייבש	ויבש	
Jonah 4:10[I]	שבן	שבין	
Jonah 4:10[II]	ובן	ובין	
Jonah 4:11	בין	בן	
Micah 1:3	ממקומו	ממקמו	
Micah 1:8	אילכה	אלכה	אי⁴לכה
Micah 1:16	הרחבי	הרחיבי	
Micah 2:6	תטפו	תטפו	תטי³פו
Micah 2:7	הולך	הלך	
Micah 2:8	ואתמול	ואתמל	
Micah 2:11	אטף	אטף	אטי³ף
Micah 5:4	בארמנתינו	בארמנותינו	
Micah 5:5	בגבולנו	בגבלנו	בגבו⁴לנו
Micah 5:13	מקרבך	מקרביך	
Micah 6:2	מסדי	מוסדי	מו¹סדי
Micah 6:6	בעולות	בעלות	
Micah 6:10	האש	האיש	הא¹ש
Micah 6:16	במעצותם	במועצתם	במⁿעצו⁴תם
Micah 7:3	להיטיב	להטיב	להי⁴טיב
Micah 7:7	אוחילה	אחילה	או⁴חילה
Micah 7:17	ממסגרתיהם	ממסגרותיהם	
Micah 7:19	יכבש	יכבוש	
Nahum 1:5	ישבי	יושבי	
Nahum 1:6	יעמוד	יעמד	יעמו³ד
Nahum 1:10	סבואים	סבאים	סבו³אים
Nahum 2:2	מצרה	מצורה	

D² Deletions:	D² Insertions:
0: complete erasure	3: supralinear
1: bar residue	4: squeezed in
2: stretched	5: remodeled

Citation	L	D¹	D²
Nahum 2:4[I]	פלדות	פלדת	
Nahum 2:4[II]	והברשים	והברושים	
Nahum 2:5[I]	ברחבות	ברחובות	
Nahum 2:5[II]	כלפידם	כלפדים	
Nahum 2:6	הסכך	הסוכך	
Nahum 2:8	לבבהן	לבביהן	לבב[1]הן
Nahum 2:11	ומבלקה	ומבולקה	ומב[1]לקה
Nahum 3:5	והראיתי	והראתי	והרא[4]תי
Nahum 3:6	שקצים	שקוצים	
Nahum 3:10	לגלה	לגולה	
Nahum 3:17[I]	ונדד	ונדד	
Nahum 3:17[II]	נודע	נדע	נו[3]דע
Nahum 3:18	אדיריך	אדריך	אדי[4]ריך
Hab 1:8	מרחוק	מרחק	
Hab 2:2	הלחות	הלחת	
Hab 2:13	וייגעו	ויגעו	ויי[4]געו
Hab 3:1	שגינות	שגיונות	שגי[0]נות
Hab 3:8	מרכבתיך	מרכבותיך	מרכבת[2]יך
Hab 3:14	עליצתם	עליצותם	
Hab 3:18	אעלוזה	אעלזה	אעלו[4]זה
Hab 3:19	ידרכני	ידריכני	
Zeph 1:6	דרשהו	דרשוהו	דרשה[2]ו
Zeph 1:9	הדולג	הדלג	
Zeph 1:15[I]	שאה	שואה	ש[1]אה
Zeph 1:15[II]	ומשואה	ומשאה	
Zeph 2:1	וקושו	וקשו	וקו[4]שו
Zeph 2:2	יבוא	יבא	
Zeph 2:5	ישבי	יושבי	
Zeph 2:8	וגדופי	וגדפי	
Zeph 2:10	ויגדלו	ויגדילו	
Zeph 2:14	קפד	קפוד	
Zeph 3:1	מראה	מוראה	
Zeph 3:9	אהפך	אהפוך	אהפ[1]ך
Zeph 3:11	עלילתיך	עלילותיך	
Zech 1:2	אבותיכם	אבתיכם	
Zech 1:3	אלהם	אליהם	אל[1]הם
Zech 1:4[I]	כאבתיכם	כאבותיכם	כאבת[2]יכם
Zech 1:4[II]	ומעליליכם	ומעלליכם	ומ[5]עלי[4]ליכם

D² Deletions:
  0: complete erasure
  1: bar residue
  2: stretched

D² Insertions:
  3: supralinear
  4: squeezed in
  5: remodeled

Citation	L	D¹	D²
Zech 1:5[I]	אבותיכם	אבתיכם	
Zech 1:5[II]	והנבאים	והנבאים	והנבי[4]אים
Zech 1:6	וישובו	וישבו	
Zech 1:8	במצלה	במצולה	במצ[0]לה
Zech 1:13	נחמים	נחומים	
Zech 1:17	תפוצינה	תפוצנה	
Zech 3:9	פתחה	פתוחה	
Zech 4:1	יעור	יער	יעור[5]
Zech 4:2	מנורת	מנרת	
Zech 4:5	הלוא	הלא	
Zech 4:11	שמאולה	שמאלה	שמא[5]ולה
Zech 5:1	וראה	וארא	וראה
Zech 5:4	עציו	עצו	עצי[3]ו
Zech 5:5	היוצאת	היצאת	
Zech 5:9	ותשאנה	ותשאינה	
Zech 5:11	מכנתה	מכונתה	
Zech 6:3	השלשית	השלישית	
Zech 6:5	רחות	רוחות	
Zech 6:8	אתי	אותי	את[2]י
Zech 6:14	לחלם	לחילם	לח[1]לם
Zech 7:2	שר־אצר	שראצר	
Zech 7:3	החמשי	החמישי	
Zech 7:5	צמתני	צמתוני	צמת[1]ני
Zech 7:7	ישבת	יושבת	
Zech 7:11	משמוע	משמע	
Zech 8:14	אבתיכם	אבותיכם	אבת[2]יכם
Zech 8:15	להיטיב	להטיב	להי[4]טיב
Zech 8:22	עצומים	עצמים	
Zech 9:5	הביש	הביש	הו[4]ביש
Zech 9:8	נגש	נוגש	נ[0]גש
Zech 9:9	יבוא	יבא	
Zech 9:15[I]	יגן	יגין	
Zech 9:15[II]	כזויות	כזוית	
Zech 10:5	כגברים	כגבורים	
Zech 10:6	והושבותים	והושבתים	
Zech 10:10	והשיבותים	והשבתים	והשבו[4]תים
Zech 11:2[I]	הילל	היליל	
Zech 11:2[II]	אדרים	אדירים	אד[1]רים

D² Deletions:

0: complete erasure
1: bar residue
2: stretched

D² Insertions:

3: supralinear
4: squeezed in
5: remodeled

Citation	L	D^1	D^2
Zech 11:5^I	קניהן	קוניהן	ק^{2}ניהן
Zech 11:5^{II}	יהרגן	יהרגון	יהרג^{0}ן
Zech 11:11	ותפר	ותופר	ות^{0}פר
Zech 11:15	אולי	אולי	אלי
Zech 11:17	זרועו	זרועו	זר^{1}עו
Zech 12:3	גויי	גוי	
Zech 12:7	והושיע	והושע	
Zech 12:8	יגן	יגין	יג^{1}ן
Zech 12:14^I	^{2nd}משפחת	משפחות	משפחת^2
Zech 12:14^{II}	^{3rd}משפחת	משפחות	משפחת^2
Zech 13:1	ולישבי	וליושבי	
Zech 13:3	ודקרהו	ודקרודהו	ודקר^{1}הו
Zech 14:12	עמד	עומד	ע^{1}מד
Mal 1:11	מבואו	מבאו	מבו^{4}או
Mal 1:12	אותו	אתו	
Mal 2:10	הלוא	הלא	הלו^{4}א
Mal 2:12	וענה	ועונה	
Mal 2:15	נעוריך	נעריך	
Mal 3:2^I	בואו	באו	בו^{4}או
Mal 3:2^{II}	בדראותו	בדראתו	
Mal 3:7	אבתיכם	אבותיכם	
Mal 3:10	והריקתי	והריקותי	והריקת^{2}י
Mal 3:11	ישחת	ישחית	ישחת^2
Mal 3:17^I	סגלה	סגולה	סג^{0}לה
Mal 3:17^{II}	יחמל	יחמול	
Mal 3:22	אותו	אותו	את^{2}ו
Mal 3:23	בוא	בא	

Appendix

Appendix A

What *Did* the Scribes Count?

Francis I. Andersen & A. Dean Forbes

A.1 The Tradition

A famous passage in the Talmud (*b. Qiddushin* 30a) reads:

> This is why the men of old were called "scribes" (**swprym**), be-
> cause they used to count (**hyw swprym**) all the letters that were
> in the Torah. They said that the **w** in **gḥwn** [Lev 11:42] is the
> middle letter of the Torah; that **drš drš** [Lev 10:16] is the mid-
> dle of the words; and **whtglḥ** [Lev 13:33] is the middle verse. In
> **ykrsmnh ḥzyr myᶜr** [Ps 80:14] the ᶜ in **yᶜr** is the middle letter
> in Psalms, and **whwᵓ rḥwm ykpr ᶜwn** [Ps 78:38] is the middle
> verse.

Variant traditions are found in *b. Sanhedrin* 106a and *Ḥagiga* 15b. The
Jerusalem Talmud makes the same word-play, but with a different object:
the men of old counted the number of ordinances in the Torah (*Sheqalim*
5.1). This is probably nearer to the origin of the tradition. Where
there is little history there will be legend. Tales grew around the folk
etymology of **swprym**, and right up to the present the reports have been
widely accepted as historical. They are said to prove that even before
the age of the *tannaᵓim* there existed a text that was fixed down to the
last detail. There existed a conscious determination to protect that text
against the slightest change. There existed a technique (counting the
letters) for ensuring the faithful transmission of that text.

Much has been made of the famous injunction attributed to the
Men of the Great Synagogue— ᶜăśû sᵉyāg lattôrâ, "make a fence
for the Torah" (*Mishnah ᵓAbot* I, 1). Rabbi J. H. Hertz was correct in
his comment to the effect that the "tradition" was the oral interpretation which protected the written Torah from misunderstanding (*Jewish
Prayer Book*, page 614). It was Rabbi Aqiba (*Mishnah ᵓAbot* III, 17)
who identified the "fence for the Torah" as **massōret**; but even then his
three following specific illustrations (tithes, vows, silence) show that this
fence maps a margin of safety against infringement in conduct. It was
only later that **massōret** was identified with *scribal* rather than legal
tradition and seen as a protection of the *text* of the Torah. This is now
the general view, in which all the terms are redefined: **massōret** changes
from traditional interpretation to scribal lore; **sᵉyāg** changes from a margin of safety for conduct to facts about the text; **tôrâ** changes from rules
for living to the text as such.

The Talmud does not say that the scribes counted the letters to
prevent changes in the text. There is no record of counting for such a
purpose, that is, checking the middle letter of the Torah to make sure
that the copy was correct. The minor tractate *Sopherim* gives many
rules for scribes but does not mention the counting of "all the letters."
It has been inferred, however, that knowledge of the total number of
letters in, say, the Torah would enable a scribe to insure that a new copy
gave the same total, ignoring that insertion errors might cancel deletion
errors to yield the correct total for an incorrect copy.

The passage from *Qiddushin* 30a is uneven. It begins by talking
about the Torah. It adds two comments about the Psalms. It says nothing about the rest of the Hebrew Bible. The acceptance of the tradition
at face value has led to exaggerations of the scope of the endeavor. It
is supposed that the enterprise covered the entire Hebrew Bible. Thus
Segal says: "It [*Qiddushin* 30a] is no doubt an abbreviation of a longer
statement embracing all the books of the Hebrew Bible." (Segal 1953)
Yeivin, in the most recent study of the Masorah—quoting the passage
once more—says: "The Masorah notes the number...of letters in the
whole Bible, in individual books,...and so on. The middle word and the
middle letter of Books, of the Torah, and of the whole Bible are also
noted." (Yeivin 1980: 73) He also refers to the poem of R. Saᶜadya
Gaᵓon, which he evidently accepts as reliable—see below.

The Talmud refers specifically to all the letters "in the Torah." It
is misleading, then, to translate this as "all the letters of the Bible,"
(Blau 1896: 343) or "all the letters in Holy Writ," (Ginsburg 1897a:
69) or "they numbered the letters of the Scriptures." (Ginsburg 1867b:
135) Eliyahu Hallevi in his influential *Massoreth Ha-Massoreth* (1538)
adorned the tale by paraphrasing the Talmud as follows: "As for the

work which the masters of the massoreth did, they worked diligently and did not rest and did not relax until they had counted (**mnw**) all the verses and words and letters in each book (**spr wspr**); that is why they are called **swprym**..." He quotes the familiar parts of *Qiddushin* 30a and adds: "and likewise book by book for the twenty-four books." (Ginsburg 1867b: 134–5) Ginsburg says: "The Massorah, in its present development, embraces almost everything connected with the external appearance of the text. It gives the number of times each letter of the alphabet occurs throughout the Bible. It states how many verses there are in each separate book. It shows which is the middle letter, which the middle word, and which is the middle verse in every book." (Ginsburg 1867a: 16)

Remarks in Philo and in Josephus have been read in the light of later concerns. Philo said: "And although many years have passed—I cannot tell the exact number, but more than two thousand—the Jews have never altered a word of what was written by Moses."[1] Josephus praises the loyalty of the Jews to the Scriptures, "beginning with birth;" they persist in them, not adding, not subtracting, not changing.[2]

The computational feats of the scribes are usually reported with a sense of astonishment, and arguments are based on their supposed historical veracity. The assiduity of the scribes is the trump proof of the integrity of the transmitted text. Thus G. E. Weil: "Their respect for the *Textus Receptus* led them to make an exact count of the verses, words, and letters of *all* [italics ours] the sacred books so that *not one letter* [italics ours] or word could be overlooked by a scribe." (Weil 1968: vi) Gordis repeatedly based his argument for textual purity on his assessment of Masoretic reckoning prowess: "That these anonymous guardians of the text, who counted the letters of Scripture, determined the middle letter and middle verse of the Torah, established the middle letter of the Bible as a whole, compiled extensive lists...—all in order to help protect it from tampering and prevent scribes from introducing changes into the accepted text—would themselves engage in wholesale changes in the accepted readings is a rank impossibility." (Gordis 1937: xiv and 19–20)

A moment's reflection indicates that the reported counting activities of the scribes were quite likely to be flawed, as the evidence of the texts themselves confirms. No two manuscripts are orthographically identical; hence, the tally of letters differs from manuscript to manuscript. Nor is there available reliable knowledge of the true counts by which to test the accuracy of any copy. And without precision, there is no (scientific) point to the claims made.

---

[1] *Political Constitution* in Eusebius *Prep. Ev.* VIII 6.

[2] *Contra Apion* VIII: 38–46.

Talmudic tradition includes a story about Rabbi Joseph, who raised with Rabbi Abbaye the question of whether the **w** of **ghwn** belongs to the first or second half of the Torah. The form of the question implies that the number of letters is even. The best-known report of the figure, that of the Leningrad Codex (**L**, B19^a), gives an odd number, 400,945 (**L**, I, 242; **BHS**, 353). This score is well-attested, notably in the *Diqduqe hatte^{c}amim* of Aaron ben Asher. If the total were in fact odd, there would be a uniquely defined middle letter belonging to neither half. The two rabbis must have had an even total. Or perhaps they had no number at all. The story goes on to say that the two scholars "did not stir from that place until the scroll of the Torah had been brought and they had counted them." Unfortunately the tradition does not tell the outcome of the experiment. The incident is to be dated to around 300 CE. This suggests that some practice of counting letters (or at least the belief that the earlier scribes did it) was already in vogue.

While there is no documentation of the use of the knowledge of the number of letters in individual books to test the accuracy of copies, there were rules for proofreading a new scroll by counting the number of letters in the old and the new column by column. This required that the very format be reproduced exactly, not such a formidable task. To compile records, to sum for the aggregate, would be more work; to preserve those records immaculate would be nearly as hazardous as the preservation of the text. "Who will guard the guardians?"

Human beings are not very good at counting. It takes time and causes weariness. One cannot relax for a moment without "losing count." Our trials suggest that just to count all the letters in the Torah by hand would take a working week, the whole Bible a working month. To find the middle letters of individual books, of sets of books, such as the Torah, and of the whole Bible, would require additional effort. (Of course, one might determine the middle letter, if any, by striking out equal numbers of consonants coming from the front and back of the text; but this would leave one with no counts of the sort given by the Masoretes.) The chances of getting any result right in one try would be slim, and the chances of getting the same answer the second time around—for confirmation— remote. Little wonder that the universal response to the amazing tales of the scribes' exploits has been admiration but not emulation.

A.2   Specifics in the Tradition

There are records of the number of *verses* in each book of the Bible in the masora. The notes in B19^a also give the middle verse of each book, and **BHS** supplies this information in marginal annotation. **L** and **BHS** annotate Lev 8:8, not 13:33, as the middle verse of the Pentateuch; they label Ps 78:36, not 78:38, as the middle verse of the Psalter.

The Torah is the only portion for which there are counts of *words*, and that is only for the Torah as a whole, not for the individual books. B19[a] identifies the middle point by words at Lev 10:16.

If the scribes did indeed count all the *letters*, the surviving results of their researches are very meager. B19[a] places the middle letter of the Torah at Lev 11:42. It does not have a masora for the middle letter of the Psalter, although it does have a letter suspended. The Aleppo Codex is the same. **BHS** also presents a datum not mentioned in the Talmud, namely that Jer 6:7 contains the middle letter of the Bible: **ḥṣy hmqr³ b³wtywt**. At Jer 6:7 Ginsburg's edition (1926) reads: **yw″d šl bbyr ḥṣy ³wtywt šl mqr³ kwlw**. This could be ascertained from knowledge of the count of letters in the Bible combined with a recount to half that number; but there is no masora giving the total count. If this knowledge ever existed, no record of it has been preserved. L. Blau, who investigated the whole matter, could not find any specific statements (Blau 1896: 344). More recently, Even–Shoshan's concordance (Even–Shoshan 1981: xxxviii) supplies a table of the number of letters in each book of the Bible. For the Torah he relies on Norzi. For the rest he simply calculates the average length of a word in the Pentateuch and multiplies this by the number of words in each book. Quite apart from uncertainty about the number of words in each book, the assumption that words have the same average length throughout the Bible is fallacious. The mean word length is smaller in the Pentateuch (3.8 letters per word) than anywhere else (Prophets: 3.9 letters per word; Writings: 4.0 letters per word). Even–Shoshan's estimates for the other books are thus too small, and his letter count for the Writings (317,400) is six percent low.

We have, then, three claims about middle letters: 1) the middle letter of the Torah (masora and Talmud); 2) the middle letter of the Psalter (Talmud, but not masora); 3) the middle letter of the Bible (editions, but not Talmud). If these identifications were ever based on actual counts of the letter totals, this information is preserved only in the case of the Torah. Such traditions are found only in the Rabbinic channels of transmission of the Hebrew Bible and have nothing to contribute to the study of other recensions or text-types which circulated in pre-Christian times. At the same time, it is acknowledged that the texts used by the Rabbis in these exercises might not have been the same as the "Masoretic" text-type now extant. The *tiqqune sopherim* attest textual adjustments, but restoring the eighteen generally recognized cases changes the letter counts in only four words for an overall difference of three letters fewer.

Having an extensively checked computer-readable copy of B19^a (our computerized text, A–F), with Josh 21:36–37 restored, allows us to examine the traditions regarding verses, words, and letters. Facsimiles of other prime manuscripts have been consulted: Aleppo Codex (**A**), Cairo Codex (**C**), and Codex Petropolitanus (**P**). All counts are based on *ktyb* texts. There is no reason to believe that the Rabbis would have used *qry* variants for their counts; but, even if they had and even if we could work out which *qry* variants they might have used, the differences in the results would be negligible in comparison with the discrepancies discussed below. If the *qry* text of **L** were used, the ten cases of *qry wP ktyb* would add ten words and thirty-two letters, while the eight cases of *ktyb wP qry* would remove eight words and nineteen letters. The Torah attracts most interest, and none of these occur in it.

A.3   Mechanisms of Divergence

We desire not only to evaluate the traditions regarding verses, words, and letters, but also to suggest possible reasons for discrepancies between tradition and received texts. Three sorts of explanations are logical possibilities (as are their many combinations):

1. *Differing Text*:
   a. *Text Changes*: Our texts may differ from those used to generate the tradition due to the insertion, deletion, or migration of blocks of text, words, or letters. Included is the possibility that the portion of text containing the designated midpoint of tradition might itself shift position.
   b. *Punctuation Changes*: The insertion, deletion, or substitution of punctuation marks could affect the location of middle words (and middle verses).
2. *Differing Definitions*:
   a. *Of Item Counted*: Consider, for example, the concept of "word:" The obvious definition of a word is that it is a contiguous sequence of letters flanked by spacers. But which symbols are considered spacers? Specifically, was *maqqep* considered a spacer? That items ligatured by *maqqep* might have been counted as single words at some places and times seems to us (and to Weil) likely.
   b. *Of "Middle"*: Did "middle" always and everywhere have the meaning of halfway *as reckoned in terms of the item under consideration*? Might a hierarchical definition have obtained? For example, might the middle letter of a book have been considered the middle letter of the middle line of the middle *seder*?

3. *Error:*
  a. *In execution:* The originators of a tradition might have been simply incorrect in reckoning counts and middle positions (or fabricated misinformation).
  b. *In transmission:* The original information might have become corrupted in transmission.

We shall refer repeatedly to these divergence mechanisms as we proceed.

A.4 Verse Counts

The verse counts in the Talmud are not very accurate if we take **L** as representative of the standard text. But to be precise, there is no such thing as a standard text. This is affirmed by Orlinsky (1966: xviii) but contested by Breuer (1976: xiii). Even if a measure of standardization was achieved by the early rabbis, in due time differences appeared between East and West (quite apart from small fluctuations due to individual errors). The Torah verse total in **L** is 5,853. For this count, each tradition has its own masora. The masora in **L** (reproduced by Even–Shoshan) has 5,845, but there are differences in versification, notably in the Decalogue. *Qiddushin* 30a says that the number of verses in the Torah is 5,888. The Talmud adds that there are eight more verses in the Psalms, that is 5,896 (actually, there are 2,527), and eight fewer in Chronicles, that is 5,880 (actually 1,765; Even–Shoshan reports 1,754). Weil (1981: 658) discusses possible reasons for the varying counts. Table A.1 gives the verse totals reported in **C**, **P**, **A**, **L**, and Ginsburg (1897b), as well as those obtained by totaling the verses in A–F. The final two rows contain the reported grand totals ("reported") and the counts obtained when we sum the various book totals ("summed").

The **C** counts are from a list in the final summary (**C**, 582). The counts reported in the Masoretic summaries of the individual books differ from those in the list for Samuel (list: 1,506, summary: 1,504) and Jeremiah (list: 1,365, summary: 1,364). The list entry for Lamentations has suffered damage. It reads: **qynwt psw mᵓtym.wᵓrb[　]wᵓrbᶜh**. If we reckon Lamentations as having 154 verses, then the grand total obtained by adding up the separate counts for **C** is 23,202. (Compare the 23,200 grand total [**kgr**] recorded in the list.)

The **P** counts are from its final summary (**P**, 224a). The counts reported in the summaries of the individual books differ from those in the **P** list for Isaiah (list: 1,272, summary: **ytqᵓ?**) and Ezekiel (list: 1,270, summary: 1,273). The list entries sum to 9,269 for the Prophets, well below the totals obtained from other lists.

The **A** counts are from the summaries following the individual books which survive.

Table A.1. Verse totals

Portion	C	P	A	L	G	A–F
Genesis	1535	-	-	1534	1534	1533
Exodus	1209	-	-	1209	1209	1213
Leviticus	859	-	-	859	859†	859
Numbers	1285	-	-	1288	1288	1289
Deut	955	-	955	955	955	959
Joshua	656	656	656	656	656	658
Judges	618	618	618	618	618	618
Samuel	1506	1504	1506	1506	1506	1506
Kings	1536	1535	1536	1534	1536	1536
Isaiah	1291	1272	1291	1291	1292	1291
Jeremiah	1365	1364	1364	1364	1365	1364
Ezekiel	1273	1270	1273	1273	1273	1273
Minor Proph	1050	1050	1050	1050	1050	1050
Chron	1765	-	1765	1765	1765	1765
Psalms	2527	-	2527	2527	2527	2527
Job	1070	-	1070	1070	1075	1070
Proverbs	915	-	915	915	915	915
Ruth	85	-	85	85	85	85
Song	117	-	-	117	117	117
Qohelet	222	-	-	222	222	222
Lam	2?4	-	-	154	154	154
Esther	167	-	-	168	167	167
Daniel	357	-	-	357	357	357
Ezra-Neh	685	-	-	685	688	685
Torah	-	-	-	5845	5845	5853
Prophets	-	-	-	9285	9294	9296
Writings	-	-	-	-	-	8064
Bible (reported)	23200	-	-	23203	23203	-
Bible (summed)	23202	-	-	23202	23213	23213

†—Ginsburg reports a verse count of 889 in words and 589 in Arabic numerals. The Hebrew numeral for 859 is misprinted n†p. In the table, we have corrected the count to 859.

The **L** counts are from the summaries of the individual books and from the *masora terminalis* of each section, where legible. The total count of verses in the Prophets list (9,285) [**L** II, 412] differs from the total of the separate counts (9,292). The count for Esther in its summary (168) [**L** III, 221] differs from that in the Writings list (167) [**L** III, 273]. **BHS**, without acknowledgment, corrects Esther's summary to read "167." The counts reported for the books total to 23,201, not to the 23,203 that the final summary asserts (L, III, 275).

The G counts are from Ginsburg (1897b: II, 450–3). The total for the Torah is duplicated in Dosa ben Elezer's *massoret* (Ginsburg 1897b: II, 338), but his total for the Prophets is 9,298 rather than 9,294. The Dosa count for the Writings is 8,063. Thus, Dosa's grand total is 23,206 verses. Ginsburg gives 23,203 as the grand total of verses; the total of his figures, corrected for Leviticus, is 23,213.

When compared with the actual verse count in A–F, the summary count for the number of verses in Genesis is one too big, due to the compound nature of Gen 35:22 which contains two *sillûq*s but only one verse terminator (Ginsburg 1897a: 74). See also G. E. Weil (1981: 658). The Masoretic summary count for Exodus is four too small, most likely because the summary count is based on a manuscript in which Exodus 20 had 22 verses (Ginsburg 1897a: 76), while **BHS** invokes 26 verses (by letting *sillûq* without verse terminator suffice to define verse boundaries). Note, however, that the portion of **L** corresponding to Exodus 20 includes only 21 verse terminators, not 22. The Masoretic count for Numbers is one smaller than the actual verse total in **BHS** because **BHS**'s Num 25:19 ends with neither *sillûq* nor verse terminator (Weil 1981: 660). Also, see C. D. Ginsburg (1897b: II, 184–5). The Masoretic count for Deuteronomy is four smaller than the actual verse total for A–F. The extra verses likely result from alternate divisions in Deuteronomy 5 (Weil 1981: 658). The Masoretic counts for Joshua reported in Table A.1 are too small by two compared with A–F. This is due to the restoration of Josh 21:36–37 into A–F (Ginsburg 1897a: 178–80). The Masoretic tally for Kings in **L** is two less than the actual total in A–F and than the totals given by **C**, **A**, and Ginsburg (1897b). We find no remaining clues which resolve the difference; nor did Ginsburg (1897a: 91). We do note that the grand total of verses given at the end of **L** is a correct sum if one recognizes the two additional verses in Kings.

To summarize: The discrepancies between verse count traditions and our texts are most simply accounted for by divergence mechanism 1.b. (*Differing Text: Punctuation Changes*). Relative to the verse count traditions, **BHS** ignored the *sillûq* in the midst of its Gen 35:22. It recognized four additional verses in the Decalogue, both in Exodus 20 and in Deuteronomy 5. It delimited a verse not so marked in **L**, Num 25:19.

It restored Josh 21:36–37 (which are not found in **L**). And it, as well as **L**, found two more verses in Kings than the reckoners of the Masoretic summaries knew. The outcome of all this is that whereas the summarizers counted 23,201 verses, **BHS** enumerated 23,213. Both sets of counts are defensible.

A.5   Middle Verses

The middle verse of each book, as designated in the margins of **C**, **P**, **A**, or **L**, is given in Table A.2. In addition, the identities reported by Ginsburg (1897b: II, 450) and reckoned by the computer for A–F are given. Note that when a book had an even number of verses, the Masoretes took the first verse of the second half as the middle verse of the book. We adopt this policy. (Following **A**, **C**'s colophon, and **L**, we have also repositioned Chronicles to precede Psalms.)

We see that the middle verses computed from A–F differ from the marginal masora and *masora terminalis* in **L** in eight instances: Genesis, Exodus, Deuteronomy, Joshua, Samuel, Torah, Prophets, and Bible. When we alter the versification of **BHS** along the lines proposed in the summary at the conclusion of the previous section, we obtain agreement in all save these three cases: 1) Samuel—it appears that **A** not **L** nominated the correct middle verse; 2) Prophets—when we make the aforementioned adjustments, the middle verse of the Prophets (by actual count) moves from Isa 17:2 to Isa 17:4, leapfrogging the Masoretic designate; 3) Bible—similarly, the middle verse of the Old Testament moves from Jer 6:2 to Jer 6:8, rather than 6:7. A simple hypothesis accounts for the overshooting of the Masoretic mark by one verse in both these cases. Suppose the determinations of the middle verses of the sections of the Old Testament were made *after* the two additional verse boundaries in Kings were marked; then the middle verse designees would in these instances be correct. (And, as noted above, the grand total in the **L** colophon would also be correct.)

A few additional observations merit noting. **P** has marginal signs indicating the middle of a book *twice* in Isaiah (opposite 33:21 and 35:8) and *twice* in Ezekiel (opposite 26:1 and 24:24). Interestingly, we find the middle *word* of Isaiah to be l‌ᵓgm in Isa 35:7; but the middle of Ezekiel by *words* is between bbᵓw and bšᶜryk in Ezek 26:10.

BHS has slightly mispositioned its middle verse indications in three instances: 1) the middle verse of the Prophets is noted opposite Isa 17:2 rather than 17:3; 2) the middle verse of Isaiah is flagged opposite 33:20 rather than 33:21; 3) the middle verse of Proverbs is flagged opposite 16:17 rather than 16:18.

Table A.2. Middle verses

Portion	C	P	A	L	G†	A–F
Genesis	-	-	-	27:40	27:40	27:39
Exodus	-	-	-	22:27	22:27	22:25
Leviticus	-	-	-	15:7	15:7	15:7
Numbers	-	-	-	17:20	17:20	17:20
Deut	-	-	-	17:10	17:10	17:8
Joshua	13:26	-	13:26	13:26	13:26	13:27
Judges	10:8	-	10:8	10:8	10:8	10:8
Samuel	???	-	1Sam 28:23	28:24	28:24	28:23
Kings	???	-	1Kgs 22:6	22:6	22:6	22:6
Isaiah	33:21	33:21	33:21	33:21	33:21	33:21
Jeremiah	28:11	28:10	28:11	28:11	28:11	28:11
Ezekiel	26:1	26:1	26:1	26:1	26:1	26:1
Minor Proph	Mic 3:12	3:12	-	3:12	3:12	3:12
Chron	-	-	1Chr 27:25	27:25	27:25	27:25
Psalms	-	-	78:36	78:36	78:36	78:36
Job	-	-	22:16	22:16	22:16	22:16
Proverbs	-	-	16:18	16:18	16:18	16:18
Ruth	-	-	2:21	2:21	2:21	2:21
Song	-	-	-	4:14	4:14	4:14
Qohelet	-	-	-	6:10‡	6:10	6:10
Lam	-	-	-	3:34	3:34	3:34
Esther	-	-	-	5:7	5:7	5:7
Daniel	-	-	-	6:12	5:30	6:12
Ezra-Neh	-	-	-	Neh 3:32	3:32	3:32
Torah	-	-	-	Lev 8:8	8:8	8:9
Prophets	Isa 17:3	17:3	17:3	17:3	17:3	17:2
Writings	-	-	Ps 130:3	130:3	130:3	130:3
Bible	Jer 6:7	???	6:7	6:7	6:7	6:2

†—Middle verse numbers in Ginsburg are regularly one too small for all books after the Torah. We have used the references of the incipits, as these are correct.

‡—Standard practice in **L** is for the word ḥṣy to be opposite the designated middle verse. In Qohelet, the word is opposite 6:12. However, Qoh 6:10 is nominated as the middle verse in the list at the end of the manuscript (**L**, III, 273).

The discrepancies between middle verse traditions and our texts are accounted for by divergence mechanism 1.b. (*Differing Text: Punctuation Changes*).

A.6   Word Counts

L gives 79,856 as the total number of words in the Torah. The differing traditions concerning the number of words in the Torah have been thoroughly studied by Weil (1981). He attributes differences in word totals to differing practices in counting proper nouns involving *maqqep*, an instance of divergence mechanism 1.a (*Definition of Item Counted*). For Rabbinic discussion on this, see *Sopherim* 37a(2)–37b(1).

For completeness and to allow comparisons, Table A.3 gives word counts for each book according to E–S = Even–Shoshan (1981: xxxviii), Weil (Cassuto 1987),[3] and A–F = Andersen–Forbes.

A.7   The Middle Word of the Torah

L identifies the middle words of the Torah as **drš drš** (Lev 10:16 in **L** at I, 126, column 2, line 7). We reckon these words to be numbers 40,922 and 40,923 out of a total of 79,983 words. They are 51.2 percent of the way through the Torah (by words). Weil reports that **yswd** in Lev 8:15 follows the midpoint in **L**'s Torah (Weil 1981). We find the middle word (number 39,992) in **L**'s Torah to be **wyqdšhw** in Lev 8:15, two words later. This difference results because we read five proper nouns in Numbers as two orthographic words each (as in **BHS**), while Weil reads them as single words.[4]

How can we account for the tradition that places the middle word of the Torah in Lev 10:16 instead of in Lev 8:15, 930 words (about eight text columns) earlier?

For the explanation to lie in divergence mechanism 1.a. (*Differing Texts: Text Changes*) would require that 1,860 words be inserted before the traditional midpoint, or 1,860 words be deleted after that midpoint, or 930 words be shifted from after to before that midpoint, or some combination of such changes.[5]

---

[3] Updated August 1988.

[4] P. Cassuto, private communication.

[5] To visualize the first change mechanism, hold up your right hand—palm in view— with your two smallest fingers folded down. The middle of the extended digits will be your index finger. Now also extend the two smallest fingers. Note that the midpoint of the extended fingers has moved one digit leftward. In terms of the text: for each *two* words added before the midpoint, the resulting midpoint moves *one* word earlier. And so on for the other mechanisms.

Table A.3. Word counts by book

Portion	E–S	Weil	A–F
Genesis	20512	20613	20613
Exodus	16723	16713	16713
Leviticus	11950	11950	11950
Numbers	16368	16408	16413
Deut	14294	14294	14294
Joshua	10015	10051	10051
Judges	9771	9886	9885
Samuel	24228	24304	24301
Kings	25345	25422	25421
Isaiah	16920	16934	16933
Jeremiah	21673	21836	21835
Ezekiel	19123	18730	18730
Minor Proph	14339	14355	14355
Chron	23801	24061	24058
Psalms	19479	19587	19586
Job	8392	8341	8343
Proverbs	6912	6915	6915
Ruth	1286	1296	1294
Song	1251	1250	1250
Qohelet	2997	2987	2987
Lam	1491	1542	1542
Esther	3045	3045	3045
Daniel	5924	5919	5919
Ezra–Neh	9062	9066	9065
Torah	79847	79978	79983
Prophets	141414	141518	141511
Writings	83640	84009	84004
Bible	304901	305505	305498

The simplest maneuver would be to remove 930 words from the back part and add them to the front part, so that the first **drš** would become the middle word. This text would still have the same overall length and content as our received text; only the order would be different. The amount of text to be transposed occupies somewhat more than eight columns in **L**. Such a migration of a portion of text is always possible when a manuscript is being copied, whether by accident or design. But it is hard to believe that such a thing ever happened to a text prestigious enough to have been the basis of a famous scribal tradition, with the altered text supplanting the old as the official text, yet not generating an altered tradition about the middle word(s). Furthermore, although we have considered the most general possibilities, it is not likely that text moved from Genesis or Exodus to Numbers or Deuteronomy. It would have to take place within Leviticus. The most likely accident would be simple loss of a portion of text following **drš drš**—1860 words ($16\frac{1}{2}$ columns or $5\frac{1}{2}$ pages of **L**). Is it likely that such a drastic change in a sacred text would go undetected, uncorrected, and that no trace of the original would survive? We conclude that it is improbable that the discrepancy over the middle word is due to divergence mechanism 1.a operating in the text of Leviticus.

Divergence mechanism 1.b (*Differing Text: Punctuation Changes*) operating in conjunction with mechanism 2.a (*Differing Definition of Item Counted*) might account for the discrepancy. Suppose that when the middle word was ascertained (we suppose this predated the counting of the words which yielded the word total of tradition), items joined by *maqqep*s were viewed as comprising single words. The Torah text of **L** contains 5,987 *maqqep*s before Lev 10:16 and 5,481 after, a difference of 506. On the hypothesized definition of word, the scribes would count 34,935 words before Lev 10:16 and 33,580 after. Thus, on this reckoning, the traditional middle word would be slightly closer to the true middle, lying 51.0% rather than 51.2% of the way into the Torah. Now, if the determination of the middle word was made on a manuscript for which certain items were systematically *not* joined by *maqqep* and these items predominated after the traditional midpoint, then words—in effect— would be added to the back "half." To cite but one example, in the Torah of **L** there are 147 more instances of lōʔ- after the traditional word midpoint than before it. In theory, there might have been a time when the distribution of *maqqep*s across the Torah, combined with a practice of counting items joined by *maqqep*s as single words, could have put the traditional middle words of the Torah at the middle of the Torah by words.

We prefer an alternate explanation, one based on divergence mechanisms 1.b (*Differing Text: Punctuation Changes*) and 2.b (*Differing*

Definition of Middle). L's Torah consists of 167 *sedarim*. The middle *seder* (number 84) runs from Lev 10:8 through 10:20 and thus contains the traditional middle words. The *seder* consists of nine lines, a blank line, 18 lines, the line containing the traditional middle words, 16 lines, a blank line, 46 lines in all. Hence, the middle line of the *seder* is number 24 (by the usual convention, the first line of the second half), five lines before the line with the middle words. Ginsburg reports manuscripts in which *seder* boundaries have jumped by a paragraph (Ginsburg 1897a: 32–65). For example, in the Torah Ginsburg reports that *Oriental 2201* marks a boundary at Gen 21:22, a paragraph earlier than the usual boundary at Gen 22:1. The *Tbilissi Pentateuch* has several shifted boundaries (Weil and Guény 1976). For example, the **L** boundary at Exod 16:4 appears in the *Tbilissi Pentateuch* at Exod 15:27, a paragraph earlier. If we hypothesize a (marginal) punctuation change wherein the boundary of the middle *seder* moves one paragraph later (down to Lev 10:12), then the line counts become: 18 lines, line with middle words, 16 lines, blank line, 36 lines in all. The middle line (the first of the second half) is now the line containing the traditional middle words. That middle line contains four words, the middle two being the traditional middle words. To summarize: If we adjust the onset of *seder* 84 of L's Torah one paragraph later, then the traditional middle words of the Torah are the middle words in the middle line of the middle *seder* of the Torah.

A.8   Letter Counts

A.8.1   Letter Counts of the Torah

Traditions regarding letters are even more flawed than those regarding words. How unrealistic some figures can be is shown by the number of letters for Genesis given in Jacob ben Hayyim's Rabbinic Bible—4395! According to Norzi, the score is 78,064. Ginsburg (1897a: 113) says 87,064—which only shows how easily a typographical error can lose the truth. Our figure is 78,069; Weil's is 78,069.

The figures in various manuscripts for the total number of letters in the Torah range from fewer than 300,000 to more than 600,000. Ginsburg's 1894 edition of the Bible gave 304,807 as the total, but his subtotals for the individual pericopes sum to 305,005. Weil (1981) tracked down the sources of the various discrepancies. Information in Hebrew MS Number 1 in the University of Madrid yields a grand total of 304,799. Blau (1896: 348) estimated 290,136 from Ginsburg's compilation of masora, but the latter's citation of 1,634 for **b** is manifestly the result of dropping a fifth digit. Using our count for **b** (16,345) with the rest of Ginsburg's figures gives a total of 304,946—a reasonable figure (see below). Elias Levita gave 600,045, which Blau has shown to be a textual corruption of the tradition in B19^a (400,945)—also corrupt! (For details, see Blau 1896: 344–5.)

In order to find out who, if anyone, was correct, Blau did not attempt to count all the letters directly. He was content to estimate the total by counting the letters on a few pages of a printed Bible and multiplying the average by the number of pages in the Torah. He did this for more than one Bible. The result was approximate, but it was enough to show that the true figure must be of the order of 300,000. This has been confirmed by the more recent and, we hope, more accurate counts given in Table A.4.

Table A.4. Letters in the Torah

Even–Shoshan	304,805
Weil	304,847
Andersen and Forbes	304,849

Divergence mechanisms 3.a and 3.b (*Errors in Execution and/or Transmission*) best account for the discrepancies. Blau (1896: 348) traces some of the transmission errors.

A.8.2　Letter Counts of the Bible

Yeivin (1980: 73) is only the most recent of a long line of scholars who have been content to point to a poem attributed to R. Sa^{c}adya Ga$^{\jmath}$on (tenth century) as sufficient proof that the sages knew the number of letters in the Bible. The poem was published originally by Elias Levita in 1538. It has often been reproduced since. The text may be found in C. D. Ginsburg's translation of Levita's *Massoreth Ha-Massoreth* (1867b); or see C. D. Ginsburg (1897b: I, 33–5). Ginsburg argues convincingly that the poem was most likely by a twelfth-century French rabbi. The poem purports to supply the counts for the individual letters. It actually distinguishes some terminal forms, and in one case distinguishes *dagesh* from *raphe*, so that twenty-eight letters in all are separately counted. The value of the numeral is protected by the ingenious method of giving the information twice, first by an acrostic (the first letters of the words are read as a numeral) and then by a series of references to scripture texts which contain the needed numbers. Perhaps it is suspicious that the numbers needed happened to be available in the Bible. Thus the score for the letter **b** (38,218) is certified by Num 1:37 (35,400) and Neh 7:11 (2,818). For each letter, Table A.5 gives the Sa^{c}adya and A–F counts and percentages. Figure A.1 facilitates comparison of the Sa^{c}adya and A–F percentages.

Table A.5. Counts of letters in the Hebrew Bible

Letter	Saᶜadya	Percent	A–F	Percent
א	42377	5.20	95683	7.99
ב	38218	4.69	65214	5.45
ג	29537	3.62	10080	0.84
ד	32530	3.99	32370	2.70
ה	47754	5.86	101962	8.52
ו	76922	9.44	129607	10.83
ז	22867	2.80	9099	0.76
ח	23447	2.88	27599	2.30
ט	11052	1.36	6310	0.53
י	66420	8.15	137867	11.52
כ	37272	4.57	29709	2.48
ך	10981	1.35	17761	1.48
ל	41517	5.09	88303	7.38
מ	52805	6.48	48523	4.05
ם	24973	3.06	50407	4.21
נ	32977	4.04	36758	3.07
ן	8719	1.07	18335	1.53
ס	13580	1.66	7635	0.64
ע	20175	2.47	44811	3.74
פ	20750	2.54	15235	1.27
ף	1975	0.24	3049	0.25
צ	16950	2.08	11355	0.95
ץ	4872	0.60	3622	0.30
ק	22972	2.82	16278	1.36
ר	22147	2.72	68065	5.69
שׂ	-	-	12124	-
שׁ	-	-	46074	-
ש	32148	3.94	58198	4.86
ת	59343	7.28	63206	5.28
Total	815280	100.00	1197043	100.00

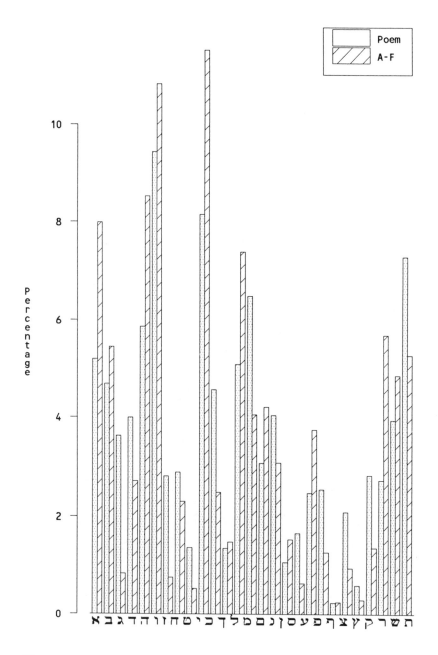

Figure A.1. Letter incidences according to Sa^cadya and A–F

Ludwig Blau (1896: 350) tried to explain the fact that the total for all the letters in Scripture yielded by this poem was less than 800,000. Blau's figure was 792,077 (echoed by Strack [1907: 69]), because he disregarded the final stanza; including it gives 815,280. The sum itself is not certain because the versions of the poem extant exhibit the usual textual variations (Blau 1896: 353). But whatever the range introduced by these variants, the total is not nearly enough for the whole Bible, which is almost 1.2 million letters. Blau argued that the total was of the right order to belong to Prophets plus Writings. He was not able to explain why such a detailed count should exist for those parts of the Bible, but not for the Torah. Yet the figures support his guess only approximately. The number of consonants in Prophets plus Writings is around 892,194 (Andersen and Forbes) or 892,179 (Weil). (The total for Torah plus Prophets [858,640] is closer to that of the poem.)

As counts of the letters in the Hebrew Bible, the numbers in the poem present two distinct problems: the grand total and the relative frequencies of the individual letters. It has not been shown that the grand total for the poem matches that of any particular portion of the Bible; but even if that could be done, the distribution of the letter counts resembles that of the Bible only roughly. The columns of percentages in Table A.5 are similar in that the same letters—**y** and **w**—are the most frequent, but their ranking is reversed. There is disagreement, however, as to the next most frequent: **t** (third rank in poem, eighth rank in Bible), **h** (third rank in Bible, fifth rank in the poem). There is general agreement as to the least frequent letters. But the biblical range of percentages is wider than the poem indicates. That is, the most common letters—**y**, **w**, **h**—are much more common than the poem says, while the rarer letters—**g**, **z**, **ṭ**, and **s**—are much rarer than the poem says. More serious is the large divergence in the frequencies of certain letters, notably **g** (the poem's frequency is far too high for biblical Hebrew) and **r** (the poem's frequency is far too low). Because of the rough fit, we are unwilling to dismiss the numbers in the poem as pure fabrication; but because of the divergences from biblical Hebrew, we cannot see how the frequencies could have been derived from the biblical text.

A.9 Middle Letters

A.9.1 The Middle Letter of the Torah

Our total of 304,849 for all the consonant letters in the Pentateuch cannot be squared with the assertion that Lev 11:42 contains the middle letter. In our text, the midpoint is consonant Number 152,425, which is the first **h** in hḥzh in Lev 8:29. This is a long way from Lev 11:42. The

w in **gḥwn** in that verse is letter Number 157,239 in the Torah. This is 4,814 positions past the true middle, or 51.58 percent through the text, about five pages too late in **BHS**.

Blau already noticed that Lev 11:42 was not on the middle page of the Torah in the editions he used. Nevertheless he did not doubt the truth of the tradition, nor did he check it. He was content to "explain" the fact that the middle letter (supposedly) was not on the middle page "by the circumstance that comparatively larger blank spaces occur in the first half of the pages than in the latter half." (Blau 1896: 346) In the Qoren edition, which has a uniform layout of block text, the Torah required 8,563 lines. The middle line is Lev 8:28.

How are we to account for the tradition? Divergence mechanism 1.a (*Text Changes*) can hardly be the explanation because the text underlying the tradition would be utterly different from any known text. Divergence mechanism 2.b (*Differing Definition of Middle*) is a more likely explanation. A scenario similar to that proposed above to explain the middle word tradition in the Torah may serve here as well: The middle letter of tradition could have been the middle letter of the middle line of the middle *seder* as demarcated by one of the alternate traditions. Word boundaries adjacent to the traditional middle letter are such that it could have been at the middle of lines of length 9, 17, 21, 29, 33, or 45 letters.[6]

A.9.2   The Middle Letter of the Psalter

The Masoretic tradition about the midpoint of the Psalter appears incorrect. There are 78,830 letters in the Psalter (Even–Shoshan—74,000 [rough estimate]; Weil—78,829). The midpoint of the Psalter is after Number 39,415, that is, after **m** in **lmnṣḥ** in Ps 77:1. The alleged middle letter (Ps 80:14) is Number 43,236, 54.85 percent into the Psalter. This is six pages further ahead in **BHS**.

Divergence mechanism 2.b (*Differing Definition Of Middle*) accounts for the apparent discrepancy: The middle "book" of the Psalms (Ps 73–89) consists of three *sedarim*. In **A** (but not in **L**), the middle *seder* (Ps 78:38–84:13) consists of 173 lines (counting blank lines). The middle line contains 27 characters. Its middle character is the elevated *ayin*. In other words, in **A** the elevated *ayin* in Ps 80:14 is the middle letter of the middle line of the middle *seder* of the middle "book" of Psalms.

---

[6] In **L**, the middle **w** is letter fifteen in a nineteen letter line; in British Museum **Or 4445**, it is letter nine in a thirteen letter line.

A.9.3   The Middle Letter of the Bible

It should be noted that there could not have been any talk about the middle letter (or verse or word, for that matter) of the whole Bible until there was such a thing as a whole Bible, with all the individual books arranged in a fixed order. Or relatively fixed. Shuffling individual books around before the book containing the middle letter or shuffling individual books around after the book containing the middle letter would make no difference, but movement of books around the middle point would change the result. Here we are reminded that the earliest tradition about the order of the books in the Babylonian Talmud (*Baba Bathra* 14b) is the same as the Masoretic Text for Torah and Former Prophets (this sequence never varied); but it presents only one of many traditions for the Writings. In any case, these are too far away from the middle to make any difference. The Latter Prophets were also subject to flux in listing.

These facts indicate that the existence of the whole Bible in a single book—an actual codex, that is—is a late development, and even then the sequence in Latter Prophets and Writings is far from settled. Goshen–Gottstein (1979) is of the opinion that the Aleppo Codex itself could be the very first complete Hebrew Bible ever made. Of course, given a fixed order in a list, the middle letter could still be calculated without the physical existence of the whole Bible as a single book, although we think that this is highly improbable.

The Talmudic sequence—Jeremiah, Ezekiel, Isaiah—is suggestive. In a book with this arrangement the middle letter *would* be in Jeremiah, the **w** in ᵓ**bwtykm** at 16:11. For such an ordering the discrepancy would not be nearly as huge as the one in our present Bible, amounting to twenty-two pages in **BHS**. If the middle letter of the Bible was worked out on the basis of the Talmudic sequence of Latter Prophets, then such a "Bible," whether made into an actual codex or merely notional, must have existed, along with the masora to Jer 6:7, before the making of the Cairo Codex, the Aleppo Codex, and the others, which have a sequence that makes the masora untrue.

But the masora, as presented in modern editions, is not true either way. Our count for the number of letters (consonants) in the Bible (1,197,043) is quite close to that of Weil (1,197,026). We could both be slightly wrong, for reasons given above, but the minute difference will not seriously affect the general result. According to our count, the middle of the Bible by letters is letter Number 598,522. This is the seventh letter in Isa 25:4, the **m** in the first **mᶜwz**. Jer 6:7 is 54.4 percent into the Bible (by letters). The overshoot is 82 pages in **BHS**. Hence, this verse can not possibly be the locus of the middle letter of the Bible.

There is a simple explanation for all this. **BHS** has altered the Masoretic marginal note opposite Jer 6:7. Its annotation is ḥṣy hmqrᵓ bᵓwtywt. **BH**³ had ḥṣy hmq̇ [bᵓwtywt]. B19ᵃ reads ḥṣy hmq̇. In the Aleppo Codex, the annotation at this point is simply ḥṣy hmqrᵓ. **D62** has ḥ hmqrᵓ. Weil (*Prolegomena* to **BHS**, page xiii) criticized Kahle's reproduction of the marginal notes of B19ᵃ "with almost photographic fidelity" as having been done "quite uncritically." Unfortunately, Weil (in **BHS**) did not place "by letters" in square brackets, thus depriving the student without access to photographs of B19ᵃ of the vital information that "by letters" is an attempt to correct a supposed error in B19ᵃ. But it is the "correction" that is in error. Jer 6:7 does not contain the middle letter of the Bible. But, as indicated in the Masoretic summary following the Prophets in **L** (II, 412), it likely was once the middle verse of the Bible. The form of marginal masora in other places which mark the middle verses of individual books should have been enough to indicate that the note to Jer 6:7 has a similar import, as should its appearance in a list of middle verses. All this suggests that the current notion that Jer 6:7 contains the middle letter is a corruption of a sound tradition that Jer 6:7 is the middle verse. Divergence mechanism 3.b (*Error in Transmission*) accounts for the discrepancy.

A.10   Conclusions

- The tradition supplies a word count only for the Torah. Its slight divergence from that of **L** has been explained (by Weil) as due to counting some items joined by *maqqep* as single words.
- The tradition regarding the middle words of the Torah may have arisen from a hierarchical definition of "middle."
- The tradition regarding the number of letters in the Torah, if originally correct for some manuscript, has been corrupted in transmission.
- The oft-cited poem of R. Saᶜadya Gaᵓon giving letter counts for the Bible remains a mystery.
- The tradition regarding the middle letter of the Torah may have a similar explanation to that of its middle words.
- The tradition regarding the middle letter of the Psalms is true for **A**, given a hierarchical definition of "middle."

Citing the traditions regarding word and letter counts as evidence of the care taken in transmitting the biblical texts is misguided. At best, the traditions involve a hierarchical definition of "middle" whose determination requires only minor reckoning skills and whose significance for text preservation is minimal. At worst, the traditions are simply incorrect.

References

REFERENCES

Abou-Assaf, A.
  1981   "Die Statue des HDYS^{c}Y, König von Guzana," **MDOG 113**:
         3–22.
Abou-Assaf, A., Bordreuil, P., and Millard, A. R.
  1982   **La Statue de Tell Fekheryeh. Etudes Assyriologiques**
         7. Paris: Recherche sur les civilisations.
Albright, W. F.
  1944   "The Oracles of Balaam," **JBL 63**: 207–33.
  1966   **The Proto-Sinaitic Inscriptions and Their Decipher-
         ment.** Harvard Theological Studies 22. Cambridge: Harvard
         University Press.
Allegro, J. M.
  1956   "Further Messianic References in Qumran Literature," **JBL
         75**: 174–187.
Amusin, J.
  1971   "4Q Testimonia, 15–17," pages 357–361 in **Hommages à
         André Dupont-Sommer,** eds. A. Caquot and M. Philo-
         nenko.   Paris: Libraire d'amérique et d'orient Adrien-
         Maisonneuve.
Andersen, F. I.
  1966   "Moabite Syntax," **Orientalia 35**: 81–120.
  1970a "Orthography in Repetitive Parallelism," **JBL 89**: 343–4.
  1970b "Biconsonantal Byforms in Biblical Hebrew," **ZAW 82**: 270–
         4.
Andersen, F. I., and Forbes, A. D.
  1985   "Orthography and Text Transmission," **TEXT 2**: 25–53.
  1986   **Spelling in the Hebrew Bible.** BibOr 41. Rome: Biblical
         Institute Press.
Bange, L. A.
  1971   **A Study in the Use of Vowel Letters in Alphabetic
         Consonantal Writing.** Munich: UNI-DRUCK.
Barr, J.
  1981   "A New Look at KETHIBH-QERE," **OTS 21**: 19–37.
  1985   "Hebrew Orthography and the Book of Job," **JSS 30**(1): 1–33.
  1988   "Review of **Spelling in the Hebrew Bible,**" **JSS 33**(1):
         122–31.
Becker, R. A., and Chambers, J. M.
  1984   **S: An Interactive Environment for Data Analysis and
         Graphics.** Belmont, CA: Wadsworth, Inc.

Beit-Arié, M.
1977   **Hebrew Codicology: Tentative Typology of Techni-
       cal Practices employed in Hebrew Dated Mediaeval
       Manuscripts**. Paris: Institut de recherche et d'histoire des
       texts: Études de paléographie hébraïque.

Ben-Zvi, I.
1960   "The Codex of Ben-Asher," **Textus 1**: 1–16.

Beyer, K.
1984   **Die aramäischen Texte vom Toten Meer**. Göttingen:
       Vandenhoeck & Ruprecht.

Blau, J.
1976   **A Grammar of Biblical Hebrew**. Wiesbaden: Harras-
       sowitz.

1982   "Remarks on the Development of Some Pronominal Suffixes in
       Hebrew," **HAR 6**: 61–67.

Blau, J., and Loewenstamm, S. E.
1970   "Zur Frage der Scriptio plena in Ugaritischen und Ver-
       wandtes," **UF 2**: 19–33.

Blau, L.
1896   "Masoretic Studies," **JQR o.s. 8**: 343–59. Also **9**: 122–41,
       471–90 (1897).

Breuer, M.
1976   **The Aleppo Codex and the Accepted Text of the Bible**.
       Jerusalem: Mosad Harav Kook.

Cassuto, P.
1987   "Liste du nombre de mots et de lettres dans la base de
       donnés bibliques faites sur le manuscrit B19a de Léningrad,"
       CATAB, CNRS, Université Jean-Moulin, Lyon III.

Chatfield, C., and Collins, A. J.
1980   **Introduction to Multivariate Analysis**. London: Chap-
       man and Hall.

Chwolson, D.
1882   **Corpus inscriptionum hebraicarum**. St. Petersburg cols.
       184–197.

Cohen, M.
1976   "The Orthography of the Samaritan Pentateuch, Its Place in
       the History of Orthography and Its Relation with the MT Or-
       thography," **Beth Mikra 53**: 413–20.

Crockett, W. D.
1951   **A Harmony of Samuel, Kings and Chronicles**. Grand
       Rapids: Baker Book House.

Cross, F. M.
1955 "The Oldest Manuscripts from Qumran," **JBL 74**: 147–72. Reprinted in Cross and Talmon 1975.
1985a "Samaria Papyrus 1: An Aramaic Slave Conveyance of 335 B.C.E. Found in the Wadi Ed-Daliyeh," **Eretz Israel 18**: 7*–17*.
1985b "New Directions in Dead Sea Scroll Research. Part I: The Text behind the Text of the Hebrew Bible," **Bible Review 1** (Summer): 12–25.

Cross, F. M., and Freedman, D. N.
1952 **Early Hebrew Orthography: A Study of the Epigraphic Evidence**. New Haven: American Oriental Society.

Cross, F. M., and Talmon, S.
1975 **Qumran and the History of the Biblical Text**. Cambridge: Harvard University Press.

Davison, M. L.
1983 **Multidimensional Scaling**. New York: John Wiley & Sons.

Degen, R.
1969 **Altaramäische Grammatik der Inschriften des 10.–8. Jh. v. Chr.** Wiesbaden: Komissionsverlag Steiner.

Delitzsch, F.
1920 **Die Lese- und Schreibfehler im Alten Testament nebst den dem Schrifttexte einverliebten Randnöten klassifiziert: ein Hilfsbuch für Lexicon und Grammatik, Exegese und Lekture**. Berlin: de Gruyter.

Diez-Macho, A.
1960 "A New Fragment of Isaiah with Babylonian Pointing," **Textus 1**: 132–240.

Dion, P. E.
1974 **La langue de Ya'udi**. Waterloo: Corporation for the Publication of Academic Studies in Religion in Canada.

Donner, H., with Röllig, W.
1962 **Kanaanäische und aramäische Inschriften**. Wiesbaden: Harrassowitz.

Dotan, A.
1977 **Ben Asher's Creed**. Missoula: Scholars Press.

Dubes, R., and Jain, A. K.
1979 "Validity Studies in Clustering Methodologies," **Pattern Recognition, 11**: 235–254.

Even-Shoshan, A.
1981 **A New Concordance of the Bible**. Jerusalem: Kiryat Sepher.

Fitzmyer, J. A.
  1967   **The Aramaic Inscriptions of Sefire.** BibOr 19. Rome: Biblical Institute Press.
  1971   "'4QTestimonia' and the New Testament," pages 59–89 in **Essays on the Semitic Background of the New Testament.** London: Geoffrey Chapman.

Freedman, D. N.
  1962   "The Massoretic Text and the Qumran Scrolls: A Study in Orthography," **Textus 2**: 87–102.
  1969   "Orthographic Peculiarities in the Book of Job," **Eretz-Israel 9**: 35–44.
  1983a "The Spelling of the Name 'David' in the Hebrew Bible," **Hebrew Annual Review 7**: 89–104.
  1983b "The Earliest Bible," **Michigan Quarterly Review 22**(3): 167–75.

Freedman, D. N., and Ritterspach, A.
  1967   "The Use of *Aleph* as a Vowel Letter in the Genesis Apocryphon," **RevQ 22**: 293–300.

Frensdorff, S.
  1876   **Die Massora Magna.** New York: KTAV [1968 reprint].

Garbini, G.
  1956   **L'aramaico antico.** Memoria Accad. Naz. dei Lincei. Classe di scienze morali, storiche e filologiche, Series VIII, Vol 7, 235–83. Rome: Accademia nazionale dei Lincei.

Garr, W. R.
  1985   **Dialect Geography of Syria-Palestine, 1000–586 B.C.E.** Philadelphia: University of Pennsylvania Press.

Gibson, J. C. L.
  1971   **Syrian Semitic Inscriptions Vol. 1. Hebrew and Moabite Inscriptions.** Oxford: Clarendon Press.

Ginsburg, C. D.
  1867a **Jacob ben Chajim ibn Adonijah's Introduction to the Rabbinic Bible.** *Prolegomenon* by Norman H. Snaith. New York: KTAV [1968 reprint].
  1867b **The Massoreth Ha-Massoreth of Elia Levita.** *Prolegomenon* by Norman H. Snaith. New York: KTAV [1968 reprint].
  1897a **Introduction to the Massoretico-critical Edition of the Hebrew Bible.** New York: KTAV [1966 reprint].
  1897b **The MASSORAH Compiled from Manuscripts.** New York: KTAV [1975 reprint].

Gordis, R.
1937   **The Biblical Text in the Making: A Study of the Kethib-Qere**. New York: KTAV [1971 reprint].

Gordon, A. D.
1981   **Classification**. London: Chapman and Hall.

Goshen-Gottstein, M.
1960   "The Authenticity of the Aleppo Codex," **Textus 1**: 17–58.
1967   "Hebrew Bible Manuscripts: Their History and their Place in the **HUBP** Edition," **Biblica 48**: 243–90.
1979   "The Aleppo Codex and the Rise of the Massoretic Bible Text," **Biblical Archaeologist 42/3**: 145–63.

Greenacre, M. J.
1984   **Theory and Applications of Correspondence Analysis**. London: Academic Press.

Hamilton, G. J.
1988   "Review of **Spelling in the Hebrew Bible**," **JBL 107**: 128–9.

Harkavy, A.
1876   **Altjüdische Denkmäler aus der Krim**. St. Petersburg.

Hartigan, J. A.
1975   **Clustering Algorithms**. New York: John Wiley & Sons.

Huffmon, H. B.
1965   **Amorite Personal Names in the Mari Texts: A Structural and Lexical Study**. Baltimore: Johns Hopkins Press.

Hughes, J. J.
1987   **Bits, Bytes, & Biblical Studies**. Grand Rapids: Zondervan.

Ihm, P., and van Groenewoud, H.
1984   "Correspondence Analysis and Gaussian Ordination," pages 5–60 in **Compstat Lectures 3**, eds. J. M. Chambers *et al.* Vienna: Physica Verlag.

Kahle, P.
1959   **The Cairo Geniza**. Oxford: Blackwell.

Kaufman, S. A.
1982   "Reflections on the Assyrian-Aramaic Bilingual from Tell Fakhariyeh," **Maarav 3(2)**: 137–75.

Kendall, D. G.
1971   "Seriation from abundance matrices," pages 215–52 in **Mathematics in the Archaeological and Historical Sciences**, eds. F. R. Hodson *et al.* Edinburgh: University Press.

Kendall, M. G.
  1980 **Multivariate Analysis (Second Edition).** London:
        Charles Griffin and Co.
Koopmans, J. J.
  1962 **Aramäische Chrestomathie, Ausgewählte Texte (In-
        schriften, Ostraka, Papyri.** Leiden: Nederlands Instituut
        voor het Nabije Oosten.
Kutscher, E. Y.
  1957 "The Language of the Genesis Apocryphon," **Scripta Hi-
        erosolymitana 4**: 1–35.
  1959 הלשון והרקע הלשוני של מגילת ישעיהו השלמה
        ממגילות ים המלח Jerusalem: Hebrew University.
Lebart, L., Morineau, A., and Warwick, K. M.
  1984 **Multivariate Descriptive Statistical Analysis.** New
        York: John Wiley & Sons.
Leiman, S. Z.
  1974 **The Canon and Massorah of the Hebrew Bible: An
        Introductory Reader.** Library of Biblical Studies, ed. H.
        M. Orlinsky. New York: KTAV.
Mardia, K. V., Kent, J. T., and Bibby, J. M.
  1979 **Multivariate Analysis.** London: Academic Press.
Naveh, J.
  1983 "Review of Z. Zevit's *Matres Lectionis in Ancient Hebrew
        Epigraphs*," **IEJ 33**: 139–40.
O'Connor, M.
  1983 "Writing Systems, Native Speaker Analyses, and the Earliest
        Stages of Northwest Semitic Orthography," pages 439–65 in
        The Word of the Lord Shall Go Forth, eds. C. L. Meyers
        and M. O'Connor. Winona Lake: Eisenbrauns.
Orlinsky, H. M.
  1966 *Prolegomenon* in Ginsburg 1897a.
Pardee, D.
  1988 "Review of Spelling in the Hebrew Bible," **CBQ 50**: 276–80.
Parunak, H. V. D.
  1978 "The Orthography of the Arad Ostraca," **BASOR 230**: 25–
        31.
Propp, W. H.
  1987 **Water in the Wilderness: A Biblical Motif and Its
        Mythological Background.** HSM 40. Atlanta: Scholars
        Press.

Qimron, E.
1986   **The Hebrew of the Dead Sea Scrolls**. Atlanta: Scholars Press.

Rahlfs, A.
1916   "Zur Setzung der Lesemutter im Alten Testament," *Nachrichten von der Königlichen Gesellschaft der Wissenschaften zur Göttingen.* Philologisch-historische Klasse: 315–347.

Rainey, A.
1983   "Review of Z. Zevit's *Matres Lectionis in Ancient Hebrew Epigraphs,*" **JBL 102**: 629–34.

Rosenthal, F.
1974   **A Grammar of Biblical Aramaic**. Fourth Printing. Wiesbaden: Otto Harrassowitz.

Rüger, H. P.
1969   " הוֹאדָא—Er: Zur Deutung von 1QS 8, 13–14," **ZNW 60**: 143–5.

Sarfatti, G. B.
1982   "Hebrew Inscriptions of the First Temple Period," **MAARAV 3**: 55–83.

Seber, G. A. F.
1984   **Multivariate Observations**. New York: John Wiley & Sons.

Segal, M. H.
1953   "The Promulgation of the Authoritative Text of the Hebrew Bible," **JBL 72**: 35–47.

Segert, S.
1975   **Altaramäische Grammatik**. Leipzig: Verlag Enzyklopädie.
1976   **A Grammar of Phoenician and Punic**. Munich: C.H. Beck.
1978   "Vowel Letters in Early Aramaic," **JNES 37**: 111–14.

Shifmann, I. Sh.
1987   **Vetkhiĭ Zavet i yego mir**. Moskva: Politizdat.

Starkova, C. B.
1974   "Les plus anciens manuscrits de la Bible dans la collection de l'Institut des études orientales de l'Academie des sciences de l'U.R.S.S." pp. 37–42 + 4 plates in **La paleographie hébraïque medievale. Colloques internationaux du CNRS No. 547 (Paris 11–13 Septembre, 1972)**. Paris: Editions du C.N.R.S.

Strack, H. L.
1907   "Die Zahl der Buchstaben im hebräischen Alten Testament," **ZAW 27**: 69–72.

Tov, E.
  1986   "The Orthography and Language of the Hebrew Scrolls Found at Qumran and the Origin of these Scrolls," **Textus 13**: 31–57.
  1988   "Hebrew Biblical Manuscripts from the Judean Desert: Their Contributions to Textual Criticism." **JSS 39**: 5–37.

Tsevat, M.
  1960   "A Chapter on Old West Semitic Orthography." Pp. 89–91 in **The Joshua Bloch Memorial Volume: Studies in Booklore and History**. Eds. A. Berger et al. New York: The New York Public Library.

Weil, G. E.
  1968   *Prolegomenon* to Frensdorff's **Die Massora Magna**. New York: KTAV.
  1971   **Massorah Gedolah iuxta codicem Leningradensem B19a**. Vol. I Catalogi. Rome: P. B. I.
  1981   "Les décomptes de versets, mots et lettres du Pentateuque selon le manuscrit B 19a de Leningrad," **Mélanges Dominique Barthélemy. Etudes bibliques offertes a l'occasion de son 60e anniversaire**, Orbis Biblicus et Orientalis 38, eds. P. Casetti, O. Keel, and A. Schenker. Freibourg/Göttingen: Editions Universitaires/Vandenhöck und Ruprecht.

Weil, G. E., and Guény, A.–M.
  1976   "Le Manuscrit du Pentateuque de Tbilissi," **Philologia Orientalis IV**: 178–209.

Weinberg, W.
  1975   "The History of Hebrew *Plene* Spelling: From Antiquity to Haskalah," **HUCA 46**: 317–487. Reprinted in **The History of Hebrew** *Plene* **Spelling**. Cincinnati: HUC Press, 1985.

Yeivin, I.
  1980   **Introduction to the Tiberian Masorah. JBL MasS 5**. Missoula, Montana: Scholars Press.

Zevit, Z.
  1980   **Matres Lectionis in Ancient Hebrew Epigraphs**. ASOR Monograph Series 2. Cambridge: American Schools of Oriental Research.